Small Countries

SMALL COUNTRIES

Structures and Sensibilities

Edited by

Ulf Hannerz

and

Andre Gingrich

PENN

UNIVERSITY OF PENNSYLVANIA PRESS

PHILADELPHIA

Published by
University of Pennsylvania Press
Philadelphia, Pennsylvania 19104-4112
www.upenn.edu/pennpress

Printed in the United States of America
on acid-free paper
10 9 8 7 6 5 4 3 2 1

A Cataloging-in-Publication record is available from
the Library of Congress
ISBN 978-0-8122-4893-7

CONTENTS

PART III. BEING AND BECOMING SMALL

PART IV. STRUGGLING WITH SCALES

PART V. GRANDEUR, IRONY, AND SMALL WORLDS

Introduction
Exploring Small Countries

Andre Gingrich and Ulf Hannerz

Take a handful of countries. During much of its half century or so as a contemporary independent state, Mali has not been much in world news. One of its cities, Timbuktu, was a medieval center of trade and learning but has more recently had a dubious claim to fame as "the end of the world." Then half the country is conquered by Islamists, the old colonial power France comes in with troops, and for some time the global news media flock there. At about the same time, the international newsweekly *Economist* (2013) devotes a cover story to "the next supermodel: why the world should look at the Nordic countries," with a portrait of a friendly but somewhat quizzical-looking Viking. A year and a half earlier, however, one of these countries had been the site of an extremist massacre. Qatar and Abu Dhabi and Dubai in what is now the United Arab Emirates used to be places where local people made a modest living from pearl fishing and trade along the shores of the Persian Gulf. Now, thanks to oil wealth, they have global museums, global sports events, and major international airlines. Singapore has been described as a First World country in a Third World region—now that the vocabulary has changed, is it a tropical part of the Global North? And in the tropics again, the Seychelles and the Maldives, out there somewhere in the ocean between Africa and India, have become celebrated tourist destinations.

All these—Mali, the Nordic countries, the Gulf states, Singapore, the island nations of the Indian Ocean—are, by some definition at least, small countries. In the global news flow, some of them may be there today and gone again tomorrow. (Mali briefly reappeared in the news in recent years, with a jihadist assault on an upscale chain hotel frequented by expatriates.) Others are more durably present. Current attention to them and their characteristics may depend on a changing international division of labor, new types of media and travel, and generally a volatile world, with new forms of violent conflict, some economies in crisis, social models under debate, and implications of demographic shifts and climate change becoming policy issues where the national and the global intersect. What the particular countries just mentioned have in common, however, is again the fact that they are in some way small. So what can smallness mean in the life of a country? The question is not so often asked, and serious attempts to answer it seem rare. At times smallness is mentioned in passing, mostly to suggest that these are countries that can be largely disregarded in the larger scheme of things. This book is an attempt by a team of anthropologists to explore the question in a more intensive fashion.

To begin with, some comments on anthropology's relationship to the study of such issues may be in order. But it also seems useful to discuss what we take these two keywords—"small" and "countries"—to mean. Their meanings are perhaps not as straightforward as they may seem.

Countries, States, Nations

First something about "countries." We take this term to be usefully preliminary, conveniently broad, theoretically more or less uncommitted. We have in mind territories with populations, primarily sovereign states. At times we will refer to them as "states"—yet if we were to do so consistently, that could risk placing too much emphasis on a political dimension and on state machineries. If we were to refer to them consistently as "nations," on the other hand, we would certainly acknowledge the linkage to a rich body of scholarly work on nationhood, nationalism, and national identity, growing not least since the 1980s (with pivotal attempts at critical overview by Ernest Gellner [1983], Benedict Anderson [1983], and Eric Hobsbawm [1991]). Yet between scholarly, official, and popular uses of "nation" and related terms there are gray zones where we would not want to lose ourselves; overtones of uniformity and of shared heritage must be held as problematic. With some of the countries that came into being with twentieth-century decolonization, their status as "nations" in such terms was at least initially not self-evident.

The popularity of notions such as "nation building" shows that nationness in any strict sense is not something to take for granted. (About Belize, Richard Wilk makes the point in one of the chapters that follow that it is a country but not a nation.) So while we will occasionally move between these partially overlapping concepts, as we deal with a wider range of phenomena and issues, the term "countries" gives us some intellectual freedom of movement.

How do we as anthropologists approach the entities to which such terms refer? It seems fair to say that anthropology has mostly not been inclined to deal with "countries" as a level of social and cultural order in its own right.[1] This is noteworthy, and may even seem odd: in other disciplines among the humanities and social sciences, scholarship focusing on the national level of social and cultural life, or simply taking it for granted, has been so much a matter of standard operating procedure that criticisms of a dominant "methodological nationalism" are increasingly often heard.[2] Frequently enough, this naturalization of the national level has been underpinned by the tendency to take the term "societies" to refer to units of this kind.

The early twentieth-century classics of anthropology, on the other hand, were about "small-scale societies," which tended to involve mostly face-to-face social relationships, and nonliterate cultures. Raymond Firth (1951: 17–18), a founding figure in British social anthropology, described this as "micro-sociology"—an intensive engagement with a thousand people or so. As anthropologists turned to peasant societies, the emphasis was still on local communities. In the study of modern Western societies, "community studies" became one prominent genre. In the British tradition again, a more explicit comparative notion of scale in earlier anthropology could be identified with Godfrey and Monica Wilson (1945) and their work in colonial East, Central, and Southern Africa. The Wilsons drew a rather broad-brush contrast where small-scale comes in a bundle of characteristics (local, face-to-face, nonliterate, low-tech, fairly homogeneous), as opposed to the kind of social order brought by colonialism, transnational mining companies, mission schools and churches, and so forth. To ideas of scale we will come back. By the mid-twentieth century, a handful of scholars, such as Robert Redfield (e.g., 1962: 364–414), also tried to think, with a certain imaginative leap, about civilizations in an anthropological way. As globalization became a major topic—whatever the term was taken to stand for—a catch formulation involved the contrast of "the global and the local." But this allowed for entities somewhere in between to be somewhat disregarded.

In passing, we might note one historical moment of confluence of world conflict with one particular theoretical tendency in American anthropology. During World War II and immediately after it, an interest in "culture and personality" was channeled into an effort to understand important adversaries or more or less problematic allies.[3] Under such conditions, "countries" became obvious units—that was how wars were fought. Unconventional ethnographic methods were employed to study varieties of "national character." But this was mostly about large countries: Japan, Germany, Russia, and to an extent Britain.

Since that period, anthropologists have shown little inclination to engage with such studies and mostly distance themselves from the notion of "national character" itself.[4] The questions we will explore here are largely not in that intellectual lineage. Nonetheless, countries are a significant kind of arena of social life, and, in our times, people's understandings of who they are and what life is like are to no small extent anchored in such arenas. While keeping our distance from methodological nationalism, then, we attempt here to fill in at least parts of a gap in anthropology, by scrutinizing small countries also within their wider regional and global contexts. Today's small countries are certainly not "small-scale" entities in the classic sense; microsociology may have a part in our inspection of them, but as wholes they are rather the subjects of a kind of macroanthropology. In pursuing this approach, however, we need not try to invent an entirely new anthropology. Rather, we suggest that a number of ideas from the intellectual inventory of past and current anthropology can be brought together and elaborated in this field.

Absolutely Small and Relatively Small

When we refer to a range of countries as "small," the first thing to point out should perhaps be that we are not focusing on the mini-countries of the world: Monaco, São Tomé e Príncipe, Nauru, the Vatican, and so forth.[5] These may sometimes offer extreme examples of the kinds of characteristics we will be concerned with, but frequently they are atypical. Their social, cultural, and political autonomy is actually quite limited; they tend to be embedded in larger entities.

While a couple of the countries discussed in the following chapters (Belize and the Maldives) have populations of less than half a million, our "small countries" are mostly considerably larger than that. We may begin by recognizing that smallness here is understood along two main dimensions. One is absolute, in the sense of referring to the size of the population and (less often) to the size of the territory. We come back to that in a moment. The other dimension is relative, contrastive. Some countries are understood to be small—by their own inhabitants or by others or by both—because there is a relevant comparison to one or more larger countries.

For a point of departure, consider Europe. It has a handful of large countries: Germany, France, Great Britain, Spain, Italy. Since the crumbling of the Iron Curtain, and after the ascension of the country into the European Union, Poland may have entered this category in the general consciousness. (Whether Russia should be counted as an integral part of Europe remains an ambiguous matter.) These countries have populations of some forty million or upward. In contrast, a considerable number of other European countries are understood to be "small." The largest of the small, the Netherlands, has a population of some seventeen million; as far as demography is our measure, we can take this figure as our admittedly arbitrary upper limit.

In Europe, the contrast between "large" and "small" has been a significant factor for a very long time and has hardly become less so during the much shorter history of the European Union. On a worldwide basis, at present, we find that some 170 countries (or more or less country-like territories) are "small" by this measure—more than 70 percent of all such entities.[6] (Naturally, they have much less than that proportion of the population; and with population growth, more countries are gradually leaving the category.) These countries are widely distributed, appearing in all world regions except North America and East Asia. They include Middle Eastern countries such as Jordan, the United Arab Emirates, and Israel; African countries like Sierra Leone, Togo, Zimbabwe, and Eritrea; Latin American countries such as Guatemala and Bolivia; all Caribbean countries, whether small or mini; in the Pacific region, New Zealand, Papua New Guinea, and Fiji; many of the countries in the Caucasus and central Asia that were formerly part of the Soviet Union; Laos, Cambodia, Timor-Leste, and, again, the city-state of Singapore.

In the European instance, however, we see how the absolute demographic measure is quickly transformed into a sense of relative smallness, as relevant comparisons are so obviously there, next door. And then when smallness is seen as a relative matter, it occasionally turns out that quite large countries are seen as small in some particular, but often glaringly inevitable, contrast.

One Canadian prime minister, Pierre Elliot Trudeau, famously described his country's relationship to the United States as like being "in bed with the elephant"—yet in every other way, Canada is certainly itself big. The relationship of Pakistan to India is another instance that may be viewed in a similar way. In one chapter, we inspect a kind of humor that flourishes in Yemen. How many Yemenites there are depends on how one counts, in particular how one views the considerable diaspora.[7] But it is particularly in comparison with neighboring Saudi Arabia that the Yemenites are inclined to see their country as small—whether the population of Saudi Arabia is much larger or not, its territory is about four times as large. And it is a much more prosperous, powerful country.

Mostly, however, our interest here is focused not on such paradoxical instances, where an "absolutely" large country becomes "relatively" small, but on countries that can be judged as small in both absolute and relative terms. We are interested in scrutinizing to what extent, and in what ways, smallness in both senses recurrently affect life and thought, sensibilities as well as structures of social relationships, in everyday life as well as in the context of critical events.

Relative Smallness: The Native's Point of View

Various historical trajectories have led to present conditions of the absolute and relative smallness of countries—colonial, imperial, local, regional. Yet such processes offer just one side of understanding how people today see their own or another country's smallness, and it is not identical with that view. Relative smallness is smallness "from a native's point of view." With a somewhat old-fashioned anthropological term, it involves an "emic" comparative dimension of the ways important routine practices, standard speech behavior, or other cultural references indicate how people in one way or another refer to their country as somehow smaller than elsewhere.

By implication, the relevant "elsewhere" usually involves one country or several countries in one's immediate or wider vicinity. This emic comparison may operate with notions of comparative smallness in a more literal sense of being demographically and/or territorially smaller. Yet that literal sense will also combine with various metaphorical and symbolic varieties of relative smallness: these metaphors will tend to indicate a relative insignificance with regard to economic success, organizational efficiency, political influence, military potentials, scientific achievements, religious relevance, ethical standing, artistic creativity, and so forth. In such ways the comparative dimensions are culturally internalized factors. The "other" country (or group of countries) is more or less ubiquitous in the local imaginary, as a latent reference to be activated any time. Don Robotham's comments in this volume on the Jamaican vocabulary are very relevant here. "Likkle" means more than just small; "Babylon" becomes a generalized big, powerful Other. Yemeni jokes as studied by Andre Gingrich make similar points.

That recurrent presence of "our" relative smallness in a small country's local imaginaries may not require any explicit position, although such ideological mechanisms of public self-limitation occur often enough. For historical and/or current reasons, a public awareness of one's country's smallness certainly prevails in several examples. In her chapter, Goh Beng Lan points out that smallness is forever present in Singapore public consciousness: "the little red dot." Jacqueline Knörr notes that it is a constant emphasis in Sierra Leonean public discourse. Yet at the same time, there are many other cases—in this book, those of Switzerland, Cuba, and the Maldives—where indigenous notions of relative smallness do not occupy any very noticeable position in the local imaginary. Indeed, such understandings may be hidden under alternative notions that could even claim the contrary. We will return to the theme of small-country claims to superiority: national David and Goliath stories.

Smallness and Its Others: Constellations

The diverse ways of conceptualizing relative smallness also remind us that certain elements of "othering" are usually inherent in perceptions about one's country's outside relations. Investigating smallness inevitably includes the examination of relational stereotypes, ideological statements connecting to issues of power. Notions of "our country" and "another country/other countries" thus often intersect with forms of alterity (Baumann and Gingrich 2004).

Outside understandings about a small country will differ from those prevailing inside it. The question whether a country is small at all, and how, is usually much more relevant inside that country and among those who identify with it. It is far less important to most outsiders, who may rarely take notice of small Others at all. Yet if there tends to be such a structural asymmetry of understandings, it may happen that in some outsiders' eyes, a small country draws more attention than it is deemed to really deserve—in her chapter, Virginia Dominguez dwells on one widely noted reference to Israel as a "shitty little country."

From a formal perspective, it seems useful to distinguish between different kinds of constellations of countries in which a small country may find itself. Three main structural constellations have appeared relevant in history and continue to be important today: binary constellations, buffer constellations, and clusters of small countries.

Binary constellations can be identified with the "Ireland/Great Britain pattern," which has analogous forms in relations such as Portugal/Spain, Austria/Germany, Belarus/Russia, Yemen/Saudi Arabia, Laos/Thailand, and New Zealand/Australia. Here the basic asymmetry discussed earlier is almost typical: the smaller side tends to care much more about this constellation, while the larger side considers it merely occasionally, as one among many other interests that are, or are at least seen as, more important.

Many of these binary constellations build on historical records of more than one generation and sometimes go back much farther than that. Yet several cases contradict any myth of characteristic longevity. Until the early twenty-first century, Greeks hardly considered their country "small" in relation to anything or anybody, nor did they see Germany as the primary Other. During the economic crises after 2008, however, some sense of being "weaker than . . ." if not "smaller than . . ." has certainly gained increasing relevance in Greek society. The example demonstrates that binary constellations may change their form and relevance. Shifting regional configurations can also mean that constellations become less dependent on spatial proximity. Greece does not border on Germany. With the coming of the European Union, the Ireland/Great Britain constellation is not quite what it was. (And even before that, as Helena Wulff notes in her chapter, with transatlantic migration, Ireland/United States emerged as another, more attractive binary set.)

The cases of Israel and Cuba as discussed by Virginia Dominguez may be interpreted as radicalized sub-versions in the binary spectrum—Israel versus the Palestinians/unfriendly Arab countries/the Muslim world; Cuba versus the United States/world capitalism. It is also true that an inventory of small countries' binary constellations at any point in time will feature transitional forms to the buffer and cluster constellations.

Buffer constellations occur when a country's "relative smallness" is acted out in relation to more than one major neighboring power whose general interests tend to differ from each other: Mongolia's position between Russia and China comes to mind, but also Switzerland's role between Germany and France (and to an extent Italy, and earlier in history the Habsburg empire). In his chapter on Serbia, Aleksandar Bošković reminds us of the in-betweenness of Yugoslavia, between Western Europe and the Soviet bloc, during the Cold War era. The position of Lebanon between Syria and Israel and that of Jordan between Israel and Iraq are Middle Eastern instances. Nepal finds itself between India and China. In Asia, too, we can take into account the somewhat different situations of the Maldives vis-à-vis Sri Lanka and India and of Singapore between Indonesia and Malaysia.

The positions of the smaller Arab Gulf states (from Kuwait to Oman) between Saudi Arabia and Iran (and Iraq before the fall of Saddam Hussein) are a Middle Eastern set of examples that can be considered as a transitional case between buffer and cluster constellations. The latter are those where a smaller or larger number of relatively small countries coexist in their regional diversity. Taken together, they may all be at a certain distance to the next large country and/or big power. In some cases, there may not be just one big power, in other constellations it may not even be clear at all who that "next" big power actually is. The best-known European example is Scandinavia, inspected by Orvar Löfgren in his chapter.

Again, we can identify intermediate cases. For nearly half a century after World War II, Finland found itself uncomfortably close to a binary constellation with the Soviet Union. A metaphorical term of "Finlandization" was indeed coined for this kind of shift toward dependence, yet in the Finnish case itself it was always to a degree counteracted by a conception of a "Nordic" cluster, where Finland joined the Scandinavian countries. In some ways the Netherlands, Belgium, and Luxembourg may be seen as a cluster, although in other ways they have formed a buffer between Germany and France. Except for Serbia, post-Yugoslav entities have shifted into a cluster since the late 1990s. Major parts of Central America and the Caribbean island world share some of these features. Belize, as discussed by Richard Wilk, may be seen to belong in two clusters: Central America as well as the Caribbean.

Then, finally, small island nations may be a special case: as Eva-Maria Knoll's chapter on the Maldives suggests, the "Big Other" here may be understood as that enormous, encompassing ocean itself.[8]

Past and present constellations of the three types just identified are often mirrored in language situations. Scandinavian languages, in their cluster, are mutually more or less intelligible, but as the countries involved are sovereign, they count as distinct languages—for, as the saying goes, "a language is a dialect with an army." The protected status of Irish in the Republic of Ireland and of Swedish in Finland in opposite ways reflect historical dyadic constellations. Austrians share German with the big country to the north. The buffer position of Switzerland is evident in its quadrilingualism—primarily of German and French, but with Italian and Romansh also present. And the historical reach of the British Empire remains globally present in the status of English as the world's only hyperlanguage and in those past colonial dyads that still make this the dominant national language of Ireland, Belize, Jamaica, Sierra Leone, and New Zealand.[9]

Meanwhile, out there in the ocean, the Maldivians speak Dhivehi.

Family Resemblances

Outlining the most general dimensions of smallness, we have done nothing to conceal the fact that small countries are a highly diverse set of entities. They differ in culture and in geopolitical situations. While some are remarkably homogeneous and cohesive by contemporary standards, others may be characterized by deep social, cultural, and political cleavages. Perhaps most important, some are prosperous, others poor; they occur in the Global South as often as in the Global North, with widely differing ramifications. If Norway and Sierra Leone are similar in population size, they do not share many other characteristics.

To try to construct some model of "the essential small country" seems consequently most probably misguided. Each small country is different. It might appear as if in exploring small countries and finding such diversity we could end up exploding "small countries" as a useful category.

Yet smallness, absolute or relative, keeps reappearing as a significant fact of life in a variety of ways. A country may have come to be small for different reasons; so in systemic terms, seen in this way, smallness may be a dependent variable. Yet interacting with the range of other factors that characterize a country—institutional, economic, political, historical, cultural, linguistic—smallness, and senses of smallness, may also appear to exercise some influence of its own on experience, thought, and action, thus becoming more of an independent variable. The challenge facing us is to grasp the contours of the complex field of possibilities here. This also involves facing a certain systematic ambiguity, a "simultaneity of contrasting possibilities," as smallness in different circumstances can have a part in shaping quite unlike social results.

This challenge is also one we should strive to confront as ethnographers. When we note, for example, that a small country is involved in a constellation of countries—dyad, buffer, cluster—this is not only a geopolitical notion but one with implications penetrating into various facets of life. Preferably we should ask, too, what people within a country we actually have in mind. It is not that "Austria" thinks this, or "Sweden" (or "Singapore" or "Belize") does that. Elite and underclass, people of city and countryside can have different experiences, sensibilities, and activities relating to smallness.

One useful notion in dealing with this rather unwieldy category of countries may be what Ludwig Wittgenstein termed "family resemblances"—later brought into anthropological thinking with Rodney Needham's (1975) "polythetic concepts." There are times when (as scholars or as laypeople) we recognize clusters of characteristics that tend repeatedly to occur together, but not always in precisely the same combination. In the case of "small countries," we may identify such a protean assemblage of features, going beyond measures of demography or territory, yet somehow not unrelated to them— but also related to various other characteristics of the countries concerned. That is to say, countries A, B, and C may share a lot; but C is also in some ways similar to D and E; and E has things that remind us of F. So even if A and F in the end seem to have nothing in common, perhaps we may discern in them variations on a collection of organizational and cultural themes?

In later chapters, our colleagues discuss implications of smallness in diverse ways. Some offer overviews of current conditions of smallness; others take a more diachronic view; a number of chapters focus on particular phenomena and events casting their special light on small-country life—a national tragedy, a celebration of athletic success, a local literary world, a careless comment by a diplomat, a widespread medical affliction. Before turning to these case materials, this introductory chapter is in large part a commentary on family resemblances, a series of comparisons within our bouquet of countries, showing parallels as well as contrasts.

The Social Fabric

We turn again to smallness in the absolute sense and primarily to smallness as a matter of national population size. (We will come back to matters of territorial size.) A major question for us as social anthropologists is how to move from a simple demographic fact to an exploration of its implications for social relationships, and relationships between relationships: toward an understanding of qualities of the social fabric and to resulting sensibilities and assumptions about social life. What a country's smallness does to its people, and what they do with it.

This is a difficult question. A satisfactory answer requires an understanding of national life both broad and deep. But the contributors to this volume are colleagues who are either themselves inhabitants of the small countries they discuss—doing a version of "anthropology at home"—or scholars with long-term commitments to research in particular countries. Thus their varied personal, practical, and research experience can help us grapple with the intricacy of smallness.

As far as conceptual tools are concerned, we noted before a certain early anthropological interest in notions of scale. A little later on, a volume edited by Fredrik Barth, *Scale and Social Organization* (1978), aimed at moving toward a more comparative viewpoint; allowing an understanding of large-scale and complex entities that would still be analytically in line with the anthropology of simpler societies.[10] In tune with 1960s–1970s developments in the discipline, network-oriented formulations were prominent here. As anthropologists had by then turned to a stronger interest in complex societies, they needed conceptual instruments taking them across the boundaries between more conventional group or institutional units of analysis, and out of local contexts. Network analysis remains attractive in its capacity for openness. As we draw on it here, however, we will not take the path of a highly technical and quantitative style of work, one direction into which network studies have also developed. Rather, it will be a matter of "thinking with networks," as one of us has put it earlier.[11] This will serve as a tool in sketching an overall perspective toward connectivity, toward possible characteristics of reach and density in social relationships and their consequences.

One point of departure comes from outside anthropology. For about fifty years already (since early experimental work by the social psychologist Stanley Milgram), social scientists have been aware of the "small world" phenomenon: even in a country as large as the United States, it takes surprisingly few actually existing network links to get from anybody to anybody.[12] You can ask someone to pass on a message toward an identified other, by way only of relationships between individuals personally known to each other; some messages will fail to reach the destination, some take more time than others, and the number of linkages used varies, but the median number of linkages in the chain, at the time of the pioneer research, was around six. This finding has even found a certain place in the popular imagination—for one thing, a play named *Six Degrees of Separation* by John Guare premiered at a New York theater in 1990.

A half century after Milgram's discovery, we may wonder what difference the social media would now make. In any case, if such "small world" phenomena may appeal to our fantasy, they also require some second thoughts. One background factor would be that each participant in the chain, looking one linkage ahead, would scan his or her entire personal network for the most suitable next connection—in principle, that could mean that many hundred possibilities are inspected in each step. In a chain of a half dozen linkages, proceeding by multiplication rather than addition, millions of people could be on the map of reachables. But then relationships are likely to cluster, so that networks are actually shared, and the map shrinks; although some individuals may have larger networks than others or networks that are more socially dispersed.[13] It is also very likely that few people are aware of people in their networks more than perhaps a couple of linkages away.

So where could such thinking with networks lead us in trying to grasp qualities of the small-country social fabric? It would seem probable that if one could get from anyone to anyone in six or so steps in American society, it would take even fewer steps in a very much smaller society. In New Zealand, Cris Shore notes, it has become a popular notion that "two degrees of separation" is typical (although a study suggests that this slightly exaggerates closeness). Yet even in such a case, the realities of the relational chains, if not known in detail, are unlikely to be directly, intentionally, acted upon. What we would point to here, on the other hand, is the possibility of a certain generalized network sensibility that may be recurrent in small countries—this may be the real significance of the New Zealander figure of speech. Because such awareness seems to be activated more frequently in similar ways, it can be part of the everyday experience, and of the repertoire of anecdotes, of people in small countries that they stumble on discoveries of "mutual acquaintances," extended kinship connections, and the like. And this may accumulate as a sense of the nature of social life, a certain expectation of relative accessibility, intimacy, or transparency. There could be less of a habitually developed taken-for-grantedness of social distance. As Sulayman Khalaf notes with regard to Abu Dhabi, the step from real community to imagined community (and vice versa) may be relatively shorter than in larger countries.

Intriguingly, Don Robotham refers to possible historical linkages between families in Jamaican plantation society—once these were families of slaves and slaveholders, now their descendants are sports stars, in Jamaica and in Britain. Helena Wulff quotes one of her Irish author informants as suggesting that just about all her writer colleagues have at one time or other met the president of Ireland. Thomas Hylland Eriksen's account of the tragedy that struck Norway in July 2011 is also a case in point. Norwegians experienced the lone extremist gunman's massacre of a large number of youths, assembled on an island summer camp, as a united nation in sorrow. But that experience involved the recognition that a great many people knew someone, or knew someone who knew someone, who was at that camp—among either the dead or the survivors.

Reading the Rankings: Trust and Freedom

"Trust" has recently emerged as a key concept in several social sciences.[14] It is tempting to translate a sense of intimacy into a sense of trust. All other things equal, in terms of social morality, a small country may be a little more *Gemeinschaft*, a little less *Gesellschaft*.[15] Perhaps in a small country it is more difficult to hide misdemeanors?

Ranking lists are now a conspicuous part of the global cultural habitat; we will have occasion to refer to several of them. Certainly one should be aware that such lists are often debatable, with regard to conception, methodology, and in other ways. Nonetheless, they may be good to think with and argue about. As far as trust and smallness are concerned, we are tempted to discern a relationship between them as we consider a ranking list of countries issued by Transparency International, the nongovernmental organization (NGO) devoted to fighting corruption around the world.[16] In its "Corruption Perceptions Index 2011," the perceived levels of public-sector corruption in 183 countries/territories around the world, the top twenty-five positions of least corrupt countries belong to (1) New Zealand; (2) Denmark and Finland; (4) Sweden; (5) Singapore; (6) Norway; (7) Netherlands; (8) Australia and Switzerland; (10) Canada; (11) Luxembourg; (12) Hong Kong; (13) Iceland; (14) Germany and Japan; (16) Austria, Barbados and the United Kingdom; (19) Belgium and Ireland; (21) Bahamas; (22) Chile and Qatar; (24) United States; (25) France.

Of these twenty-five countries, seventeen are by our standards "small." One could quibble about the concept of "corruption perceptions"—does this mean really least corrupt, or just that those doing the perceiving are more sweetly innocent about what is actually going on? Yet either way, well-founded or misplaced, a sense of trust may be involved. Regina Bendix notes in her chapter how a number of major corruption scandals in Austria, involving high levels of government, caused the country's index ranking to slide downward several notches. So small countries are clearly not immune to such phenomena. But possibly the breach of trust is then constructed as a greater scandal than it would be where corrupt practices are more common-place? In any case, other small countries are scattered throughout the Transparency International list. The bottom position, moreover, belongs to Somalia (with a population of about ten million). So being a small country does not always help.

Moreover, we can discern here a certain ambiguity—indeed, a simultaneity of contrasting possibilities—in the domestic lives of contemporary small countries. If there is some sense of intimacy, transparency, and trust, one may take a bottom-up view and argue that this suggests something like a healthy civil society, seeing to it that members of the elite do not get out of line. Alternatively, one can take the top-down view: for the rulers, it is easier to keep a small population under surveillance. Small countries may lean in different directions here. Probably Singapore would often be understood to be of the latter kind; although in her chapter, Goh suggests that the case is no longer so clear-cut.

Consider also another global ranking list: the annual "World Press Freedom Index" by Reporters Without Borders for 2013 features a number of counterintuitive results.[17] The best rankings for large countries in this index are 17, 20, 22, and 26 (Germany, Canada, Poland, Australia), while Great Britain (29) and the United States (32) compete with much smaller, more fragile countries such as Cape Verde (25), Suriname (31), and Lithuania (33) for their respective positions regarding liberal and democratic rights. As if that were not remarkable enough, the fifteen best positions in this ranking are held by small countries (by our criteria), from three continents.

Obviously the index first of all highlights the question of democratic pluralism—those countries that are last on the list are Turkmenistan, North Korea, and Eritrea. Yet the matter also includes complicated factors that cannot be adequately addressed here: the rising relevance of new social media and the general downward slide of print dailies and weeklies. Still, some of the world's largest countries, including those with the most stable democratic records, perform badly in these rankings. If we look at the qualifying criteria and indicators underlying the "freedom of press" ranking, accuracy of reporting and featuring different opinions are central. This is where the size of a country may come into play.

In domestic social conditions of relative proximity and intimacy, "local news" can readily become countrywide news from the outset; getting from real communities and regions to the imagined community of the nation is not such a big step. It is relatively easy to report "accurately" in a small country—there are fewer local news stories to report in the first place, and if the newspaper *Tiroler Tageszeitung* ignores them, then people will know about them from the broadcasts of Radio Tirol. And what goes on in a Tyrolean valley might interest the townspeople at Klagenfurt, at the other end of Austria. Furthermore, a diversity of opinions is more difficult to ignore or suppress. Public communication in a small country generally depends less exclusively on print and electronic mass media. Even before the current era of "social media," news about a major avalanche disaster in that Tyrolean valley, and reports about the authorities perhaps handling the situation badly, could spread to all parts of the country: rumors, leaflets, political speeches reach all other parts of the small nation, so people can judge at an earlier point whether media reports adequately reflect different opinions and possible dissent. At least under those conditions of liberal democracy, whatever kind of "mass" media actually exist in a small country, they tend to come under greater pressure to integrate diverse opinions, because everybody would know if they ignore or distort them.

By contrast, the more radical anonymity of a country like India, Brazil, or the United States makes "local news" less interesting for people in other corners of the country. In addition to not caring about what goes on in northern Iowa if you live in Brooklyn, and in addition to the sheer quantity of information that could not be digested even if it were reported, it is also much more difficult to assess whether a diversity of opinions and perspectives is "accurately and fairly" represented in a media item or genre. Perhaps that is why national reporting is relatively thin in many larger countries, while most consumers take more interest in local media.

Such arguments do not exclude the possibility that other factors will also play their part—such as, for instance, the structure of the current national media landscape, power and property relations among the major media enterprises, or people's habits of media consumption. Among these phenomena some lead to the other side of the spectrum of contrasting possibilities. Power and property relations in many small countries, for instance, feature public television stations that control large segments of the relevant market. Dating back from historical contexts when no other initiatives were capable of establishing an appropriate infrastructure, these monopolies have gone through series of legal deregulations and regulations that nevertheless leave them in influential market positions—as in the cases of public radio and television in large parts of Europe.

What Small Countries Do with Standard-Size Structures

Media organization may often be rather sensitive to facts of scale at national and local levels. Smallness, however, is not always directly mirrored in nation-level organizational forms. Take sports as a very clear example, showing up in many of our chapters.

In the contemporary world, sports form one context where the expression of nationalist sentiments largely remains publicly legitimate. This is also one domain where the David and Goliath motif is recurrent in the small-country imagination—there is often very concentrated national attention to the performance of local stars in international contests, and someone who succeeds is likely to become a national hero or heroine. This is a major topic in Robotham's chapter on Jamaica, focusing on responses to athletic achievements in the 2012 London Olympics. And in both Switzerland and Austria, Bendix notes, Alpine sports stars are celebrated.

But note also for example what Shore says about New Zealand's pride in the All Blacks, its national rugby team. Team sports may indeed engage the David and Goliath motif in a particular way—perhaps because they involve collective efforts, with some special affinity to the idea of the nation, but also because of their particular relationship to scale. Consider, hypothetically, a Brazil-Norway soccer game. Brazil has a population of about two hundred million, Norway one of close to five million. This does not mean that Norway fields a team of eleven players, and Brazil proportionately one of somewhere over four hundred—both teams are only allowed to have the same number of individuals on the field at any one time. So in a way there is "a level playing field." If Brazil would be expected to win the game, however, it would in large part be because its team can be recruited from a much larger pool of talent. (Other factors also play a part—otherwise China and India would be major soccer nations, which they have not been so far.)

In fact, there was once a Norway-Brazil soccer game, in Marseille in the 1998 World Cup. Norway did win, 2–1. Brazilians may have forgotten this soon enough. In Norway it became a mythological event, even celebrated several years later in an opera.

Anyway, it would seem that a somewhat parallel view can be taken toward the relationship between various other nation-level structures and their variable-scale surroundings. The sociologist John W. Meyer and his collaborators (e.g., Meyer et al. 1997; Meyer 1999) have argued that "nation-states" have become a globally dominant mode of political organization; more-over, as notions of modernity and rationality diffuse among these states, their formal role structures tend to become isomorphic. But, we would suggest, at this level they, like the soccer team, may not be very sensitive to scale. This may turn out to be a financial burden not least to the poorer of small countries. Moreover, the recruitment of personnel to these structures occurs under rather different conditions in large and small countries. There are offices to be filled; yet, as in the case of the soccer team, the small country has fewer people available to populate a structure of roles rather like that assembled in some much larger country.

What do small countries do when nation-level structures are a bit on the large side? Will they shrink these structures in one way or another? Or will they allow a rather larger proportion of the total population to be drawn into them than would be needed in a larger country? Or will the result be one of role combinations that might seem surprising to an observer from a country of another size? One of us once commented a little playfully on politics in the Cayman Islands (not really a "country" but at that time a British crown colony) that it made him think of operettas and comic novels about invented mini-states, where the same people show up in many roles, knowing each other and perhaps knowing too much about each other (Hannerz 1974: 7). The countries we deal with here are considerably larger, but several of the problems of fitting smaller populations to less scale-sensitive structures may again show up.

It is occasionally suggested that nepotism rather than corruption is likely to be a recurrent weakness of small countries, but precisely how this relates to complexities and contradictions of scale still seems to demand more precise analysis. Perhaps nepotism actually becomes a slightly less powerful concept in small countries, where there is a smaller population to recruit from for various positions. There is simply a rather higher probability that relatives, friends, old schoolmates, or cronies will appear in closer proximity in the state apparatus or other major institutions. If Transparency International were to construct a global "Nepotism Perceptions Index," how would its ratings compare to those on perceptions of corruption?

In this volume, particularly Richard Wilk's chapter on Belize (which happens to end with yet another, less triumphant, comment on a David and Goliath soccer game—David lost), deals with the problems of stretching a small population to meet international requirements. For one thing, Belize cannot have embassies everywhere. Elsewhere, Khalaf notes that in Abu Dhabi, of the small proportion of the population that is of local origin, 90 percent are employed in the state bureaucracy. This may be taken as a way of meeting international standards. On the other hand, it could also be an example of how an exceptionally affluent state can afford to create sinecures for citizens.

Zero-Sum Thought

If limited scale and transparency might just possibly generate trust, the other side of the coin could, also just possibly, be a tendency to disapprove of originality and too much success. Envy is undoubtedly a widespread human sentiment, occurring at various interpersonal or social levels, but it seems worth noting that forms of it are given a kind of public recognition in some small-country vocabularies. In Sweden, one somewhat old-fashioned and paradoxical term is *kungliga svenska avundsjukan*, "royal Swedish envy" (which has nothing to do with the monarchy—the label seems rather more to indicate the ubiquity of the phenomenon, coterminous with the kingdom itself). In Scandinavia more generally, there is also the "Jante Law," a term originally coined by the Danish-Norwegian writer Aksel Sandemose in the 1930s, but quickly adopted throughout the region to indicate a multifaceted pressure toward conformity, as contrasted with individual achievement. Apart from extensive academic references in several European languages (e.g., Michel et al. 2001) about conceptualizing a "society of envy/envious society," popular German-language puns play on the similarity between the terms for oath (*Eid*) and envy (*Neid*). This includes the much-publicized occasion when a president of Switzerland, the country officially being referred to as the "Oath Association" (*Eidgenossenschaft*), warned that Switzerland must never turn into a *Neidgenossenschaft*, that is, an association of envy.

Then in a quite different area, anthropologists of the Caribbean have reported on a related notion of "crab antics": if you have a bucket full of crabs and one of them tries to climb up and escape, it will be drawn down again into the bucket by other crabs (see particularly Wilson 1973). And this serves as a revealing metaphor for local human social behavior. In his chapter on New Zealand, Cris Shore also turns it into a traveling metaphor.[18] In this volume, too, we have the instance of Singapore. Here a strong elitist emphasis is present in the nation-building strategy from the late twentieth century onward; but in recent times, there has been a popular dissatisfaction with the resulting inequality, which Goh Beng Lan relates to its particular conspicuousness in a small society.

If ideas and idioms of conformism and envy are a less attractive side of egalitarianism, such zero-sum thought about the distribution of social and material resources may occur most readily at a local level, where the conduct and achievements of neighbors are readily observable. From the heritage of anthropology we may retrieve George M. Foster's (1965) conception of "the image of limited good," drawing on ethnography from Mexican peasant society. Yet we may sense that varieties of similar thinking may grow also with the characteristic historical pasts of at least some small countries: among somewhat marginal peasantries at the outskirts and in the buffer lands of Europe; in societies reacting to their beginnings in plantation slavery, as in Jamaica, or elsewhere in the Caribbean; or among those New Zealand settlers, leaving a deeply stratified mother country behind.

On the other hand, there are small countries that at least now organize life according to quite different conditions. One of our contributors, Sulayman Khalaf (1992; see also Chapter 13 in this volume), indeed, in discussing contemporary affluent Arab Gulf society, suggests an "image of unlimited good."

Borders and Copresences

Thinking of smallness in absolute terms, we have mostly been concerned with implications of a limited population size. Yet smallness may also be a spatial matter. True, population numbers and territorial extent do not always covary. Some inhabitants of small countries, population-wise, would seem to have a chance to really stretch their legs: Libya, with some 6.5 million people, Chad, with some 10.5 million people, and Mauritania, with a little over 3 million people, are all among the thirty largest lands in the world (out of some two hundred). But then in each of these instances, much of that space consists of inhospitable Saharan desert, and most of the population is concentrated in a rather limited part of the territory. Mali is also rather like that: the crisis we noted at the beginning of this introduction started as the relatively few people living in the northern half of the country (in large part Tuaregs), who had long felt neglected, got hold of arms and a mobilizing ideology. In other regions, countries with small populations and large territories (with comparable amounts of steppe and desert portions) include, for example, Botswana, Namibia, and Mongolia. We do not come across so many countries where the small population is evenly distributed across the large land. In the striking case of the Maldives, discussed in Eva-Maria Knoll's chapter, the country stretches over a very large area, but much of it is sea.

If smallness really is a matter of limited space, however, what might be its consequences for national life? We see at least two possibilities. One is simply that borders are always nearby: the whole country may be more or less a borderland. There is now a well-developed genre of border studies in anthropology, and while most of these studies may deal with the border areas of larger countries—that between the United States and Mexico drawing by far the greatest attention—the accumulating understandings in this field may well be relevant to small-country studies.[19] What can it mean to be always close to a border? That depends greatly on what is on the other side. Some borders, such as those between prosperous member states of the European Union, are now rather less significant. You hardly notice when you cross them. If the country on the other side is enemy country (actual or potential), or a much poorer or richer country, border consciousness may be a more conspicuous part of crises or of everyday life. An extreme case is that of Israel: a great deal of life may go on as if the country were an island, but it is a continuously important fact that much of it is, or would be, within firing distance from surrounding lands. In Helena Wulff's chapter on Ireland, we learn that the northern border of the republic never seems far away; and around it is the land of troubles. Gingrich and his coauthors provide examples of how the proximity of Israel is reflected in Palestinian jokes.

The other consideration involving a small space we want to point to is of a rather different kind. It involves the possibility of running into particular other people more or less by chance. One of us has used the term "traffic relationships" to describe the mostly unfocused, brief copresences in public settings that are one characteristic of cities (Hannerz 1980). These are minimal relationships, involving people passing one another, avoiding bumping into each other, queuing, and so on, mostly managed so as to avoid closer contact. In the city, they tend to be characterized by anonymity. Here, however, we would argue that when a limited population share a limited space, there is also a possibility that traffic relationships will rather more often involve recognition: mutual or one-sided. You just may run into a TV star in the supermarket aisle when you go shopping or a government minister half naked on the beach. Of course, traffic relationships with such a potential for serendipitous recognition may be unevenly distributed in public space; there is no doubt a particular microgeography of traffic relationships.

What is the significance of such encounters? They may well remain matters of mere copresence. Perhaps later in the day, as a conversational resource, you mention whom you just saw to others. Such people spotting could be deemed mostly trivial, although possibly it contributes marginally to a sense of intimacy and relative accessibility. Robotham notes, for example, that any Jamaican has a chance of running into one of the country's athletic heroes or heroines in the street or at some entertainment nightspot. Perhaps these encounters also do something to blur the contrast between "public" and "private." Then, however, traffic relationships may be transformed into something not so trivial, if one party insists on turning them into something different. Copresence in a public space can be a source of danger, not least for someone readily recognizable. Ulf Hannerz offers two examples in his concluding chapter.

Umbrellas and Ditches

In what has been discussed up to this point, there may be some chance of discerning where more absolute or more relative smallness is the most influential. But there are certainly many areas of small-country life where these two dimensions interact. In the remaining parts of this introduction, we will mostly not insist on trying to sort out such complexity very explicitly. In what follows next, however, our point of departure is in what was said above about networks.

In his own contribution to *Scale and Social Organization*, Fredrik Barth (1978) made an exploratory attempt to map his personal network, taking careful note of all his interactions, including telephone calls and written correspondence. He was surprised at his findings: if an investigating anthropologist had asked him to generalize about his network, Barth concluded, he would have been a poor informant.

He did, however, venture to make two generalizations. One was that "English-speaking anthropologists above 40 years of age make up a small world of high density"; the other was that "Norwegian 'public' persons in arts, sciences, and mass communication are largely known to each other" (Barth 1978: 177). Some decades later, the first of these appears strikingly untrue—evidence of the global growth of the anthropological discipline in the intervening years. The second statement, about the cohesion of Norwegian public life, is more immediately relevant to our interests here. It suggests a certain transparency or intimacy of the national scene, of the kind we have identified before. It can also remind us of a statement by another anthropologist, at about the same time. In *Changing Jamaica*, Adam Kuper (1976: 122) wrote of this Caribbean nation that

> perhaps 30,000 men rank as potential men of influence, on the most liberal count. Most of them were educated in a handful of grammar schools, which link them in loyal cliques even as ageing men, and they are further organized in the network of clubs and associations I have described. . . . Members of this category will be familiar with others in it, at least by name or reputation, or by some contact with their family. I believe, further, that every member of this category has the possibility of personal contact, through no more than one intermediary with a member of the cabinet, or a leading member of the opposition.

Kuper makes the point that a small number of schools had an important part in creating linkages early in the lives of those influential Jamaicans, and that certain organizational memberships contributed to social cohesion at later points. Even as they accumulate into nationwide webs of relationships, networks are in large part far from random creations. They are shaped by particular contexts: often enduring, often institutional in nature. To understand the particularly effective reach of certain networks in creating the social cohesion of small countries, one must identify those institutions that hold particularly large umbrellas over significant parts of the population. Educational establishments may often be important here, bringing people together early in life and for extended periods. Many of the current generation of prominent Irish literary figures, Helena Wulff notes, know each other from the time when they were all students at University College Dublin. But other kinds of institutions can have a comparable role. Commentators on Israeli national life have often pointed to the part of the Israel Defense Forces as an effective machinery for bringing a people of notably diverse backgrounds together.

When the inhabitants of a country cannot really form direct relationships with one another, a particularly unitary media structure can at least foster a sense of continuous common experience, of "I know that you know"; where more or less everybody reads the same morning newspaper or watches the same evening TV show, there is the shoulder-to-shoulder relationship of recognizably shared attention. Major calendrical events—of a secular national nature or involving a shared religion—can similarly cultivate a sense of wide togetherness. In the final chapter, Hannerz notes some such umbrella devices in Sweden, including the festivities around the annual award of the Nobel Prizes. Most remarkably, João de Pina-Cabral points to the enduring influence of the Roman Catholic Church as an overarching structure through much of Portuguese history.

Then, on the other hand, there are small countries that face greater obstacles in getting to such connectivity and cohesion. Instead of umbrellas, they have ditches, more or less deep. Religious, ethnic, or racial divides may leave their mark on countries that may or may not have been rather arbitrary constructs on the map. The internal diversity of our category of small countries certainly includes cases where major social cleavages run through the social fabric. Again, in Mali, the Tuaregs have felt left out. In his chapter about Jamaica, Robotham shows how the society was built from scratch around the deep chasm of plantation slavery, the traces of which remain durably important (even as they combine, presumably, with the old school ties referred to by Kuper). Writing about Sierra Leone, Knörr points to another historical divide formed in the wake of the slave trade: that between the Krios of Freetown and the populations of inland.

There are thus small countries where ditches may indeed be deep. Yet certain institutions can even then be important in building bridges. Possibly the growth of a plethora of new NGOs, as well as more traditional-style but updated secret societies, as also described by Knörr, can play a part in building cohesion in post–civil war Sierra Leone, after older institutions were destroyed or discredited before or during the war.

Then again there is the language issue. Language-dependent institutions may contribute less to national cohesion where there are two or more strong languages, and where people may turn some of their attention to the educational and media structures operating in these languages in neighboring countries. Instead of building shoulder-to-shoulder relationships, there may be back-to-back relationships of limited attention and engagement.

Becoming a Small Country: Responses to Shrinking

Our concerns here are mostly with small countries in the present; but it would not be a good idea to go entirely presentist. Thoughts of smallness may have much to do with historical change. Several of our chapters deal with such circumstances.

Mostly used somewhat pejoratively, the term "Balkanization" refers to a small-country creation process going too far. It is a kind of process, however, with two sides. As new national boundaries are drawn, some present-day small countries have become countries. Others have turned small.

The crumbling of empires has had much to do with this. Already early in the nineteenth century Greece was reborn, as the Ottoman Empire began coming apart. After World War I, the Russian and Habsburg empires were no more, but Finland, the Baltic countries, and Czechoslovakia came into being as sovereign entities, and Yugoslavia was put together. The independence of Ireland around the same time foreshadowed what would come during the following decades after World War II, when the British, French, Dutch, and Belgian empires withdrew from most of Asia, Africa, and the Caribbean. A great many new countries, large as well as small, appeared on maps around this time. Portugal withdrew from what remained of its overseas territories a little later. The independence of Singapore came as it was found too much to swallow for the recently created Malaysia—Goh notes differing interpretations of what then happened. In the Middle East, after both the Ottoman and the British empires left, the Zionist success story of creating Israel stands as the most dramatic example of a new country coming into being. But in the Arab world surrounding it, there were several others. Nearby, a rather arbitrarily carved-out territory of mostly desert constructed itself as the Hashemite Kingdom of Jordan, proclaiming a direct genealogical connection of its leadership to the Prophet Muhammad. Among the principalities on the Persian Gulf that had been under British protection, some went their own way, like Qatar. Others, including Abu Dhabi and Dubai, joined together in the United Arab Emirates. And then, as the twentieth century was coming to an end, the disintegration of the Soviet empire led to the reappearances of a number of countries with ancient identities, on the Baltic, in Eastern Europe, in the Caucasus, and in central Asia.

But again, some old countries are now smaller than they once were. Portugal, as João de Pina-Cabral describes its volatile history, may seem to have been more a process than a state, a project growing on land and across the seas from the modest domain of the Count of Portucallem to something stretched out over four continents—and then shrinking. Austria can identify itself as a core successor state to the Habsburg empire. In Scandinavia, as Orvar Löfgren shows, both Denmark and Sweden have histories of growing and shrinking. Serbia, discussed by Aleksandar Bošković in another chapter, achieved its independence from the Ottoman Empire, became the dominant core of a not-so-small Yugoslav kingdom before World War II and of the federal republic of Yugoslavia after, and then found itself on its own again, rather small, and moreover losing Kosovo.

How do the citizens of these countries respond to such changes? What is the place of shrinking in national sensibilities? Very possibly there are mixed feelings, but one can discern that there are differences in the way memories are, or are not, carried into the present. In Austria, Habsburg memories may mostly take the form of nostalgia.[20] One hardly wants old territories back, but one treasures, seriously or playfully, the souvenirs from the great past. Offering important historical depth in her contrast of Austria with Switzerland, Bendix shows how the former juggles with its memories of grandeur, while the latter has a sense of great continuity in its current shape. In Scandinavia, Norway, still relatively young as an independent country, celebrates its nationhood joyfully every year on 17 May, while Denmark and Sweden seem inclined toward historical amnesia. To them what was before the twentieth century is not very important; what matters more is the rise of the modern welfare state and its updated versions.

Claims to Superiority, Risks of Embarrassment

In the past, the cultural management of the state was mostly internalist, turning local people into citizens and patriots. Now nations as brands compete with each other in an external market for investors, tourists, and general goodwill.[21] This tends to go well with another current key concept, "soft power"—if you can gain the approval of others for what you do or who you are, you can increase your influence.[22] These notions show up in several chapters. Your soft power may also reflect what you have been. A notion of Austria as "a cultural superpower" can continue to feed on a Habsburg, or Viennese fin de siècle, artistic and intellectual past. Jacqueline Knörr reports that the Krios of Sierra Leone, present-day descendants of an early educated elite, fondly refer to their capital Freetown as the "Athens of West Africa" (see also Knörr 2010: 211). Yet one may sense that the brands, whether oriented toward the past or the present, can actually face two ways: toward the outside world and toward a public at home. As Robotham shows, the aesthetic of defiance that is a Jamaican gift to the world grew initially on one side of that deep divide through plantation society.

Later chapters in this book bear witness to the fact that in some way or another, small countries often claim a greater importance than their mere size would warrant—even if they are not always what Virginia Dominguez terms "chutzpah countries."[23] But the national brands they promote are of a variety of kinds, sometimes through key phrases suggesting particular places in the global landscape. A particular specialization may turn into claims to expertise, perhaps recognized by others; at times this is enacted in some special niche that cannot be adequately embraced by larger neighbors. Fields of niche expertise may include competencies in diplomatic arbitration, military peacekeeping, or monitoring of elections (activities in which Scandinavian countries, Switzerland, Austria, and New Zealand have been engaged; Shore touches on this fact in his contribution, and Hannerz again in his concluding chapter). Here, part of the brand message may indeed be that "small is beautiful" in its own right—the small country cannot aim at achieving domination in its own right, hence is not dangerous to others.[24] Similarly, but with a more internalist emphasis, small countries are sometimes held, in their own view as well as that of outside commentators, to function well as laboratories where social experiments can be performed—even as sites for utopian thought turned into practice. Such assumptions about potentials for social engineering may draw on the possibilities of accessibility, transparency, trust, and control referred to above. Cuba under Castro may come to mind as taking these possibilities in one direction, Singapore under Lee Kuan Yew in another. Again, recent transformations of the Scandinavian sociopolitical landscape, toward a new blend of a market economy with a lean yet functioning welfare state, may serve as another instance. Cris Shore discusses a similar development in New Zealand.

Some countries may even make internal accessibility a part of their brand. In his *Our Last Best Chance* (2011: 135), a combination of autobiography and national manifesto, King Abdullah II of Jordan makes the point that the Diwan, that is, the Royal Court, is an adaptation of a traditional system through which "every Jordanian citizen has the right to petition the king directly . . . when I visit rural areas of the country, people will frequently come up to me directly and hand me a piece of paper with their petition written on it." In his chapter, Khalaf makes a similar point about sheikhly accessibility in Abu Dhabi. Again, small is beautiful.

As another set of specialized qualifications, certain economic and fiscal practices come to mind: various financial opportunities from commercial services via offshore banking to "tax havens." Richard Wilk finds Belize engaged in such business. Goh Beng Lan notes in her chapter that Singapore is now less inclined to look at Israel for a parallel experience—a small heroic country in hostile surroundings—and leans toward seeing Switzerland as the proper model. The United Arab Emirates offers another example. One or the other of sets of specialized economic "small-country expertise" is combined with cultural productions, creative industries, and tourism. In the opening paragraph we noted how Gulf countries could convert oil wealth into other assets. Objects of the world cultural heritage are acquired for new museums, while the local heritage also takes on a higher profile. The striking example here is that of Abu Dhabi, as reported on by Sulayman Khalaf. The emirate has a Louvre Abu Dhabi and a Guggenheim Abu Dhabi, yet gives a new shape to a public culture of camel racing and falconry as well. Another emirate, Qatar, operates a global television news channel competing with CNN International and BBC World. In other cases the goods and services of tourist and cultural industries form a fairly independent set, as in the case of the Maldives. These fields of niche expertise need not remain a matter of top-down policies: they also have their impact in education, the job market, and biographical choices.

If small countries may set forth various claims to greatness, however, there is also some risk involved. The claims may be disputed or simply ignored. The inhabitants of small countries may be aware, too, that there are facets of national life that they do not want to put on display—in Erving

Goffman's (1959) dramaturgical terms, there may be a front stage and a back stage. The notion of "cultural intimacy" offered by Michael Herzfeld (1997), one anthropologist more recently engaging with the complexities of national cultures, is relevant here. As Herzfeld points out, there is a level of informal exercise of culture and power, not quite in line with official rules, quite familiar to the locals, but also a source of embarrassment when it comes to the attention of outside observers. Herzfeld draws examples from many countries, large or small, without emphasizing differences in scale. We suspect, however, that not least in its dimension of external embarrassment, cultural intimacy may be a particular concern in small countries. Representatives of a large, powerful country may perhaps readily shrug off any outside reminder of its possible blemishes, and, given its position in the world, these may be difficult to conceal anyway. But people from a small country might prefer if nobody notices what might cause them to blush. Pina-Cabral notes that the Portuguese enjoy their self-deriding jokes but resent it when these are told by foreigners. It is a continuous theme of Shore's chapter that New Zealand's external brand of small-country strengths does not match domestic policies particularly well.

Backstage, such sensibilities may be addressed in many different ways. They may cover the critique of an elite's unwavering willingness to let one's country be pushed around, yet they can also extend as far as collective irony on the verge of self-humiliation—as in Yemeni jokes about the average Yemeni's willingness to walk as long as it takes, just to get a job in the Gulf region. The theme of inferiority thus also includes its limits, as in "small, but . . ."—small but also unwilling to cope with it, or small but surprisingly creative/intelligent, small but proud and conscious of one's own virtues, and so forth. These topics may be addressed through various media formats: literature, performative and visual arts, popular jokes, or riddles. At times a trickster-like element also becomes evident here.

Creativity at the Periphery

Some of the prevalent understandings of the characteristics of small countries, particularly those involving relative smallness, may remind us of more or less classic social-science conceptions of relationships between center and periphery or metropolis and province. Very small states can be world centers of some kind, such as the Vatican. But mostly centers are big countries, or somewhere in big countries, and small countries are in the periphery. Center-periphery relationships, however, are not all alike.[25]

As first described by the sociologist Edward Shils (1972, 1975), these were consensual relationships of dominance and deference. The center had vitality and creativity, while the periphery was unimaginative, petty, narrow. So the periphery, if it had a choice, it was one between impoverished autonomy and enriching dependence. In the passage of culture, the center would be the donor, the periphery the recipient.

That view of center-periphery relationships may at one time have depicted what we have described as binary constellations. The notion of "cultural cringe," mentioned by Cris Shore, suggests sentiments of inferiority, but where Shils saw consensus, one might now often see contested hegemony. While not discarding the conceptual pair as a relic from the past, we are more likely to find an active periphery accepting this, rejecting that, and synthesizing whatever is imported with what is already in its own cultural inventory. There may even be some periphery-center counterflow.

Meanwhile, the center may not be so good at attending to the outside. The formulation by one prominent British diplomat and international relations thinker, Robert Cooper (2003: 97–98), is interesting here:

> Perhaps there is a general difficulty for the powerful in understanding the outside world. First, they have less need to understand others than do the weak. . . . Second, a large country with a big bureaucratic or imperial machine will have such difficulty reaching an internal consensus that listening to foreigners or taking account of their concerns may sometimes simply be too difficult. If you sit in the middle of a big country, in a big capital city, in a big administration, then even remembering that the outside world exists can sometimes be a problem.

So here is a suggestion of some advantage of the weak and small, acutely aware that the rest of the world exists. In the final chapter, Hannerz cites a Swedish newspaper columnist who argues that the small-country person becomes a true internationalist because he knows "he lives his life on the edge of the plate." The advantage may be enhanced if the periphery engages with multiple centers. Such a periphery can at best work out its own synthesis of selections from the centers (together with whatever may be useful at home), a David learning to maneuver successfully between Goliaths. Intellectual historians in Finland have seen a local flowering of philosophical thought as resulting from the varied European travels and sojourns of its leaders: "While it is possible to ignore London in Paris, and Paris in London, both centers are present in Helsinki" (Strang 2011).

Cosmopolitanism—or Neo-Nationalism?

Such commentary on center-periphery structures also suggests that recent debates over cosmopolitanism in many human sciences may offer connections to the study of cultural life in small countries.[26] An openness across borders may involve some of that openness to diversity characteristic of the cultural, intellectual, and aesthetic stance of cosmopolitanism.

Yet we must confront again that simultaneity of contrasting possibilities. Small countries can also have their nationalisms. Perhaps nationalism flourishes in more fertile grounds here for two reasons that frequently occur together: threats from the outside are perceived as more obvious, while the threat of nationalism in a small country does not impress outsiders very much (Gingrich 2006, 2011). Combinations of small-country nationalism and right-wing extremism have resulted in the forms recently described as neo-nationalism (ranging from the rise of Jörg Haider in Austrian politics in the 1990s to the Norwegian massacre in 2011). Yet fusions between small-country nationalism and left radicalism (as in Cuba or in certain phases in the history of the Irish Republican Army) cannot be ignored either. At any rate, small-country nationalism often activates one form or another of "cultural pessimism," as in "what will happen to my country's education/language/other traditions if all these neighboring/foreign/ immigrant/ secular/ other religious/global influences become increasingly stronger?"

Moreover, elements of cultural pessimism may combine in a small country more easily with a second factor, one of economic chauvinism (Gingrich 2006). As we have seen, a small country's situation sometimes results in a degree of affluence that is quite distinct within the wider region, as in cases such as Singapore, Israel, the Maldives, the United Arab Emirates, and Switzerland. Economic chauvinism can thus be identified as the widespread reluctance in a small country to share wealth with others. In combination with a fear of downward social mobility, it seems to represent a relatively independent source for the emergence and maintenance of small-country nationalism.

Small Is Vulnerable

Small countries may risk being embarrassed; yet that is hardly the most weighty of the risks they may face. A sense of vulnerability is a recurrent and multifaceted characteristic among them. Goh Beng Lan senses it in Singapore; and an extreme present-day instance would seem to be the Maldives, discussed in this volume by Eva-Maria Knoll. It is not only a matter, for these low-lying islands, of the sea level rising due to global warming, so that the country could vanish. There is also the widespread occurrence of a hereditary blood disorder, creating a need for blood donations from the outside. Another drastic sense of vulnerability could involve a fear that one's small country will simply be swallowed by some big neighbor—as happened to Austria, with *Anschluss*, before World War II, and with Kuwait, briefly turned into the nineteenth province of Saddam Hussein's Iraq, in 1990.

Another of those recently prominent global ranking lists seems relevant here. There is now a notion of "failed states," or (slightly more tentatively) "failing states." A list of such states is published regularly by *Foreign Policy* magazine (Acemoglu and Robinson 2012). Here Somalia, worst on that Transparency International list of perceptions of public corruption, moves from the bottom to the top. Among the twenty "most failed," we also find other small countries: Chad, Haiti, Guinea-Bissau, and Burundi. Yet among the failures are also large countries such as Pakistan, Iraq, the Democratic Republic of Congo, and Nigeria. So size does not in itself seem to matter much. In any case, the *Foreign Policy* list, the methodology used in constructing it, and the very notion of "failed states" have been debated and questioned.

Vulnerability, however, can also take a variety of economic forms. If "freedom of expression" promotes diversity, "free markets" do not always do so. It seems somewhat easier in small countries to establish a variety of economic monopolies or quasi-monopolies. For instance, more than 70 percent of the consumer food market in Austria is controlled by three major supermarket chains. On the Maldives, two companies control most of the market for cell-phone network providers. In Belize, on the other hand, Richard Wilk notes, the limits of the marketplace are such that local firms have a hard time establishing themselves at all, in competition with imported goods. And where some sort of externally based, or externally oriented, economic enterprise becomes overwhelmingly strong in a small and weak country, discomfort may also grow. One could consider here the recent financial crises in several small European countries (Iceland, Ireland, Cyprus), following the border-crossing outreach of some of their commercial banks. Illicit enterprises can also become too powerful; there have been signs that transnational narcopolitics has a strong influence in certain small West African countries, and it is present in Belize as well. In her chapter, Jacqueline Knörr can point to the very disruptive influence of diamonds in Sierra Leonean affairs, with impoverished youths connecting to smugglers and warlords. Under such conditions of external connectedness, closeness at home may not breed trust and social control but rather a sense of disgust as power and wealth are visibly hoarded in small groups. Knörr refers to the politics of the belly, for some time a root metaphor in African political studies. And in *A Small Place*, the novelist Jamaica Kincaid's (1988: 41) sharply critical essay on Antigua, her Caribbean island country of origin, with pervasive kleptocracy, Kincaid suggests as the view of every ordinary Antiguan that "the government is corrupt. Them are thief, them are big thief."

Cultural pessimism need not be so acute or pervasive. It can involve a vaguer sense that the country's identity and way of life are threatened, perhaps by insidious, creeping influences. Larger countries may well face some of the same general types of problems—narcopolitics, for example, has been dramatically present in a large country like Mexico as well. However, the danger may be felt more quickly in a small country: there is a sense of approaching some kind of tipping point.

Migration—In or Out

Among those problematic facts of life that small countries face, one of the more important is sometimes that people move. Transnational migration is a widespread phenomenon, but in countries with small populations it may contribute to a sense of vulnerability in particular ways.

On the one hand, if the country is attractive to migrants, or actively recruits migrants for one reason or another, there can be a perceived risk of takeover, of being swamped. Again, in post–World War II northern and western Europe, small and relatively prosperous countries have had anti-immigration, sometimes xenophobic political groupings. Eriksen's chapter reports on the Norwegian case, Bendix on that of Switzerland. But difficulties in coping adequately with immigration are not limited to Europe. Persian Gulf countries need to recruit labor forces from abroad—for the oil industry, for construction work, for services and various other purposes. Yet they do not want these migrants to become citizens or permanent residents, turning them into legitimate members of national society. Sulayman Khalaf touches on this in his chapter on Abu Dhabi, with a remarkably small proportion of native Emiratis. So in various ways, such migrants are allowed only restricted rights, for limited periods; undeniably present but not really recognized.[27]

On the other hand, people moving out can also become a threat if the emigration proportionately occurs on such a scale as to constitute a real or potential depopulation. Early in the twentieth century, when one-fifth of the Swedish population had already gone to the United States, and emigrant ships continued to cross the Atlantic, a government commission was established to propose policies that would halt this rush toward the exit; perhaps by now it is most remembered for a short book on Swedish folk mentality that was an early contribution to the genre of national character studies (Sundbärg 1911). The commission report also contained close to three hundred personal accounts by emigrants to North America who often described the oppressive class structure as a major reason for leaving. But it also provided groundwork for varied reforms pointing forward to the future welfare state and certainly did something to persuade people to stay home.

Then later in the century, before the "Celtic Tiger" arrived, one joke in Ireland, a classic emigrant country, was the request "Will the last person to leave please switch off the light!" Meanwhile, in Singapore, there is also some concern with people leaving, as Goh reports in her chapter—well-educated, English-speaking "cosmopolitans," rather than less-educated, Chinese-speaking "heartlanders." Yet the demographic issue to which the Singapore government tries to attend with various well-intentioned remedies is another one: the low birthrate especially of the former of these categories.

Among the emigrants themselves, there is probably less worry about the future of the country they are leaving and more hope for their own future wherever they are going. A remarkable example is in Charles Piot's (2010) recent study of the small West African republic of Togo (population about six million). The continuation of a dictatorial family dynasty, and a weakening post–Cold War economy under global neoliberalism, appears to have made emigration an attractive prospect for just about everybody. A striking number of Togolese seem to participate in the green-card lottery of the local American embassy, dreaming of a new life in the United States. A complicated local structure of expertise has developed around ways of getting past all formal obstacles. Not many succeed, of course. For those who remain behind in Togo but who have links to those who manage to get out, there may yet be significant gain: migrants' remittances to the home country now constitute an important part of the global economy. Belize, as Richard Wilk shows in his chapter, depends greatly on remittances. But without such incomes, there can be vulnerability of sorts for a country without migrants as well.

In this context, we may also be reminded that some small countries have strong diasporas. Wilk notes that there are probably more Belizeans in Los Angeles than in their home country's capital. Often enough, certainly, migrants and their descendants figure noticeably only in the small-scale circles of family, kin, and neighbors back home. Yet there are those notable instances where diasporas leave a major mark on national life. If they achieve some strength in countries of settlement that are themselves big and powerful, they can affect their countries of origin in different ways. The instances of Jewish (not in the strict sense of Israeli), Irish, and Cuban diasporas in the United States are the most obvious: in two cases as important political allies when their corresponding countries of allegiance have been involved in enduring conflicts, and in the third case in large part as an important adversary. Dominguez, in her chapter, mentions an argument in an Israeli cabinet meeting where the prime minister at the time, Ariel Sharon, supposedly expressed his view that the political influence of the diaspora in the United States was indeed strong. The Armenian diaspora in western Europe, the Lebanese and Syrian diasporas in Central and South America, the Portuguese diaspora in North America, and the Greek diaspora in the Middle East and Africa are noteworthy examples for less politicized patterns, yet with enduring commercial and financial affinities with the respective countries. The Jamaican diaspora is visible in Robotham's account of Jamaican cultural power. In Sierra Leone, Knörr reports, the ambiguous position of the Krios, resulting in a certain exodus during the civil war, seems to have

improved after it, when members of the diaspora have also engaged in re-
constructing the nation.

Small Countries, Global Openings

Questions of mobility, finally, take us to one important set of issues for an
understanding of small countries (but in the end, not only them), at present
and in the future: that of transnational linkages.

With growing global interconnectedness, notions of relative smallness
can change in a very general way. It may now matter a little less for Ireland
and Austria that they are next to Great Britain and Germany, respectively—
but rather more that they are also small in comparison with the United
States, India, and China. Even Germans may occasionally sense that they
belong to a "small country," when compared to the Chinese.

More specifically, these connections involve varieties of greater openness. We have assumed here that countries are significant containers of
social life. But these containers do leak. (Probably the country that has attempted to be most self-contained has been North Korea—not an absolutely small country, but relatively small in some historically significant
ways—but that has had its costs.) The greater openness may affect everybody
in small countries, for better or for worse, although probably some of their
inhabitants more than others.

One reaction to small-country life that is sometimes mentioned is that it
is boring—not enough variety, not enough going on, nowhere to escape to.
Locating boredom at the national level may seem, at first glance, like an odd
idea. But in any case, perhaps it is, at least nowadays, not so likely to be true.
Even when people stay put inside the borders, the power of media may allow
them to know of a wider range of the global cultural inventory and engage
with it. Increasingly, some people may be in a country but not quite of it.

That may seem like a straightforward widening of choice, but particularly in the small country it could also have other consequences. Some of
what we have referred to as umbrella institutions no longer cover quite everybody. Part of their power may have entailed cultural brokerage: they have
been sources of understandings of the outside world. Now when you can read
the New York Times every morning on the Internet and watch BBC World or
Al Jazeera on your television screen, some people may share less with those

sticking to old consumer habits. With the *Economist* and the *New York Review of Books* readily available, whatever may have been their nearest media counterparts locally may seem less attractive, even less necessary.

Then there are again those questions of mobility. These natives are not likely to be "incarcerated," as Arjun Appadurai (1988) has put it. The American labor economist Robert Reich (1991) once identified the emergent category of "symbolic analysts," people engaged in the nonstandardized manipulation of all sorts of symbols—words, data, oral and visual representations. They were people who identified and solved problems, sometimes strategic brokers; people whose skills were mobile. They could be involved in finance, technology, the arts, academia. "The creative class" is another label for more or less the same set of people (Florida 2002). One senses the distinction in Goh's discussion of the "cosmopolitan/heartlander" divide in Singapore.

Writing in his American context, Reich warned that the symbolic analysts were no longer so reliably attached to their nation. That may have been so even there, but their potential for footlooseness may be greater in a small country. The readiness to move may be a matter of "push" as well as "pull." Particularly where certain slots in the small-country opportunity structure are very limited in number, there may just be no openings at a given moment, and nothing coming up in the foreseeable future. The national scene may seem to offer a zero-sum game. For those aiming for such positions, the solution may be to seek them elsewhere.

But it could also be a matter of aiming higher. If you ask what you can do for your country, perhaps a great deal; if you ask what your country can do for you, possibly not so much. Those who seek a perch at the higher echelons of world business are less likely to find it in a small country, more probably in one of the "global cities." If you are in a field of artistic creativity, you may still be tempted to spend at least some of your time in Paris or New York rather than Stockholm.[28] Or consider the academic field. There are now global ranking lists here as well; that compiled annually by the Shanghai Jiao Tong University is among the best known.[29] Of the top one hundred academic institutions on the 2015 list, nineteen were, by our standards, in small countries. A respectable proportion perhaps, but the best placed of them, a Swiss institution, was in twentieth place. As with others among recent ranking lists, those comparing universities are debatable. The way these lists are constructed, they tend to foreground some disciplines and may favor institutions in English-speaking countries. Yet the fact remains: if you want to get your education at one of the really top universities of the world, or have your career there, you will not stay all the time in the small country. The presence of a Sorbonne Abu Dhabi or a campus of New York University in the same emirate, as noted in Sulayman Khalaf's chapter, may be designed to alleviate such inequality in the global academic order but also makes it more obvious.

In cases when people do move away, the migration may be permanent; another instance of what has been termed "brain drain." Yet if they return, or in some other way make themselves useful to their countries of origin, there can be some "brain gain" as well. But a point that may be especially relevant to small countries is that even then there could be some loss in what we have thought of as transparency and access. That is, if people, including some of "the best and the brightest," return from sojourns elsewhere, those network linkages that might have been shaped in more fully inclusive umbrella institutions at home may not be present to the same extent. When some in the business elite come out of Harvard Business School, they may know more of "what" but less about "whom." So perhaps that sense of "small world" risks being weakened with greater global interconnectedness.

Yet some of that, and many of these other structures and sensibilities that cluster as family resemblances among small countries, will probably still be in place for the foreseeable future. At the same time, we have to take into account the point with which João de Pina-Cabral ends his chapter: if the global economy offers no more empty spaces, for the Portuguese or for anybody else, modernity's model of growth may face its limits. If that is so, the expression "small world" could refer to something other than those strikingly ramifying social networks discovered a half century ago. It takes on a very different meaning for everybody; but that is mostly another story.

Notes

1. Some examples would include works in rather varied styles by Adams (1970) on Guatemala, Kuper (1976) on Jamaica, and Durrenberger and Pálsson (1989) on Iceland. Lloyd A. Fallers's *The Social Anthropology of the Nation-State* (1974) tends to see the anthropological contribution to nation-level studies as a focus on microcosms, dwells rather more on what divides countries than on their cohesion, and does not stay very consistently on the topic. John H. Bodley's *The Small Nation Solution* (2013) is strongly policy oriented, and Bodley's flexible notion of "nations" ranges from what we would

regard as "small countries" to entities such as the Asháninka people of Amazonia. Our coverage and aims are thus not so similar.

2. For critiques of methodological nationalism, see, for example, Wimmer and Glick Schiller (2002) and Beck (2005). Malkki's (1992) discussion of "the national order of things" is also relevant here.

3. Among the scholars prominently involved in national character studies at the time were Ruth Benedict, Margaret Mead, Gregory Bateson, and Geoffrey Gorer; a volume edited by Mead and Métraux (1953) casts light on concepts and methods. For a later critique, see Neiburg and Goldman (1998).

4. In other disciplines, or quasi-academic fields of application, generalizations about character traits of nationalities may even thrive. Conspicuous instances are in the field of "intercultural communication" studies. Anthropologists tend to be critical of these; see Breidenbach and Nyíri (2009: 262–304).

5. An early anthropological contribution to the study of these entities is that by Benedict (1966; see also Benedict 1967).

6. For population and territorial data on the countries and territories of the world, see www.geohive.com/earth.

7. Yemeni statistics rest on a version of jus sanguinis. Persons who are now regarded as citizens of the countries where they reside—Saudi Arabia, Great Britain, the United States—continue to be counted as Yemeni citizens because of Yemeni ancestors.

8. Eriksen's (1993) overview of the island as reality and metaphor in anthropology is relevant here.

9. On the global language order, see De Swaan (2001).

10. Yet more recent work by Jean and John Comaroff (e.g., Comaroff and Comaroff 2003), writing about South Africa—and aware of the previously mentioned work of the Wilsons as an intellectual heritage—likewise identifies scale as a key problem in doing ethnography; they envision and develop an "imaginative sociology" drawing on varied ethnographic sources in productive interplay with theory. While the key questions of their "ethnography on an awkward scale" involve globalization and modernity rather than nation units, their style of work is perhaps not entirely different from what we envisage here.

11. See Hannerz (1980, 1992) on network understandings of urban life and the global ecumene respectively.

12. For the beginnings of "small world" research, see Milgram (1969) and Travers and Milgram (1969).

13. Jeremy Boissevain's (1974) early exploratory study of the networks of two Maltese men covered only their own direct, "first-order" relationships. One of them named 638 contacts, and the other 1,751—a notable difference. Another classic study, Mark Granovetter's (1973) analysis of "the strength of weak ties," argues that social entities need weak ties, of acquaintanceship rather than friendship, not immediately leading back to the same dense clusters of interconnectedness, to cohere on a larger scale.

Through the weak ties new contacts are made, information spreads, initiatives are taken.

14. See, for instance, Fukuyama (1995), who only discusses large countries.

15. *Gemeinschaft* and *Gesellschaft* were the terms classically used by Ferdinand Tönnies for contrasting types of social order, presumably established in a global social-science vocabulary because the terms of the English-language translation, *Community and Society* (Tönnies 1957), have seemed less rhetorically effective.

16. The Transparency International list is at cpi.transparency.org.

17. The Reporters Without Borders ranking list for press freedom is at en.rsf.org /press-freedom-index-2013.

18. One may object that the "tall poppy syndrome," a notion that seems to be particularly closely linked to Australia, would speak against any direct connection between scale and this kind of restrictive social judgment—yet the egalitarian inclination to cut off the stalks of those human poppies who grow taller than others seems to have been identified in Australia already in the late nineteenth and early twentieth centuries, when the country had a considerably smaller (and more homogeneous) population than it does now.

19. The wider anthropological view of borders and border zones has for some time depended greatly on the work of Hastings Donnan and Thomas G. Wilson (e.g., Donnan and Wilson 1994; Wilson and Donnan 2012).

20. For a discussion of "Austronostalgia" in parts of the Habsburg empire that were Balkanized, and of later "Yugonostalgia" after Yugoslavia had split up, see Baskar (2007).

21. On cultural branding and nation branding, see Holt (2004) and Aronczyk (2013); for an ethnographic study of nation branding in Macedonia, see Graan (2013).

22. The notion of "soft power" introduced by the political scientist Joseph Nye (e.g., 2004) has rapidly entered a more general vocabulary.

23. The term "chutzpah" may not be familiar to every reader. The Hebrew expression means "audacity" or "insolence"; after moving into Yiddish it has spread from a primarily American base into the global vocabulary largely through American literature, television, and film, also taking on more favorable connotations of courage.

24. The phrase "small is beautiful" is linked to the views of the economist E. F. Schumacher (1973). Schumacher was primarily concerned with criticizing industrial capitalism and its environmental consequences, not with small countries.

25. For a review of the development of social-science understandings of center-periphery relationships and related concepts, see Hannerz (2001).

26. The debate over cosmopolitanism has grown rapidly since the 1990s; see, for example, Vertovec and Cohen (2002), Hannerz (2004), and Werbner (2008).

27. The discussion of "waiting" by Ehn and Löfgren (2010: 9ff.) is relevant here. Kanna (2011) offers an anthropological view of the situation of labor migrants in Dubai, where they constitute 95 percent of the workforce.

28. Studying young Swedish sojourners in New York in the late 1980s, Wulff (1992) found that in various kinds of professional pursuits, they judged that a period in New York was essential to their continued careers.

29. The Shanghai Jiao Tong ranking list for world universities is at www .shanghairanking.com.

References

Abdullah II (King of Jordan). 2011. *Our Last Best Chance.* London: Penguin.

Acemoglu, Daron, and James A. Robinson. 2012. Failed States: The 2012 Index. *Foreign Policy* 194 (July/August): 85–91.

Adams, Richard N. 1970. *Crucifixion by Power.* Austin: University of Texas Press.

Anderson, Benedict. 1983. *Imagined Communities.* London: Verso.

Appadurai, Arjun. 1988. Putting Hierarchy in Its Place. *Cultural Anthropology* 3 (1): 37–50.

Aronczyk, Melissa. 2013. *Branding the Nation.* New York: Oxford University Press.

Barth, Fredrik. 1978. Scale and Network in Urban Western Society. In Fredrik Barth, ed., *Scale and Social Organization.* Oslo: Universitetsforlaget.

Baskar, Bojan. 2007. Austronostalgia and Yugonostalgia in the Western Balkans. In Bozidar Jezernik, Rajko Mursic, and Alenka Bartulovic, eds., *Europe and Its Other.* Ljubljana: Department of Ethnology and Cultural Anthropology, University of Ljubljana.

Baumann, Gerd, and Andre Gingrich. 2004. Debating Grammars: Arguments and Prospects. In Gerd Baumann and Andre Gingrich, eds., *Grammars of Identity/Alterity.* Oxford: Berghahn.

Beck, Ulrich. 2005. *Power in the Global Age.* Cambridge: Polity.

Benedict, Burton. 1966. Sociological Characteristics of Small Territories and Their Implications for Economic Development. In Michael Banton, ed., *The Social Anthropology of Complex Societies.* ASA Monographs 4. London: Tavistock.

———, ed. 1967. *Problems of Smaller Territories.* London: Athlone.

Bodley, John H. 2013. *The Small Nation Solution.* Lanham, Md.: AltaMira Press.

Boissevain, Jeremy. 1974. *Friends of Friends.* Oxford: Blackwell.

Breidenbach, Joana, and Pál Nyíri. 2009. *Seeing Culture Everywhere.* Seattle: University of Washington Press.

Comaroff, Jean, and John Comaroff. 2003. Ethnography on an Awkward Scale: Postcolonial Anthropology and the Violence of Abstraction. *Ethnography* 4 (2): 147–79.

Cooper, Robert. 2003. *The Breaking of Nations.* London: Atlantic Books.

De Swaan, Abram. 2001. *Words of the World.* Cambridge: Polity.

Donnan, Hastings, and Thomas M. Wilson, eds. 1994. *Border Approaches.* Lanham, Md.: University Press of America.

Durrenberger, E. Paul, and Gísli Pálsson, eds. 1989. *The Anthropology of Iceland*. Iowa City: University of Iowa Press.

Economist. 2013. The Next Supermodel: Why the World Should Look at the Nordic Countries. 2–8 February, 8–13.

Ehn, Billy, and Orvar Löfgren. 2010. *The Secret World of Doing Nothing*. Berkeley: University of California Press.

Eriksen, Thomas Hylland. 1993. In Which Sense Do Cultural Islands Exist? *Social Anthropology* 1 (1b): 133–47.

Fallers, Lloyd A. 1974. *The Social Anthropology of the Nation-State*. Chicago: Aldine.

Firth, Raymond. 1951. *Elements of Social Organization*. London: Watts.

Florida, Richard. 2002. *The Rise of the Creative Class*. New York: Basic Books.

Foster, George M. 1965. Peasant Society and the Image of Limited Good. *American Anthropologist* 67 (2): 293–315.

Fukuyama, Francis. 1995. *Trust*. New York: Simon & Schuster.

Gellner, Ernest. 1983. *Nations and Nationalism*. Ithaca, N.Y.: Cornell University Press.

Gingrich, Andre. 2006. Urban Crowds Manipulated: Assessing the Austrian Case as an Example in Wider European Tendencies. In Rik Pinxten and Ellen Preckler, eds., *Racism in Metropolitan Areas*. Oxford: Berghahn.

———. 2011. Nation, Status and Gender in Trouble? Exploring Some Contexts and Characteristics of Neo-Nationalism in Western Europe. In Gerd Baumann and Steven Vertovec, eds., *Multiculturalism: Critical Concepts in Sociology*, vol. 4, *Crises and Transformations: Challenges and Futures*. London: Routledge.

Gingrich, Andre, and Marcus Banks. 2006. Introduction: Neo-Nationalism in Europe and Beyond. In Andre Gingrich and Marcus Banks, eds., *Neo-Nationalism in Western Europe and Beyond*. Oxford: Berghahn.

Goffman, Erving. 1959. *The Presentation of Self in Everyday Life*. Garden City, N.Y.: Doubleday/Anchor.

Graan, Andrew. 2013. Counterfeiting the Nation? Skopje 2014 and the Politics of Nation Branding in Macedonia. *Cultural Anthropology* 28 (1): 161–79.

Granovetter, Mark S. 1973. The Strength of Weak Ties. *American Journal of Sociology* 78 (6): 1360–80.

Hannerz, Ulf. 1974. *Caymanian Politics*. Stockholm Studies in Social Anthropology 1. Stockholm: Department of Social Anthropology, Stockholm University.

———. 1980. *Exploring the City*. New York: Columbia University Press.

———. 1992. The Global Ecumene as a Network of Networks. In Adam Kuper, ed., *Conceptualizing Society*. London: Routledge.

———. 1993. The Withering Away of the Nation? An Afterword. *Ethnos* 58 (3–4): 377–91.

———. 2001. Center-Periphery Relationships. In Neil J. Smelser and Paul Baltes, eds., *International Encyclopedia of the Social and Behavioral Sciences*. Oxford: Elsevier.

———. 2004. Cosmopolitanism. In David Nugent and Joan Vincent, eds., *Companion to the Anthropology of Politics*. Oxford: Blackwell.

Herzfeld, Michael. 1997. *Cultural Intimacy*. London: Routledge.

Hobsbawm, Eric. 1991. *Nations and Nationalism Since 1780*. Cambridge: Cambridge University Press.

Holt, Douglas B. 2004. *How Brands Become Icons*. Boston: Harvard Business School Press.

Kanna, Ahmed. 2011. *Dubai: The City as a Corporation*. Minneapolis: University of Minnesota Press.

Khalaf, Sulayman N. 1992. Gulf Societies and the Image of Unlimited Good. *Dialectical Anthropology* 17 (1): 53–84.

Kincaid, Jamaica. 1988. *A Small Place*. New York: Farrar, Straus.

Knörr, Jacqueline. 2010. Out of Hiding? Strategies of Empowering the Past in the Reconstruction of Krio Identity. In Jacqueline Knörr and Wilson Trajano Filho, eds., *The Powerful Presence of the Past*. Leiden: Brill.

Kuper, Adam. 1976. *Changing Jamaica*. London: Routledge & Kegan Paul.

Malkki, Liisa. 1992. National Geographic: The Rooting of Peoples and the Territorialization of National Identity Among Scholars and Refugees. *Cultural Anthropology* 7 (1): 24–44.

Mead, Margaret, and Rhoda Métraux, eds. 1953. *The Study of Culture at a Distance*. Chicago: University of Chicago Press.

Meyer, John W. 1999. The Changing Cultural Content of the Nation-State: A World-Society Perspective. In George Steinmetz, ed., *State/Culture*. Ithaca, N.Y.: Cornell University Press.

Meyer, John W., John Boli, George M. Thomas, and Francisco O. Ramirez. 1997. World Society and the Nation-State. *American Journal of Sociology* 103 (1): 144–81.

Michel, Karl Markus, et al., eds. 2001. *Die Neidgesellschaft*. Kursbuch, Heft 143. Berlin: Rowohlt.

Milgram, Stanley. 1969. Interdisciplinary Thinking and the Small World Problem. In Muzafer Sherif and Carolyn W. Sherif, eds., *Interdisciplinary Relationships in the Social Sciences*. Chicago: Aldine.

Needham, Rodney. 1975. Polythetic Classification: Convergence and Consequences. *Man* 10 (3): 349–69.

Neiburg, Federico, and Marcio Goldman. 1998. Anthropology and Politics in Studies of National Character. *Cultural Anthropology* 13 (1): 56–81.

Nye, Joseph S., Jr. 2004. *Soft Power*. New York: Public Affairs.

Piot, Charles. 2010. *Nostalgia for the Future*. Chicago: University of Chicago Press.

Redfield, Robert. 1962. *Human Nature and the Study of Society*. Chicago: University of Chicago Press.

Reich, Robert B. 1991. *The Work of Nations*. New York: Knopf.

Schumacher, E. F. 1973. *Small Is Beautiful*. London: Blond & Briggs.

Shils, Edward. 1972 *The Intellectuals and the Powers*. Chicago: University of Chicago Press.

———. 1975. *Center and Periphery*. Chicago: University of Chicago Press.

Strang, Johan. 2011. Den perifera eklekticismens gränser och potential. *Historiska och Litteraturhistoriska Studier* 86. Helsinki: Svenska litteratursällskapet i Finland.

Sundbärg, Gustaf. 1911. *Det svenska folklynnet*. Stockholm: Norstedts.

Tönnies, Ferdinand. 1957. *Community and Society*. East Lansing: Michigan State University Press.

Travers, Jeffrey, and Stanley Milgram. 1969. An Experimental Study of the Small World Problem. *Sociometry* 32 (4): 425–43.

Vertovec, Steven, and Robin Cohen, eds. 2002. *Conceiving Cosmopolitanism*. Oxford: Oxford University Press.

Werbner, Pnina, ed. 2008. *Anthropology and the New Cosmopolitanism*. Oxford: Berg.

Wilson, Peter J. 1973. *Crab Antics*. New Haven, Conn.: Yale University Press.

Wilson, Thomas M., and Hastings Donnan, eds. 2012. *A Companion to Border Studies*. Malden, Mass.: Wiley-Blackwell.

Wilson, Godfrey, and Monica Wilson. 1945. *The Analysis of Social Change*. Cambridge: Cambridge University Press.

Wimmer, Andreas, and Nina Glick Schiller. 2002. Methodological Nationalism and Beyond: Nation-State Building, Migration and the Social Sciences. *Global Networks* 2 (4): 301–34.

Wulff, Helena. 1992. Young Swedes in New York: Workplace and Playground. In Rolf Lundén and Erik Åsard, eds., *Networks of Americanization*. Uppsala: Department of English, Uppsala University.

PART I

Nationhoods: Mirrors and Magnifying Glasses

CHAPTER 1

"100% Pure New Zealand":
National Branding and the Paradoxes
of Scale

Cris Shore

In his *Imagined Communities*, Benedict Anderson (1983: 6) famously observed that nations "are to be distinguished, not by their falsity/genuineness, but by the style in which they are imagined." Similar arguments could be made for the idea of "smallness." Echoing Anderson, albeit from the perspective of political ecology, J. Christopher Brown and Mark Purcell (2005) note that while the concept of "scale" is increasingly referenced in debates around globalization, the properties of scale are often taken as a given or ignored. "Scale," as they argue (2005: 607), "is socially produced rather than ontologically given." Put simply, how we conceptualize scale with regard to a country is usually a matter of cultural classification. One consequence of this undertheorized treatment of scale is that it creates what Brown and Purcell (608) call the "scalar trap," whereby people typically assume that organizations, policies, or actions at a particular scale are inherently more likely to have desired social effects than arrangements at other scales. It is often assumed that environmental sustainability, social justice, and democracy are most likely to be achieved by the devolution of power to local-scale actors and organizations. Whether it is the principle that "small is beautiful" and indigenous remedies are best, or the obverse idea that "bigger is better," normative assumptions about scale and the relationships it produces continue to shape cultural understandings of space, nation, identity, and morality.

Understood as geographically isolated and considered sparsely populated with a population of only 4.5 million on a land mass of 268,680 square kilometers (slightly greater than that of the United Kingdom and Italy), New Zealand offers an exemplary site for investigating some of these tensions around scalar relations, cultural understandings of smallness, and the "spatialization of politics" (Cox 1998; Murdoch and Marsden 1995). Much has been written in anthropology about the discipline's traditional preoccupation with small places, peripheral situations, marginality, and "remoteness" (Hannerz 1986; Ardener 1987; Das and Poole 2004). From this background anthropology has often struggled to find suitable units of analysis—and methodologies—appropriate for the study of larger-scale phenomena (including whole countries) and wider global processes. Bounded, temporally fixed cultures were always a product of anthropology's own imagination. In an increasingly intertwined, transnational world, the challenges have become more acute.

This chapter explores some of these theoretical issues of scale in the context of Aotearoa/New Zealand. More specifically, I examine how the *idea* of New Zealand as a small country—and the discourse of "smallness"—has been utilized by the New Zealand state as part of a wider project of national branding. My argument is that the notion of "smallness" in the New Zealand context has ambiguous and contradictory meanings, particularly in terms of the way it is experienced and represented. While New Zealand's relative small size is a source of vulnerability and potential weakness, it is also a strategic asset that successive governments have exploited, particularly in the fields of trade and international diplomacy, to promote New Zealand's status as an "honest broker" and internationally "trusted small nation." Smallness, I suggest, is a floating signifier, which, in the context of New Zealand, also operates as a "master symbol" (Wolf 1958; Ortner 1973).

In order to contextualize my argument, let me first say something about my own positionality. I am a British-born anthropologist whose main areas of ethnographic expertise are Europe and the European Union. However, in 2002 I took up a position at the University of Auckland and moved to New Zealand the following year. In 2007 my family and I took up citizenship and since 2008 I have also been conducting ethnographic research in New Zealand, with a particular focus on cultural politics and the engagement with neoliberalism (Taitz and Shore 2009; Shore 2010; Shore and Taitz 2012). This chapter is therefore written from a dual perspective of insider and outsider.

In terms of the larger theoretical themes of smallness and scale that frame this volume, three aspects of New Zealand culture and society stand out as particularly salient. The first concerns the normative assumptions that underpin the discourse of New Zealand as a small country. This typically includes a set of associated adjectives and images highlighting the virtues of smallness. Terms like "plucky," "enterprising," "pragmatic," and "punching above our weight" are recurring motifs in the way New Zealand narrates itself. The second concerns New Zealand's identity vis-à-vis its larger neighbor Australia—and to a lesser extent Britain and the United States—the way that small-country status is constructed and imagined by New Zealanders, and its implications for social relations, cultural intimacy, and national self-understandings. The third concerns the ways in which assumptions about scale and the moral qualities pertaining to smallness are used for national diplomacy and as part of the state project to brand New Zealand as a tourist destination. I suggest that the imagined community of New Zealand is one of both relative and absolute smallness, augmented and tempered in turns by subjective scales that are both projected onto the world and reflected back into New Zealand as part of a project of identity construction. These themes, particularly the interplay between insider and outsider perspectives, are exemplified in an ethnographic vignette describing a visit to Auckland by the secretary-general of the United Nations Ban Ki-moon.

Morality and the Paradoxes of Scale: Smallness and the New Zealand Imaginary

The invitation arrived by e-mail one morning in August. "His Worship the Mayor of Auckland Len Brown and the Chancellor of The University of Auckland Roger France are pleased to invite you to a Public Address by the Secretary-General of the United Nations, His Excellency Mr. Ban Ki-moon, who will be speaking on *New Zealand and the World: Sustainability and Security in a Time of Global Transition* at the University of Auckland at 12 noon on Tuesday 6 September 2011."[1] Some two thousand people turned out to listen to the speech. A buzz of excitement hung over the crowd as the vice-chancellor strode to the rostrum to introduce the speaker. This was a historic event; the first time a UN secretary-general had ever attended a Pacific

Island Forum or visited the University of Auckland, and the first high-level UN visit to New Zealand since Kofi Annan in 2000. Ban Ki-moon was aware of the symbolic importance of the occasion. While his main themes were peace, security, and global climate change, his speechwriters had prepared him well. He began by flattering his audience with remarks about the pleasure he felt being in this "most beautiful country," and especially at this "famous university," whose alumni included the prime minister of Samoa (Tuilaepa Lupesoliai Sailele Malielegaoi) and Helen Clark, the first woman ever to head the United Nations Development Program. He applauded New Zealand for its leadership in promoting global peace and security, remarking playfully; "I sometimes feel we could all use a little of the spirit of Auckland alumna Lucy Lawless—Xena the Warrior Princess." He joked about the similarities between the Pacific Island Forum, and the Rugby World Cup, the other "game in town" being hosted by New Zealand at that time: "In rugby, you lose teeth. In diplomacy, you lose face." And just as "rugby scrums confuse anyone who doesn't know the game," so too with UN debates. His next comments earned even greater applause from the audience. Rugby, he pronounced, is "a celebration of common values and a way of life: Teamwork, mutual respect, solidarity. The qualities of grit and determination—all very useful, I have found, in the world of diplomacy." Finally, he paid tribute to the character of the New Zealand people, leading the world in terms of sustainable energy solutions and sustainable security:

> It is fitting that New Zealand plays host to the world. Kiwis are famed for warmth and hospitality—also for your global perspective, your outreach to the world. I know that the "OE"—the Overseas Experience—is a meaningful part of the individual lives of so many New Zealanders. In fact, it defines your national character. More than almost any other country, you are people of the world. And you have helped lead the world, proving yet again that small countries can often have outsized influence. Long ago, New Zealand was the first nation on earth to embrace universal suffrage. Today, you are a strong and consistent supporter of the Millennium Development Goals— and a major donor to your neighbours in the Pacific. I thank you for your leadership.

Ban Ki-moon concluded his lecture to rapturous applause. While his comments were widely reported in the national media, they attracted little reflection or analytical commentary. Yet his speech highlights many of the points I wish to make about how New Zealand likes to portray itself.

New Zealand: Small Country, Big Destination

As a nation New Zealand imagines itself small in some ways but large in others, with contradictory juxtapositions evident on many fronts.[2] In terms of its military presence, New Zealand joins a host of other small countries that take pride in the small size of their armed forces and the modesty of their spending on defense. This stance was epitomized by the decision of the Labour government in 2001 to disband its air combat wing, a decision that provoked stinging condemnation from the Australian press and some politicians who accused New Zealand of "abandoning its Anzac tradition" (*Australian*, 9 May 2001).[3] Yet in international diplomacy and in matters of global ethics, including nuclear proliferation and environmental protection, New Zealand's "soft power" is far greater than its limited economic and political standing in the world would suggest. The country occupies a disproportionally important place in international organizations such as the United Nations and the World Trade Organization (WTO). The same contradictory largeness/smallness pattern is reflected in its agriculture and sports, where New Zealand handles a third of the world's dairy trade (NZTE 2012) and boasts one of the world's most highly regarded national rugby teams, the All Blacks. Similarly, when marketing itself as a tourist destination, the rhetoric of "bigness" is frequently deployed to portray New Zealand as a land of vast natural wonders, native bush, and wilderness. These large/small juxtapositions often occur in a direct, binary manner; for example, in the simultaneously important images of New Zealand's pristine "naturalness" and the contradictory hugeness and efficiency of its dairy industry—whose 3.85 million cows and other polluting livestock paradoxically pose the greatest challenge in the country's attempt to reduce carbon dioxide (CO_2) emissions. Agriculture and the natural environment thus provide powerful, yet ambiguous, symbolic resources for constructing New Zealand's image on the world stage.

Smallness and largeness in this context, however, refer not only to scales of political power or economic might but also to the relative scales of distance (physical and social) between people, institutions, and realities. New Zealand has a proud history of being in the forefront of social change: it was the first country to introduce universal suffrage (1893), the first English-speaking country to provide a state-funded old age pension (1898) and to introduce a comprehensive welfare state for all citizens (1938); and one of the first postcolonial states to grant voting rights to its indigenous population.[4] These progressive traditions emerged in the context of a small settler society proud of its ties to the "mother country," yet also keen to distinguish itself from the British traditions of class hierarchy, privilege, and inherited status.[5] Like other Anglophone settler societies, New Zealand society is characterized by a strong ethos of egalitarianism and a traditional resentment of those who adopt an air of superiority (or "being up themselves," as it is referred to colloquially). Peter Wilson's book *Crab Antics* (1973) is often cited as the ethnography that best captures the tensions typical of small societies where values of "respectability" and the drive toward stratification come into conflict with the dynamics of reputation management and the drive toward equality.[6] However, this much celebrated history of progressive civil rights and innovative social development stands in sharp contrast to other, more recent aspects of New Zealand's modernity. During the early 1980s, New Zealand became the first developed nation to embark on the wholesale dismantling of its welfare state as the Labour government pursued a breakneck program of comprehensive free-market reforms. As John Gray (1999: 29) observes, this program was the most ambitious attempt to construct the free market as a social institution to be implemented anywhere in the twentieth century. The model—known as the "New Zealand Experiment"—was hailed by the World Bank, the *Economist,* and the Organization for Economic Cooperation and Development (OECD) as an exemplar for the rest of the world to follow (Kelsey 1997: 2).

New Zealand thus provides a good illustration of another feature of small countries: their capacity to act as "laboratories" for experimenting with new social and economic policies or testing out new models of social organization (Castles 1996: 88–89). However, the net result of the past three decades of market-led reforms has radically changed New Zealand society and undermined its egalitarian self-image. A recent OECD report (2011) shows that over the past twenty-five years, the gap between rich and poor in New Zealand has risen faster than any other developed country—with the exception of Sweden (Rashbrooke 2013). New Zealand also has one of the world's largest prison populations per capita, and one of the highest young adult suicide rates in the industrialized world (Romanos and Garrett-Walker 2012). For all its claims about social inclusion and biculturalism, the unresolved tension between Maori and the state over the expropriation of land under the Crown and successive settler governments remains a key political fault line. That said, the settlement process initiated by the establishment of the Waitangi Tribunal in 1975—a permanent commission charged with making recommendations on claims brought by Maori relating to actions of the Crown going back to 1840—represents one of the most far-reaching attempts by any settler society to redress historical grievances resulting from colonialism.

Yet despite these social realities, New Zealand continues to promote an image of itself as a progressive, safe country; an island paradise in the Pacific, or "God's own country" as the New Zealand poet Thomas Bracken described it in 1890. Young couples who have returned from overseas often comment that "New Zealand is a great place to bring up your children," yet it has one of the highest rates of child poverty, domestic violence, and child abuse of any developed country (Every Child Counts 2013). Contrary to its well-cultivated reputation for environmentalism and sustainability, New Zealand also has one of the worst records of any country for environmental destruction, species loss, and environmental degradation. As a recent World Wildlife Fund report (2012) states, the country has failed to meet any of the major environmental commitments it agreed to under the Kyoto Protocol.

Significantly, these features, which epitomize the contradictions of New Zealand as a small country, are not well known outside of New Zealand. Here we see at work some of the principles of what Michael Herzfeld (1997: x) termed "cultural intimacy": those "sore zones of cultural sensitivity" that constitute part of the "private lives of nations." The image New Zealand presents to the outside world—as a small, courageous, trustworthy, and environmentally engaged country—has none of these negative characteristics that are widely acknowledged by cultural insiders.

Smallness and Sibling Rivalry: Relations with Australia

Relative smallness tends to be understood in relation to a particular "Other." For New Zealand, that larger and more prosperous neighbor is Australia, with a population of twenty-three million and growing—over five times bigger than New Zealand—and covering an area 28.6 times larger. Trans-Tasman relations are often characterized by a degree of sibling rivalry, perhaps more so on New Zealand's part, as Australia's living standards and income levels have rapidly outstripped those of its smaller neighbor. While New Zealand continually benchmarks itself against Australia—in everything from government spending and home detention policies, to university rankings and quality of life measures—national politicians speak wistfully about the ever-more elusive goal of "catching up" with Australia economically.

Like Ireland in relation to England, or Canada in relation to the United States, New Zealand continually defines itself against its larger neighbor. Nothing fuels national pride more than beating Australia at rugby, cricket, or some other competitive sport. The competition is all the greater for the fact that Australians share so much with New Zealanders. Australian policies and practices are often replicated in some form in New Zealand (and sometimes vice versa), and the two countries have a long history of cohesive political and economic action. The Australia–New Zealand Close Economic Relations Trade Agreement, for example, is one of the world's most comprehensive and wide-ranging free-trade agreements and saw the complete elimination of tariffs and restrictions by 1990 (New Zealand Ministry of Foreign Affairs and Trade 2010). Recent movements toward a trans-Tasman single economic market, which would see the two economies effectively merged, emphasize how dependent New Zealand has become on its larger neighbor. The relative absorption of New Zealand into its larger neighbor can even be taken to a literal level, as Australia's Department of Immigration and Citizenship estimates that as of June 2012, some 647,863 New Zealand citizens lived in Australia (Australian Government 2013), over 14 percent of New Zealand's entire population. As Robert Muldoon, New Zealand's prime minister from 1975 to 1984, once caustically remarked, New Zealanders moving to Australia "raises the IQ of both countries."

This fragility is also manifest on the broader worldwide stage, as New Zealand struggles to maintain its own identity in the face of more powerful allies and neighbors. This is typically reflected in the national media. For example, one such story reported that New Zealand's prime minister John Key was approached by U.S. president Barack Obama at a UN summit not once, but twice. Obama's statement that "I hope to be seeing a lot more of you," coupled with the reported fact that the American president paid more attention to the New Zealand prime minister than to many others, was front-page news in New Zealand's newspapers (Tait 2009). Bordering on starstruck, this level of excitement from both the prime minister and the media high-lights how New Zealand's smallness creates a sense of fragility.

Relations with Britain and the United States: The David and Goliath Syndrome

In many respects, New Zealand was forced toward greater independence by Britain's entry into the European Economic Community (EEC) in 1973 and by its de facto expulsion from the ANZUS military alliance with Australia and the United States in 1985 following its banning of nuclear armed ships from New Zealand waters. As a result of these traumas, New Zealand has invested heavily in developing a role in international diplomacy. In doing so, it joins several other small countries as recognized "havens of stability and diplomacy." This is evidenced both in New Zealand's disproportionally large presence in the areas of international diplomacy and peacekeeping and in its reputation as a business-friendly country. According to the Swiss-based International Institute for Management Development's *World Competitive Yearbook* (IMD 2011), it is one of the world's most politically stable nation-states, and it is regularly classed among the world's most open and business-friendly countries. In terms of Transparency International's "Corruption Perceptions Index," New Zealand is consistently ranked as one of the world's "least corrupt" countries. Again, this external reputation belies the some-what different internal reality of a low-wage economy characterized by harsh, antiunion legislation and arcane employment practices. The transition from a heavily protected welfare state to a totally deregulated market economy was a period of dramatic instability. As historian James Belich (2001: 463) wrote, in 1960 New Zealand society was characteristically "homogeneous, conformist, masculist, egalitarian and monocultural" and "subject to heavy formal and informal regulation." By the year 2000, however, it had become "one of the least regulated societies in the world, economically even more than socially."

Much of New Zealand's image as a small but courageous nation stems from its reputation for championing diplomatic morality on the world stage. David Lange, prime minister from 1984 to 1989, presided over an era that regularly pitted little New Zealand against the mighty United States. Lange banned U.S. nuclear warships from entering New Zealand waters, despite American retaliatory sanctions and accusations that the country had reneged on its treaty obligations. The highpoint of this stance came in 1985, when Lange won a televised debate at the Oxford Union on the indefensibility of nuclear weapons, coining the memorable quote against his opponent Jerry Falwell, "I can smell the uranium on your breath." With its strong presence at the United Nations, its involvement in international peacekeeping missions, and its resolute adherence to a nuclear-free policy, New Zealand has extended its reputation for independence into the new millennium.

However, while governments have tried to make a virtue out of New Zealand's small size and proud independence in some contexts, in others they have demonstrated the complete opposite. The dispute over the filming of *The Hobbit* in New Zealand is a good illustration. When the tiny actors' union Equity sought to negotiate a collective employment contract for its members commensurate with international standards, Warner Brothers threatened to shoot the movie in the Czech Republic instead. As documents later showed, Warner Brothers had no intention of relocating overseas but used the dispute to extract further subsidies from a compliant government (Kelly 2011). The National government, already well known for its antiunion policies, colluded with Warner Brothers to create a narrative claiming that the actors' union was threatening jobs and destroying New Zealand's film industry. Sir Peter Jackson, the director of *The Lord of the Rings* trilogy, and government ministers also used the fact that Equity was affiliated to a larger Australian-based union called Media Entertainment and Arts Alliance (MEAA) to fuel nationalistic sentiment against the alleged threat of predatory unions from Australia (another example of "largeness" culturally coded as antithetical to New Zealand's self-image). These claims were subsequently used to justify removing the employment rights of workers in the New Zealand film industry. Henceforth, the actors were reclassified as "free contractors" rather than as "employees," thus ensuring by law that wages, benefits, and entitlements for domestic workers would be inferior to those enjoyed by foreign actors working in New Zealand. While one government was prepared to stand tall and defy the world's leading military state on the highly emotive issue of nuclear power, standing up to a major Hollywood studio was another matter altogether.

New Zealand's identity as a country is therefore woven together by imagined (and often contradictory) strands of largeness and smallness, independence and dependency, principled ethics and economic expediency. Because of the smallness of its military ambitions, New Zealand can afford to imagine itself large in its diplomacy. Yet even this does not capture the complex whole. New Zealand has a strong warrior tradition in both its Maori roots and its heavy involvement in two world wars. Military sacrifice forms an important part of New Zealand's national identity, and the continued participation in worldwide peacekeeping efforts demonstrates the enduring relevance of the noble warrior image. The huge popularity of Anzac Day, a national day of remembrance for the lost New Zealand and Australian soldiers in all wars, yearly reminds us of this point.

The vulnerability of being a small country gives rise to what is often referred to as "cultural cringe." New Zealand is often criticized for its lack of self-confidence and for its tendency to copy or mimic the policies of other countries. As two New Zealand intellectuals summed it up, "Our colonial past makes us super-globalizers (settlers, that is to say, are avant-garde in their capitalism): we act out the historical design-drive of globalization in our 'fast-following' tendencies—our inherent slavishness to metropolitan models" (Sturm and Turner 2012: 3). Ironically, this radical "fast-following" can sometimes generate novel conditions that transform small countries into social laboratories, as was the case with the neoliberal reforms of the 1980s.

Small States, Diplomacy, and National Branding

This final section brings us back to the theme of the strategic uses of "smallness." Is there anything distinctive about diplomacy, nationalism, and identity construction in small countries? Many small countries cultivate forms of patriotism that make a virtue of their relative smallness; what we might term "Lilliputian nationalism." Here, smallness itself comes to serve as a marker of national identity and basis for pride. In some cases this can produce a sense of self-righteousness (for example, Australians often accuse New Zealanders of being sanctimonious about their country's stance toward its indigenous Maori population, which has fared much better than Australia's Aborigines). According to this logic of Lilliputian nationalism, small countries have moral qualities and capacities—like trustworthiness, moral integrity, a better record on human rights—that larger states lack. But smallness can also lead to inferiority complexes and fears about being left behind. These preoccupations feature prominently in New Zealand discourses about trade and international relations and may partially explain the extraordinary lengths to which New Zealand goes to join transnational networks and international organizations. There is also a clear recognition of the strategic advantages of global networks for a small country dependent on trade. The threats and opportunities posed by international conglomerations have provided a powerful stimulus for successive New Zealand governments to mobilize different sectors in defense of the national interest. According to Christine Ingebritsen and her colleagues (Ingebritsen et al. 2006), small states must adopt particular forms of action to be effective on the international stage. These include countering power by having "superior commitment," being more "innovative" and creating more tightly knit domestic institutions, and being better at setting agendas or acting as "norm entrepreneurs."

This is also how New Zealand politicians and diplomats typically represent their country. As Jim McLay (2011: 126–27), former New Zealand ambassador and permanent representative to the United Nations, argues, "a small country has real options to operate in the Security Council professionally and credibly and with nimbleness and flexibility. On the great issues of the day, small states are often less weighed down by their history, and are less constrained by domestic constituencies, or by an international leadership role, or by past international actions; put simply, they come with less baggage—and are often more willing to seek creative, pragmatic solutions." Not having the military or economic capability to act unilaterally beyond their own borders makes small countries more predisposed to seek bilateral and multilateral relationships—which makes them seem more trustworthy, independent, and able to act as "honest broker." As New Zealand's former ambassador to Russia noted, this soft power can be turned into economic and political capital:

> A small country like New Zealand can increase its chances of getting what it wants by being quick on its feet, and even exploiting the fact of its smallness. We sometimes call this being nimble. Smallness does bring with it some advantages—consultative processes at home tend to be less formal and more speedily resolved, and there tend to be fewer special interest groups to be placated on particular issues. The range of issues requiring resolutions is often more restricted anyway. By being nimble, and being innovative, it is sometimes possible to steal a march on larger and more slow-moving competitors. (Elder 2009: 5)

The assumption here is that New Zealand's small size makes it is easier to unite people behind the policies of government; that New Zealand's small scale and "two degrees of separation" that connect most people somehow render political and ideological differences less relevant and make *Gemeinschaft*-like relations more prevalent.[7] This idea is also expressed in the term "NZ Inc.," a phrase used in different contexts where the state and private business are brought together to defend the national interest. The slogan was originally imported from Japan in the 1980s, at a time when "Japan Inc." was widely used to describe Japan's extraordinary economic development. Transplanted, "NZ Inc." became a mobilizing metaphor for economic nationalism. It sought to overcome the problem faced by New Zealand (and other small countries with too many small firms) by bringing government agencies and business into alignment to shape a competitive nation.

This strategy of presenting a united front later culminated in a shift toward the promotion of New Zealand as a national brand state, particularly with the "100% Pure" marketing strategy developed by Tourism New Zealand. Launched in 1999, that campaign has proved to be remarkably successful in raising New Zealand's profile overseas and in attracting increasing numbers of tourists. As the Tourism New Zealand website declares, in a narrative punctuated by evocative images of young people riding mountain bikes and happy couples walking barefoot on gentle beaches with dramatic volcanic backdrops: "Few countries in the world can boast New Zealand's range of natural features—from high peaks and glaciers in vast mountain ranges to sub-tropical rainforests, lush rolling farmland to geothermal activity, white and black sand beaches to desert-like plains, and unpopulated islands—all within one compact land" (Tourism New Zealand 2013).

The branding of New Zealand as a tourist destination has been spearheaded far more by government than by big business. This reflects perhaps another interesting feature of many small countries: the extent to which national identity and branding in an age of neoliberalism are projects driven by government ministries rather than private-sector interests or corporations. Margaret Werry (2011) explores many of these themes in her book *The Tourist State*. She writes:

> For much of the new millennium, New Zealand has been the global ticket. . . . No longer the dreary sheep farm at the end of the world, the *new* New Zealand—Aotearoa New Zealand—is at the world's fresh cutting edge: clean, green, technologically capable, aesthetically innovative "Islands of Imagination" whipped by the Pacific's brisk winds of change. Yet in 2001, when Aotearoa New Zealand strode onto the world stage, it did so not as a cosmopolitan, competitive,

Asia-Pacific knowledge industry hub. Instead, it made its entrance as sublime scenic backdrop to a premodern fantasy Europe that never was: "Home of Middle-earth," where the race of Man battled savage hordes in an epic struggle for supremacy. (Werry 2011: ix)

Werry's argument is that New Zealand has been "not so much imagined as *imagineered*" (2011: x). By that she means that tourism lies at the heart of the project of nation building in New Zealand and represents "the hub of the machine of state" (Werry 2011: xii). Ever since the nineteenth century when New Zealand was constructed as an Anglo-Saxon paradise, national branding has been used to consolidate tourism as New Zealand's primary foreign exchange. Tourism in New Zealand is implicated in virtually every sector of economy and society. Significantly, Prime Minister John Key also held the portfolio of minister for tourism. In packaging their national identity, countries draw selectively on their history, environment, and cultural traditions. In New Zealand, this has resulted in a curious mix of myths, stereotypes, and externally projected touristic images in which New Zealand is variously marketed as a "scenic wonderland," "a patchwork history of Māori, European, Pacific Island and Asian cultures," and a "melting pot" whose "pioneering spirit" and "resourcefulness and ingenuity" have given rise to the unique national character of "Kiwi culture" (Tourism New Zealand 2013). As Claudia Bell observes, these "official, governmental and commercial programmes to raise New Zealand's profile promulgate particular notions of nationhood to external audiences" which "inevitably spill over into the nation's own population, and become part of national identity constructs" (Bell 2005: 14). For example, the Tourism New Zealand website and marketing campaigns typically suggest that New Zealand has far lower levels of pollution and environmental degradation than other parts of the world. These slogans, as Bell says, have proved very effective in avoiding issues of environmental degradation and land contestation. According to a recent government report, drinking water contaminated by feces actually increased in New Zealand between 2010 and 2012 as a result of intensive farming, and over 2.4 percent of the population were drinking water with excessive numbers of E. coli bacteria (Johnston 2013). Despite being confronted with clear evidence of this, John Key reiterated the Tourism New Zealand slogans in an interview for the BBC's *HARDtalk* program in 2011. New Zealand's water and air quality, he proclaimed to the bemusement of his interviewer, Stephen Sackur, "are 100 percent pure."[8]

However, this image was severely tarnished in August 2013 when the dairy giant Fonterra announced a wide-scale recall of its whey products after apparently discovering botulism-causing bacteria in safety tests. The recall affected seven countries, including New Zealand's largest markets, China and Australia. While the botulism scare eventually proved to be a false alarm, several countries imposed import bans on New Zealand milk products and the country's reputation for food safety took a major hit. An editorial article published on several major Chinese news websites described New Zealand's "100% Pure" campaign as a "festering sore," and went on to criticize New Zealand for its unswerving faith in neoliberalism, which, so it argued, had severely undermined health and safety standards: "One could argue the country is hostage to a blinkered devotion to laissez-faire market ideology. Many New Zealanders fell victim to this when the construction industry was deregulated two decades ago resulting in damp and leaky homes that quickly became uninhabitable" (cited in Adams 2012). Elsewhere, the British news website *Daily Mail Online* derided New Zealand with a headline describing the country's green claims as "pure manure" (Gray et al. 2013; Quilliam 2013). Even New Zealand's largest circulation newspaper, the *New Zealand Herald*, ran with the headline "100% Tainted" on its front page.

Conclusions: The New Zealand Brand

New Zealand illustrates many of the problems and contradictions around the idea of smallness as an analytical category for classifying countries. Yet, more important, it also shows how scale and smallness are implicated in the way countries are classified internationally and, in turn, how they classify and define themselves. As I have tried to show, smallness is an ambiguous, shifting, and relative concept whose characteristics are contradictory and difficult to pin down with any precision. What I have focused on, therefore, is the way the discourse of New Zealand as a small country has been mobilized by government to promote a national imaginary that highlights the positive qualities of diminutive scale. This typically plays upon the positive tropes and stereotypes usually associated with diminutive scale, including friendliness, integrity, nimbleness, and the capacity to "punch above its weight." Many of these supposed characteristics are rendered more salient because of the presence of its larger neighbor, Australia. This strategic deployment of smallness is particularly evident in the way New Zealand conducts its economic and foreign policies. But I suggest that this is not so much an illustration of the "scalar trap" as a form of auto-essentialism, one in which assumptions about smallness have been strategically mobilized by both state and nonstate actors in order to gain competitive advantage. New Zealand elites seem to have embraced Ingebritsen's (2006) arguments about the special role that small states can play in international diplomacy. However, they have done so with a particularly local interpretation of the role of the state in developing a modern free-market economy, one that differs notably from the United Kingdom and Australia, two larger countries that provide implicit points of comparison. In the New Zealand version of neoliberalization it is government ministers and officials rather than private entrepreneurs and business who have been the main drivers. The same corporatist ideology also underlies the "NZ Inc." approach, which, while not unique to small countries, seems to provide a particularly useful strategy for these countries in developing their trade and external relations policies.

The second interesting conclusion to draw from New Zealand concerns the ambiguities and contradictions around branding and tourism. The "NZ Inc." approach is particularly evident in government attempts at rebranding New Zealand as "Middle Earth," following the success of Peter Jackson's *Lord of the Rings* and *Hobbit* film trilogies. Significantly, Tourism New Zealand recently announced it had signed a one-year Memorandum of Understanding with the national carrier Air New Zealand, valued at over $20 million, to undertake joint marketing activity promoting travel to New Zealand in selected international markets (Travel Biz Monitor 2013). On its website, Tourism New Zealand (2013) carried a story headlined "Hobbit Stars Find Perfection in NZ." Yet behind the carefully constructed marketing images of New Zealand as a pristine, "100% Pure" country inhabited by happy, friendly, and innovative folk, there is another face to contemporary New Zealand that reflects the cultural intimacy of a different narrative—that of an increasingly unequal society and low-wage economy where basic employment rights are sacrificed to corporate interests. If branding New Zealand serves to project an external image of unity and cohesion, it also operates internally to reinforce a set of neoliberal political projects related to free trade, commercialization, and deregulation.

Finally, New Zealand provides a good illustration of how small countries can become social laboratories or experimental testing grounds for developing new economic and social models. Samuel Butler's famous utopian novel

Erewhon, published in 1872 about a country supposedly discovered by its protagonist, was inspired by the period he spent in the new colonial settlement of Christchurch in New Zealand's South Island. From its position as a pioneering champion of the welfare state, New Zealand became a site for testing the neoliberal policies of Chicago School economists. More recently still, China's decision to sign a free-trade agreement with New Zealand in 2009—the first such agreement China has signed with another country—was also motivated by what some have termed the "demonstration effect." Not only was China able to demonstrate that it was open to such agreements, but "its negotiators also had the opportunity to cut their teeth on a relatively straightforward small-scale agreement before going on to more difficult negotiations with more intransigent trading partners" (Elder 2009: 6). Compared with China, New Zealand is a tiny country, yet once again, as the ideology shared by so many leading politicians and policy makers would have it, smallness was turned into a strategic asset and New Zealand "punched above its weight." As these examples illustrate, small country politics offer strategic opportunities for testing new social and political forms, but these experiments also carry social costs and have contradictory and unforeseen consequences.

* * *

I would like to thank my colleagues at the University of Auckland for their insights, over many conversations, into the specificities and character of New Zealand as a small country. I particularly want to acknowledge Susanna Trnka and Sasha Maher for helpful feedback on an earlier draft of this chapter. I also want to acknowledge Robert Falconer for his help in collecting materials for this chapter and in framing the argument. Finally, I wish to thank Ulf Hannerz and Andre Gingrich for their helpful copyediting and editorial suggestions.

Notes

1. All quotes from the secretary-general's speech are taken from Ban Ki-moon (2011).

2. "New Zealand: Small Country, Big Destination" is an advertising slogan used by the New Zealand Tourist Board (Tourism New Zealand 2013).

3. The Anzac tradition or Anzac spirit is a concept which holds that Australian and New Zealand soldiers share special characteristics and values arising from the battlefields of the First World War, particularly the disastrous Gallipoli campaign. These values include endurance, courage, ingenuity, good humor, "larrikinism," and mateship.

4. In 1867 the New Zealand government established four Maori seats and Maori were able to vote without needing to meet the usual property requirements.

5. This was not the case throughout New Zealand. In the settlement of Christchurch, for example, the Canterbury Association that oversaw the city's development consciously sought to transplant the English class system to the new colony, and these social and spatial divisions are still evident today (see King 2007: 148; *Te Ara* 2013).

6. Wilson's ethnography was based on fieldwork in the tiny Caribbean island of Providencia, but many would argue that his insights could apply equally to the fabric of social life in small communities anywhere. Wilson himself spent the last twenty-seven years of his life living and working in the small university town of Dunedin in New Zealand's South Island.

7. The New Zealander notion of "two degrees of separation" is a variation of the U.S. idea of "six degrees of separation" as discussed in the introductory chapter of this book. This is a strong popular view, expressed all the time in the media and in everyday conversation—there is even a major mobile phone company called "Two Degrees Mobile Ltd." Some years ago, a researcher from the New Zealand Department of Statistics set out to test this assumption in the case of the labor market and found that in the network of wage and salary earners two random people are able to connect within four steps on average.

8. John Key, interview, BBC *HARDtalk*, 5 September 2011.

References

Adams, Christopher. 2013. 100% Pure "Festering Sore"—China News Sites. *New Zealand Herald*, 6 August.

Anderson, Benedict. 1983. *Imagined Communities*. London: Verso.

Ardener, Edwin. 1987. Remote Areas: Some Theoretical Considerations. In Anthony Jackson. ed. *Anthropology at Home*. London: Tavistock.

Australian Government, Department of Immigration and Citizenship. 2013. *Fact Sheet 17: New Zealanders in Australia*. Accessed 13 June. http://www.immi.gov.au /media/fact-sheets/17nz.htm.

Ban Ki-moon. 2011. Text of speech delivered to Auckland University, 6 September. http://www.un.org/apps/news/infocus/sgspeeches/statments_full.asp?statID =1280#.Ub0vpGaN03E.

Belich, James, 2001. *Paradise Reforged*. Auckland: Allen Lane/Penguin.

Bell, Claudia 2005. Branding New Zealand: The National Green-Wash. *British Review of New Zealand Studies* 15:13–29.

Brown, J. Christopher, and Mark Purcell. 2005. There's Nothing Inherent About Scale: Political Ecology, the Local Trap, and the Politics of Development in the Brazilian Amazon. *Geoforum* 36 (5): 607–24.

Castles, Francis G. 1996. Needs-Based Strategies of Social Protection in Australia and New Zealand. In Gøsta Esping-Andersen, ed., *Welfare States in Transition: National Adaptations in Global Economies*. London: Sage.

Cox, Kevin R. 1998. Spaces of Dependence, Spaces of Engagement and the Politics of Scale, or: Looking for Local Politics. *Political Geography* 17 (1): 1–23.

Das, Veena, and Deborah Poole, eds. 2004. *Anthropology in the Margins of the State*. Santa Fe, N.M.: School of American Research Press.

Elder, Chris. 2009. Gaining a Voice: A Small Power's Strategy. *New Zealand International Review* 34 (4): 2–6.

Every Child Counts (Wellington). 2013. Accessed 14 June. http://www.everychildcounts .org.nz/resources/child-abuse/.

Gray, John. 1999. *False Dawn*. London: Granta Books.

Gray, John, Rebecca Quilliam, Kate Shuttleworth, and Brendan Manning. 2013. Fonterra Apologises to Consumers. *New Zealand Herald*, 7 August.

Gupta, Akhil, and James Ferguson. 1992. Beyond "Culture": Space, Identity, and the Politics of Difference. *Cultural Anthropology* 7 (1): 6–23.

Hannerz, Ulf. 1986. Theory in Anthropology: Small Is Beautiful? The Problem of Complex Cultures. *Comparative Studies in Society and History* 28 (2): 362–67.

Herzfeld, Michael. 1997. *Cultural Intimacy*. London: Routledge.

IMD (Institute for Management Development). 2011. *IMD World Competitiveness Yearbook*. Lausanne: IMD.

Ingebritsen, Christine. 2006. Conclusion: Learning from Lilliput. In Christine Ingebritsen et al., eds., *Small States in International Relations*. Seattle: University of Washington Press.

Ingebritsen, Christine, Iver Neumann, Sieglinde Gstöhl, and Jessica Beyer, eds. 2006. *Small States in International Relations*. Seattle: University of Washington Press.

Johnston, Kirsty. 2013. Drinking Water Contamination Spike. *Stuff.co.nz*, 30 June.

Kelly, Helen. 2011. The Hobbit Dispute. *Scoop Independent News*, 12 April.

Kelsey, Jane. 1997. *The New Zealand Experiment*. Auckland: Auckland University Press.

King, Michael. 2007. *The Penguin History of New Zealand Illustrated*. Auckland: Penguin.

McLay, Jim. 2011. Making a Difference: The Role of a Small State at the United Nations. *Juniata Voices* 11:121–34.

Murdoch, Jonathan, and Terry Marsden. 1995. The Spatialization of Politics: Local and National Actor-Spaces in Environmental Conflict. *Transactions of the Institute of British Geographers*, n.s., 20 (3): 368–80.

New Zealand Ministry of Foreign Affairs and Trade. 2010. Australian Trade and Economic Links. Accessed 25 April 2013 at http://www.mfat.govt.nz/Foreign-Relations /Australia/1-Trade-and-Economic-links/index.php.

NZTE. 2012. *The New Zealand Dairy Industry*. Wellington: New Zealand Trade and Enterprise.

Ortner, Sherry B. 1973. On Key Symbols. *American Anthropologist* 75 (5): 1338–46.

Quilliam, Rebecca. 2013. UK Paper Rubbishes NZ's Green Claims as "Pure Manure." *New Zealand Herald*, 9 August.

Rashbrooke, Max, ed. 2013. *Inequality: A New Zealand Crisis*, Wellington: Bridget Williams Books.

Romanos, Amelia, and Hana Garrett-Walker. 2012. Fresh Ideas Sought to Tackle Youth Suicide. *New Zealand Herald*, 25 April.

Shore, Cris. 2010. The Reform of New Zealand's University System: "After Neoliberalism." *Learning and Teaching in the Social Sciences (LATISS)* 3 (1): 1–31.

Shore, Cris, and Mira Taitz. 2012. Who Owns the University? Institutional Autonomy and Academic Freedom in an Age of Knowledge Capitalism. *Globalisation, Societies and Education* 10 (2): 201–19.

Statistics New Zealand. 2011. International Investment Position Statement—Stock by Country: March 2011. Wellington.

Sturm, Sean, and Stephen Turner. 2012. Excellent Universities, Here, There and Everywhere. *Inquire: Journal of Comparative Literature* 2 (2).

Tait, Maggie. 2009. "Look Forward to Seeing a Lot More of You," Obama Tells Key. *New Zealand Herald*, 24 September.

Taitz, Mira, and Cris Shore. 2009. Discipline and Punish: The Cultural Politics of Smacking Children. In Roger Openshaw and Elizabeth Rata, eds., *The Politics of Conformity in New Zealand*. Auckland: Pearson.

Te Ara—The Encyclopedia of New Zealand. 2013. Accessed 25 April 2013 at http://www.teara.govt.nz/en.

Tourism New Zealand. 2013. 100% Pure New Zealand. http://www.newzealand.com/int/.

Travel Biz Monitor. 2013. Air NZ, Tourism New Zealand Sign Marketing Alliance. *Travel Biz Monitor*, 14 June.

Werry, Margaret. 2011. *The Tourist State*. Minneapolis: University of Minnesota Press.

Wilson, Peter J. 1973. *Crab Antics*. New Haven, Conn.: Yale University Press.

Wolf, Eric. 1958. The Virgin of Guadalupe: A Mexican National Symbol. *Journal of American Folklore* 71 (279): 34–39.

World Wildlife Fund. 2012. *Beyond Rio: New Zealand's Environmental Record Since the Original Earth Summit*. Wellington: WWF–New Zealand.

Wright, Susan, and Sue Reinhold. 2011. "Studying Through": A Strategy for Studying Political Transformation; or, Sex, Lies and British Politics. In Cris Shore, Susan Wright, and Davide Però, eds., *Policy Worlds: Anthropology and the Analysis of Contemporary Power*. Oxford: Berghahn.

CHAPTER 2

After 22 July 2011:
Norwegians Together

Thomas Hylland Eriksen

Driving toward the center of Oslo on a spring morning in 2013, I noticed that my wife suddenly made an unexpected right turn. Then I remembered: several of the main streets were closed because of the reconstruction work still going on, almost two years after the terrorist attack on 22 July 2011.

It must have been the country's most sustained presence in the global media world since Amundsen beat Scott in the race to the South Pole in December 1911. The country was in shock. The world was incredulous. In peaceful, slightly dull Norway—a small, rich country where nothing usually happens—a man had inflicted major damage on several government buildings, killing eight and injuring dozens, with a homemade bomb, before driving to the site of a political summer camp, where he killed sixty-nine, many of them teenagers. The media images from central Oslo that afternoon, with smoking ruins forming the backdrop for bleeding victims, visibly upset policewomen, and scattered debris, were reminiscent of a civil war scene, not of a sleepy northern city in midsummer.

The terrorist attack took place in the middle of the summer holidays, a period when the country runs well below its usual capacity and routinely finds itself in a condition of drowsiness. Many Norwegians are on holiday abroad, others take their vacations at a campsite or in a family cottage. Both the ministries under attack and the police were accordingly understaffed. Thus the casualty numbers in central Oslo were less, and the police slower to react, than would otherwise have been the case.

My family and I were spending July in our summerhouse on the coast south of Oslo, but on 22 July I happened to be in town because my son was going to play in a football cup in Denmark and needed transportation to the ferry. We were outside in the garden and heard the blast, but mistook it for thunder. By the time we were updated on the facts, it was still widely believed that the perpetrators were Muslim terrorists. I heard of one worried Muslim father who drove into town to pick up his daughter, so that she would not have to take the metro home. The leader of the populist Progress Party went on TV that afternoon, describing the attack as "an assault on Norway." She would later learn that the terrorist had been a member of her own party for ten years.

The entire country was now edgy and nervous, nowhere more so than in central Oslo. My son and I had to take a cumbersome detour in order to get to the port. We soon noticed that the queue to the ferry bound for Denmark moved much more slowly than usual since all vehicles were checked by the police before being allowed to enter the boat. While waiting to get our boys on their way, one of the other soccer dads received a text message from his wife, who had heard rumors about shooting at Utøya, that idyllic island on a lake north of Oslo where the youth wing of the Labor Party (AUF) held their annual summer camp with more than six hundred participants from all over the country. We looked at each other. Any connection? No, that was unthinkable. After a moment of hesitation, we waved our boys good-bye and returned home. Only later that evening did it become clear that the Utøya shootings were indeed connected with the attack on the government houses. The experts all agreed that this had to be an operation planned by a professional organization. Al-Qaeda and "the Libyans" were mentioned.

Reactions to 22 July

When the extent of the atrocities became known, and it became clear that all the horrors had been carried out by a single, from all appearances very ordinary person, the Norwegian terrorist attack made headlines across the world. The foreign demand for Norwegian voices commenting on the tragedy was such that I, for one, ended up spending a week's worth of holiday time speaking to journalists from perhaps twenty different countries on my mobile phone, from my summerhouse terrace, and spending the evenings writing short pieces for publications in various countries.

My personal and professional engagement with the terrorist attack on Norway is easy to explain. First, although right-wing extremism is not my field of research, cultural diversity is, as well as nationalism and ethnicity. Second, I have firsthand experience of the Islamophobic kind of right-wing nationalism, having found myself on the receiving end of unpleasant attacks for years.

One perspective on Norway from the international press, which came to predominate after the initial shock had subsided, was a sense of wonder and puzzlement over the Norwegian reactions to the massacre. Rather than spending energy demonizing the perpetrator and blaming people who shared his worldview, official Norway, represented by royalty and politicians, came out with pleas for compassion and solidarity. A spontaneous "rose procession" (*rosetog*) was organized in Oslo already on 24 July, with thousands of participants coming together to share their grief. The rose does not only signify compassion and love in this context. It is also a symbol of the Labor Party. The general feeling was nevertheless that this show of solidarity, replicated in many other Norwegian cities and towns, expressed the sentiment that everybody in the country had been bereaved, had somehow lost a family member.

Following the arrest of Anders Breivik on 22 July 2011, during the lengthy trial in spring and early summer 2012, and in the subsequent period, the terrorist attack and its various contexts were analyzed from various perspectives by domestic and international commentators. Some focused on Breivik's ideology and related it to other Islamophobic and nationalist tendencies. Others were concerned with the inefficiency of the police at Utøya and the lacking security measures around Oslo government buildings. Yet others have looked into Breivik's class background in an affluent Oslo neighborhood, or into his complex upbringing by a neurotic single mother, the father being mostly absent following divorce. There have been debates about the limits of the freedom of speech (understandably, given that the terrorist acts were inspired by hate speech on the Internet), and about the quality of the state support given to the bereaved and survivors. This chapter is not meant as a contribution to these debates. My focus is on the Norwegian reactions in the days and weeks following 22 July. To what extent can the Norwegian responses to the terrorist attack be understood in the context of the smallness—relative as well as absolute—of Norwegian society?

Relative Smallness and the Norwegian Self-Understanding

A standard response of mine when asked, be it on a radio show in Scotland or in a Chilean newspaper, to explain the surprisingly dispassionate Norwegian response to the terrorist attack, had to do with smallness. Norway is relatively small in population (five million) and remotely located. Partly for this reason, I explained, there is a widespread sense of vulnerability on behalf of the nation and a strong feeling of cohesion. The Norwegian Constitution Day, 17 May, is celebrated by more than 90 percent of the population, most of them taking part in one or several public events. The tropes of family and kinship invoked in nationalist rhetoric function well in the Norwegian context and could thus be mobilized easily in the aftermath of the terrorist attack. The photos of slaughtered teenagers in the newspapers created a sense of recognition. It was *our* metaphorical sons, brothers, daughters, and nieces who had been murdered.

Relative smallness is an important aspect of any national construction seen as small, since nationhood is—like all forms of identification—relational. Whether a country is small or large depends on the relevant horizon of comparison, and this holds true for other entities as well. In Mauritius, a relatively isolated oceanic island with a total population of slightly over a million, my villager friends were deeply worried when, in the autumn of 1986, I revealed my plans to move to the capital. That is a really big city, they said, with pickpockets and conmen, traffic jams, and a furious pace. As a matter of fact, the population of Port Louis was at the time around one hundred thousand, and by European standards the city ambience was rather sleepy and peaceful. Yet, compared to the coastal village where I had lived, it appeared to be a big and scary place.

In other contexts, Mauritians see their island as fairly tiny and insignificant. Regarding Norway, it would have made a difference if its main horizon of comparison had been, say, Iceland. Compared to Iceland, Norway has a pleasantly temperate climate, a large and diverse population, a relaxed attitude to linguistic nationalism, not so much fish, and inexpensive beer. Yet the historically predominant comparisons that were constitutive of Norway in the nineteenth century were toward the closest neighbors, Denmark and Sweden.

Indeed, both Denmark and Sweden can be considered small countries. Denmark is densely populated and highly urbanized, but it has a tiny surface area (compared to Norway and Sweden). Its population is, today, roughly the same as the Norwegian one. However, until the Napoleonic Wars, today's Denmark formed the core of an imperial state stretching from Greenland to the North Cape, with Norway as a rural province. Thus, from the Norwegian point of view, Denmark is urban and differentiated, as opposed to the (proverbially) rural and homogeneous Norway.

With Sweden, the situation is different, and it illustrates the importance of relationality with regard to size. Certainly, Swedes often see their country as small, since they tend to compare themselves not to Finland or Norway, but to France and the United States. (There are exceptions, though: In winter sports, notably skiing, Norway and Sweden are rivals, with Norway getting the better of its larger neighbor in recent years, with the Swedish media taking on a suitably humiliated attitude on the day after a major competition.) As a rule, however, Sweden is more important to Norway than Norway is to Sweden. Finland, Denmark, and Norway have about five million inhabitants each. Sweden, geographically in the middle, has ten. Sweden thus looms large in the imaginations of the three other Nordic countries.

In small countries, there is a constant yearning for attention from the larger neighbors or, as the world has become more interconnected, from anybody out there. And the attention increases in symbolic value along with increasing size and importance in its country of origin. For a Norwegian artist, being "big in Hollywood" is something qualitatively different from being "big in Reykjavik," but both kinds of success will be noted by the Norwegian media.

Countries portraying themselves as small relative to their neighbors may emphasize their simplicity, homogeneity, and cohesiveness as virtues that go with smallness. This has historically been the case in Norway, and the post–22 July responses suggest that it is still an important part of the collective self-understanding. This in turn has consequences for the mechanisms of inclusion and exclusion at work; a country with a self-understanding as being homogeneous and simple may not be the best place for immigrants from remote areas. And the lack of aggression witnessed in the Norwegian population and media after the terrorist attack may have had something to do with the fact that Breivik, the terrorist, was "one of us," to use the title of Åsne Seierstad's (2015) acclaimed book, from a middle-class suburb of the capital.

Absolute Smallness, Networks, and Scale

Yet although relative size matters, absolute size and scale also matter and may shed light on the aftermath of the terrorist attack in important ways. In very small societies, most members are known to each other even if they do not know each other personally. This would be the case in societies integrated at the level of the village or small town, but also quite often in a country such as Iceland (pop. 250,000). Some years ago, a Swedish friend of mine telephoned a colleague in Iceland, let us call him X. However, he had the wrong number, so when my friend asked for X, the person at the other end said, "Oh no, you have reached a number in Akureyri, and X lives in Reykjavik—hold on, and I'll find the correct number for you." That would have been less likely to happen in New York City.

In societies where the scale is small in absolute terms, anybody can risk being recognized by others any time. There is no way you can walk down the main street of a small town on a Saturday afternoon, if you have lived there all your life, and not meet someone you know. In Mauritius, bank robberies are unheard of. There are few possible hiding places on the island, one of the bank employees would probably recognize the robbers, and people would get suspicious anyway when young men known to be penniless suddenly began to spend money conspicuously. This kind of transparency seems to be characteristic of societies below a certain threshold and with fairly evenly distributed social networks.

The scale of a social system can be defined as the number of statuses necessary for the system to be reproduced (cf. Barth 1978). There can be no simple delineation of any social system, however, since subsystems (religion, labor market, politics, and so on) operate on different levels of scale. Yet it makes sense to state that the scale of the labor market, say, in a society such as Mauritius, is modest compared to that in countries like Malaysia or Madagascar. As already pointed out by Burton Benedict (1966), a strike in a sugar mill in Mauritius would have more severe repercussions throughout the national economy than an identical strike in India. By the same token, individual potentials for careers are less diverse the smaller the scale. All other things being equal, there are fewer jobs and fewer opportunities for success in a small society than in a large one. Thus V. S. Naipaul, himself from a small plantation island, once commented on the Mauritian politician Gaëtan Duval that if he had been from a larger country, he might have become a rock star, but in Mauritius he had to settle for glamour in politics.

As with relative smallness, absolute smallness is also characterized by an obsessive interest in the outside world's views of oneself. Whenever someone from Mauritius encounters success overseas, he or she automatically becomes a celebrity at home. In Norway, five times the size of Mauritius in terms of population, the expression "world famous in Norway" is occasionally used about people whose success is restricted to the domestic stage, while the appreciative description "better known abroad than in Norway" is its opposite.

It is possible, on a lucky day, for a local to walk down the main street of Oslo without meeting an acquaintance. There is a real possibility of anonymity. In other respects, however, the scale of Norwegian society is small enough for encompassing, dense networks to be possible. Size is a necessary but not sufficient factor in this regard. All other things being equal, the chance of a Norwegian knowing someone who knows the prime minister is twice that of a Swede and eight times that of a Spaniard. This fact made a difference in the aftermath of the terrorist attack, when elite members of society made impassioned speeches to the nation: they were speaking as neighbors, family members, and colleagues, not as leaders from the higher echelons of society. The king took on an avuncular role, the crown princess spoke as a metaphorical sister and daughter, the mayor of Oslo as everybody's sympathetic neighbor.

Scale and network density are a function not simply of size but also of internal organization. In societies that are strongly segregated along class or ethnicity, networks rarely cross boundaries. The degree of crosscutting identification may therefore be modest. Norway is interesting in this respect. Although inequality has been on the rise since the 1980s, it ranks as one of the least unequal countries in the world. Moreover, although local identities are strong and linked to dialects, food, and other regional traditions, national identity is more powerful.

Social distances are generally short in Norway. Norwegians tend to know people outside their own social class and, because of the geographical mobility associated with modernity, their region. The majority of Norwegians have taken part in some kind of voluntary community service (*dugnad*) to the benefit of the school marching band, the local children's ski club, or the housing cooperative. Especially in the spring and autumn, "work parties" are organized to raise money for the maintenance or improvement of some shared asset. I remember once in Oxford, following a seminar at the Institute of Social Anthropology, when I had to leave the pub early to catch a flight home. As I explained, I was enrolled to sell hot dogs at the local football stadium on the next day. This raised some eyebrows. The point, however, is that through such activities, as well as membership in various organizations, Norwegians get to know a broad variety of other people personally. Partly as a result of this kind of practice, national identity is relatively undifferentiated. Just as all Muslims or Christians are equal before God, every Norwegian is equal before the nation.

This has not always been the case. In the 1930s, when labor relations were conflictual and the labor movement had a strongly international orientation, people who marched under the red banners of May Day would usually not march under the Norwegian flags of 17 May, dismissing the celebration of Constitution Day as class collaboration. By now, this does not seem to be an issue. The labor movement has become more moderate politically, the nation is portrayed as a community of equals. There is a small, rich upper class and a small lumpenproletariat of drug addicts and others who have somehow fallen off the welfare map, but the remaining vast majority of the Norwegian population is integrated through denser and more egalitarian networks than in most societies of comparable complexity.

Finally—and this is arguably a function of egalitarianism just as much as of scale or size—trust is generally high in Norway. When asked by quantitative social scientists, a comfortable majority of Norwegians agree with the statement "Most people are to be trusted" (while the figure in, for example, the United States is much lower). Studies are sometimes carried out where a handful of wallets with some money and some ID papers are placed around in European cities (ten in each city), and the researchers record how many are returned or handed over to the police. Oslo consistently makes the top place—before Copenhagen, and way ahead of Rome and Athens.

The Metaphorical Family and the Others

Both relative and absolute smallness play a part in creating this imagined community. In the traumatic situation experienced after 22 July 2011, the country's political leadership and media elites could presuppose solidarity and a widespread family feeling. Nations are metaphorical families, witnessed through the usage of metaphors such as "fatherland," "mother tongue," or "brothers and sisters of the nation." In the Norwegian setting, that family can be mobilized when need be, and this was palpably operative in this situation of crisis.

At the same time, the dominant metaphorical family was now faced with serious difficulties following the terrorist attack. Since the very cohesiveness (and vulnerability due to smallness) of the Norwegian family had been emphasized in all standard national narratives, it was difficult to find a cultural script for Breivik and what he did. Like in many small countries, Norwegians have access to several scripts involving foreign invaders and heroic resistance. The dominant narrative about World War II remains that of the small people heroically standing up to the bad Nazis—while actually far more Norwegians took employment with the Germans than were active in the resistance. It is undercommunicated that Norwegians did little to protect the country's Jews. In more recent years, several Norwegians—including a few elderly gentlemen with a background in the Resistance—have drawn a parallel between the German occupation and current non-European immigration, seeing both as threatening the integrity of the nation. Other dramatic narratives about the country's past have also chiefly involved foreign invaders or enemies (the Swedes played this part for many years), while no strong national myths involve enemies from within.

Breivik associated himself with right-wing opposition to immigration, posing in a homemade uniform allegedly representing the Knights Templars, and extending his genealogy back to the Crusades. Strongly influenced by the imagery of fantasy literature and online games, Breivik nevertheless served as a reminder that the Norwegian population was in fact severely divided over issues of cultural pluralism and immigration. Many Norwegians, perhaps as much as half the population, are to varying degrees dissatisfied with the extent of contemporary immigration. From a modest beginning around 1970, the numbers of immigrants, mostly non-European, have grown and then skyrocketed. As late as 1995, the number (including immigrants and their children) was 250,000 or 5 percent of the population; by 2013, there were more than 650,000, or 13 percent. Although the largest new immigrant groups are European (Poles, Swedes, and others), the main public concern is with non-Europeans, especially Muslims. Several of the websites perused, and contributed to, by Breivik have tens of thousands of users every month, routinely publishing material indicating that the government and parliament lie to the public about immigrant numbers and failed integration.

The point is that Breivik symbolizes a deep divide in the Norwegian population. Taking this fact as a point of departure in the post–22 July attempt to come to terms with the attack would have implied placing the responsibility partly on those who shared some of Breivik's convictions. It was therefore convenient for some commentators to define Breivik as a lunatic, thereby effectively isolating him from the dark undercurrents of Norwegian nationalism, and even from the counterjihadist and anti-immigrant Internet networks of which he was part. The reactions were likely to have been different if he had been a Muslim. Analytically, however, this is a more interesting situation since it is less obvious: a small, wealthy country with a strong sense of nationhood and cohesiveness is betrayed from within. Should it place the traitor in the madhouse or discuss his ideology? Although Breivik was declared insane by the first team of psychiatrists who examined him (their verdict was later overturned), he was sentenced to prison, yet he was scarcely seen as a political terrorist. Could this be because the mechanisms of inclusion and exclusion in Norway were incapable of accommodating a deep internal division along ideological lines? Was Norwegian society so based on perceived similarity and equality that it could not afford fundamental disagreement? To this question we now turn.

Inclusion and Exclusion in a Small Country

Every society has boundaries, but no boundary is so solid as to prevent everything from seeping in and out. The boundaries of a society may be seen as semipermeable membranes: they allow certain substances (people, ideas, goods, and so on) to flow in and out, and the rules regulating the inflows differ from those regulating the outflows. Using this analogy, the differences between the main challenges of tiny, small, and large countries become clear.

For a tiny country, a main challenge consists in developing a minimum of relative autonomy and showing its ability to reproduce itself. It is hard to keep a full assortment of domestic media going. Newspapers tend to be thin and flimsy, local TV productions derivative and low budget. These countries strive to fulfill the minimal obligations needed for them to be considered full-fledged countries; such things as having a UN ambassador, a currency, a national football team may matter considerably.

In a large country, the internal differentiation is such, and social distances usually so huge, that a main challenge is to create a minimum of cohesive structures, institutions, and persuasive symbols for a collective identity to be possible at all.

What about those countries that are neither large nor tiny? Their main challenge, I suggest, consists in reconciling their *Gemeinschaft*-like ideology of common culture and intimacy with modernity and difference. A typical anxiety voiced in Norway, faced with growing diversity, concerns the future of the institutions generating trust, and the welfare state as such (the metaphorical father and mother of the imagined community). Taking its cultural homogeneity for granted and modeling itself on the family, or perhaps the local community, it has difficulties building its identity on anything but similarity. Simply by virtue of size, it seems, larger countries—at least in Europe—avoid this conceptual straitjacket since their internal diversity is undeniable.

By the same token, it would have been far more difficult in a larger country—Germany or Italy—to generate a sense of collective grief comparable to that experienced in Norway. People saw the newspaper pictures of the slaughtered teenagers and immediately felt that they knew them. In addition, the absolute smallness and egalitarian social organization of Norway ensures that a vast number of Norwegians were affected directly or indirectly by the massacre. One of the victims was the son of the canteen lady at my wife's workplace, and the hundred persons who used the canteen had all heard her talk proudly about her bright son who had decided to go into politics to make the world a slightly better place. As for myself, I had met one of the young victims on a couple of occasions and was asked to speak at his funeral. It seemed as if—just as a great number of Norwegians know somebody who knows somebody who knows the prime minister—most people *knew about someone* who had been affected directly by the massacre—a sibling, a parent, a survivor, a teacher, a neighbor.

This is how Norway works in a situation of crisis. A couple of critical questions must still be raised. One, which I have been asked by numerous foreign journalists, is whether the situation is now easier for ethnic minorities. The question makes sense for two reasons. First, several of the young people who were killed at Utøya, and several of the survivors visible in the media afterward, had a minority background. As I sometimes pointed out, they were in a certain sense better integrated into Norwegian society than I was at the age of eighteen; they were members of the youth wing of a leading party and committed to "the Norwegian model" of egalitarianism and social democracy. So through their sacrifice, they showed right-wing Islamophobes that Norwegian Muslims were not all religious fanatics. Second, the target of Breivik's attack was exactly multiculturalism. Against this background, one might reason, a reaction from society could be a determination not to let him have it his way, to embrace those impurities and cultural instabilities that Breivik detested, and to show that mainstream Norway did not share his negative views of people with a different cultural background.

But the answer to the question is no: there is no indication that Norwegian society is either more or less at ease with its growing diversity today than it was before the terrorist attack. Somehow, the political context of Breivik's attack has become anathema—the mere mention of his name in connection with anti-Muslim or anti-immigrant discourse immediately releases a stream of indignant replies (see Bangstad 2014 for details). As a right-wing populist politician said a few weeks after the terrorist attack, the most serious effect of this event could be that it would now be difficult to "tell the truth about Islam."

To recapitulate: the initial reaction to the terrorist attack was collective grief, mourning and large-scale public displays of compassion and solidarity. Subsequently, Breivik was treated by the public as an anomaly, a deviant, a psychological mystery, and a mad psychopath. As a result, Norway never had to take the political context in which he operated seriously. Perhaps the semipermeable membranes surrounding Norwegian society are forced to eject persons like Breivik, just as they reject begging Roma women, unemployed Somali men and criminal gangs from the Baltic region. Foreigners can always be thrown out physically. Individuals like Breivik cannot; they have to be digested or else isolated as singularities, anomalies, exceptions that confirm the rule. The price to pay for moving displays of solidarity and cohesion is the silencing of fundamental divisions in society. Paradoxically, the very tendency that Breivik devoted his life to fighting—mixing, pluralism, and cultural instability—may eventually serve to undermine the very conditions for this kind of *Gemeinschaft*-like coziness. Some trust may be lost, some openness may be gained (see Eriksen 2014 for a full analysis).

Is This Really About Smallness?

During the Breivik trial, I had several telephone conversations and some e-mail correspondence with a Japanese journalist, writing for a major Japanese newspaper. I went on about size, scale, egalitarianism, and network structure, pointing out that Libya, with roughly the same population, did not display anything remotely reminiscent of Norway with regard to social solidarity. I even made an excursion into kinship studies and classic political anthropology in order to explain what kind of imagined community Norway was, and how this shed light on the collective experience. It was similar, I went on, whenever there was some international sport competition. Indifference or hostility toward the Norwegians did not go down well then, so we were talking about a particular kind of small country.

My interlocutor listened politely but made an interesting objection. Following the earthquake, tsunami, and nuclear fallout in Fukushima in March 2011, he said, Japanese reactions were quite similar to the Norwegian ones after the terrorist attack: mourning for the dead, concern for the survivors, a collective determination to help them rebuild their communities and recreate their lives. Japanese culture, he said, was also by and large a culture of consensus, based on strong ideas of cultural commonality.

There is just one problem. While Norway has 5 million inhabitants, Japan has 130 million. Does this mean that there is something flawed with the very conceptualization of the small country, or with my analysis of Norway as a particular kind of small country?

The preceding argument has presented Norway as a *relatively* small country (giving a sense of vulnerability plus strengthening the internal solidarity) and an *absolutely* small country (with short social distances and dense networks). This is a recipe for strong social cohesion and made it difficult to frame the events of 22 July as an attack from within, since the "inside" is by default not only cohesive but also good. Additionally, emphasizing the ideological motivation for Breivik's massacre would have created a conflictual situation since a substantial part of Norway's population shares some of his views of Islam, multiculturalism, and immigration.

Japan is a very different country: it has an ancient feudal history and is less egalitarian than Norway. For most Japanese, there is no way to reach the prime minister, or another leader at the national level, through just two or three removes in a network. It is also common to argue that the predominant Japanese concept of personhood differs from egalitarian individualism and can instead be described as a form of collectivism where loyalty is valued highly.

It may initially appear as if Norway and Japan are almost exact opposites of each other regarding some key variables. Yet it seems that there are also some interesting convergences. First, Japan is in important respects relatively small. Its significant Other was for centuries China and has been the United States in the postwar period. It is an island state, vulnerable to invasions and prone to isolation.

Second, the collectivism of Japanese society, as demonstrated in its corporate culture (where lifelong employment used to be the norm and still is an ideal) and its local communities (where social control is such that crime rates are very low), parallel the Norwegian ideal of the local community as the template for society and voluntary community work as a morally valuable activity. These parallels between Japan and Norway may thus lead to similar results, unlike what one would find in deeply divided and conflictual societies such as the United States or South Africa.

Trust, loyalty, solidarity, and a collective identity based on a notion of sameness appear to be comparable in Norway and Japan, though for different reasons (see Nakane 1972 for a classic statement; Hendry 2012 for an updated account). In both countries, national identity is based metaphorically on *Gemeinschaft*-like communities, where family and locality are essential; in Japan, the corporation adds to this. Most Japanese people must be assumed to be separated by more degrees of separation from the leadership of the country than in Norway.

Yet this fact does not seem to play an important role in the creation of a cohesive moral community. Although it encompasses twenty-six times as many persons in Japan as in Norway, the imagined community functions on the same principle, as a metaphorical extension of the community, and presupposing cultural similarity. The widespread perception of homogeneity and local integration led Japanese across the country to identify with those directly affected by the Fukushima earthquake. They could see themselves and their neighbors in the victims.

As in Norway, ethnic minorities have struggled to achieve recognition in Japan, and immigrants are not easily "digested." Their grammar of alterity, to follow Gerd Baumann and Andre Gingrich's typology (2004), is mainly that of orientalization: we have something that the other lacks. The community as metaphor for the nation offers security, at the expense of sacrificing openness.

It could be that relative smallness does play a part, in Japan as well as Norway: again, the Japanese may also perceive themselves as relatively small compared with China and the United States. Yet the direct effect of smallness on community responses to events like those of 22 July will evidently not be the same everywhere. Even before speaking to the Japanese journalist,

I was aware that smallness did not in itself explain the Norwegian reactions to the terrorist attack. Discussing the event and Norwegian reactions with a Scottish colleague (population size in Scotland is the same as in Norway), he insisted that Scots would have looked for those directly or indirectly accountable in a similar situation, blaming anyone from police and government politicians to the Islamophobic fringe groups. The Scottish ethos, he added, was not based on an egalitarian individualism, but rather on a combative, competitive individualism intersected by deep class differences and regional rivalries. What the Scottish and Japanese comparisons suggest is that beyond the level of face-to-face relations, size does not in itself matter for the strength of national cohesion. In this, small countries are different from tiny ones, where the majority of inhabitants are aware of each other's existence. Against this background, I emphasized network types and imagined homogeneity, which I nevertheless also related to both relative and absolute smallness.

All things considered, smallness, both absolute and relative, helps. Networks are more likely to overlap, mutual acquaintances are often discovered at chance meetings, and since people often have to play several public roles in order to fill up the requirements of a complex society, multiplex relations abound. Social distances are also shorter, if nothing else because less wealth accumulates in few hands in a small country than in a big one (again, all other things being equal). In winter, the prime minister goes skiing in the forest north of Oslo and says hello to the people he meets; the most famous TV comedian in the country lives in an ordinary house just up the street from me (not at a secret address), and "people who matter" know each other, or are at least aware of each other. This would not be the case in Japan, although instead, people can identify with each other, assuming that they share the same culture. The aim of strong national cohesion can be achieved in several ways, and smallness is only one. But the downside of exclusion and exclusivity is also the same, be the country small or large.

References

Bangstad, Sindre. 2014. *Anders Breivik and the Rise of Islamophobia*. London: Zed.

Barth, Fredrik, ed. 1978. *Scale and Social Organization*. Oslo: Universitetsforlaget.

Baumann, Gerd, and Andre Gingrich. 2004. Foreword. In Gerd Baumann and Andre Gingrich, eds., *Grammars of Identity/Alterity*. Oxford: Berghahn.

Benedict, Burton. 1966. Sociological Characteristics of Small Territories and Their Implications for Economic Development. In Michael Banton, ed., *The Social Anthropology of Complex Societies*. London: Tavistock.

Eriksen, Thomas Hylland. 2014. Who or What to Blame: Competing Interpretations of the Norwegian Terrorist Attack. *European Journal of Sociology* 55 (2): 275–94.

Hendry, Joy. 2012. *Understanding Japanese Society*, 4th ed. London: Routledge.

Nakane, Chie. 1972. *Japanese Society*. Berkeley: University of California Press.

Seierstad, Åsne. 2015. *One of Us: The Story of Anders Breivik and the Massacre in Norway*. New York: Farrar, Straus and Giroux.

CHAPTER 3

The Scandinavian Cluster:
Small Countries with Big Egos

Orvar Löfgren

"I was bored in a fjord. And I curse the heart and soul of Scandinavia" is the start of British singer Morrissey's "Scandinavia" from 2011, declaring that he despises "each syllable in Scandinavia." But then someone comes along, and the song turns to love: "I kiss the soil, I hug the soil, I eat the soil . . . I'd be so happy to die in Scandinavia."

So what kind of soil or soul is Scandinavia? A successful brand with a shared identity, a political model, or a way of life held up as an admirable example—or criticized as the wrong way to go? Like Morrissey's, international opinions tend to fluctuate, but most can agree that the label Scandinavia is a successful example of both a clustering strategy and transnational integration.

Outsiders frequently bundle these countries. Is Copenhagen the capital of Sweden, do Norwegians speak Danish? Or as an American official put it in 2002: "the Norwegian countries" (quoted in Witoszek 2011: 12). They blend as clean and well-run but not overexciting little welfare systems—boring nanny states, populated by blond girls and slightly gray but effective bureaucrats, with Finland as the wild card.

Using Scandinavia or "the Nordic countries" (Denmark, Finland, Iceland, Norway, and Sweden) as my case, I want to discuss the political and cultural dynamics of clustering that seem to be typical of small nations. Is clustering a label imposed from the outside, or a conscious strategy for small nations vis-à-vis the outside world? Small countries can engage in supranational relations like dyads, buffer zones, or clusters. My focus is on the analytic potential of the concept of cluster. Although there might be other constellations, most examples of clustering seem to deal with small nations. My Scandinavian examples will show what clustering can do to small countries, as a resource or a problem. A cluster must have some coherence; it is not just a random collection of small states.

What are the different origins and strategies of small-nation clustering? When applied as a label from the outside, it often has a negative slant. "That bunch of small countries out there, whose names I keep forgetting!" To be part of a cluster is a way of being rendered insignificant, just bundled together with some neighbors. Identifying clusters may also be a way of economizing or pointing to similarities, like the use of another term, that of "regions."

Operetta Kingdoms and Banana Republics

The belittling approach is found in the derogatory talk of small nations as cute but comical. We find it in concepts like "banana republics" in Central America, or early twentieth-century Balkan "operetta kingdoms." Although such countries tried to use the established forms of modern nationhood— passports, standing armies, national assemblies, banks, and museums—the miniature scale made them look a bit ridiculous. One could not quite remember their individual names.

In popular culture they have often showed up as fictions. A model for that became Ruritania, invented as a small central European kingdom in Anthony Hope's novel *The Prisoner of Zenda* (1894). The emergent genre involved books ranging from Winston Churchill's early novel *Savrola* to the boys' book hero Biggles and his flying adventures in the conflict between Maltovia and Lovitzna. It offered popular parodies in Hollywood films like the Marx Brothers' *Duck Soup* from 1933, taking place in the bankrupt Balkan country of Freedonia. Ruritania entered academic research as an example of a hypothetical country in international law and economics, but also in other social sciences, as in Ernest Gellner's *Nations and Nationalism* (1983), where the Ruritanians living in the "Empire of Megalomania" develop their own national project. In her book *Inventing Ruritania: The Imperialism of the Imagination* (1998), Vesna Goldsworthy discusses it as a "narrative colonization" of small Balkan countries.

The belittling dimension is also found in the Latin American world of "banana republics"—a term often used to describe small countries with unstable economies and corrupt leadership (and originally an American banana company in control). A more recent similar cluster label is "Absurdistan," used since the 1970s, and increasingly after the fall of the Soviet empire, often focusing on immature nations with authoritarian profiles.[1]

These three labels have different histories and geopolitical foci, but they are all used to describe diffuse clusters of small, often failing nations. But there are other kinds of clusters, created from the inside as neighboring countries enter forms of cooperation to fortify or advertise their positions in relation to big nations. It may be a strategy of pooling resources, of making a greater political or cultural impact by becoming a bigger bloc—clustering can have many aims. Drawing on the Scandinavian case, I want to avoid discussing only the discursive aspects of clustering, as branding, political rhetoric, or outside stereotyping—focusing also on aspects of Morrissey's "soil." What kind of experiences and processes have occurred on the ground, at an everyday level, making this cluster of countries share not only a common history but also an integration based upon common institutions, cross-border movements, and cooperations creating shared practices, interests, and values? This calls for a historical perspective.

Shrinking Empires and National Amnesia

Scandinavia is a somewhat fluid concept. There are two cluster labels at work here, often used interchangeably. Scandinavia actually consists of three core countries: Denmark, Norway, and Sweden, but as a successful brand name, it has often become a synonym for the wider cluster of the five Nordic countries. Finland is sometimes seen as the special case, although I would not go as far as Richard D. Lewis (2005) does with his book *Finland, Cultural Lone Wolf.* For linguistic as well as geopolitical reasons, Finland has a special situation, but it is firmly placed as a Nordic country. The concepts used are thus Scandinavia and the local term *Norden* (simply "The North") or the Nordic countries. In the following I will mainly use "Scandinavia," but sometimes also the "Nordic" prefix.

Scandinavia constitutes a rather special cluster, in several ways. It is often presented as a group of almost timeless, well-integrated, and homogeneous nation-states; classic examples of small, peaceful countries with stable "natural borders." In reality, they are the product of a rather late breakup of two smallish northern maritime empires with a long history of military aggression and intra-Scandinavian warfare. Their current Nordic smallness is the result of an accidental but well-timed breakup of these empire-like states, just before the boom of modern nationalism.

While the Nordic countries were briefly united for a period in the fourteenth century, they were organized in the kingdom of Denmark, including Norway, Iceland, Greenland, the Faroese Islands, and the German duchy of Schleswig-Holstein (an Atlantic empire) and the kingdom of Sweden, including Finland and Baltic territories (a Baltic empire). Slowly these two kingdoms shrank. Sweden took big chunks of Denmark in the seventeenth century, while German states and Russia gnawed away at both empires. In 1809 Finland became part of the Russian empire until 1917, and in 1814 Sweden as a compensation took Norway from Denmark, a forced union lasting until 1905. In 1864 Denmark lost its southern territories (and a third of its population) in the war with the alliance of German states. Iceland became independent from Denmark in 1945.

In this gradual process Sweden, Denmark, Norway, and Finland turned into smaller and much more homogeneous nations. After the loss of Finland the slogan in Sweden was "let us regain Finland within the new Swedish borders." In Denmark, several times on the verge of disappearing as an independent country, a similar rallying cry was heard after the traumatic losses in 1864.

The new rhetoric of smallness was formulated in different ways. In Denmark it laid the ground for "Lilliput chauvinism"—small but great (see Jenkins 2011: 46). In Finland the virtues of tiny but tough were extolled during the two wars with the Soviet Union during World War II. The author Väinö Linna ended his famous war novel *The Unknown Soldier* with a soldier joke: "The Union of Soviet Socialist Republics won, but little tough Finland came in a close second!"

So behind the images of stable, peaceful Scandinavian history there is a long history of conflicts and changing borders—a history often forgotten or put aside. Danes rarely think of Norway as an old part of their country, Swedes seldom reminisce about the Finnish connection—although these linkages existed since the Middle Ages. Turning inward, both Denmark and Sweden lost touch with their geopolitical past (see Østergaard 1997).

During the first two decades of the twenty-first century, several anniversaries have commemorated the drastic shifts: two centuries since the loss of

Finland in 1809 and since the loss of Norway in 1813, one century since the breakup of the Swedish-Norwegian union in 1905. It is striking how little popular interest there has been in these commemorations (especially in the losing countries). Borders have become naturalized and populations integrated in ways that make Nordic countries think of themselves as distinct and homogeneous entities, and this has helped make a stronger clustering possible. Already in the mid-nineteenth century the old combatants fostered an intellectual movement of Scandinavianism, talking of their Nordic neighbors as brothers, not as old enemies or colonizers.

To understand this rapid shift we must turn to the effective nationalization of the Nordic countries during the nineteenth century. The old empires became distinct nations without revanchist ambitions. Unlike the cases of Austria and Serbia (see Bendix's and Bošković's chapters in this volume), there is little nostalgia for a grander past.

Cultural Nation Building—Scandinavian Style

The result of this process was that the nations were also shrinking in another way: through an intense cultural nation building in the nineteenth and twentieth centuries they became much more integrated and homogenized. The nation-state became tangible in many more everyday situations, through new communication networks from newspapers to railways, but also through national institutions and practices. During the nineteenth century, nation building was intense, perhaps most intense in Norway (in forced union with Sweden, but with great autonomy) and Finland (also with considerable autonomy, as an archduchy of Russia).

The countries often used their Nordic neighbors as contrasts, but often within a shared platform. When searching for a suitable past, the simple virtues of peasant history were extolled in all countries, but the choice of symbolic heritage was done in the tradition of national othering. The Finns focused on the folklore of the slash-and-burn peasants of Karelia—very non-Swedish. The Norwegians chose the mountain peasantry, as far removed from the Danish peasants of the rich plains as possible. Sweden chose to celebrate the region of Dalecarlia.

The same tension between similarity and difference was found in the nationalization of nature. All the Nordic national anthems emphasize the importance of nature, rugged cliffs, smiling woods, billowing cornfields, and blue waters. This focus on nature is shared with other northern countries, who have felt they must make up for a lack of grandiose history by an abundance of unspoiled nature. Marginality was turned into an asset. We may lack grand heritage monuments, but we have fantastic, wild landscapes! (Löfgren 2000: 33ff). The preoccupation with nature is still strong. In Nordic exchanges of TV shows, nature programs dominate. The image of the perfect summerhouse is a small cottage on a quiet lake or by the sea.

An even more striking similarity in the nation-building process had to do with a feeling of being in the periphery of Eupe. The wish to catch up was typical of the Nordic countries from the late nineteenth century and onward. Scandinavians became early adopters, keen on new technologies, ideas, and institutions, and this innovative mentality was often linked to a firm belief in progress: "being progressive was perceived as a moral quality," as Kazimierz Musial (2000: 10) has put it in his discussion of the Scandinavian model.

In this process there was an enthusiastic drive to nationalize modernity, especially in the interwar years and the decades after the World War II. During the 1950s and 1960s Scandinavia was often talked of as the most Americanized region in the world, but in retrospect we can see that it was precisely during these decades that intense investments in a welfare society made Scandinavia very Scandinavian. The welfare state became more visible in everyday life than in many other countries, in day-care centers and housing estates, in leisure and at work. The making of "Scandinavian modern" took shape, not only in design and fashion, but also in family politics, child rearing, gender equality, and social policies. When in a 2005 report the Nordic Council tried to define Nordic "core values," it was about egalitarianism, trust, small power distances, informality, flexibility, respect for the environment, Protestant work ethic, and an aesthetic sense (see Harvard 2011: 22). It is striking that many of these "soft values" were institutionalized and elaborated during the years from 1945 to 1975. The nationalization of everyday life went further here than in many other Western countries. A kind of soft informality also became a strong element in domestic life—an elusive dimension of coziness called *hygge* in Danish, *kos* in Norwegian and *mys* in Swedish. The other side of this development has been described by the Finnish historian Henrik Stenius (1997: 171): "All the doors are open—to the living room, the kitchen, the larder, the nursery, not to question the bedroom—and they are not just open: society marches in and intervenes, sometimes brusquely."

Much work has been done by historians and sociologists on what has been called the Nordic or Scandinavian model, discussing the roots of a special kind of welfare capitalism in peasant egalitarianism, Protestant work ethic, and the strong political position of social democratic parties (see Sørensen and Stråth 1997; Esping-Andersen 1990). Questions have centered around whether this Scandinavian modernization constitutes a *Sonderweg* in European history and how deep its historical roots are (see Götz 2003).

Although the position of the Social Democrats has been weakened in all Nordic countries, the party's heritage is so strong that even when parties of the right gain power, they define themselves as guardians of the welfare state, committed to "the Nordic model." This successful nationalization of modernity also came to mean that the Nordic nations saw themselves as no longer old-fashioned chauvinist. Ideas of national pride were hidden in notions of modernity, normality, and rationality, thus often becoming invisible to the natives.

One example of that is the use of flags. Scandinavians often talk of other nations as "flag-waving" ones. Flags are waved in the United States, France, or Britain, but not here. This attitude has a long history. In a critique of the Swedish lack of cultural pride in 1916, author Carl G. Laurin hastens to add: "The idea is of course not that we should become as blue-and-yellow as the Americans are 'star-spangled'" (quoted in Löfgren 2007: 137). On the other hand, today there seem to be more national flags per square mile in the Scandinavian countries than in most other countries. It is perhaps no surprise that it was a British sociologist, Richard Jenkins (1998), who pointed to the use of Danish flags as a symbol for everything, from a happy party mood to a great discount sale. Flags are everywhere, on birthday cakes and Christmas trees. Visitors landing at Copenhagen Airport will be surprised by the number of flag-waving Danes waiting for arriving kin or friends. On charter tourist destinations Germans and Britons very rarely take along miniature flags to fly from the balcony of the rented *apartemento*, whereas Scandinavian flags have become common (see Eriksen and Jenkins 2007).

The Nordic cult of the flag is not unproblematic. The Norwegian national day shows a happy parade full of flag-waving children, but when in 2013 a schoolteacher suggested that immigrant children could carry flags that were Norwegian on one side and their original home country flags on the other, this was not at all applauded. "Flexibility" was one of the core values in the Nordic list above, but it has not been a striking feature in Nordic attempts to integrate immigrants during recent decades. Jenkins (2011) has pointed to the tendency for Danish (as well as Scandinavian) identity to be rather self-congratulatory: we know best and we represent not only normality but also the future. Accepting cultural diversity can be difficult within such a mental framework. All Scandinavian countries have comparatively weak records when it comes to bringing immigrants into both the labor market and the public sphere. Especially the influx of non-European refugees and asylum seekers has met with ambivalent responses. The rise of anti-immigration parties is another phenomenon shared by Nordic countries. Thomas Hylland Eriksen scrutinizes the Norwegian case in Chapter 2.

The Baltic Contrast

The Scandinavian historical experience can be compared to that of the Baltic cluster.

Across the Baltic Sea from Scandinavia, Estonia, Latvia, and Lithuania do not constitute a strong cluster. Above all it is a cluster mainly imposed from the outside. The three Baltic states share a turbulent but very different history, with different languages and geopolitical orientations. They are a good example of how clustering may occur in given situations. During the Soviet occupation from World War II to 1991, these states were incorporated in the Soviet Union as republics, but often bundled together as "the Baltic republics" or "the Soviet West." They were often seen as more Western, with more contacts to the West and better access to Western goods and trends. "The Baltic republics" were the place to go for Soviet citizens. As the Soviet empire started breaking up, political cooperation between the Baltic republics was important—presenting a united front in the struggle for independence. As free nations again, they all joined NATO and the European Union (EU), but in the post-Soviet era different political, social, and cultural developments made integration and a common identity less striking. In short the Baltic cluster has above all been created by outside labeling. It is a very different cluster from that of Scandinavia.

The fall of the Soviet empire opened up an interest in an expansionist Scandinavia. Should the Baltic states be included in a Scandinavian cluster? A lot of new forms of cooperation and initiatives were developed, but this

Scandinavian growth potential has only been partly successful (Weaver 1992: 96ff.).

Branding Strategies

At a city branding conference in 2012 one of the makers of the slogan "Stockholm—the capital of Scandinavia" was asked why they didn't choose "Nordic" instead. "We thought about that," he said, "but found that 'Nordic' opens up an image of something cold and remote, with polar bears in the street, 'Baltic' didn't work either, but 'Scandinavia' was a much more attractive label, evoking tall and sexy blonds, great design and quality products."

How did Scandinavia become such a great brand that Finland often wants to share the label? Earlier I mentioned the political movement of "Scandinavianists" of the mid-nineteenth century. A bit later the prefix "Scandinavian" became popular in commercial branding. Instead of being the Swedish Bank, it was grander to call yourself the Scandinavian Bank. This was a way for local firms to grab a label signaling a bigger ambition than just the national.

Gradually "Scandinavian" became a label also understood abroad. Beyond tourist clichés, the idea of Scandinavia as not only picturesque but avant-garde started slowly to take over. This expansion occurred mainly in the 1950s and 1960s, when Scandinavian modern life was materialized in the successful export commodities of Scandinavian design, followed by another export commodity: images of blond beauties and a sexually permissive society. ("Swedish" or "Danish" films became a pornographic genre.) The prefix "Scandinavian" started to spread in many arenas, as dreams or lifestyles. This was frontier modernity—informal and natural living, but also a restrained and minimalist aesthetic. As often happens, the brand was reinforced through links between different arenas: fashion, architecture, design, family politics, welfare policies, children's culture, film, popular music. The ideas of "Scandinavian modern" were also successfully linked to a Nordic past. The immensely successful 1980s traveling art exhibition "Northern Light" showed romantic paintings from the decades around 1900. Modern minimalism, landscape painting, and simple peasant life came together. Folk costumes and ultra-new furniture could coexist.

Once the Scandinavian brand was securely established, it could be reinvented in new forms. In the early 2000s the export wave of crime writing, films, and TV series created the image of "Nordic noir," showing the darker sides of Scandinavian life.

Behind this successful brand is a constant collective effort of marketing. State institutions have played a central role, tirelessly organizing cluster activities of Scandinavian design shows, art exhibitions, and workshops. There is the usual bickering about what country actually contributed the most—was Danish design not most important, Finnish architecture the best, Sweden the main exporter of children's culture? Despite such national vanities, most actors realized that it was advantageous to be on the shared bandwagon.

The success in Scandinavian branding also entailed a heavy investment in promoting the Scandinavian model of welfare capitalism as innovative, cool, and trendy. In this self-understanding there is a strong focus on Scandinavian states being small but flexible, open to the new: be it digital worlds, the experience economy, or the fashion industry (Löfgren 2005; Riegels 2012). Scandinavian modern has resulted in a new kind of tourism, interested in contemporary social life as much as in fjords and folk costumes. Journalists write pieces like "In Search of the Scandinavian Dream: What's It Like to Live the Nordic Life," where Susie Mesure makes a pilgrimage to day-care centers, bicycle lanes, nature reserves, and trendy restaurants (*Independent* [London], 12 June 2013). Again the focus is not on the particularities of each country, but on overall "Scandinavity." The general hyping of Scandinavia also means that the media are eager to spot flaws in paradise, as when suburban riots hit Stockholm in 2013 or in the Breivik massacre in Norway. Maybe these little countries are not so perfect after all?

The Happiest Nations in the World?

Clustering can be observed in different forms. As shown in the introduction to this book, some small nations tend to cluster in different forms of global rankings, from corruption indexes to the freedom of the press. Looking at such listings, it is even more striking that the Nordic countries tend to form a very close cluster. They end up together—at the top or the bottom—in many global statistics, where attempts are made to rank national characteristics or profiles of "national characteristics." Take for example the Gallup World Poll that tried to measure happiness, based on interviews in 155 countries in 2005–2009. Here the four top listings are Denmark, Finland, Norway, and Sweden (with Iceland only number twenty-three—but this was during a grave financial crisis). The ranking was carried out according to levels of perceived satisfaction—the percentage of citizens defining themselves as thriving. Similar results are found in other rankings trying to measure well-being and happiness. Such rankings and sweeping generalizations are a rather dangerous pastime, but what interests me here is this recurrent clustering of Nordic nations. In this world of rankings they are united by similar marks for high levels of femininity and informality, or small power distances. Other examples of clustering occur in measurements of eco-friendliness, gender equality, and trust of the state.

Whatever is actually measured here, the Nordic figures may tell us something about a shared social and political history with the production of a similar everyday habitus in some arenas, but they also give rise to grand egos. "I thought I could organize freedom, how Scandinavian of me," sings the Icelandic artist Björk in her 1997 song "Hunter." Critics point out that the Nordic nations like to see themselves as moral superpowers, ready to export Scandinavian virtues to the rest of the world. "Norm entrepreneurs" is a term coined for these Scandinavian ambitions (Ingebritsen 2002).

The self-congratulatory stance became striking as the Nordic countries discussed EU membership. The high degree of EU skepticism tended to produce a stronger Nordic self-image. "Do we up here in the good North, with our peaceful and well-run little welfare states, really get involved with the messy (and Catholic) South? We are ready to export our way of life, but could we really learn something from them down there?"

The Norwegian scholar Terje Tvedt (2007) coined the ironic phrase "the regime of goodness" as a label for Norway's moral and political ambitions. He was inspired by the former prime minister Gro Harlem Brundtland's claim that "it is typically Norwegian to be good." In her study *The Origins of the "Regime of Goodness,"* Nina Witoszek (2011) discusses the makings of this Norwegian and Nordic self-understanding. In recent decades the Nordic countries have been very active in international arenas: as peace brokers, conflict negotiators, development aid providers, keeping a high profile in organizations such as the United Nations (similarly to New Zealand). To be small and nonthreatening but also well-behaved opens up certain windows of opportunity for small countries.

"The regime of goodness" is also seen as an arena where the state has been very active in defining this kind of outlook on the world and designing practices. This also has Witoszek discussing a *Homo scandinavicus*, a peace-loving creature not good at defending itself, and in any uncertain situation looking for the help of the state (interview in *Weekendavisen* [Copenhagen], 12 May 2012). This resonates with a longer tradition of seeing Scandinavia as a cluster of "nanny states." While such portrayals risk entering the dangerous territory of national mentalities, they raise the question of how Scandinavian policies and ideologies are received in the rest of the world. There are some striking fluctuations here, oscillating between Scandinavia as utopia or dystopia (see Andersson 2009). Already in the 1930s the Scandinavian model was debated, when Marquis W. Childs wrote his *Sweden: The Middle Way* (1936). It was followed by more critical reports such as Roland Huntford's book on Sweden, *The New Totalitarians* (1972). In the years after the 2008 economic crisis, the Nordic countries again had good press, culminating in the *Economist* cover story of 2013 referred to early in the introduction to this book.

Nordic Sharing

Statistics show that there are indeed many common traits in social and economic development (as well as some striking differences). But how does Scandinavian social and cultural integration look on the ground? Is there a Scandinavian everyday habitus? Have Scandinavians become more alike (and in what ways)?

First of all it is striking that the political ideology and social values of "the Nordic model" have a strong background in the many voluntary associations and popular movements that emerged during the nineteenth century in all Scandinavian countries and created a grassroots political culture, in free churches, temperance lodges, labor unions, and many other forms of local associations.

Second, during the twentieth century a Nordic political infrastructure was developed, like the Nordic Council from 1954 and later the Nordic Council of Ministers (parliamentarians meeting to discuss questions of cooperation) and a number of state-financed shared institutions. There is a Nordic Investment Bank as well as the Nordic Battlegroup, a military force for use in international crisis situations, but more important the grassroots network spun by the Norden Association, started in 1919, with many local branches and the aim of promoting Nordic cooperation and understanding. Even if the association may have seen its best days—sometimes it is now described as "a bunch of aging schoolteachers"—it has definitely been important in putting Nordic issues on local maps.

Yet one should not underestimate the many successful attempts to homogenize the Nordic countries, from the common marriage legal framework created in the 1920s to the Nordic Passport Union that was formed in 1952 to make mobility between the Nordic countries easier and also by later granting citizens from other Nordic countries rights to work and draw social benefits. More grandiose plans of cooperation, on the other hand, have failed over the years: a common currency union, a defense union, dreams of a Nordic federation (an idea first aired in the enthusiastic young "Scandinavianist" movement in the mid-nineteenth century). Scholars tend to agree that really "hard matters" of integration have been bypassed for more symbolic markings of Nordic unity. The death or demise of Nordic cooperation has often been predicted, but the cluster keeps reappearing, sometimes in new forms.

Cluster cooperation is often used to get advantages of scale and greater international visibility—from the cluster of Nordic embassies built in Berlin to joint Nordic exhibitions abroad. In the academic world there is a fair amount of Nordic cooperation. There are Nordic research institutes and academic journals, as well as Nordic conferences. Another population segment that has benefited from Nordic cooperation is the world of culture: writers, artists, and filmmakers enjoy joint funding, Nordic prizes, and scholarships.

One area where cooperation has been less successful is that of media. Although Danes, Norwegians, Swedes, and Swedish-speaking Finns are supposed to understand each other, this is not often the case. Films are subtitled, books translated. In the 1960s, Swedish children's television was extremely popular in other Nordic countries, which had the side effect that one generation found it easier to understand Swedish.

Over the last 150 years of peaceful coexistence, the Nordic countries with their cultural, lingual, and social similarities have favored migration within the cluster, creating all kinds of networks binding the nations together. Swedes who could not afford to emigrate to America took jobs in Denmark and Norway at the end of the nineteenth century, and these Swedish minorities were very quickly assimilated—there is hardly any trace of them today except for Swedish surnames. After World War II there was a great Finnish labor migration to Sweden. The open borders and shared welfare benefits since the 1950s have made such movements easier. Scandinavians are not seen as "real" immigrants in other Nordic countries; they are often symbolically represented not as aliens but as friendly neighbors or siblings (the most marked exception being the slow integration of Finnish-speaking working-class Finns in Sweden).

There have been different waves of Nordic migration, in different directions. With the help of EU policies favoring transborder regions, several regions in Scandinavia have recently engaged in strong cross-border cooperation. It is interesting to note that these border zones have benefited from the fact that all Nordic countries have different currencies (only Finland is in the Eurozone), resulting in fluctuating exchange rates and prices. The landscape of opportunities on the other side of border is constantly changing. What are cheaper, better offers, what is forbidden or regulated? Paradoxically it is to a great extent such small differences, resting on a platform of common understandings, that have created large numbers of Scandinavian "regionauts," benefiting from cultural similarities and moving easily between the countries (see Löfgren 2008).

The constant flow across the borders has created all sorts of cluster links. In 2012 there were nearly twenty-one million Nordic cross-border visits to Sweden, most of them day trips and holiday tours—but after shopping, the most common reason for travel given was "visiting friends and relatives."

Cluster Dynamics—Sibling Rivalry and Solidarity

"If we believe in the idea that Nordic brothers shall stand up for each other this is a good occasion." This was how a Swedish politician commented on the debate about the Nordic countries taking over the surveillance of Icelandic airspace after the Americans had withdrawn (*Svenska Dagbladet*, 12 June 2012). The Scandinavian cluster is often described in metaphors of family. Nordic countries are siblings. When asked if he was not worried by the great influx of Danes after the construction of the bridge across from Copenhagen, the mayor of next-door Malmö answered: "We don't see Danes as immigrants, they are our brothers!"

Family metaphors are common in small-nation clusters but can work in different ways. What kinds of siblings do we find inside the Scandinavian cluster? Definitely one "big brother." A big brother is always open to criticism for being too dominant or arrogant toward smaller siblings. Other Scandinavian countries have accused Sweden of claiming ownership of the

Nordic model, representing it as "the Swedish model." Critics point out that many Swedish welfare policies were originally copied from Danish social programs in the interwar years. Norwegians will argue that today "the Norwegian model" is triumphant. There are other big brother problems. Is Sweden also a Big Brother in another metaphorical sense, too much focused on state control and intervention?

This constant comparison and positioning is typical of family squabbles.

Outsiders are often surprised at the amount of energy Scandinavians invest in pointing out important national differences within the cluster. Othering becomes a family matter. Small differences become highly visible. There is a reification of the national and a production of stereotypes like "typically Norwegian," "very Danish," or "'the Swedish ways of doing things." Almost two centuries of modern Scandinavian nation building has produced a nationalizing gaze, a persuasive model for simplifying differences by presenting them in national terms. Ignoring variations involving class, gender, generation, or region, they could avoid much complexity and ambiguity. In order to understand these stereotyping dynamics we could turn to the Freudian notion of a narcissism of small differences: the closer we feel to others and the more we recognize of ourselves in them, the more important it becomes to emphasize differences in order to create a necessary distance. Family bickering is also a special form of togetherness. Slovenian philosopher Slavoj Zizek (2005) has pointed out that storytelling and antagonism on a verbal level kept Yugoslavia together. It was when people stopped telling stories about stupid Bosnians that the crisis was felt in the air.

There is a long and rich tradition of Nordic stereotyping that also mirrors shifting power balances. Anders Linde-Laursen (1995) has analyzed these dynamics over the centuries. During the nineteenth century, Denmark was often seen as most advanced, more continental and urbanized. Swedes called Danes "the Arabs of the north" because of their commercial skills. They were tough business negotiators. The Danes, on the other hand, often talked of the Swedish as a still uncivilized peasantry of the forests, drinking too much aquavit and carrying knives. (Later on Swedes used the same stereotypes for Finns.) During the first part of the twentieth century the power balance changed. Sweden became a dominant economic power with rapid industrialization, and so there were new stereotypes. For Danes, the typical Swede became an uptight bureaucrat in a pin-striped suit, obsessed with regulating everyday life. Swedes started to describe Danes as happy southern bohemians, perhaps a bit too laid-back. It has been said of the Danes that their self-understanding is helped by the wonderful fact that they are surrounded by cultural norths: the real Prussians south of the border, and on the other side the Prussians of the North—the Swedes.

In recent years the sibling hierarchy has been challenged by the impressive economic performance of both Norwegians and Finns. It is important here that the members of the cluster tend to measure their performance against other cluster members, not against big neighbors like Germany and Russia. Who has the best BNP figures, most Michelin stars, or gold medals in the Olympics? Who are the most egalitarian (us Norwegians, of course), who are the happiest nation (us Danes, of course), who are the most innovative (us Swedes, of course). And we Finns surely have the best schools in the world.

This comparative framework helps make Scandinavian egos grow, as it provides a safe terrain for comparisons. People find their own cherished values also loved by those across the border. Scandinavia works as a reassuring echo chamber: we are doing fine!

Family dynamics of cluster identities also mirror the model of segmentary opposition. The Nordic cluster is often seen as "a second-best" national alternative. When faced with outside enemies the Scandinavians rally, and when they meet in distant holiday destinations they feel safe among their Scandinavian siblings. This secondary identification brings up the question of what is actually shared within the cluster. If a question of "Have you ever been abroad" is answered by a Swede, by "Yes, I have been to Norway," the reply might well be, "No, I mean *really* abroad." Migrating to another Scandinavian country can be described as "Exile Lite."

Conclusion: Strategies, Ideas, Practices

What are the lessons from the Scandinavian case of clustering? First of all it shows how clustering creates an alternative and flexible identity that does not have to compete with national identities but rather complements them. You can choose when to use it or to opt out.

Second, the cluster may create a special family landscape of competition and comparison. Who is best, first, happiest, or smartest among us? In other situations it is similarities and common interests that stand in focus. Dynamics like these may change the importance of a cluster—is it weak or strong, temporal or long lasting? Is it an example of an active clustering or a result of being clustered together by outsiders?

Third, clusters create a family dynamic of sibling relationships. There is often a big brother, like Serbia in the post-Yugoslavian cluster. Some members may slide in and out of the cluster or only be accepted in certain situations, and there may also be closer and weaker dyads within the cluster. Some clusters may be shaped by strong asymmetries, as with the very strong position of Abu Dhabi in the Arab Emirates, or Serbia in ex-Yugoslavia. There might also be competitions for big brotherhood, as between Jamaica and Trinidad in the Anglophone Caribbean.

While some clusters have emerged out of empires or disintegrating nations, it seems difficult for modern clusters to take the step into a federation or conglomerate states. Why did this tight Scandinavian cluster not evolve into a political union, a new state? Looking back on the last two centuries of modern nationalism the cluster has hardly seen systematic attempts at constructing strong supranational institutions. In this case strong nation building has been a prerequisite for successful cluster cooperation.

Fourth, clusters open up certain strategic possibilities for small countries. Being surrounded by small siblings may help boost egos. In the Scandinavian cases we can see how different kinds of smallness are activated, from cuteness to "small and flexible." The Nordic case also illustrates that if you are small and in the periphery you have to work very hard to be at the cutting edge.

Clustering can be a strategy for meeting the world empowered but also a way of sheltering among equals and breeding a kind of inward-looking insularity. In the Scandinavian case clustering has quite clearly been an ego-boosting strategy: we are small but great! The fact that the Scandinavian cluster has acquired a special political and cultural profile has often been combined with a strong feeling that being different means being ahead—other nations will catch up when it comes to welfare, eco-friendliness, or gender equality. This idea has been central in Scandinavian self-images, yet it is also possible to think of Scandinavia moving from a model for the future to an increasingly eccentric deviance from normal patterns.

Again and again, it is stated that the Nordic model is now outdated—a thing of the past, pure nostalgia, but this is not really the case. As an alternative and sometimes dormant identity it is activated for certain aims, by certain actors, in certain historical situations. Scholars are eager to point out that

Scandinavia is an elite invention, but as I have tried to show, inventions need cultural resonance on the ground to survive. Over time Scandinavia has become a territory sharing a lot, from legal frameworks and political values to habits and aesthetics. The commitment to a Scandinavian unity has never been evenly distributed, and it is constantly changing. Yet it has created a kind of communality based not only upon ideas and images but on everyday practices as well. Not just soul but also soil.

Note

1. Good overviews of the debate of "Ruritania" and "banana republics" are found under these headings in Wikipedia. See also http://tvtropes.org (Ruritania), which lists the uses of fictive small nations in popular culture.

References

Andersson, Jenny. 2009. Nordic Nostalgia and Nordic Light: The Swedish Model as Utopia, 1930–2007. *Scandinavian Journal of History* 34 (3): 229–45.

Björkman, Jenny, Björn Fjæstad, and Jonas Harvard. 2011. *Ett nordiskt rum: Historiska och framtida gemenskaper från Baltikum till Barents hav.* Riksbankens Jubileumsfonds årsbok 2011/2012, Göteborg: Makadam.

Childs, Marquis W. 1936. *Sweden: The Middle Way.* London: Faber & Faber.

Eriksen, Thomas H., and Richard Jenkins, eds. 2007. *Flag, Nation and Symbolism in Europe and America.* London: Routledge.

Esping-Andersen, Gösta. 1990. *The Three Worlds of Welfare Capitalism.* Princeton, N.J.: Princeton University Press.

Gellner, Ernest. 1983. *Nations and Nationalism.* Ithaca, N.Y.: Cornell University Press.

Goldsworthy, Vesna. 1998. *Inventing Ruritania: The Imperialism of the Imagination.* New Haven, Conn.: Yale University Press.

Götz, Norbert. 2003. Norden: Structures That Do Not Make a Region. *European Review of History* 10 (2): 323–41.

Harvard, Jonas. 2011. Det nya Norden—hårt eller mjukt? In Jenny Björkman, Björn Fjæstad, and Jonas Harvard, eds., *Ett nordiskt rum: Historiska och framtida gemenskaper från Baltikum till Barents hav.* Göteborg: Makadam.

Huntford, Roland. 1972. *The New Totalitarians.* New York: Stein and Day.

Ingebritsen, Christine. 2002. Norm Entrepreneurs: Scandinavia's Role in World Politics. *Cooperation and Conflict* 37 (1): 11–23.

Jenkins, Richard. 1998. *Fra Amalienborg til Kvickly: Dannebrog i dansk dagligliv.* Skive: Skive Museums Forlag.

———. 2011. *Being Danish: Paradoxes of Identity in Everyday Life.* Copenhagen: Museum Tusculanum Press.

Lewis, Richard D. 2005. *Finland, Cultural Lone Wolf.* Yarmouth: Intercultural Press.

Linde-Laursen, Anders. 1995. *Det nationales natur: Studier i dansk-svenske relationer.* Copenhagen: Nordisk Ministerråd.

Löfgren, Orvar. 2000. *On Holiday.* Berkeley: University of California Press.

———. 2005. Cultural Alchemy: Translating the Experience Economy into Scandinavian. In Barbara Czarniawska and Guje Sevón, eds., *Global Ideas: How Ideas, Objects and Practices Travel in the Global Economy.* Malmö: Liber.

———. 2007. A Flag for All Occasions? The Swedish Experience. In Thomas Hylland Eriksen and Richard Jenkins, eds., *Flag, Nation and Symbolism in Europe and America.* London: Routledge.

———. 2008. Regionauts: The Transformation of Cross-Border Regions in Scandinavia. *European Urban and Regional Studies* 15 (3): 195–210.

Musial, Kazimierz. 2000. *Roots of the Scandinavian Model.* Baden-Baden: Nomos.

Østergaard, Uffe. 1997. The Geopolitics of Nordic Identity; From Composite States to Nation States. In Øystein Sørensen and Bo Stråth, eds., *The Cultural Construction of Norden.* Oslo: Scandinavian University Press.

Riegels, Marie Melchior. 2012. Understanding Contemporary Links of Fashion, Museum and Nation. *Ethnologia Europaea* 42 (1): 54–61.

Sørensen, Øystein, and Bo Stråth, eds. 1997. *The Cultural Construction of Norden.* Oslo: Scandinavian University Press.

Stenius, Henrik. 1997. The Good Life as a Life of Conformity: The Impact of the Lutheran Tradition on Nordic Political Culture. In Øystein Sørensen and Bo Stråth, eds., *The Cultural Construction of Norden.* Oslo: Scandinavian University Press.

Tvedt, Terje. 2007. International Development Aid and Its Impact on a Donor Country: A Case Study of Norway. *European Journal of Development Research* 19 (2): 614–35.

Weaver, Ole. 1992. Nordic Nostalgia: Northern Europe After the Cold War. *International Affairs* 68 (1): 77–102.

Witoszek, Nina. 2011. *The Origins of the "Regime of Goodness."* Oslo: Universitetsforlaget.

Zizek, Slavoj. 2005. *Interrogating the Real.* London: Continuum.

PART II

Aspiring for Success

CHAPTER 4

Red Dot on the Map:
Singapore, Size, and the Problems of Success

Goh Beng Lan

As a Malaysian academic who has worked and lived in Singapore since 1999, I consider Singapore as now my home. For me, a main attraction in working in Singapore is the intellectual vibrancy and the professional academic culture that Singapore offers. As a Malaysian researching on Malaysia and Southeast Asia, I find that my base in Singapore lends me more room and recognition of my work. To me Singapore is an extremely conducive place: Malaysia, my field site, is just next door, and I am located at a regional hub where the study of Southeast Asia is taken seriously and graduate education generously supported. This provides me with the privilege of having a hand in training a future generation of Singaporean and Southeast Asian researchers. Evidently, my personal experience is contrary to the popular imaginary of Singapore as an affluent but highly regulated society where freedom to think and act is lacking. I am, however, conscious of my privileged location as an "expatriate" and aware of recently growing domestic unhappiness over income gaps and immigration. Like anywhere else there are challenging dimensions of everyday living in Singapore. My encountered difficulties are, however, less about personal constraints than institutional intricacies. Two struggles come to mind: the first has got to do with regional academic relations; and second, a competitive and fast-changing work environment. With regard to the former, as an academic based in a Southeast Asian studies department, I have learned that tensions arising from Singapore's uneasy relationship in the region can sometimes be replicated in academic relations, thus requiring delicate treading to avoid awkwardness. An incident that occurred during my early years in Singapore illustrates what I mean. A top university in the Philippines had organized a regional meeting on doing Southeast Asian studies in Asia. Most major regional institutions were invited, except my department. This had set my department head fuming, whereupon he wrote to the organizers and invited himself. The incident tells a lot about Singapore's uncomfortable place in the region. The second point is about the relentless quest for excellence in academic culture. Certainly the arrival of a corporatized audit culture at the university is by now a global phenomenon. In Singapore, however, the process can be pursued to almost perfection. For better or worse, this has created a climate of rapid change in work life. I have resigned myself to this fate. My sentiment is perhaps not unique: there is a local joke that change is the only constant factor in Singaporean life. This condition is inevitably reflective of a wider work ethic that values the tenacious quest for competitiveness and betterment. After all, it was out of sheer determination that Singapore turned itself within a short span of time from a backwater into a globally competitive economy.

*   *   *

Contributing to this volume provides an opportunity to show how smallness shapes everyday Singaporean life. As I will suggest, smallness, as both a form of psychosis and scale, works as a double-edged sword. All that Singapore excels in also comes back to haunt it, the result of which is a society at a crossroads. Managing the underside of its virtuoso excesses will require a reformation of even its best practices of planning and leadership. There are comparisons to be made, but first a brief overview of the effects of smallness, as a national psychosis and in scalar terms, on governance and social life in Singapore is necessary.

Red Dot Psychosis

"It's OK with me, but there are 211 million people [in Indonesia]," he says. "Look at that map. All the green

[area] is Indonesia. And that red dot is Singapore.
Look at that."

> —Ex-Indonesian president B. J. Habibie
> (Borsuk and Chua 1998)

To many Malaysians, the red dot is simply an
irritating pimple which refuses to burst.

> —Shamsul Akmar, columnist,
> *New Straits Times* (2002)

Smallness is ingrained in the Singaporean psyche. Singaporeans refer to their home as "the red dot," a label derived from an infamous spoof on Singapore's representation as a dot (albeit not always red) on global maps which was made by the ex-Indonesian president B. J. Habibie, just after the fall of his country's New Order government in 1998. Adding insult to this injury, "the red dot" was sarcastically equated to "an irritating little pimple that refuses to burst" by a Malaysian national daily in a commentary over territorial disputes with Singapore that erupted in 2002. Inevitably, Singapore's diminutive size, predominantly Chinese population, and near complete dependency on food, fuel, and water imports have placed it precariously vis-à-vis its immediate neighbors, Malaysia and Indonesia, both of which are larger countries having domestic tensions involving their ethnic Chinese populations. Outstanding bilateral issues on trade, military exercises, land reclamation, and territorial disputes have further strained Singapore's relationships to its neighbors. The country's tiny size—a mere 715.8 square kilometers[1] that cannot even be adequately delineated on the world map—consistently signals its vulnerability.

Since Singapore broke away from Malaysia (although the latter would insist that Singapore was expelled) in 1965, this vulnerability has lent legitimacy to pragmatic top-down rule by the People's Action Party (PAP). Stepping out on its own, it was utterly necessary that Singapore succeeded as an independent country, for its own sake and to prove itself to Malaysia and the world. The imperative to overcome smallness was present from the founding moment of Singapore's nation building. The only way for a future was to overcome the limits of its smallness by sheer human courage and determination. The country's leaders knew that they had to do the job right. There would be no second chance. This dire need to succeed and preempt all

obstacles gave rise to a national character called *kiasu*, a Hokkien word referring to the fear of losing. If there is a small man syndrome, then *kiasu* is
the equivalent of Singapore's national psychosis of smallness.

Small, without resources and faced with bigger neighboring countries
armed with resources and population numbers that it could never match, the
nascent nation-state was confronted by the inevitable issues of national
security and economy. The Singapore state had no choice but to be clever.
National survival meant a dire need to constantly remain on top of all circumstances. In this way the Singapore situation is comparable to that of
Israel, another small country that also has to constantly outwit both its natural impediment as a desert land as well as potential hostilities around it.
However, unlike Israel, Singapore is not in a war mode. Switzerland's path
as a safekeeping haven for wealth, keeping it out of World War II, may be a
more relevant geopolitical strategy. That Singapore has of late become a tax
haven for the superrich and its 2012 establishment of a tax-free gold trading
market (Wallop 2013) are indications that it might be heading down the
Switzerland way in preparation against perilous power configurations in
a fast changing Asia-Pacific region. Nevertheless, in the early days, such a
measure was still out of the means. Rather, the imperative then in the 1960s
was to kick-start a robust economy.

Meritocracy became the guiding principle of governance, to find the
best minds to build the nascent nation-state. The turn to meritocracy was
unsurprising, as Singapore had departed from Malaysia precisely because of
differences over a preferential system of rule. In its ideal form, meritocracy
is a practice presuming that all individuals have an equal and fair chance of
succeeding on their own merit. Meritocracy quickly became the foundation
of Singapore's political system. A pool of smart and committed individuals
soon took on the onerous task of planning for national survival. They set in
place a dogged quest for foolproof strategies in which thoughtful, comprehensive, meticulously calibrated plans became the hallmark of government
policy and bureaucracy. Through a concerted strategy of economic openness,
Singapore's leaders proved the assumptions about the inability of smallness
to influence global markets wrong. The last remnants of capital controls
were removed by 1978, and Singapore was able to attract trade, capital, and
financial flows (Abeysinghe and Choy 2007: 2). A rigorous planning system
compelled by "kiasuism"' paid off by the 1980s, when Singapore was rapidly
transformed from a land of scarcity to an unparalleled economic success. It

was this top-down model of engineering success that gained Singapore its global reputation as a poster child for a brand of "soft authoritarianism."

Ever since, Singapore's growth model has attracted immense global attention. While there are other small countries that equally lack natural resources and are reliant on human capital for their economic successes, these countries have not caught the world's attention as has Singapore. Arguably, Singapore's status as a small newly successful non-Western capitalist economy, its authoritarian state practices, and its strategic geography have combined to provide fodder for international attention. Opinions on Singapore are, however, deeply divided between those who admire and seek to learn its secrets of high productivity and competitiveness, on the one hand, and those who are critical of its model of "soft authoritarian" rule and the limitations on human freedom, on the other. Singapore's incongruous image as an affluent yet highly regulated society is nowhere more famously captured than in the aphorism "Disneyland with the death penalty," penned by the novelist William Gibson (1993). While divergent views persist, a new call for a serious examination of the virtues of Singapore's governing and strategic practices has appeared of late. Thomas Friedman (2011), Pulitzer Prize–winning journalist, and Joseph Stiglitz (2013), the Nobel Prize–winning economist, are two influential opinion makers who have contributed by postulating Singapore's coherent governing practices, its inclusionary society, and its strong performing education system as possible lessons for the United States. Inevitably, economic crises and rising social inequality in America and Europe have compelled their societies to be on the lookout for lessons from other countries. By the new millennium, Singapore's record of having done everything right to remain economically competitive coupled with its privileged location in a booming Asian region have elevated its importance as a key player of interest to many countries.

Ironically, however, these international praises occur at a juncture of an emerging critical public sphere within Singapore. Free-market and immigration pressures arising from a globalized economy have created widening income gaps, unaffordable housing, and strains on public amenities, which led to an unprecedented unleashing of citizenry frustrations over related policies during the general elections in 2011. Having enjoyed a one-party dominance since independence, the PAP suffered its first significant loss of parliamentary seats—seven out of eighty-seven. The election result compelled the government to respond quickly with policy changes and more avenues for dialogue with the people.² All these indicate a swiftly changing political and social landscape.

That internal and external responses to Singapore's model of governance are so reversed at this juncture suggests that capitalist societies, big and small alike, are at a crossroads and searching for a more viable future. What does Singapore have to offer? Alec Barrett (2011), writing for the *Harvard Political Review*, has suggested that the greatest lesson Singapore has for the West is "the delicate balance between integration and assimilation, between diversity and conformity." This is an astute observation, but only insofar as it pins down the question of "balance" as the crux to the search for sustainable societies. In a country where excellence is pursued to an almost perfection, moderation may not be Singapore's greatest virtue. The question of finding the right balance in strategies of growth is a challenge confronting the country today. Furthermore, this challenge is made doubly hard by the psychosis and scale of smallness that act to intensify, magnify, and compress both the virtues and problems of policy. As much as absolute smallness facilitates regulation, order, and rapid success, it also magnifies contradictions and excesses and quickens the risk of a meltdown. It does not require much political acumen to realize that in a small country, once agitation gains popular momentum, there is a real risk of catastrophe; in a small pond, a swell can quickly turn into a dangerous tsunami. It is to the double-edged sword of smallness and its impacts on everyday Singaporean life that we next turn.

The Heydays and the Bad Hair Days of Smallness

If anything, up until the end of the twentieth century, Singapore has proven right the adage "small is beautiful." While its strategic geography as a hub of international commerce is a comparative advantage, it has also benefited from its tiny size. Absolute smallness had facilitated efficient rule and rapid success. Everything remaining equal, scale matters to any state administration.

A vast geography is definitely much harder to administer than a tiny territory. This fact is easily evident if we were to just compare Singapore and Malaysia. The job of running Singapore could perhaps be equated to that of administering a high school, that of Malaysia to managing a university with two campuses. By the early 1980s, after barely two decades as an independent state, the quick result of Singapore's strategic planning was already evident when it was recognized as one of the most successful economies in the world (Lim 1983). Since then Singapore has continued to maintain its high productivity and competitive ratings. In just four decades, Singapore has become a cutting-edge economy and one of the most livable, green cities in the world. Its public institutions, transportation, and infrastructure enjoy a reputation for efficiency and reliability. In particular, Singapore's high performing education system, especially pupil achievements in math and science benchmarks, has received international accolades.

Singapore's top-down model of an efficient nanny state delivering material comfort in return for social acquiescence from citizens worked pretty smoothly until the entry of the new millennium. Until recently, there were no substantial grounds for social disgruntlement except for the state's reputed intolerance of opposition. The state had done all that responsible states should do: it invested in education, health care, public housing, an efficient public transportation system, a livable city. However the tide has somewhat changed in the new millennium. Singaporeans have become increasingly expressive of their thoughts on governance and the future of their society. This is a significant milestone for a predominantly docile society. The catalyst behind this change, as I will show, arises not from any sudden awakening but rather from the compression effect of smallness over time, which has magnified the accumulation of social stress and increasingly eroded the foundations of the rule of meritocracy.

Social Compression: Stress, Work, and Life

No society is free from the stress of modern life. Yet in a small city-state like Singapore where there is no escape to hinterlands or outlying areas, stress levels can intensify quickly, producing a pressure-cooker effect on society. Not unlike the animal world, where miniature creatures must often work harder than larger ones, the dire need to succeed has forced Singaporeans into a nation of worker bees. The firm belief in meritocracy has seen competitiveness put on a pedestal, deemed as the premium vehicle to bring out the best in individuals. Competitiveness is an endless quest to better performance, constantly raising the bar of benchmarks achieved. Without balance, it can create a hard-nosed environment where individuals are constantly kept on their toes and pushed to continuously outdo others in order to remain on top. No wonder, therefore, that Singaporeans live a highly stressful life-style.

This has been confirmed by various studies that have found Singaporeans to be a highly stressed, unhappy lot. The Global Stress Index of 2007 placed Singapore as the top sixth country (Grant Thornton IBR 2010). Interestingly Hong Kong, another small advanced Asian capitalist society, in the words of Rey Chow (1992), perpetually caught "in between colonizers," came in next, in seventh place. In sharp contrast are Sweden, Denmark, Finland, and Austra-lia, located at the lowest end of the stress index. Similarly, when it comes to happiness, the Happy Planet Index of 2012 ranked Singapore a lowly nineti-eth of 150 countries studied. Again, Hong Kong was the only other Asian entity that ranked lower than Singapore. Surprisingly, Vietnam, a formerly war-torn and less affluent Southeast Asian economy, was ranked second hap-piest country in the world. In the matter of libido, Singaporeans did not fare any better. Global Sex Surveys by the condom maker Durex, for the years 2002 and 2003, placed Singapore at the bottom of the respective lists of twenty-two and thirty-four countries studied when it came to the frequency of having sex (Goh 2005).

With high stress levels, it is not surprising that Singapore has a low fer-tility rate. With a below-replacement fertility rate of 1.25, Singapore's future is in jeopardy. It is faced with a growing aging population without enough younger replenishment. While the phenomenon of a below-replacement birthrate is shared by many economically advanced societies, in a society where people are its greatest resource, this problem becomes an extremely grave concern. The concern is so great that the country's founding father, the late Lee Kuan Yew, warned that if this continues, Singapore would have to "fold up" (Lim 2012). In extra efforts to boost the country's birthrate, a deci-sion to cut down work from a five-and-a-half to a five-day workweek was implemented in the public and private sectors in 2004. The aim was to pro-mote better work/life balance, with the hope that it could improve the fertil-ity rate. Various other piecemeal measures were also taken to improve on work/life balance. One of these is the annual "Eat with Your Family Day," launched on 25 May 2007. This day, which falls before the start of the mid-year school break, is meant to encourage Singaporeans, known to work long hours, to create time to sit down and take a meal together with their families (Reuters 2007). However, all these efforts have not seemed to work. When it comes to the female body, the Singapore state is up in arms; so far it has not been able to convince women to obey its plea for more babies. The state has had no choice but to turn to immigration as a solution, but this has in turn created more competitive stress for an already strained population.

The hullabaloo over work/life balance indicates that Singapore, a latecomer to the Asian economic success club, is equally plagued by the phenomenon of overwork as was Japan, an earlier success story. While Japan is much bigger than Singapore, the former shares a similar characteristic of being a contained island nation-state. In Japan, the work stress level is much worse—there is a sudden-death syndrome called *karoshi*, which literally means death from overwork. Could the feature of overwork be part and parcel of a new capitalist culture emerging from rapidly expanding Asian economies? Or could size and containment have something to do with magnifying social stress? Suggestively, so far this phenomenon seems not to have yet affected China, a super huge country and a rising economic giant.

The Critique of Meritocracy

In a highly competitive society, the magnifier effect of absolute smallness exposes cracks within a system that can lead to social resentment. One of the biggest problems gripping contemporary Singapore is a backlash against its revered institution of meritocracy.

After more than four decades of delivering on its promises, meritocracy, a key principle of governance and leadership in Singapore, has come under increasing public criticism for inculcating elitism. In part, the resentment against elitism comes about from widening class gaps that have become apparent in the new millennium. There are visible signs of a growing divide between the haves and have-nots in Singapore.

While poverty is generally hidden in Singapore, due to the availability of public housing, class fissures are still quickly showing. Despite being one of the most affluent societies in the world, Singapore has one of the highest measures of income disparity with a Gini coefficient at 0.478 in 2012 (Yue 2013: 7). Yet there is no official poverty line. Inevitably, the poor in Singapore have access to basic necessities of food and housing but contend with relative poverty. Attaining the minimum standard of living norms in this affluent city-state is a struggle for them.[3] Poorer households typically live in one- or two-bedroom public housing flats. The poorest among them will be those in subsidized smaller units reserved for those who cannot afford housing.[4] In public housing estates, housing blocks are differentiated by unit size, which makes poorer households identifiable by particular blocks in local neighborhoods. Recent media hype over cases of poverty has also heightened public sentiments over class disparity. In particular, the emotional breakdown of a popular young female opposition candidate when recalling a meeting she had with a poor female resident from her constituency who could not afford to pay the eighty-dollar tuition fee for her child on top of her flat rental helped propel the plight of poor income families to public attention during the 2011 general election campaign.

An earlier debate on "cosmopolitan versus heartlander" mooted by the then prime minister Goh Chok Tong in 1999 was a forerunner of an official recognition of growing class divides. This debate, which referred to two different segments of the population, the "cosmopolitans" and the "heartlanders," was couched in cultural terms rather than as a class divide, as it was aimed at addressing the problem of emigration. The "cosmopolitans" are supposedly those with a tendency to emigrate: more fluent in English than in Mandarin; holding suave international outlooks; comfortable anywhere in the world. In contrast, the "heartlanders" are deemed the backbone of Singaporean society: they live in public housing estates; are more conversant in Mandarin and Chinese dialects; hold strong family values; and are deferential to authorities. Nonetheless, it is clear by now that more insidious than a cultural divide is the problem of gaps between a growing "cosmopolitan" segment whose education, employment, and income profiles supersede those of "heartlanders" stuck in public housing estates.

In a society where the rule of meritocracy reigns supreme, access to education and employment is a primary determinant of class differentiation. Education is a foremost vehicle of social mobility in Singapore. The bottom line of class difference in Singapore is often that between university and non-university education. This is because there is a wide gap between the salary structure of degree holders and those without degrees. Overall, the former are more privileged than the latter. However, those who are a cut above are those educated in elite schools, as they stand a better chance of winning competitive scholarships and eventually top positions in the civil service or private sectors. Entry into an elite school is crucial in determining one's future. Elite schools are known for their higher cut-off entry points compared to what are called "neighborhood" schools. There is hence enormous pressure for families to get their children into elite schools. It is an open fact that Singaporean parents spend an enormous amount of money on private tuition in order to help boost their children's academic performance. Evidently financial means make a difference to a student's education opportunities.

Elitism becomes a problem when children of elite-school graduates turn out to be the predominant ones gaining entry into elite schools. In a small country, where there is a small population pool from which talent is tapped, there is a danger of a swift concentration of a narrow elite group whose privilege will further benefit their subsequent generations. Such a pattern is a harbinger of the loss of a level playing field; a closed elitist system is in the making.

Inevitably, there is a growing entrenchment of a small elite segment as they perpetuate themselves through generations. Meritocracy might have worked well for the pioneering two generations or so. These earlier elites had gotten to where they were by sheer hard work as the privileged were few and far apart in a newly independent society largely consisting of immigrants. As long as they had equal access to public education, all had the same opportunity to compete and get ahead. This explains why many early generations of political and corporate leaders in Singapore have much to boast about their humble beginnings (K. Tan 2008: 17–18). Problems, however, kick in when their subsequent descendants become the prevalent qualifiers into elitist schools and the winners of top jobs in the public or private sectors. There are no available data on student profiles of elite schools. In an article on education reform in Singapore, however, Leonel Lim (2013) culls a snapshot from newspaper reports on speeches given by Lee Kuan Yew as he visited elite and neighborhood schools in 2011. Lim notes that 60 percent of student population in Raffles Institution, a top elite school of which Lee Kuan Yew was himself an alumnus, reportedly had parents who were graduates. At neighborhood schools, this percentage fell significantly, with the highest at 13.1 percent (based on available data from four schools).

As income and class boundaries become harder, it can no longer be assumed that everyone can compete equally. That meritocracy is narrowly defined in terms of educational and professional qualifications and commercial success has also made matters worse (K. Tan 2008: 14). This has seen an ascendancy of a closed elitist network whereby the higher echelons of government and private sectors hail from a few top schools. The turn to foreign talent for top jobs has added foreigners as another elite segment. This has added salt to the wound: beyond having to compete domestically, Singaporeans now also have to compete with outsiders. Highly publicized recruitments, whenever top-class scientists are lured to work in Singapore's recently prestigious biomedical research hub, have only helped fuel public resentment against what is seen as a growing class divide. This has made the state immigration policy highly unpopular. In an intensely networking society, new social media have further fanned public criticisms. There is a growing perception that the state has lapsed in its protection of national interests. It is against such a background that an explosion of criticisms against meritocracy has appeared.

In analyzing the critique of meritocracy, many commentators have pinpointed its inherent problems as a cause of Singapore's current dilemma. They have highlighted how the assumption of similar starting points for everyone places minority groups at a disadvantage. They have also pinpointed the problem of a closed network that tends to produce conformity and similar worldviews among elites. Nevertheless, the fact remains that meritocracy is a principle upheld all over the world. By itself, it is not a bad thing. Singapore is not alone in having elite schools that produce political, administrative, and corporate leaders.

All over the world, there are elitist education systems playing the same part in creating social elitism. In the United States there are the Ivy League universities, premium academic institutions where entry is highly selective and graduates often go on to become part of America's elite. In France there is the *grandes écoles* system, existing outside the main university framework largely to train top civil servants, selecting students for admission based chiefly on merit in competitive exams at the national level. In Japan, leading national universities, with the University of Tokyo topping the list, are elite institutions where entry is by competitive public exams and where graduates often get far ahead in their careers.

Yet many of these elitist systems have remained intact over time. Why has Singapore's young meritocratic system met with disapproval so quickly, just within four short decades? As a start, it is useful to remember that meritocracy, no matter where and how it is practiced, will only be effective as long as the system remains open to everyone in that any individual coming from any race, gender, class, creed, and so on is theoretically able to compete equally and be rewarded in the system.

Huge population sizes could be a significant factor for the preservation of those exclusive institutions within their respective countries. In a big country, pockets of elitist concentration are more easily dissipated than in a small country, where cliques become easily conspicuous and grab attention.

Singapore has no luxury of a huge population. That its young merito-cratic system is so quickly in a tight corner could be in part due to small-ness. As the cornerstone of Singapore's progress, merit as the basis for reward has become sacrosanct in a society plagued by the fear of having missed the boat. The *kiasu* psychosis has molded a regimented implementation of the rule of merit by a rule-observant bureaucracy. When I first sat on scholar-ship selection panels as part of my job, I found it puzzling that no students would ever talk of their financial difficulties during interviews, even though some came from working-class backgrounds. Their parents' occupation, family backgrounds, and places of residence provided telltale signs of their financial situations. But I soon understood the students' conduct; in a sys-tem where merit is sacred, it would be a taboo to cite one's financial difficul-ties as a reason for reward.

Nevertheless, citizenry backlash in the watershed elections of 2011 resulted in quick remedies to improve on shortcomings in the merit system. Three months after the elections, a change was observed in the selection process of the President's Scholarship, Singapore's most prestigious scholar-ship and a central vehicle for selecting future political and administra-tive leaders. Among the four recipients of the scholarship that year was a male student from an elite school, the Hwa Chong Institution, who did not score straight As for his A-level exams. He was selected reputedly because "his grades were good enough" and "he had leadership qualities and an out-standing co-curricular record" (A. Tan 2011). In responding to queries, the rewarding body, Singapore's Public Service Commission (PSC), explained that not all President's Scholarship holders have straight As because it "rec-ognizes that grades alone are not necessarily an indication of a student's cali-ber, leadership potential and commitment to the Singapore public service." Reiterating the same point, the chairman of the Government Parliamen-tary Committee for Education said, "It is good that the PSC does not look at academic performance when choosing [scholarship holders] but at the over-all development of a student. Academic performance is an important mea-sure but it is not the only measure." In 2012, another record was made when one of the awardees became the second Malay student to have received the President's Scholarship, forty-four years after the first Malay won the schol-arship in 1968.

There has also been an ongoing reformation of the schooling system to allow for the development of more diverse sets of talents among school students. An elitist separate track for talented students called the Gifted Education Program has been gradually abolished at the secondary school level. In its place is an ability-driven education philosophy that seeks to develop every child's talent and abilities to his or her fullest potential (Lim 2013: 5). Furthermore in order to offer students with artistic interests a chance to pursue an arts academic curriculum, the School of the Arts, the country's first independent, pretertiary arts school was opened in 2008.

There has also been expeditious response by the Singapore state to address citizenry frustrations over class gaps. A fortnight after the 2011 elections, the PAP showed that it took resentment against elite domination seriously by doing away with the positions of minister mentor, held by Lee Kuan Yew, and senior minister, Goh Chok Tong, the second prime minister of the country. This move was revolutionary, given the stature of Lee Kuan Yew as the patriarch of Singapore society and his role in political life even after retirement. In addition, almost immediately after the elections, an independent committee was set up at the end of May 2011 to review the salary of ministers. The multimillion-dollar ministerial salary structure that made politicians in Singapore the best paid in the world has been highly unpopular. To no avail, Singaporeans had been angered by the way the state had justified the salary hike with rationales of a need to attract talent from the private sector and to deter corruption. With approval ratings at stake, the government finally gave in, and the prime minister's salary was sliced by 36 percent followed by 51 percent for the president's annual salary.

Cognizant that without inclusive growth, social resentment would get higher, concerted steps were also taken to amend income inequality. A first step taken was a decision to raise the income ceiling of a Workfare Income Supplement, so as to benefit more low-wage workers. It is expected that approximately the bottom third of Singaporean income earners will benefit. A month later, there was a review of the Employment Act in an effort to make more workers eligible for overtime pay.

Rising social discontent has forced the state to respond quickly to pacify its citizenry. A picture of a Singapore state held in check by its citizenry is a new one. Arguably this is the sting of smallness. The compression effect of smallness has magnified social discontent and now works to facilitate citizens' keeping a tight rein on the state. The PAP government might have been socially responsible, but until recently it has generally been a top-down administration. Nonetheless, the table seems to have turned recently. Caught in a reverse tide, the state has had no choice but to accede to the demands of its people. The rapidity of its response is yet another hallmark of smallness. Quick responses to popular sentiments have seen the PAP recapturing one lost seat in the September 2015 general elections, winning eighty-three of the eighty-nine contested seats. Indeed, speed has rendered an experimental and futuristic quality to Singapore's capitalist growth. Its future will depend on how well it succeeds in exploiting the flexibility that smallness offers, while avoiding the excesses and intensities that come with the paranoia and scale of smallness.

Critical Spaces of the Future

Singapore's history has always been constituted by a meeting of outside and inside forces. Its providence can only continue if an openness to people, capital, goods, and ideas remains in the future.

Yet, as we have seen, openness brings with it impingements on national economy and society, which have caused cracks to the founding pillars of Singapore's success story. Free-market pressures and the uncertainties of today's neoliberal capitalism have spurred and pulled in diverse directions. As a result there is an explosion of human creativity and ingenuity, both absorbed by and in opposition to market logic. Singapore is not spared from such transformations. Evidently the thinking, doing, and desiring of its people have changed tremendously and will continue to mutate in the future. The days when the Singapore state apparatus can push its citizens too hard and too fast may now be limited. Younger Singaporeans are increasingly rejecting the "Singapore Dream," or what is known as the five *c*'s—cash, car, credit card, condominium, and country club membership. Many have abandoned successful careers in order to pursue more low-key alternative lifestyles better suited to their interests. Leadership, too, has to change. No longer can the PAP handpick successors. Capable and committed leadership has emerged at the opposition front, insisting on being codrivers of the state.

Such changes all suggest that the ultimate challenge ahead may be for Singapore to develop its own intricate parameters of a good life, not dictated by market logic alone and also integrative of its citizens as well as outsiders temporarily in the country. This is a tall mandate.

Nevertheless, Singapore's recent ambition to become an Asian paradigm of futuristic economy and a regional hub for the arts has created an unexpected path toward future possibilities. It has turned this city-state into a site for political expressions via the arts. Singapore has long provided opportunities for employment and political escape for its neighboring populations, as demonstrated by the influx of rich Indonesian Chinese during the 1998 Indonesian riots. However, the current promotion of the arts has brought in an entirely different population of cultural producers, deeply engaged in the creation of political spaces against consensus and exclusion. Inevitably, investments in the arts have led to a flourishing of activities providing opportunities for regionally based visual and performing artists, to exhibit, perform, and talk about their work. In this process, many sensitive art works of Southeast Asia, sometimes banned in their local countries, have found expressions in Singapore in recent years.

Ironically, this political expression is enabled by a professionalized, often commoditized and apolitical environment. It is precisely Singapore's uniqueness as a pint-sized capitalist and apolitical haven that has created a free space for political critique, otherwise unavailable in the artists' home environments. These activities have unintentionally turned Singapore into a site for political expression beyond a mere tax haven or safe abode of the rich. It is interesting that while Singapore has little room for the freedom of political expressions, politicized contemporary art appears to be good for business. Clearly Singapore is not an isolated case of this, as art is increasingly vital to the creation of the economic value of global cities today. Nevertheless, in a society where rigid social boundaries continue to prevail, artistic expressions can provide effective counteractions as they tend to shake up homogenizing definitions of economy, self, and community. Disinterested contemplation of the arts by authorities and the official patronage of arts exhibitions by museums further help conceal the potency of artistic visibilities and enable their public dissemination. While premature, it is not inconceivable that such critical spaces may have subsequent impacts on Singaporean society itself, given the current pervasiveness of transnational influences. The Singapore case may yet throw light on the power, ironies, and surprises of the politics of smallness in the context of futuristic subjectivities arising from the schisms of a new global age.

Notes

1. Land reclamation has seen Singapore grow from 622.6 square kilometers in 1997 to 715.8 today.

2. An "Our Singapore Conversation" series was introduced during Singapore's National Day in 2012 as a platform for the government to engage ordinary Singaporeans in the country's future plans. See https://www.reach.gov.sg/read/our-sg-conversation.

3. Low-income households were officially defined in 2013 as those in the bottom 20 percent of household incomes (Yue 2013: 2). The average monthly household income from work figures in 2011–2012 shows that the bottom 10 percent of households were earning $440 per month while the next ten percentile above were earning $856 per month, in contrast to the median of $2,127.

4. Only families with a total monthly household income of less than $1,500 are allowed to rent at monthly rates of from $26 to $205 for one-room and from $44 to $275 for two-room flats (Yue 2013: 18).

References

Abeysinghe, Tilak, and Keen Meng Choy. 2007. *The Singapore Economy: An Econometric Perspective*. New York: Routledge.

Akmar, Shamsul. 2002. Vital for Singapore's Leadership to Address the Discomfort of a Neighbor. *New Straits Times*, 9 March.

Barrett, Alec. 2011. Sizing Up Singapore. *Harvard Political Review* [online], 18 May.

Borsuk, Richard, and Reginald Chua. 1998. Singapore Strains Relations with Indonesia's President. *Asian Wall Street Journal*, 4 August.

Chow, Rey. 1992. Between Colonizers: Hong Kong's Postcolonial Self-Writing in the 1990s. *Diaspora: A Journal for Transnational Studies* 2 (2): 151–70.

Friedman, Thomas L. 2011. Serious in Singapore. *New York Times* [online], 29 January.

Gibson, William. 1993. Disneyland with the Death Penalty. *Wired*, September/October.

Goh, Victor H. H. 2005. Sexuality, Ageing, and Fertility in Singapore. *Innovation* 5 (1).

Grant Thornton IBR (International Business Report). 2010. Heavy Workload and Economic Climate Upped Stress Levels for Business Owners in Singapore. News release, 17 March.

Happy Planet Index. 2012. Singapore Achieves a Happy Planet Index Score of 39.8 and Ranks #90 of All the List of Countries Analysed. Accessed 17 June 2013 at http://www.happyplanetindex.org/countries/singapore/.

Lim, Leonard. 2012. Get Married and Have Babies, Migrants a Temporary Solution: LKY. *Straits Times* [online], 11 August.

Lim, Leonel. 2013. Meritocracy, Elitism, and Egalitarianism: A Preliminary and Provisional Assessment of Singapore's Primary Education Review. *Asia Pacific Journal of Education* 33 (1): 1–14.

Lim, Linda Y. C. 1983. Singapore's Success: The Myth of the Free Market. *Asian Survey* 23 (6): 752–64.

Reuters. 2007. Eat with Your Family Today, Singaporeans Told. *Reuters* [online], 25 May.

Stiglitz, Joseph E. 2013. Singapore's Lessons for an Unequal America. *New York Times* [online], 18 March.

Tan, Amelia. 2011. See, He's a President's Scholar. *Straits Times*, 13 August, Prime, A3.

Tan, Kenneth. 2008. Meritocracy and Elitism in a Global Age: Ideological Shifts in Singapore. *International Political Science Review* 29 (1): 7–27.

Wallop, Clementine. 2013. Singapore Considers Gold Fix. *Wall Street Journal* [online], 16 April.

Yue Jie Zheng Bryan. 2013. Being "Low-Income" in Singapore: The Relative Dimensions of Poverty. Honors thesis, Department of Southeast Asian Studies, National University of Singapore.

CHAPTER 5

"Wi Likkle but Wi Tallawah": Soft Power and Smallness in Jamaica

Don Robotham

"Wi likkle but wi tallawah"—"we may be small but we are strong" (powerful, influential, resilient)—is a phrase frequently on the lips of Jamaicans at home and abroad. Usually said in a context of some exceptional achievement by an individual or the nation as a whole, it speaks to an image that many Jamaicans have of themselves and their country and the close attention that Jamaicans pay to how they are seen on the world stage.

To begin with, which societies are "small" and which "big" is a matter of size of territory or population. But smallness is also a geopolitical issue: it is difficult to discuss smallness in isolation from the global system where each small society occupies a definite niche and from which it receives a steady stream of messages concerning its size and significance. Today more than at any other time, one has to examine the specific position a nation occupies in the global hierarchy of cultures and nations. Drawing on language from the nineteenth-century period of high imperialism, the question really is one of who is and is not a "Great Power," and what consequences follow. Which countries carry commanding weight on the global scene, with wealthy economies and overwhelming military might, capable of intervening decisively outside of their national borders and of defying "international law" with impunity? Societies that achieve this enviable "hard power" state are "big." The rest, on the other hand, suffer from degrees of "smallness."

From this standpoint, issues of smallness connect with that old work of Carl Schmitt and others in which liberal international law is ridiculed as a system designed to mask the hard realities of gross national power inequalities (Kelsen 1952; Schmitt 1976). While rejecting Schmitt's extreme conclusions about the hollowness of liberal fictions of the formal equality of nations—he argues that some nations are "lions," others "mice"—it is hard to deny that a sharp distinction must be drawn between formal equality and harsh power politics. From this brutal viewpoint, the United Nations General Assembly is a collection of "mice," while in the Security Council the "lions" roar.

However, Jamaicans very much think of themselves as "lions in Zion"—to use the Rastafarian formulation—irrespective of where and how "Babylon" may rank them. "Babylon," in the Old Testament narrative that still pervades Jamaican popular culture, refers not only to the "principalities and powers," within and without the country, that perpetrate specific acts of oppression (the Jamaican policeman being the quintessential enforcer). "Babylon" is above all a *system* of all pervasive oppression and negative "livity" (way of life) characterized by "rich-quick" ("Mammon") self-centeredness taking hold of people's minds on a mass scale. The consequence is that "Babylon" becomes deeply internalized, posing huge challenges for mass "deprogramming" and "emancipation from mental slavery." As a Rastafarian lamented to me in 1999, "Babylon" (and thus "smallness") rests above all on self-subordination at the social psychological level: "material crave, material crave—a it is the problem also. Because, this man set up him system, and him system is not fe benefit I and I. But I and I find pleasure in him system, which is only temporary pleasure" (Easy Skanking 1999).

Possibly because of this tendency to see themselves as struggling against a system of global and local psychological oppression, the Jamaican approach has been to deploy soft power. Achievements in the London 2012 Olympics have made assertions of "tallawahness" ever more frequent—helping to reveal how a society of 2.7 million people on the doorstep of the leading world power manages its identity and sense of purpose. Amid the euphoria, the most frequent refrain was for Jamaicans to "big up" the athletes and to "big up" Jamaica, coinciding as the Olympics did with the fiftieth anniversary of Jamaica's independence from Britain. According to the *Urban Dictionary*, the term "big up" is of Jamaican origins, going back to sometime in the 1980s as "an expression of support or encouragement." Whatever the truth of that etymology, Jamaicans were heard in both visual and print media making statements about their star sprinter such as "Usain Bolt, yu a di big man of di place," or "Usain Bolt, you are the real big man—you are a lion in Zion," or "Big up unnu [your] self, you have made Jamaica so proud and I am so proud to be a Jamaican—Big up Jamaicaaaaa!" Or, "A Jamaica wi seh! . . . To the worl' a we dat [that's us]! . . . You hear wa Bob Marley seh? 'Dem a go ti-yad fi si wi face, can't get wi outta di race'" and more words along those lines (*Jamaica Gleaner* 9–11 August 2012).

Soft Power and External Smallness

Some small countries—Singapore would be a classic case, Qatar another—use hard power to "punch above their weight" on the global stage. Jamaica, at least since the 1990s, has come to rely almost wholly on soft power. There is much talk of "Brand Jamaica"—not just a generic Caribbean of sun, sea, and sand but "a paradise with an edge": the land of dreadlocks, reggae, ganja, and jerk chicken—"once you go, you know," as television advertisements mysteriously proclaim. "Jamaica Irie" (Jamaica is sweet)—home to Bob Marley and Usain Bolt. This carefully crafted image can be seen regularly on American network television, incorporated as placements in regular programming. Many episodes of that quintessential piece of TV Americana *Wheel of Fortune* are filmed in Jamaica, and the announcement that a prize-winner will be going there invariably produces screams of delight. Recently, a Volkswagen Super Bowl advertisement featured a German speaking with a rather odd rendition of a U.S. version of a Jamaican accent. Some viewers were offended, regarding the advertisement as patronizing, even racist. But many Jamaicans saw this as another affirmation of how culturally "tallawah" Jamaica had become. The upshot was a visit to Jamaica for the German actor, courtesy of the Jamaican Tourist Board pleased by new prospects of marketing "Brand Jamaica" in Europe.

This soft power imagery is also increasingly evoked internally and especially in the Jamaican diaspora, with the narrative of the country as a happy-go-lucky, endearingly offbeat society with a unique culture—"A yah so nice!" ("It's *here* that's really nice!"), rambunctious and alluring but also defiant and dangerous. "'Jamdown" or "Jamrock" are untranslatable terms of affection frequently used by Jamaicans to refer to their native land. This emphasis on cultural edginess was dramatically brought home while watching on television the ecstatic response in both London and Jamaica to the performance of Jamaican athletes in the 2012 Olympics. Throughout the games Jamaica basically came to a halt, with pandemonium erupting after races such as the men's 100- and 200-meter finals. The Jamaican diaspora in New

York responded similarly. The real climax came on the last day when the Jamaican men's relay team beat off a strong challenge from the United States. Ah, sweet victory!

In the context of these Olympic triumphs, "Wi likkle but wi tallawah" (tough, bold, irrepressible—"hard man fi dead" and so on) was heard more commonly than ever. At the end of the 100-meter final in which he won a silver medal, Yohan Blake addressed the country thus, "Jamaica we 'likkle but we tallawah,' it's been great and tomorrow is going to be a special moment for us on the podium" (Lowe 2012a). It was one thing to make your mark on the world stage, as musicians like Bob Marley had done before. It was another thing to do this while defeating the team of the powerful neighbor to the north, in whose shadow Jamaicans continuously live. An intense wave of patriotism swept over the country, starting with the athletes themselves. One expression came at the end of the men's two hundred meters, in which Jamaica won all three medals. In a kind of secret gesture to the Jamaican audience and their London "homies," the bronze medalist Warren Weir (from the village of Refuge, of which more later) turned to the cameras at the end of the obligatory postrace BBC interview and mischievously called out in a deep rural Jamaican accent, "Nuh English, straight patwa!"—"No English, real Jamaican speech only!" The puzzled interviewer did not get it, but many young white Britons probably did—such has been the impact of Jamaican urban talk on the speech of especially London youth.

A year before, in a commentary on the London riots that achieved much notoriety, the English historian and TV commentator David Starkey had complained bitterly about how, in his view in Britain, "The whites have become black . . . black and white, boy and girl, operate in this language together, this language which is wholly false, which is this Jamaican patois that has been intruded in England" (Quinn 2011). It is common to overhear youth in London greeting each other in Jamaican style—"Whaa gwaan?" ("What's going on?"). To Jamaicans at home and abroad, Weir's audacious assertion of cultural nationalism was particularly striking because of its inhouse nature: you had to be an initiate to get it. This was not the official nationalism of flag and anthem, but the nation "from below" (Jamaicans would say "Yaad")[1]—the often disregarded "roots nation" of African descent and "broken English"—live and in your face, on global television no less. The Empire biting back: you "intrude" on me and I "intrude" on you.

The "investment"' in its Olympic athletes has paid off handsomely: Usain Bolt alone has 2.6 million Twitter and over 10 million Facebook followers;

Yohan Blake has 214,500 followers on Twitter. But this is not just exercising soft power in the Anglosphere. Jamaica's cricketers are familiar to fans in India, Pakistan, Bangladesh, Sri Lanka, South Africa, as well as Australia and the United Kingdom. The country's musicians—Bob Marley being the exemplar—have likewise achieved global iconic status. What is more, the worlds of sports and music greatly overlap: many of the leading sportsmen are ardent music and dance fans, go to each other's events, and follow each other on Twitter and Facebook. Bolt's sports bar in Kingston attracts visitors from all over the world, and there are plans to expand its operations to London and New York. One of the iconic images of athletics on YouTube is a video of Bolt and Asafa Powell dancing Jamaican-style on the track at the end of the men's relay in the 2009 World Championships in Berlin. Other clips of Bolt and Powell holding a "dance-off" doing the "gully creeper"[2] at the post-Olympics party in in Beijing in 2008 have over 118,765 hits and can be found on many Internet sites, not to mention the tumultuous dancehall session at the "Puma Yaad" in Brixton in 2012, featuring performances by Bolt, Weir, and Powell. Usain Bolt presented the trophy to Rafael Nadal, the winner of the French Open tennis title in 2013. Another example: Yohan Blake, world class sprinter, music lover, and avid cricketer, was given the rare honor of "ringing the bell" that signaled the start of play in the England versus South Africa cricket match at Lord's Cricket Ground, shortly after the 2012 Olympics.

Slavery and Internal Smallness

One of the striking features of this soft power strategy is its internal dynamics, linked to the country's distinctive history. The Jamaican global cultural figures all originate in the lower strata of a highly stratified society, riven by class and racial divisions. In a Twitter post on 7 November 2012, Hansle Parchment (@HansleParchment), the 2012 Olympic bronze medalist in the 110-meter hurdles, tweeted some familiar lines from Bob Marley's song "War," but with an interesting and probably unconscious modification. He wrote: "Now until the philosophy which hold one class superior and another inferior is finally and permanently discredited, dis ting will be war." Marley's actual words are:

Until the philosophy which holds one *race* superior
And another
Inferior

Parchment's substitution of *class* for *race* captures the social context in which the Olympic victories were received: a contemporary Jamaica in which a black middle and upper-middle professional stratum has been superimposed on old colonial racial hierarchies, modifying but not destroying the color-class relationships inherited from slavery.

All this by way of explaining the cultural-political reception of the Olympic victories and why, in such a context, Jamaicans say "little" rather than "small": like so much else in Jamaican culture, this word speaks not only to the sense that Jamaica's problem has been constituted by global forces—by "the system" (see Popcaan's song below)—and therefore must unavoidably locate itself somewhere on the global stage. It goes further. The point of "likkle" here is not just small but "small and vulnerable." But the even more important point involves "internal smallness." The view held by large sections of a population is that the more privileged strata of the society view themselves as "big men" and the rest as "small," of little consequence. Thus the emotional implications in Jamaica's case have to do with the sense not only of belonging to a vulnerable nation but also of being a disadvantaged social stratum—the "grass roots"—and therefore the necessity to be "talla-wah" and "big 'bout ya"—to be resilient and to show fortitude at all times, to be on the alert for acts of oppression and disrespect, to be pugnacious ("no skin-up") when necessary, although, people will also be quick to add, "coward man keep sound bones."

The Jamaican "edgy tropical paradise" narrative is thus inextricably intertwined with another, perhaps even more powerful one, one that is not so readily exportable and that speaks more clearly to the internal structure and culture of Jamaican society today. This is the popular narrative around the experience of slavery, repeatedly evoked at the time of the 2012 Olympic victories. Commenting on the victorious performance of the Jamaican men's relay team, one person, identified significantly as "Rasta," wrote the following in a leading local newspaper:

> What some people don't remember that Jamaica is one of the most talented countries. Jamaica is always leading. From Boukman leading Haiti to its independence, Garvey teaching the world of black empowerment and Bob Marley who motivated the world through his music. Remember that the strongest Africans were brought to Jamaica through slavery. So it's been the same, never to change, Jamaica will

always be in charge. Small in size but huge with talents. Bolt and the rest, great job. Haters get use to it.

In response to which another commenter, "Bolt's#1fan," added: "Exactly. Jamaica being one of the furtheresr [*sic*] countries to get to during the middle passage voyage the weakened slaves were left off first only the fittest of the fittest made it to Jamaica . . . Long Live the Determination and Resilence [*sic*] of the Jamaica spirit !!!!!!!!" (Lowe 2012c). Resorting to the slave narrative was by no means unique to these commenters. Another—"Evanarchere"—responding to a story on the origins of many athletes in the old sugar parish of Trelawny, observed: "The people of Trelawny had been introduced to advanced industrial technology, at an early stage—that may have contributed to the optimistic and progressive disposition of most of those native to that area! All this, with a commendable history of resistance, to the oppression of slavery!!!" (Spaulding 2012).

To understand why the Olympic victories evoked these references to slavery one must understand history as well as the current society. Jamaica is a case not only of absolute and relative smallness, but also of a long history of plantation slavery, which imparts very particular qualities to its sense of being "likkle." Unlike other societies, small and large, Jamaica was not simply "inserted" into globalization. On the contrary, this is a society constituted by global processes themselves—the European expansion into the Americas from the fifteenth century, the plantation system, the Atlantic slave trade, limited postslavery indentured Indian, Chinese, Lebanese, and some German migration. It is a country that has had and continues to experience substantial migrations, first to Panama, Central America, and Cuba in the nineteenth century, and then to the United States and Britain. One consequence is that Jamaica connects deeply into British history, including connections to Prime Minister David Cameron's family (Manning 2013).[3]

Another consequence is that Jamaica does not have an indigenous precapitalist past out of which an idyllic *Gemeinschaft* nationalist narrative can be constructed. This does not prevent a constant invocation by Jamaicans of a narrative of a "sweet-sweet Jamaica nah lef ya." The "first" Taino population did not long survive the Spanish colonization after 1494, and what remained has been assimilated into the larger population with little cultural impact. Nor should one forget that after the Spanish period Jamaica was under the control of a single colonial power for 307 years. At the English conquest in 1655, the country was established not as a nation, but as a Cromwellian business venture: it was a "plantation," part of the Protector's "Western Design," supervised by a committee of the Privy Council. Not only was it a plantation, but this was a system of *racialized* plantation *slavery*. Between 1655 and the ending of the British slave trade in 1807, 1,083,369 enslaved Africans were sent to Jamaica, with 915,204 arriving. Jamaica was by far the single most important recipient of Africans traded in by the British, receiving 40–50 percent of the total between 1720 and 1790. Mortality was such that during the eighteenth century, 575,000 enslaved persons were needed to increase the enslaved population by about 250,000 (Burnard and Morgan 2001: 207). At emancipation in 1838, the enslaved African population numbered a mere 317,000. Jamaican plantation ownership was heavily absentee, and the plantations were large compared to those in the southern United States (Higman 1976: 70). The frequency of revolt was high, the disadvantages of smallness being offset by the rugged mountainous terrain. At the same time, there were many smallholdings, with the result that a large number of "small whites," as well as many free coloreds and blacks, owned slaves. The stereotypical picture of a slave-master oligarchy confronting an enslaved mass is only a partial truth. There was significant small-scale "domestic" slavery with 24.3 percent of all slaveholdings in lots under fifty.

Nevertheless it is the plantocratic image that most Jamaicans have, and the "warrior cause" narrative of enslavement and resistance is deeply embedded in contemporary consciousness and sustained by popular music in particular. The Olympics evoked this narrative largely because of the manner in which plantation slavery was brought to an end, as the Jamaican sociologist Peter Espeut (2013) recently pointed out. In his article "No Closure to Slavery," he remarks on the popularity of the lyrics of Vybz Kartel, one of the leading Jamaican dancehall artistes who openly rationalizes the large-scale defrauding of Americans by Jamaican scammers, singing, "Big up de scamma . . . me call it reparation."

Kartel was only continuing in a tradition established even more forcefully by others. In an earlier song, "Warrior Cause," the Jamaican DJs Elephant Man and Spragga Benz chant to a heavy bass line:

Well mi come fi big up all di warrior from the present to the past
An who know dem fight fi a cause (cause)
Big up all di warrior from the present to the past
An who know dem fight fi a cause

Well some say dem a badman and no know di half a it
Don't know a big gill nor a quart a it
Whappiking and Rhigin was the start a it
Feathermop an Burry Boy was di class a it
Tony Brown an George Flash come master it
Jim Brown fight the struggle inna di heart a it
Starkey an Daley the bloodbath a it
Bucky Marshall an Tek-Life di rath a it[4]

In this remarkable piece of dancehall music, a whole string of colorful Jamaican inner city characters—Whappiking, Rhigin, Feathermop, Burry Boy, Tek-Life, and many others who found themselves on the wrong side of the law—are assimilated into the pantheon of Jamaican national heroes celebrated as "Warriors" who died fighting for a cause: stealing from the (Jamaican and Caucasian) rich to give to the poor. Jamaicans say, "Tief from tief, God laugh"—no need to shed any tears for the rich if they are plundered by the poor.

In a song very much in the "Warrior Cause" tradition characteristically entitled "The System," Popcaan, an artist popular with the athletes, sings as follows:

Sad to say
But, white people ah bawl
Indian people ah bawl
Black people ah bawl
Chinese people ah bawl.
Di system, design fi set we up
Yeaaaa dem give we di guns and
Dem same one come wet we up yaaaaa . . .

. . . suh
If we sell weed ah problem dat
If we do a robbery a problem dat
Di whole world a pray fi di problem stop.
Nobody nuh cater fi solving dat[5]

No one cares—"nobody nuh cater fi solving dat"—not the state, the church, nor the larger Jamaican society, not the world. One is on one's own in the face of "the system." And—in a feature that, while not being altogether absent from left-wing popular music in the 1970s, is really new—individual acts of criminality are treated as part of the long-standing Jamaican tradition of popular resistance. The point to note is that "the system" in question is depicted as both global and local. "Babylon" abroad sustains "Babylon" at home. The popular musical artist Burning Spear asked rhetorically in his album *Chant Down Babylon*

Do you remember the days of slavery?

And how they beat us
And how they worked us so hard
And they used us
'Til they refuse us . . . ?[6]

The vast majority of Jamaicans even today, 175 years later, would very likely respond with a resounding "Yes!"

This is the "rebel" cultural milieu in which many of the male athletes move, as do many other young Jamaicans. Espeut argues that such lyrics resonate because the British carefully crafted the ending of slavery to ensure that the plantation system survived. Since subsequent economic and social development has been built on this post-emancipation foundation, there is a felt continuity between the slavery past and today. Although postcolonial education-driven upward mobility has dramatically "blackened" the Jamaican upper-middle class, the top of the sociocultural pyramid is still light-skinned. Because of liberal democracy, the Anglophone Caribbean is that unique part of the world in which the political system is controlled by descendants of formerly enslaved people. Jamaicans of African descent control the state and the political system and dominate popular culture but do not control the economy and do not define the status hierarchy. Those at the base of the society now are still the direct descendants of those who were at the base when slavery ended (Robotham 2000).

It is not uncommon for working- and middle-class Jamaicans to say, half seriously, "I am going to slave"—meaning "I am off to work"—or to describe an exacting supervisor as a "slave driver." People will frequently say in a jocular fashion, to children preparing to go back to school at the end of the summer holidays or to a recently married male, "Your free paper [manumission document] burn," meaning that your days of freedom are over. Or they will show their disdain for a particularly bossy person in language drawn straight from the eighteenth century, that he or she is behaving like a "bucky massa" (slave master). Very recently, a person reminiscing with mild bitterness about growing up poor in rural Jamaica in the 1950s said to me, "I was the slave in that yard."

In the case of the Olympics, these old global-local historical connections produced a link, which was deeply ironic, yet cannot be regarded as entirely coincidental. One year before the 2012 Olympics, the British newspapers revealed that Sebastian Coe, former Olympic long distance gold medalist, retired British member of Parliament, and chairman of the Organizing Committee for the 2012 London Olympic Games, was a direct descendant of English slave masters from the parish of Trelawny in Jamaica. Lord Coe's ancestors owned 297 slaves and received today's equivalent of seven hundred thousand pounds sterling in compensation money at emancipation (Singh 2011). In fact, on his mother's side, Coe's family (Clarke) is from Hyde, just outside the present-day Clark's Town, in the still operating sugar estates with a factory where Captain Morgan rum was once distilled. British newspapers focused on the fact that Usain Bolt was also from Trelawny, ignoring the fact that Bolt's community—Sherwood Content—is many miles away toward the western end of the parish. But the two-time women's 200-meter Olympic gold medalist Veronica Campbell-Brown is from a nearby community, as is Warren Weir.

Refuge, the village from which Weir's family originates, was one of eight church-founded free villages established by Baptist missionaries in the parish of Trelawny after the passage of the Ejectment and Trespass Acts at emancipation. The point of those acts was to evict the formerly enslaved from the small plots of land on the hills of the plantation (including house plots), which they had occupied for over a century. The aim of the planters, supported by the British government, was to ensure that this would provide them with a dependent labor force to continue working on the plantations. In response, the missionaries bought abandoned properties near to the plantations and subdivided them into small house plots for the recently freed to reside on, while insufficient for farming purposes. The missionaries sought not to create an independent peasantry, but to limit the exploitation of housing tenancy arrangements by the planters, and to improve the bargaining position of the freed, still destined to work on the old plantations but now as a "sugar proletariat" (Paget 1949/1950; Mintz 1958). Weir, like Coe, is five generations in direct descent from this typically Jamaican, global-local historical process. It is therefore not at all farfetched that Coe's ancestors encountered Campbell-Brown and Weir's ancestors during the eighteenth and nineteenth centuries in a master-slave, planter-tenant relationship. Weir's mother's surname happens to be Clarke.

This connection between Coe and Trelawny did not escape some Jamaicans during the 2012 celebrations. "Don't forget Seb Coe, the organiser of the Olympics," a commenter, going by the name "Voice of Reason," remarked. "His ancestors lived in Trelawny for generations" (Spaulding 2013). Interestingly, this was not written in an antagonistic spirit. This was not the time for divisiveness: the euphoria generated by the Olympic celebrations made that impossible. All the athletes, including Coe himself, as people said repeatedly, "had helped to put Jamaica on the map."

"Putting yourself on the map" is critical for any small country today. A history such as Jamaica's in a small space is no easy matter to overcome. The narrative of racial oppression and divisiveness rumbles along just beneath the surface in popular music in particular, and this is what is being repackaged for export and branded as "edginess." Part of the reason why the Jamaican soft power strategy is so popular with nearly all strata within this divided "nation" is because it tells a tale of "tallawahness" overcoming "littleness" to different audiences. Globally speaking, this narrative of contesting the entire Western global project ("Babylon") from a romantic anti-capitalist standpoint is at the heart of the broad appeal of Jamaican music. Reggae—in particular Bob Marley—as *Zivilisationskritik* mourning the loss of a precolonial, pre-neoliberal *Gemeinschaft*—has had an enduring appeal to the European '68 generation (Robotham 2008). To the Jamaican in the diaspora and those at home from the upper reaches of society, the musical and Olympic triumphs are a story about Jamaican success on the world stage. To the mass of Jamaicans at home as well as to the less successful youth abroad, however, this goes beyond global success. For it is not only global obstacles that these cultural icons have had to overcome. They have had to do battle against the homegrown ones as well. In order to succeed on the global stage they first had to overcome the oppressive structures of Jamaican society. "Tallawahness" of necessity begins at home and from an early age.

No surprise then that the idiom of congratulatory statements called on Jamaicans to "big up" the athletes and themselves: "Big up to the one Shelly [Ann Fraser-Pryce, gold medalist in the women's one hundred meters]. Big up to sister VCB [Veronica Campbell-Brown, the bronze medalist]. Big up all yaad massive." And again: "Big up all the winners, it couldn't have come at a better time when we are celebrating our 50th anniversary. BLACK, GREEN AND GOLD MAKE ME SOOOOOOOOOOOO PROUD. God Bless u all!" (Lowe 2012b).

In a Twitter post on 29 November 2012, Blake (@YohanBlake) wrote: "Popcaan—Cyah Believe (Raw) [Reservoir Riddim] Sept 2012 home chilling and playing this song real talk POPCAAN mad." In the opening lines of this haunting song—"Cyah Believe" (I can't believe it) about which Blake tweets—Popcaan laments how

> Dem nevah know when mi hungry
> Dem only see di smile
> Dem nuh see di sad time, yeah
> Dem only see di good time
> Dem nuh see di bad time.[7]

Tallawahness is needed globally but also locally, where "cold ground is your bed, and rockstone is your pillow," to paraphrase the words of Marley's "Talkin' Blues." Not long after Blake tweeted, in an unrelated Twitter post on 3 December 2012, Parchment (@HansleParchment) indignantly wrote: "RT@dwightwebley: A weh yuh did deh wen mi a suffer to rahtid, wen mi a go a school ina one suit a khaki!" (Where were you when I was suffering to hell?—when I was going to school with only one suit of khaki [school uniform]!). Especially in this vivid imagery using Jamaican talk, these are expressions resonating deeply with most Jamaicans, especially those from the countryside where having only one school uniform was common. People will tell you how they would wear a single uniform for two days, come home on Tuesday, wash it quickly, hang it on a clothesline to dry overnight, wear it again on Wednesday, to be washed again on Friday. Others will describe the shame they felt having to go to high school with only one pair of shoes and having to stuff these with newspaper when the soles wore out. Given the substantial upward mobility in Jamaican society with the middle and upper-middle class overwhelmingly originating among the rural poor, these are memories shared by a broad cross section of Jamaican society.

Parchment's and Blake's sentiments therefore are by no means isolated ones. As an anonymous commenter, identified only as "Guest," in her public congratulation of the mother of Warren Weir put it,

> Congratulations Ms. Clarke. What a blessed and thrilling moment.
> Your "baby" . . . an Olympics medalist! After injury, nay-saying, pain,
> perseverance and anguish. His nose did run, but him foot dem run
> faster yesterday . . . and took him to the Olympic podium.
>
> Missis, mi happy suh till . . . The whole Jamaica is happy for you
> and your son. Me know seh you did go through all the trials and
> tribulations with him when he moved through the issues that tested
> him. And mi know that you were at work running like the dickens
> along with your son yesterday. (Kelly 2012)

"Him nose did run, but him foot dem run faster yesterday" and a life of "trials
and tribulations." Jamaicans say, "if you want good, yu nose haffi run," meaning that there is no achievement without sacrifice and suffering. The reaction
among Jamaicans to the achievements of Jamaican athletes and musicians is
therefore tied into the fact that they all originate in the lower tiers of Jamaican society. The photograph of Hansle Parchment's father that appeared in
the newspapers was that of a typical dreadlocks Rastafarian of the older generation. Without a working television, this furniture maker from the village
of Cashew Bush had to rush to a neighbor's home to watch the race. On the
fringes of one of the oldest sugar plantation areas, the very name Cashew Bush
is archetypically rural Jamaican—a country in which colorful village names
such as "Wait-a-Bit" and "Mi no sen', you no come" abound. The name Cashew
Bush speaks to the post-emancipation policy of confining the recently free to
villages in the "bush," preserving the best lands for the sugar plantations. Blake
is from Bogue Hill, west of the resort town of Montego Bay, not far from
luxurious villas filled by North American celebrities in the winter months.

This touches a deep cultural-historical nerve in Jamaica. Erupting in
jubilation at Parchment's unexpected run, some villagers shouted, "Cashew
Bush to the world!" Others, when asked about Parchment only receiving
a bronze medal, retorted, "Hansle bronze is Cashew Bush's gold!" (Ellington
2012). Narratives of bootstrap achievement by Jamaicans abound. The unpleasant realities of Jamaican society—harsh conditions of life for the majority, in a context of relative elite affluence and a stagnant economy—are
both affirmed and denied amid these bouts of euphoria.

The feeling is therefore that the athletes and musicians have overcome
great odds, locally and abroad. This is at the core of their immense local popularity. Moreover, none of them deny their origins. On the contrary, they
make a point of giving back not only to their community but to low-income

communities, especially schools, across the island. Bolt, for example, spent substantial sums to refurbish the local health center, rewiring the Sherwood Content Basic School and providing his old high school with its own school bus. It is common for the athletes to give children not only gifts but also motivational talks or free coaching. Among themselves, they are in the process of setting up a fund whereby the more successful stars will assist the lesser known and younger generation, where most cannot afford even food and transportation to come to training regularly. But perhaps the most critical fact is that the leading athletes have turned down lucrative offers to locate and train abroad, particularly in the United States. They not only train in Jamaica but are coached by Jamaicans. This means that it is a fairly common thing to see them in public, in traffic, and, in the case of some, on the extremely active Jamaican nightlife circuit. Almost without exception they are extremely approachable. Athletic achievement at their level is extremely demanding, and people respect the great sacrifices made by athletes and their families. To be so "tallawah," yet remaining humble and "roots," guarantees them a permanent place in Jamaican hearts.

Smallness and Society

The history recounted above has not only produced a sense of vulnerability and divisiveness, but also a strong individualism rooted in the peasant-plantation past. As Jamaicans like to say, "Man free." The right to own your own property, to speak your mind, to not be oppressed by "Babylon," to be able to travel where you want and live where you want, locally as well as globally, preferably to work for yourself rather than for another (proletarian employment notoriously grates on the Jamaican psyche)—all the things that slavery denied—are inalienable "natural" rights not conferred by any state or government. At the same time the "man" being referred to above is not only the individual but "humanity"—"people," the community. Referring to no one in particular, Jamaicans will commonly say, for example, "All a wi a one," meaning that these rights are public rights and should be available to all. The tradition of individualism in Jamaica is not the abstract neoliberal formal legal one but is derived from the synthesis of African communal traditions and nonconformist religions—Baptist, Methodist, and Moravian (Sammons 2013).

Therefore this freedom must be substantive. It must result in real material gains to the individual and real transformations in the standard of living of the community. When this idea confronts a society and a world that constantly celebrate formal freedoms while in fact constructing a reality of entrenched material, social, and cultural "bigness," then the sense of being regarded as "likkle" is hugely intensified. Because of their history, Jamaicans see this "big/likkle" contradiction as rooted at the global level—it is "Babylon." Of necessity it must therefore be contested both locally and globally. Over the last thirty years, Jamaica, like other islands in the Caribbean, has been undergoing a painful transition away from the plantation system that has defined it, both in reality and in past anthropological literature. The sugar plantations have long been downsized and the major ones sold to the Chinese, currently engaged in a rapid modernization program with high levels of mechanization and automation. Tourism, the culture industries, and the service sector now define the region and its economic future (Robotham 2009).

This chapter argues that the issue of smallness is principally a geopolitical one—"bigness" and "smallness" arise in the context of the global order. As long as Jamaicans face what they regard as an unjust local and global "system," the necessity to demonstrate "tallawahness" will arise. Since Babylon's method is one of mental enslavement, the soft power strategy of addressing smallness recommends itself. Yet the strategy does not overcome the sense of vulnerability that Jamaicans feel but to some degree exacerbates it. What Jamaica primarily supplies is the "raw material" of soft power. Only to a limited extent is the technology that makes Jamaican soft power a global force generated locally. Advanced tourism, music, and sports consultancies "to the worl" have emerged, with, for example, Jamaican global tourist consultants playing a modest part in the development of the tourist industry in Egypt. But these are still very minor parts of the economy. Apart from this dependence of the soft power strategy on First World sports, media, and marketing corporations, the contrast between the personal success of the leading personalities and national socioeconomic failure seems to be leading a number of these figures to "think hard" about the vulnerabilities of the present.

Paradoxically, it is this relative failure (so far) of making what I have elsewhere referred to as "the third transition" that keeps Jamaica significantly rural—with about 40 percent living in the countryside. Thus the Jamaica of Cashew Bush, Sherwood Content, Refuge, and Bogue Hill remains alive. This is the Jamaica from which reggae and dancehall spring and the "Sweet Jamaica—mi soon fahwud" (sweet Jamaica, I shall soon return) of which the athletes tweet. Out of these rural communities also comes that driving Jamaican "ambition"—a quality endlessly dinned into the ears of children, without which neither musical nor athletic achievement would be possible. It is this encounter with global history and its local inequities that has produced not only the athletes and musicians but also the aesthetic of defiance that is the secret behind the appeal of Jamaican culture, including both "conscious lyrics" and "slackness music." Without this no "tallawahness" is possible, and Jamaicans would remain, in their own eyes, merely " 'likkle."

Notes

1. "Yard" or "home." Jamaicans commonly refer to their residence as their "yaad" or "gates," since the norm for generations in Jamaica has been for every individual residence to be fenced and gated where possible. Such a place is your "yaad" where you and your family live, by extension the entire country, especially if you are in the diaspora. Hence the expression "Yardie."

2. A popular Jamaican dancehall style, wildly popular at street dances and Jamaican nightclubs at home as well as in the diaspora.

3. Another striking but by no means isolated example: the ninety-four thousand pounds with which Thomas Wildman purchased Newstead Abbey from Lord Byron in 1818 came from the fortune made exploiting more than eight hundred slaves in Jamaica. The Wildman family in turn obtained the Jamaican properties from William Beckford, the author of *Vathek* and the builder of the famously extravagant Fonthill Abbey in Wiltshire in 1796, also from a very wealthy slave-owning family. There is a Wildman Street in Kingston and a Beckford Kraal in the parish of Clarendon, named for Edward Hyde, 1st Earl of Clarendon and chancellor of Oxford University.

4. Lyrics accessed 30 June 2016 at http://motolyrics.com/elephant-man/warrior -cause-lyrics.html.

5. Lyrics accessed 30 June 2016 at http://urbanlyrics.com/lyrics/popcaan/thesystem .html.

6. Lyrics accessed 30 June 2016 at http://genius.com/Burning-Spear-slavery-days -lyrics.

7. Lyrics accessed 8 July 2016 at http://popcaanmusic.blogspot.com/2012/10/cant -believe-it-lyrics-popcaan.html.

References

Burnard, Trevor, and Kenneth Morgan. 2001. The Dynamics of the Slave Market and Slave Purchasing Patterns in Jamaica, 1655–1788. *William and Mary Quarterly* 58 (1): 205–28.

Easy Skanking. 1999. Interview. Taylor Hall, University of the West Indies, Jamaica, 24 June.

Ellington, Barbara. 2012. Cashew Bush Is Jubilant! *Gleaner* (Kingston, Jamaica), 10 August.

Espeut, Peter. 2013. No Closure to Slavery. *Gleaner*, 12 April.

Higman, B. W. 1976. *Slave Population and Economy in Jamaica, 1807–1834*. Cambridge: Cambridge University Press.

Kelly, Daviot. 2012. Warren "Go Hard and Done." *Sunday Gleaner* [online], 10 August.

Kelsen, Hans. 1952. *Principles of International Law*. New York: Rinehart.

Lowe, André. 2012a. Hurricane Bolt. *Gleaner* [online], 6 August.

———. 2012b. "Pryceless"! Shelly, VCB Open Ja[maica]'s Medal Account. *Sunday Gleaner* [online], 5 August.

———. 2012c. We Were Never Worried About the US. *Sunday Gleaner* [online], 12 August.

Manning, Sanchez. 2013. Britain's Colonial Shame: Slave-Owners Given Huge Payouts After Abolition. *Independent* (London) [online], 24 February.

Mintz, Sidney W. 1958. Historical Sociology of the Jamaican Church-Founded Free Village System. *De West-Indische Gids* 38 (1–2): 46–70.

Paget, Hugh. 1949/1950. The Free Village System in Jamaica. *Caribbean Quarterly* 1 (4): 7–19.

Quinn, Ben. 2011. David Starkey Claims "the Whites Have Become Black." *Guardian* (London), 12 August.

Robotham, Don. 2000. Blackening the Jamaican Nation: The Travails of a Black Bourgeoisie in a Globalized World. *Identities: Global Studies in Culture and Power* 7 (1): 1–37.

———. 2008. Review of *Bob Marley: Herald of a Postcolonial World*, by Jason Toynbee. *Global Media and Communication* 4 (3): 366–68.

———. 2009. *The Third Crisis: Jamaica in the Neoliberal Era*. Kingston: University of the West Indies Press.

Sammons, Edward. 2013. Much Too Much Selfishness: Neoliberalism and the Practice of Freedom in a Jamaican Farmtown. Ph.D. dissertation, City University of New York.

Schmitt, Carl. 1976. *The Concept of the Political*. New Brunswick, N.J.: Rutgers University Press.

Singh, Anita. 2011. Sebastian Coe's Roots Go Back to Sugar Cane Baron Who Kept 300 Slaves. *Telegraph* (London), 20 August.

Spaulding, Gary. 2012. Sensational Talents from Trelawny. *Sunday Gleaner* [online], 11 August.

CHAPTER 6

On Chutzpah Countries and "Shitty Little Countries"

Virginia R. Dominguez

Is Israel a revealing example of a small country that refuses to act small and succeeds in getting the attention of much larger countries (some of it positive, much of it negative), or an example of a problem country perceived by many not to play by the "rules"? Or is Israel a fairly unique case of a country whose refusal to act small is so extreme that it can only be treated as a rogue state or a pariah state, like North Korea and Iran?

This chapter explores the question by examining a media incident that began in December 2001: Israel was referred to as "that shitty little country Israel." A French diplomat using this phrase at a private party in England was exposed in the British press, then excoriated in traditional and electronic media, partly defended by the French government, and later transferred to a diplomatic post in North Africa. That the phrase offended, inspired, and went viral demands exploration, but that the phrase continues to have a social and rhetorical life more than a decade later also warrants commentary. This chapter explores the surprising fact that the phrase "that shitty little country" remains, with few exceptions, a referent to Israel.

To put it in perspective, I consider countries whose governments resist pressure from contemporary megacountries (to the point of periodically looking brave and foolhardy at the same time), chutzpah countries, countries with hubris. Of course, not all contemporary megacountries support the same smaller countries, nor do they always have unchanging policies toward each of those smaller countries. But I am nonetheless treating as chutzpah countries those countries whose governments have over more than a few years (and across different political eras) shown what some applaud as laudable independence and others as annoying resistance. I recall Tito's Yugoslavia being celebrated in the United States during the Cold War for exhibiting autonomy toward the Soviet Union, while Castro's Cuba was typically seen as a pawn or satellite of the Soviet Union. But to overpersonalize it by thinking of chutzpah as only pertaining to certain leaders of certain countries in particular periods, or of some small countries being put up by megacountries to do their intelligence, military, or political work for them, is too limiting. It simply fails to consider that some countries resist acting small.

My question is not whether Israel resists political pressure from other countries. There is ample evidence that it does, since independence in 1948, and not just from Arab or Muslim countries (cf. Dominguez 1995, 2013; Kimmerling 2005). Over the years Israeli governments have bemoaned but also severely critiqued UN condemnations of Israeli policies vis-à-vis Palestinians. And numerous U.S. presidents have supported Israel's right to exist as a country, while trying to pressure Israeli governments to settle its conflict with Palestinians and other neighboring Arabs. Given the Holocaust, official European critiques of Israel have been complicated. More strongly in recent years, it has involved a human rights or political rights message about making peace with the Palestinians, ending injustices, and avoiding racism, ethnicism, and discrimination. Israeli politics have changed over the years, with governments seen as more right-wing beginning in 1977 when Menachem Begin's Likud Party won the Knesset election, but there have also been national unity governments and more socialist/left-wing prime ministers since then. While some outsiders (as well as insiders) condemn specific Israeli government policies and actions as not furthering the cause of peace, Israel is used to harsher criticism of its very existence, or of the Zionist idea that Israel is a country privileging Jews as inhabitants and citizens. It is therefore not news that Israel resists political pressure, including from large European countries that support its existence.

Is a reference to Israel as a "shitty little country" just a reference to chutzpah countries, or an indexing of chutzpah countries, or even an indexing of small countries in today's contemporary world? The particular matters here, but so does the larger question about size and the expectations of size in the contemporary nation-state system. Clearly Israel is a small country both relatively and absolutely, but its strong critics and supporters alike often seem to exceptionalize Israel, thereby suggesting that there is nothing like it in the world. I choose here to look at Israel as a way of looking at the topic of smallness and power, nationness and the semi-veiled expectations of smallness in today's "nation-state" system, and even at some of the ways sovereignty is invoked, undermined, defied, critiqued, and asserted. Putting it in sharp relief, I ask whether Israel is just a chutzpah country that periodically gets more attention than others, or a chutzpah country whose hypervisibility is regular, expected, and in need of explanation, or even an extreme subcategory of chutzpah countries, revealing the limits of possibility in the contemporary geopolitical world.

To make it crystal clear, the issue is not about Israel as a poor country, an unclean country, or an unhealthy country, the epithet "shitty" in the offending phrase notwithstanding. It is quite clear that "shitty little country Israel" does not refer to poverty, underdevelopment, poor infrastructure, or bad hygiene. The country's statistics tell a different story. The phrase instead exudes criticism, even disgust, and implies moral failure. As a form of name-calling, it resembles others known in social, cultural, and linguistic anthropology—from witchcraft accusations to hate speech (Beidelman 1964; Evans-Pritchard 1937; Favret-Saada 1981; Green and Mesaki 2005). As a speech event, it is more performative than descriptive, to borrow a distinction familiar from the writings of Michael Silverstein (e.g., 1976). As I aim to show, the force of criticism is more important than the veracity of the claim. What does it mean for Israel to be (at least in that social field that keeps it viable) that "shitty little country Israel" and not just a chutzpah country?

Something is afoot here. I spent months looking for print or online references since the original incident to "that shitty little country," "shitty little country," and "shitty little countries," and I have found little evidence of people around the world using the phrase (or even a variant of it like "crappy little country") to refer to other countries of its relative size—or even dozens of countries smaller than Israel in population or territorial size. Something else is clearly in play, and the social life of its terminology is worth considering in light of this volume's focus on "small countries," and even my identification of certain of them as "chutzpah countries."

The Incident and Its History

"That shitty little country Israel." The phrase has an origin and a provocative social life. In a 1986 U.S. movie (*Iron Eagle*), one of the characters called an unnamed Middle Eastern country, holding the main protagonist's father captive, a "shitty little country." The imagined country could have been any one of at least a dozen. I doubt the filmmakers intended it to be Israel, yet the phrase has become tied to Israel. Credit goes to Daniel Bernard, then French ambassador to the United Kingdom, who used the phrase in December 2001 at a private dinner party in England hosted by the publisher of the *Daily Telegraph*, Lord Conrad Black. Barbara Amiel, Black's wife, clearly offended by the phrase, later quoted (indeed exposed) Ambassador Bernard in that paper. After first denying the allegation, Ambassador Bernard subsequently sent the following letter to the *Daily Telegraph*:

> Over the past few days, I have been the subject of grave accusations because of a comment I am reported to have made during a conversation with Lord Black. The facts are: while we were discussing the Israeli-Palestinian issue, I pointed out to Lord Black that this tragedy was taking place in a geographically limited area (I even specified that it was the equivalent of three French departments) that for 40 years had been suffering from a conflict whose equitable solution seems more out of reach than ever. Of course, I never meant to insult Israel or any other part of that region. The deliberately biased presentation of this conversation in some circles, accompanied by malicious accusations, is deeply shocking and insulting.

Media attention was quick in England, France, Israel, and cyberspace. A BBC story discussed the incident under the heading "'Anti-Semitic' French envoy under fire." Reports appeared in traditional print and online media. The ambassador's spokesman tried to defend him, the French government tried to diffuse the situation, and the Israeli government criticized his words as evidence of anti-Semitism. But it is the social life of his words in cyberspace, and the life the phrase has continued to have, that are worth pondering. A great deal of the initial reaction to Bernard's statement named anti-Semitism as the real story behind his words, or challenged that framing of it. What was presumably shitty about Israel appears frequently to have been assumed, not discussed explicitly.

Of interest to me here is that the issue was not this French ambassador's reference to Israel as a "little country" that captured the limelight but his reference to Israel as "that shitty little country." Ariel Sharon, long known as a right-wing military man and politician, was prime minister of Israel at the time, and this incident took place just three months after the tragedy of 9/11. But it would be a mistake to see the incident as strictly tied to its historical moment (Dominguez 1989). When a high-level diplomat from a major European country calls Israel "that shitty little country," the incident becomes a lightning rod for something deeper.

Consider some of the immediate reporting. An entry in Wikipedia (retrieved 24 January 2012) on Ambassador Bernard is nearly all about this December 2001 incident and public reactions to it. Drawing on several sources—from the *Guardian* to the *Daily Telegraph* and the *Irish Examiner*—it details that reaction as follows:

> The British press saw a firestorm as a result, as comment on the 23 December 2001 in the Daily Telegraph exemplifies. One British journalist, Deborah Orr, did defend Bernard.
>
> British Labour MPs Jim Murphy and Gwyneth Dunwoody wrote to French president Jacques Chirac asking that Bernard either resign or be removed from his position. . . .
>
> In Israel, the remark sparked outrage, with Raanan Gissin, spokesman for Israeli Prime Minister Ariel Sharon, calling Bernard's statement "a pure anti-Semitic expression" and further stating that the French government "should draw the conclusions of a senior representative of a nation making an anti-Semitic remark." Gissin also stated that "If the French government does not take action, it would imply that the French government condones it and I think that would be inconceivable."
>
> In the United States, the Anti-Defamation League stated that "It is highly troubling that a French government official would make such crude anti-Israel statements" [ADL 2001]. . . .
>
> The French Foreign Ministry . . . dismissed the charges of anti-Semitism. A Ministry spokesman stated that "These malevolent insinuations have been addressed very clearly by our ambassador in London and I suggest you refer back to that."
>
> The French press was also largely supportive of Bernard, while recognizing that he was a flamboyant character (*Le Monde* 2 May 2004). His obituary in *Le Monde* in 2004 [Vernet 2004] also illustrates the same points.

These reactions range from categorical defense of the accused country to humor, agreement, disgust, pride, and outright dismissal, with the former much more typical of defenders outside the accused country than within it. One hypothesis worth contemplating is that Israel is just a very visible "chutzpah country." Israel certainly qualifies as a "chutzpah country." The problem is that a number of other countries in the late twentieth and early twenty-first centuries do, too—Cuba, Libya, Venezuela, North Korea, Syria—and some of these qualify as small countries. Moreover, while I anticipated seeing people since December 2001 borrowing the phrase to refer to some of these countries, little of that is in evidence. Indeed the Bernard incident, its handling outside Israel, and the relative nonextension of the phrase "shitty little country" all seem to exceptionalize Israel in noteworthy ways.

As I will try to show, there is a moral denigration or even disgust that seeps through in references to Israel as "that shitty little country." Its quality as a form of name-calling is worth examining. The anthropological literature has ample examples of other forms of name-calling—some of it more clearly indexical (even nonreferential) and some of it more open, literal, and arguably referential, but all clearly performative. This includes what in the United States is being called "hate speech" but also accusations of use of "hate speech"—not unlike witchcraft accusations and their critique. Critique, even moral ridicule or at least denigration, dominates each of these forms of speech in their contexts. There is little subtlety in the message sent. Someone is hailed, named, and identified as deficient in each case.

Likewise, "that shitty little country Israel" simultaneously performs and enacts an Us/Them mentality that indexes something other than poverty or prosperity, absolute population size, or even spatial density. Interestingly, it is not its perceived Otherness that enables and arouses name-calling, but rather Israel's perceived kinship with North Atlantic countries presenting themselves as "Western democracies." One could argue that the perception of kinship with North Atlantic countries (Western European countries, the United States, and Canada) is stronger in Israel than in those countries, but there is also ample evidence of European complicity with such a picture—from long-standing European inclusion of Israel in its annual Eurovision Song Contest to its inclusion of Israeli teams in European leagues. Hence, I lean toward the argument that it is Israel's perceived (but problematic) Westernness, and its parliamentary system and rhetoric as a Western-style democracy that fuel both the graphic name-calling and the range of reactions among those taking sides.

More provocatively, I sustain that the name-calling points to continued undercurrents of tacit imperialism and colonialism found in the North Atlantic even at the start of the twenty-first century, understandings peppered with both anti-Semitism and Orientalism. I do not say this lightly, nor has it been my first, second, or third hypothesis. I have contemplated specific aspects of Israel that could be factors, including Israel being a state with a neighboring or domestic population with which it is often at war or quasi-war. But even this unflattering characterization would not explain its widespread discursive exceptionalization. Countries like Serbia, Rwanda, Zimbabwe, Syria, Sierra Leone, Yemen, or Libya would all seem easy targets for related discursive accusations, yet my research has not yielded evidence of any such extension. Likewise, I have contemplated countries that nearly all U.S. governments have considered enemy countries, including Cuba, Venezuela, North Korea, Grenada (under Eric Gairy), Syria, and Libya, but they, too, largely seem exempted. The graphic and intensely negative picture depicted in the phrase "that shitty little country" seems primarily reserved for Israel.

Relativity—Size, Territory, Population, and Their Invocation

Clearly the idea that "small" is relative is a useful starting point for our analysis here. But it risks missing much of the work it takes to sustain the ontology of smallness and its utility for social, cultural, economic, military, and intergovernmental purposes. It is not just that a country may be small relative to another, but rather that X calls Y a small country and Y may or may not agree with that conception of itself (see also Dominguez 2012). In all cases, the invocation, dubbing, and declaring are crucial aspects of the meaningfulness of "smallness" and demand attention as politically mediating speech acts.

Consider this from a different angle. At present the United Nations consists of 193 member states. As of June 2016, only thirteen have populations exceeding one hundred million, and two-thirds are arguably within our volume's categorization of "small countries." By the standards of the small number of megacountries, nearly all the countries in the world are small countries. So, key questions are: When and under what conditions is "small-ness" proclaimed, including by whom, and toward what end? Who is the audience for the proclamation? And how is the ontology of smallness sustained? I think it worth extending this to ask whether smallness is proclaimed in order to reduce anxiety about another country, diminish the expectation that a perceived enemy is dangerous, infantilize the country or patronize it with praise while seeking to extract long-term, consistent allegiance and co-operation.

This may be especially the case with what I have dubbed "chutzpah countries." I have often been struck by the discursively normalized practice in the United States of describing Cuba as small (especially in the Castro years, 1959 to the present) while treating it for decades as its main rival in the Western Hemisphere—continuously counting U.S. medals vis-à-vis Cuba's medals in the Pan American Games, and implying that the success of the United States is to be measured relative to Cuban teams' wins and losses. But when two populations are that different in size (eleven million versus three hundred million), the idea that the larger one (indeed a giant one) has something to gain by beating the smaller one calls attention to itself. If Cuba is a "small country" and the United States a "big country," is the United States not setting itself up for embarrassment if it does not whop Cuba in the Pan Am Games? What does the United States gain by first conceptualizing Cuba as small? One answer is that for years the United States was really comment-ing on the Soviet Union, its system for training and supporting athletes, and its use of the military in dubbing athletes amateurs—and seeing Cuba as a Soviet satellite. Another related answer was that the competitive accounting really entailed measuring capitalism against Communism, proving that U.S.-style capitalism always prevailed in the end. Calling Cuba small but implying that it was a threat to the United States made little sense without this larger context.

Parallels also exist in the military arena, not just in the colonial era. First, the U.S. military invaded the Caribbean country of Grenada in the early 1980s, and then it gloated about its speed and efficiency. Not long thereafter, it invaded Panama and proceeded to gloat about that. Both Grenada and Panama are significantly smaller in land mass and population size than Cuba, and yet gloating over the defeat of the incomparably smaller country has been a factor in all three cases. Clearly then it is not the success the United States has with these countries that is noteworthy but, rather, the gloating. When the country conquered is that much smaller than the mega-country, it would make more geopolitical sense for the United States to downplay the size differential and background the enormous difference in population size. Clearly something else is the key message, and some audience (domestic or foreign) is discursively being targeted.

Something then about the performativity of dubbing some countries as small becomes clearer when exploring the "shitty little country" incident and its continuing legs—for most countries may, under certain circumstances, be dubbed "small" but not "shitty and small" like Israel was at the end of 2001. More countries are de facto in the shitty category, though are not called that. It is not their size that gets highlighted in that grouping. Rather, it is their alleged immorality vis-à-vis the overwhelming majority of the world's countries, at least in the eyes of the accusers.

But the whole name-calling incident that made "that shitty little country Israel" a noted phrase over the past decade combines an ontology of size with an ontology of anger/annoyance/immorality. Our question ought to be not only whether Israel deserved it, what it referred to, and how Israelis responded to it, but also whether the name-calling illuminates an underlying set of ideas about nations and latent imperialism, hidden discursively behind seemingly objective concepts of size.

While I believe that underlying ideas about countries and a kind of Pax Americana cause this eruption of name-calling, a comparison between Israel and Cuba is also revealing in that the term "shitty little country" has not been extended to Cuba. In my eyes, both are "chutzpah countries," thorns in the side of bigger countries that helped establish them, although both have long functioned as dependent states (of one or another megastate).

So I ask myself what the invocation of size might really index. High on my list of suspicions is that the issue is the perceived violation on the part of the smaller country of something best described as dependent status. I have considered other possibilities, including the explicit or implied accusation of human rights violations, and the two-way nature of that discourse; potential domestic uses of references to better standards of living at home rather than abroad; relative hierarchies of racism or oppression (within or vis-à-vis the accused country); and, in narrower terms, a smaller country's government's tendencies not to collaborate with (or at least always agree to) the bigger country's demands. But relative smallness coupled with dependent status and behavior that defies that dependent status may play the biggest role in invocations of size in the case of both Israel and Cuba. And yet we need to ask why more countries are not dubbed "shitty little countries," at least publicly. Could it be that they are not powerful enough to deserve the label—or not European enough, not independent enough, not cohesive enough, not prosperous enough?

An exhaustive search of online sources of many types has helped me locate many contributions to the debate about Israel as "that shitty little country." But again, an equally diligent search has resulted in very few examples of the phrase being applied to other countries. There are some telling exceptions: the recent accusation (especially by Lithuania) that Austria is "a shitty little country," a 2011 reference in a blog post about Cuba as a "shitty little country," and a Canadian critique of Canadian nationalist discourse in 2008, with reference to Togo and Olympic medals (Kavkaz Center 2011; Devil's Excrement 2011; Crowe 2008).

Israel and Cuba: Chutzpah Countries Compared

Arjun Appadurai's *Fear of Small Numbers* (2006), subtitled *An Essay on the Geography of Anger*, bears reflection. While most of Appadurai's text concerns minorities—both "substantive minorities" and "procedural minorities"—and seeks to understand violence to these populations within several countries, some of his thinking about smallness may apply here. There is the matter of fear—fear by a self-labeled "majority" toward smaller populations that do not conform to the presumed majority's vision, expectations, or worldview. Appadurai (2006: 53) writes that "small numbers represent a tiny obstacle between majority and totality or total purity . . . in a sense, the smaller the number and the weaker the minority, the deeper the rage about its capacity to make a majority feel like a mere majority rather than like a whole and uncontested ethnos." Might there be a parallel that applies to the whole world and its many countries rather than to majorities and minorities within a given country? And might the fear of at least some small countries not backfire, perhaps by stimulating the accused countries' can-do sense of itself, a form of national pride (despite internal debates)? Later in his chapter on fear of small countries, Appadurai adds that "more broadly, small numbers always carry the possibility of what in the liberal vernacular of the United States are called 'special interests' and thus pose threats to some idea of the 'general interest'" (Appadurai 2006: 62).

What if that logic were to apply as well to countries, and not just sectors of the United States, for example? And what if "general interest" were to mean general interest as interpreted by the megacountry (in this case, the United States) and "special interest" were the megacountry's framing of ideologies, values, and actions on the part of the "small country"? It would seem that without the framing of a country as "small" it would be harder to equate such a country with a "special interest" group at home and, therefore, hard to evoke fear of its apparent unwillingness to just accept "majoritarian rule."

Israel arguably looks ill-fitting as a "small country," especially if the expectation is that a "small country" is at the same time small and less developed, if not downright poor and in need of special privileges, and perhaps especially if it is framed as "other." Note all of the following:

1. Israel has a reasonably large European-origin population and educated elites (though perception of the proportion of the European-origin population is often wrong).
2. Israel has large European-origin and educated diasporic communities, traveling populations both old and new, largely rooted in other countries.
3. Israel arguably consists of many prodigal sons (and daughters)—since the majority of Israeli Jews in leading political, intellectual, cultural, and legal circles have long been those with close family ties to European countries, so even if their relative numbers make them a numerical minority in Israel, there are enough of them to warrant being seen as somehow European expatriates.
4. Israel was never really a colony of a North Atlantic power, but has come close (through its dependence on foreign aid from the United States), and it did experience quasi-colonial status: the British Mandate over Palestine is central in all stories of the emergence of Israel in 1947–1948.
5. Israel has long-standing public and private discourses sustaining the view that its citizens are clever (Katriel 1986).
6. Israel also has a strong sense of being like many European countries— in playing roles on the larger world scene (vis-à-vis Iran, South Africa, the United States, the Soviet Union, Western Europe, and Eastern Europe). Paralleling this is Israel's sense of itself as a Western democracy, a persistent self-reference since its founding.

7. Israel plays off bigger powers and has for decades (the United
States and the Soviet Union; the United States and the European
powers).

Despite all this—while ironically related to it—talk of smallness pops up
at times, repeating long-standing rhetoric, or indexing strategic geomilitary
issues. Good examples of this are references to how narrow Israel is and
therefore how vulnerable. Invocation of the few kilometers between the
Mediterranean and the West Bank often functions to stress the need for a
high wall keeping West Bankers out of Israel (Markowitz 2013).

Consider some of the talk surrounding the "shitty little country Israel"
incident. Angst, domestic anxiety, morality, anger, and dissent are all loud
and clear. Tel Aviv University psychology professor Carlo Strenger (2007),
wrote the following in *Haaretz* (Israel's leading, high-brow, largely liberal
newspaper), in a column titled "On the Way to a Pariah State":

> Israel's way of dealing with the Palestinians and Lebanon in the
> last few decades has led to a long-term process in which the Western
> world is beginning to see Israel as a pariah state that has no true af-
> finity to Western values. Hence, it is not on the "right" side of the
> clash of civilizations, as was reflected in the French ambassador to
> Britain calling Israel "that shitty little country" not long ago.
>
> This development is consistently disregarded by Israeli decision
> makers. Short-term political bickering is on their minds more than
> the survival of Israel, which in theory is their main goal. Any criti-
> cism of Israel's policies is dismissed as an expression of the New Anti-
> Semitism. The proof often provided is that we are not judged by the
> same standard as our neighbors: "Jordan, Syria, Iraq and Saudi
> Arabia can get away with inhuman behavior a lot worse than ours,"
> the argument runs.
>
> My point is simple: the day we are no longer judged by the stan-
> dards of the West is the beginning of Israel's end, because it means
> that the West has decided we are no longer part of it, and hence will
> not be committed to Israel's existence. . . .
>
> . . . Morally and strategically, the continued occupation and sub-
> jugation of the Palestinian people has put us on the wrong side of
> history.

Before that, a few weeks after the 11 September 2001 events in the United States, the Hebrew-language radio station Kol Yisrael reported that an acrimonious argument erupted, during the Israeli cabinet weekly session, between Israeli prime minister Ariel Sharon and his foreign minister Shimon Peres. Peres warned Sharon that refusing to heed incessant American requests for a cease-fire with the Palestinians would endanger Israeli interests and "turn the U.S. against us." According to a critic, Sharon reportedly yelled at Peres, saying "don't worry about American pressure, we, the Jewish people, control America."[1]

Note that "smallness" is selectively and strategically invoked and that it is either denied or at least downplayed by others. Note as well that a primary relationship with at least one megacountry (or quasi-country like the European Union) looms large in the framing of Israel as small, where the affective element (patriotism or at least caring for the nation) becomes central. For Israel it is clear that its relationship with Europe is at stake, or more broadly its relationship with "the West." Israel does not want to see itself as Other to "the West" and has undertaken many policies over the years to affirm its ties to it—from those determining immigration to those concerning educational institutions, popular culture, and even sports. Despite the Middle Eastern and North African countries of origin of large numbers of Jews in Israel (and the presence of more than a million Arabs within Israel's 1967 borders), Israel's cultural policies, institutions, practices, and educational priorities have long favored "the West" and have consistently promoted values seen as coming from "Western democracies" (Dominguez 1989). And yet it is really only Israel that keeps getting invoked as "that shitty little country."

Consider Cuba once more, a country geographically very close to the United States, seen by all U.S. governments as a thorn in its side since Fidel Castro toppled the right-wing, pro-U.S. military dictatorship of General Batista in 1959. If there is one country that might be a good candidate for "shitty little country" talk (at least in the United States), it is post-1958 Cuba. But very little has surfaced drawing on that colorful phrase. One insightful commentary appearing in the online *Cuba Journal* asks if Cuba really is a small country (Schlachter 2006). It cites some geographical and demographic facts, but does so to call into question the perception of smallness. "There are 89 other nations," it says, "that occupy a smaller area than the Caribbean island." So why, then, has Cuba traditionally been referred to as a small—almost tiny—country? The suggested answer is that it involves geopolitics and has a long history: first with Spain as the seat of Spanish imperial power and, more recently, with the United States.

This text questions the idea that Cuba is small, but it contains little reference to anxiety, morality, anger, or even competitiveness. It is indeed meant to get readers to wonder why anyone thinks of Cuba as small—and more precisely, who does. And it alludes to the idea that Cubans may or may not think of their country as small.

Consider the Israel-Cuba comparison differently. It is not likely to be the most obvious to readers, because we tend to place countries within geographical regions or as parts of former empires, and assume that those are logical comparisons. However, a different logic applies if we consider both "chutzpah countries." Both countries report very high literacy rates and very high rates of physicians per capita. Both report very low infant mortality rates and high to very high health and education expenditures. In a number of these and other socioeconomic statistics, one or both countries have better statistics than many European countries associated with prosperity, wealth, or high standards of living, like Austria, Finland, and England.

Cuba and Israel both have large militaries and employ them for defense as well as to advance national policies and causes. Both have film industries, serious universities, large tourist sectors attracting foreign vacationers, and both admirers and critics (often intensely one or the other) around the world. Cuba is, of course, not a democracy in the U.S. and Western European sense of the word, while Israel is. And, yet, only Israel among these chutzpah countries gets labeled "that shitty little country."

Why? My conclusion is that ambassador Bernard's comment in London in 2001 hit a nerve in Israel, and among supporters of Zionist Israel outside Israel, because the relationship of (largely) Jewish Israel to the largely Christian European continent remains fragile, even more than sixty-five years after World War II and the exposing of Hitler's genocide of millions of Jews. Moreover, "moral outrage" is always a possibility on the Israeli side vis-à-vis Nazi Germany and its collaborators. In that sense, "shitty little country Israel" was and is a part of a discursive, moral, political, and affective field of continued mutual suspicion, lack of trust, and dissatisfaction with "the Other." The subtext remains human rights violations affecting millions of people. In this sense, then, "shitty little country Israel" may largely be a European corollary—perhaps more a Western European corollary—entailing response and reciprocal accusation to Israeli charges of anti-Semitism in Europe. It would thus be something not generalizable even to Cuba or Serbia, Rwanda, Libya, Syria, or Zimbabwe. They may be small (in space and/or population) and arouse the ire of at least some larger, prosperous, and self-labeled Western countries, but they do not by their very existence keep the discourse of anti-Semitism on the table.

A Troubling Look at Mutuality?

So any account of small countries needs to take into account not just size, absolute or relative, but also specific histories and mutual forms of othering, selving, framing, and distancing. Moreover, it needs to take into account the social field of accusations, the basis of those accusations, and the work to sustain often-competing visions of morality. I have argued here that the incident involving Ambassador Bernard made sense in light of the long-standing but fraught relationship between Israel and much of Europe, from the perspective of Israel and its defenders, but also clearly from the perspective of its detractors. Israel's smallness mattered, but mostly because its visibility and impact in much of the world greatly exceeds its size, or even the size of its population. Central was a perceived mismatch between size and power, size and its assertion of sovereignty and independence, contrary to expectations and the implicit rules of the contemporary geopolitical world. Putting it in sharp relief, it is clear that Israel indeed operates as a chutzpah country, that even as a chutzpah country it periodically gets more attention than others, and that it is a chutzpah country whose hypervisibility is regular, expected, and in need of explanation—an explanation deeply rooted in its originary Europeanness. It is not clear that it is exceptional in the world, even if and when generalized rhetoric sustains such a vision, whether through mundane accusations or vividly palpable, colorful imagery that reeks of offense and calls attention to itself.

Note

1. A critic's comment shortly before the incident but contextualizing part of the discursive, political, and affective atmosphere within which the name-calling ("that

shitty little country Israel") occurred; it suggests, or implies, how and why Israel is different, thinks of itself as different, and is seen as different by others (Khodr 2001).

References

ADL (Anti-Defamation League). 2001. Letter to the Foreign Minister of France, 21 December. http://archive.adl.org/israel/letter_france.asp.

Appadurai, Arjun. 2006. *Fear of Small Numbers: An Essay on the Geography of Anger.* Durham, N.C.: Duke University Press.

BBC. 2001. "Anti-Semitic" French Envoy Under Fire. *BBC News* [online], 20 December.

Beidelman, T. O. 1964. Intertribal Insult and Approbrium in an East African Chiefdom (Ukaguru). *Anthropological Quarterly* 37 (2): 33–52.

Bernard, Daniel. 2001. Comments on Israel "Distorted." *Daily Telegraph* [online], 22 December.

Crowe, Jonathan. 2008. In Defence of Shitty Little Countries. *DFL*, 14 August. http://www.mcwetboy.net/dfl/2008/08/in-defence-of-shitty-little-countries.html.

Devil's Excrement. 2011. Deputy Ramos Teams Up with Alek Boyd to Ask Some Tough Questions. *Devil's Excrement* (blog), 29 October. http://devilsexcrement .com/2011/10/29/deputy-ramos-teams-up-with-alek-boyd-to-ask-some-tough -questions/.

Dominguez, Virginia R. 1989. *People as Subject, People as Object: Selfhood and Peoplehood in Contemporary Israel.* Madison: University of Wisconsin Press.

———. 1995. Invoking Racism in the Public Sphere: Two Takes on National Self-Criticism. *Identities: Global Studies in Culture and Power* 1 (4): 325–46.

———. 2012. Are There Umpires and Quasi-Umpires Outside the Baseball Field: Claiming and Asserting Social Identities in U.S. Society. In Benczik Vera, Frank Tibor, and Geiger Ildikó, eds., *Tanulmányok Bollobás Enikő 60*, 37–52. Budapest: ELTE School of English and American Studies.

———. 2013. Falling in Love with a Criminal? On Immersion and Self-Restraint. In Fran Markowitz, ed., *Ethnographic Encounters in Israel: The Poetics and Ethics of Fieldwork.* Bloomington: Indiana University Press.

Evans-Pritchard, E. E. 1937. *Witchcraft, Oracles, and Magic Among the Azande.* Oxford: Clarendon Press.

Favret-Saada, Jeanne. 1981. *Deadly Words: Witchcraft in the Bocage.* Cambridge: Cambridge University Press.

Green, Maia, and Simeon Mesaki. 2005. The Birth of the "Salon": Poverty, "Modernization," and Dealing with Witchcraft in Southern Tanzania. *American Ethnologist* 32 (3): 371–88.

Katriel, Tamar. 1986. *Talking Straight: Dugri Speech in Israeli Sabra Culture.* Cambridge: Cambridge University Press.

Kavkaz Center. 2011. Shitty Little Country Austria Licks Boots of Russians—Aggressive and Armed Enemies of Civilization. Kavkazcenter.com, 17 July. http://kavkazcenter .com/eng/content/2011/07/17/14754.shtml.

Khodr, Mohamed. 2001. Sharon to Peres: "We Control America." *Media Monitors Network*, 20 November. http://www.mediamonitors.net/khodr49.html.

Kimmerling, Baruch. 2005. *The Invention and Decline of Israeliness: State, Society, and the Military.* Berkeley: University of California Press.

Markowitz, Fran, ed. 2013. *Ethnographic Encounters in Israel: The Poetics and Ethics of Fieldwork.* Bloomington: Indiana University Press.

Schlachter, Alexis. 2006. Is Cuba Really a Small Country? *Cuba Journal*, 23 March. http://cubajournal.blogspot.co.at/2006/03/is-cuba-really-small-country.html.

Silverstein, Michael. 1976. Shifters, Linguistic Categories, and Cultural Description. In Keith Basso and Henry Selby, eds., *Meaning in Anthropology.* Albuquerque: University of New Mexico Press.

Strenger, Carlo. 2007. On the Way to a Pariah State. *Haaretz* [online], 25 September.

Vernet, Daniel. 2004. Obituary of Ambassador Daniel Bernard. *Le Monde*, accessed 2 May 2015 at http://www.lemonde.fr/cgibin/ACHATS/acheter.cgi?offre=ARCHIVES&type _item=ART_ARCH_30J&objet_id=851903&xtmc=daniel_bernard&xtcr=29.

Wikipedia. Entry on Ambassador Daniel Bernard. Accessed 24 January 2012 at https://en .wikipedia.org/wiki/Daniel_Bernard_(diplomat).

PART III

Being and Becoming Small

CHAPTER 7

Portugal and the Dynamics of Smallness

João de Pina-Cabral

"Portugal is not a small country." In Portugal, the poster map (Figure 1), where the country's colonial possessions at mid-twentieth century are superimposed in red upon the map of Europe, continues to have a *succès de scandale*—one of the most famous instances of the kind of vacuous imperial bravado that my generation of left-leaning anticolonialists so deplored (Vale de Almeida 2004; Sanches 2006). The map was conceived and produced in the mid-1930s by one of the more extraordinary figures of the period: Henrique Galvão was the most inspired propagandist of the early fascist regime and of Portugal's African empire. At the time, he was the founder and first director of the National Radio Agency and a very widely read writer of colonialist novels focusing on daring tales of hunting deeds. He was the organizer of the first colonial exhibition in Oporto in 1934 and was deeply involved in the organization of the important Exhibition of the Portuguese World of 1940 (see Pina-Cabral 2001).

What *was* going through his head when he produced this map? Formally, he was validating António de Oliveira Salazar's constitutional claim that the colonies were an integral part of Portugal just like the Atlantic islands or the European metropolis, as it was then called. But can it be as simple as that? Surely not. The very caption of the map makes it clear that doubts do legitimately arise; that he needed to counter some kind of assumed smallness.

Yet the ambiguities do not stop there. Considering that Galvão always had deep personal links with Brazil, one wonders why the Latin American giant is not part of the map (staining in red all of Russia . . .). At the time, he would probably respond that Brazil was no longer part of Portugal like

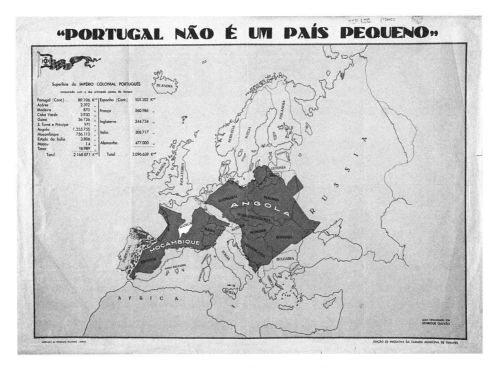

Figure 1. "Portugal is not a small country." Henrique Galvão, ca. 1935. Câmara Municipal de Peniche.

Mozambique and Angola. But that answer would always leave out the fact that, when Salazar finally put him in prison in the early 1950s, that is where he escaped to. At the end of World War II, he became one of the best-known critics of the dictator, after they fell out due to his outspoken reports as a member of the National Assembly representing Angola. He famously denounced the horrors of forced labor in the African colonies (Galvão 1975).

Subsequently he became one of the first international terrorists who manipulated the media for political purposes, with the televised hijacking of the luxury liner *Santa Maria* in 1961. Galvão's media-oriented operation (involving taking over the liner mid-Atlantic and handing it over to the Brazilian authorities, without any risk to the life of the passengers) was a political call for the plight of the people in Africa and in Portugal who were suffering under the yoke of the dictatorship. Galvão was even invited to speak at the United Nations against Portugal's fascist and colonialist regime in the late 1960s.

Yet he was to die in 1970 as a lonely and deranged old man in a public asylum in Rio de Janeiro—a fitting end for someone whose life was always lived as a romantic tale, from the days of his youth as one of the military cadets that organized the failed putsch of the dictator Sidónio Pais in the early 1920s.

The least that can be said is that Henrique Galvão must have had a flicker of laughter in his eye as he produced his patently mischievous map. One thing is certain—and the survival of the map to this day suggests just that— he was pointing his finger at an important issue. He was sapping a significant ideological vein: Portugal's recurrent confrontation with a problem of national feasibility.

The assessment of the smallness of a country does not depend only on what counts as a country but also on how one conceives the encompassing political order at a specific historical moment. Witness the recent debates as to whether Catalonia and Scotland do or do not count as nations. Furthermore, the relevant smallness is not that conceived by the external analyst, but that which is part of the assessment of their own condition by the politically active members of that country. Smallness, therefore, is the outcome of a judgment of viability within a dynamic process of acquisition of the means to political and cultural autonomy.

But even that autonomy cannot simply be assumed. Today, we automatically interpret "country" to mean "an independent nation-state," but that interpretation is in some ways deeply misleading. The notion of the world as an international field is a fiction that never allowed for the actual complexity of the processes of enchainment that historically produce the world as a political field. Independence is hardly a simple thing as the case of the European Union or the British Commonwealth amply validate. To give another example: in the 1820s, was it Brazil that became independent from Portugal, or Portugal that became independent from Brazil? After all, the capital of the kingdom was in Rio de Janeiro at the time. The senior branch of the royal family is that of the emperors of Brazil, not that of the subsequent kings of Portugal. Over most of its nine centuries of existence as a political entity, and even though its European borders are probably the oldest in the continent (having been broadly established in 1249), Portugal cannot be said to be territorially closed in any way.

There are two senses in which this is the case, and they correspond to the two axes of ecumenic proximity (Figure 2; cf. Mintz 1996) that continue to play a role today in the political condition of this country/nation/state/ people . . . well, let us leave that undecided for the moment (Pina-Cabral and

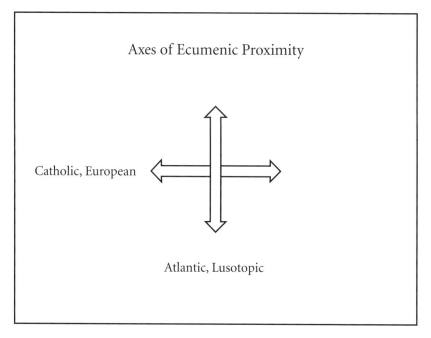

Figure 2. Axes of ecumenic proximity: European/Catholic versus Atlantic/ Lusotopic.

Feijó 2002). The *first axis* is clearly the insertion in Europe's Catholic world, represented by the allegiance to the pope. One of the most bitterly debated questions, leading to a series of revolts and revolutions at the beginning of the twentieth century, was precisely that one. Can Portugal be conceived at all as a lay state along the liberal logic of separation between church and state? If so, can it continue to be itself without the association to the Catholic Church? The so-called Integralists adopted that name precisely because they claimed that the nation's integrity was being wrenched apart by the instituting of a lay state. Those who attempted to restore the monarchy in the north with Henrique Paiva Couceiro in 1911 had at the top of their list of demands the ending of the civil registry of births, claiming that Catholic baptism should be the only source of civic existence (see Pulido Valente 2006). It was as a response to the unresolved nature of that debate between Republicans and Integralists that the following generation turned as a compromise to the church-inspired republican totalitarianism governing Portugal up to 1974.

In fact, this allegiance to the Catholic Church as a politically relevant entity must not be seen as unidirectional. From roughly 1460 to roughly 1911, the Portuguese Crown was entrusted by the pope with overlooking the well-being of the church in its territories, including the management of church property and the appointment of bishops and priests—the famous Padroado Português (see Neto 1993: 265–83). This sense of interpenetration has deep political implications not only in the way in which this royal authority shaped the social and religious institutions of the various lands ruled by the Portuguese Crown, but also in the way they created allegiances that went well beyond the boundaries of anything that can be considered today a "country," a "state," or even an "empire."

Two very distinct examples will suffice to clarify this. The first is how the Monomotapa kings based at the Great Zimbabwe, in what is today the eponymous country, had a personal guard of around four hundred Portuguese soldiers for about a hundred years, from the mid-sixteenth century to the mid-seventeenth, and were ultimately "converted" to Catholicism by members of this guard. Yet these men are more aptly called Catholics than Portuguese. Most of them belonged to the mixed populations that arose throughout the Indian Ocean at the time, and whose links to European Portugal were never too certain (see Axelson 1973).

The second example of this is my own personal discovery, when studying the Eurasian population of Macau in the 1990s, that its notion of collective identity in an ethnically divided city could in no way be described simply as Portugueseness. In fact, it constituted a compound of three factors that counted in equal terms as both differentiating and identifying features: (1) some form of mixed phenotype; (2) some sort of connectedness to the Portuguese language or culture; (3) some kind of allegiance to Catholicism (even if merely formal; see Pina-Cabral 2002b).

But there is a *second axis* of ecumenic proximity that crosses the European, Catholic axis. It is constituted by the links formed across the Atlantic through a sense of shared cultural past, which I have elsewhere called Lusotopy, claiming that it forms an ecumene in the sense that Ulf Hannerz (1992) and Sidney Mintz (1996) have given to the word. As a political entity, Portugal was launched in the early twelfth century by the crusader movement in a process of political expansion of the Catholic Church—the so-called *Reconquista*. From the beginning, it found itself territorially enclosed by the growing presence on its back of Léon and Castille as a political entity. However, its location facing the sea provided it with considerable assets. At first, its feasibility was ensured by its strategic position on the commercial and military sea route from the North Sea to the Mediterranean. After the fifteenth century, when the technological means for offshore sailing became available, this set the country on its way to territorial expansion through conquest (see Pina-Cabral and Feijó 2002).

From this perspective, the expansive nature of Portugal's smallness makes for a very different kind of smallness from that, for example, of Switzerland. It casts the trope of smallness into a dynamic mode more akin to that of naval potentates like ancient Athens, Holland, or England. That is probably why the Portuguese continue to look at Galvão's map with a kind of bemused surprise. It points to a form of collective existence that is belied by the hegemonic notions of "country," of "nation-state," of "state," or even the notion that the world's order is represented graphically in New York in the General Assembly of the United Nations.

Allow me to refer here to a verse in a song by a very popular Oporto rock star, Rui Veloso (the words are by Carlos Tê). When I first heard it on my car radio I could hardly believe how true it was, but I trust it was written in that tone of self-deriding humor that the Portuguese so readily engage upon, but that they so resent when enacted by foreigners. I have tried it out on a number of friends and acquaintances, and they invariably responded with a smile. My own belief is that—like most jokes—what makes this one work is that it states something that is both obviously untrue and yet, somehow, inescapable.

The verse goes: "Portugal é Guimarães, tudo o resto são conquistas"— literally, "Portugal is Guimarães, all the rest is conquered land." Guimarães is the small town where the Count of Portucallem, a vassal of the king of León, had his seat in the early twelfth century (see Mattoso 1993: 11–21). In short, Portugal was originally constituted as a movement of conquest southward on the part of a military elite. What the song implies is that, the original seat being insignificant, the dynamic of outward conquest and subsequent retreat is all there is to Portugal.

In the course of the tenth century, the small Christian kingdoms of the north of the Peninsula started pushing southward across lands that had been in disputed Muslim control for around three centuries since the fall of the Visigoth Empire (the area is still called "Beira," etymologically meaning border, even though today it is in the middle of the country—see Pina-Cabral 1989). This southward conquest was achieved with the help of groups of crusaders coming from the North Sea, sailing round the Peninsula in order to reach the Holy Land. With them came the North Sea merchants that contributed to the wealth of Portucallem (today's city of Oporto), whose name the country eventually adopted.

From 1139 onward, as his land increased, the count conceived of becoming politically autonomous and assumed the title of king. In 1147, with the help of crusaders coming from Dartmouth in England, he finally managed to conquer Lisbon—the only large natural port on the western coast of Iberia. By 1179, Pope Alexander III recognized him as king of Portugal, finally freeing him of vassalage to the king of León, later of León and Castille.

Roughly one century later, in 1249, his descendants had conquered all the land to the south of his original possessions, and the country's present frontiers were finally established. As Portugal expanded to the south over lands previously controlled by the Almoravids, so did Léon and Castille. The result is that Portugal found itself bound by a political entity that was always to remain both larger and wealthier, due to the vast fertile plains to the interior (today's Andalusia and La Mancha in Castille).

The Black Plague arrived in 1348 and decimated nearly half the population before it receded in the last decades of the fourteenth century. As the plague receded (1385), there was a failed attempt on the part of Castille to take over what was no longer a mere fiefdom, but a nation with a sense of its own political identity and its own language. The resistance by the urban merchant sectors connected to the naval trade led to the eviction of the Castillians and the consolidation of a new native dynasty. Once again, English support was decisive—the new queen was a daughter of John of Gaunt and sister to Henry IV of England. The population was growing fast and the dynasty needed to establish its own moral legitimacy, so the process of expansion into the Atlantic started immediately with the conquest of Ceuta in 1415. The island of Madeira was populated in 1418 and the Azores from 1427 onward. The first shipment of sugar from Madeira reached Bristol in 1456.

However, the occupation of North Africa did not lend itself to the sort of permanent erasure of Muslim presence that had been possible in the southern provinces of Portugal. By the time the Portuguese lost Tangiers in 1437, it had become clear that a new policy of expansion was required. A movement of exploration in the Atlantic toward the south was launched. The Cape Verde Islands were occupied from 1456 onward, and by 1482, the fort of St. George of Elmina (São Jorge da Mina) was built in what is today Ghana, starting a long and dark history of Atlantic slave trading.

Over the following half century the Portuguese established a commercial naval empire reaching as far as Japan. They were permanently present

on the China coast from the mid-1540s until they handed over the administration of Macau to the People's Republic of China in 1999 (see Pina-Cabral
2002b). With the possible exception of Goa, however, none of this involved
permanent extensive administrative occupation. Their control of the naval
routes was based on the establishment of strategic, territorially insignificant
commercial forts. The only real possibility of the kind of extensive administrative occupation that had characterized the conquests of southern Portugal arose in Brazil, and it demanded the massive importation of African
slaves. The Portuguese had established a claim to the Brazilian coast in 1500,
but it was only with the foundation of the city of Salvador, half a century
later, that the process of territorial administration started in earnest.

The aim of this historical sketch is to highlight my principal argument:
Portugal's smallness is as politically questionable as it is territorially obvious.
Thus it establishes a dynamic imbalance in political terms. As Rui Veloso's
song implies, either Portugal is nothing but the few square kilometers of the
count's stronghold at Guimarães or, if not, where does it stop precisely?

The question is not really rhetorical as one might be tempted to believe.
For example, when the regent moved to Brazil in 1807 impelled by the Napoleonic invasions, he founded a new political entity called the "United
Kingdom of Portugal, Brazil, and the Algarves" with its capital in Rio de Janeiro. Eventually, his son would declare himself emperor of Brazil, but only
after the Portuguese forced the king to return to Portugal in 1820. They did
so by preventing the landing in Lisbon (on his way back from Rio) of William Beresford, the British governor who had ruled the country for the king
during the Peninsular Wars.

Now, in 1815, the king's Brazilian title included three named territorial
entities: Portugal and Brazil seem obvious, but he added also "the Algarves."
Etymologically, this last word derives from *el-Garb*, short for *garb el-Andalus*,
the Arabic name of the Western part of the Almohad Empire in the Peninsula. Note, however, that, in the king's title, it is always used in the plural.
It describes not only the southern province of Portugal in Iberia, to the
west of the Strait of Gibraltar, but also the possessions in Africa conquered
after 1415 and last abandoned in 1769 when the population of Mazagão, the
strong fortress, was taken to Brazil, there to refound the city in the Amazo-
nian basin (see Vidal 2005), where it is still today. Ceuta was by then Spanish, having failed to acknowledge the Duke of Bragança's claim as king when
Portugal recovered its independence from eighty years of Castillian dominion in 1640.

In the late fourteenth century, Manuel I's royal title had been "By the Grace of God, King of Portugal and of the Algarves *on this side and that side of the sea in Africa*, Lord of Guinea and of the Conquest, Navigation and Commerce of Ethiopia, Persia and India" (my emphasis). The plural concept of the Algarves *on both sides of the sea* captures this processual nature of conquest and shows that, in the constitution of this political entity, smallness is merely the starting point.

My point is essentially that the notion behind this title that the Portuguese kings used for three and a half centuries (from 1471 to 1815) cannot be grasped in purely territorial terms. It has to be understood as one of political movement. It is imbued with a post-Renaissance view of power as outward conquest; it implies a notion of development, of expansion, of growth by colonizing freely available land. This is a movement that follows on the crusader expansion; it did not start with Pedro Álvares Cabral, Amerigo Vespucci, or Christopher Columbus. Rui Veloso's song is right: "Portugal is Guimarães, all the rest is conquered land." As a political project, Portugal is a process of expansion and retraction. That is why historians have argued convincingly that we cannot speak of one imperial process, but must distinguish three distinct imperial drives: the Asian commercial empire in the sixteenth and seventeenth centuries; the Brazilian slave-based empire in the seventeenth and eighteenth centuries; and the African colonial empire in the twentieth century (Clarence-Smith 1985). In that sense Portugal is not different from many other Western nations. Bertrand Russell (1934: 290) makes this point in a characteristically racialist and bigoted passage from his essay "The Settlement of the West": "The men who conquered the West had courage, tenacity, hope, self-reliance, and a fundamental instinct towards civilised society. To understand their achievement, one should compare it with what happened in most parts of Latin America, where a thin stream of white blood was lost amid Indians and negroes, leaving most of the primeval jungle untamed, while the government, such as it was, combined tyranny and anarchy." Geographic difference, economic difference, demographic factors, cultural differences, slavery, racial violence and discrimination, genocide—all go to the winds, and we are left with a John Wayne–type cowboy ideology that balances all modern imperialisms one against the other, coming out with a clear preference for those who speak Russell's own language and share his own racial prejudice.

But the passage continues with some really prophetic words. Remember, the essay was written at the time of the Great Recession—a period not at all unlike our own—and Russell must have had that in mind as he finished his essay on the following troubled note: "They succeeded in the conquest of the earth; they succeeded in preserving political freedom; but economic freedom was lost by a process which we can now see to have been inevitable. They did their work well, but their philosophy depended for its success upon the empty spaces, and cannot solve the problems of our more crowded world" (Russell 1934: 290). What we have to ask is: in what sense were those spaces really empty? What allows for the mirage of emptiness in southern Iberia, North America, or Africa? Were the vast prairies of Alentejo and Andalusia really empty, or did the crusader kings just simply slaughter, convert, and push off the earlier occupiers? Were the western prairies really empty of Amerindians? Were the green hills of Africa really depopulated, as Henrique Galvão so often stated (see Pina-Cabral 2001)? We all know what the balance of today's answer is likely to be. My interest in this passage, however, goes further. Is today's world (after all, Russell was writing more than eighty years ago) no longer empty? If the earlier emptiness was nothing but a mirage, is today's fullness an equally immeasurable phantom?

To my mind, Russell's observation signals the coming to an end of the modern mode of imperial expansion outward. He was merely ahead of his time in seeing the economic implications of continuing to treat the world as if it were permanently expandable, without taking into account what, some eighty years later, seems blatantly obvious to us all: there are no longer any empty lands out there. And that's not because there is no land, but because no one will allow us to ravage it as if it were free for the taking.

For the Portuguese, the moment of reckoning came at the time of the Bandung Conference in April 1955. Suddenly, it became clear that Portugal might be a small country. The immediate response of the elite who surrounded the aging dictator was to grasp on the Brazilian model. People like Marcello Caetano and Adriano Moreira believed that they could prevent Portugal from confronting its smallness at the end of the colonial era by building a new ideological formulation of transcontinental integration. The humanist, Lusotopic ideas of the Brazilian anthropologist Gilberto Freyre (a disciple of Franz Boas—see Freyre 1946 [1933]) were used in an attempt to open up the path for new political solutions, since simple colonial domination was patently unsustainable (see Pina-Cabral 2012). These attempts failed for a number of reasons, one of them being the very nature of the process of political binarization that characterized the Cold War.

Come what may, by the time the Portuguese democratic revolution took place in April 1974, the country found itself in need of building a new national project. For a while it looked like the Atlantic, Lusotopic axis had simply faded beyond repair (see Pina-Cabral and Carvalho 2004). Naval routes had lost their earlier significance, imperial expansion was unavailable, ex-colonies were aligned with the Soviet bloc, and the country was still blocked off by Spain from access to what was seen as the only path to economic well-being, Europe. The Portuguese had to reinvent themselves.

The answer came in the form not of conquest but of assimilation, into the European Union. For about fifteen years after 1986 it looked like the European axis had absorbed Portugal, allowing for a bypassing of Castilian oppression. The Portuguese responded enthusiastically: the infrastructures were fully renewed, the educational system completely renovated, scientific research institutions were launched with considerable success, Portuguese business carved an important position in Eastern Europe and Latin America, the administrative system became far more competent and modernized, public services were standardized, and, on the whole, levels of corruption were brought down significantly (with the exception of the internationally controlled banking sector).

By the early 2000s, it looked like Portugal was on the way to a new form of political and economic viability. In political terms, Portugal's participation in the common institutions of the European Union was ample and seemingly successful. European federalism as personified by the charismatic figure of President Mário Soares became a widely supported option (cf. Soromenho-Marques 2002). However, there were clouds already forming on the horizon: soon, together with all of Western Europe, the Portuguese economy simply stopped growing. The ever more insistent application of neoliberal cures only sped the train further toward its inevitable wreckage. By 2008, although Portugal had a rate of sovereign debt smaller than that of Germany, France, or Britain, it had no firewall when faced with financial blackmail coming from Wall Street, then desperate to recoup its own losses.

It may seem incredible that I should need to point this out, but most people do not know that Portugal did not have a banking crisis then, never had a construction bubble, and never had a problem of administrative and political enforcement like Greece or Italy. The Portuguese economy was stopped in its tracks and a whole generation of young people left out of economic life for the simple fact that Portugal is small. The heirs of Bertrand

Russell succeeded in giving life to their prejudices by first enforcing economic atrophy (under the neoliberal banner of reducing the size of the state) and then throwing Portugal in the hands of international usurers (under the name of "austerity"). Never in its history has Portugal felt as small as it feels today. With the collapse of the ideals of European integration at the hands of northern European populist politicians, it utterly lacks any project of a viable political future.

In truth, new phenomena do emerge that are, to say the least, unexpected and interesting, since they point toward new forms of activation of the Atlantic, Lusotopic axis of ecumenic proximity (see Pina-Cabral 2002a and 2005). Most of the large Portuguese firms with significant international presence are in fact owned and headed today by representatives of the government of Angola, in a process that has now gained increasing speed due to the alliance of Angolan capital with Chinese commercial interests. Portugal's largest commercial private bank is a case in point. The sale by the Portuguese government under orders from the International Monetary Fund of Portugal's electricity provider to Chinese interests was mediated by Angolan capital. When faced with sudden, long-term unemployment, Portugal's now educated youth are finding employment in extraordinarily large numbers in both Angola and Brazil, but principally in the United Kingdom.

Yet another question arises, however: is this problem really particular to Portugal? Is this really a matter of the lack of viability of a country that is an outlier in Europe, too small to possess its out financial firewalls in a world where international finance is essentially deregulated? We return to the open ending of Russell's paper on North America's settlers: are there any more empty lands to conquer out there? We have lived through a period of growing financial deregulation at the global level, during which the impossibility of growth through expansion has been camouflaged by processes of financial hyperaccumulation. Such at least seems to be the assessment of a number of reputed economic analysts.

I conclude, therefore, that the problem of smallness is no longer really one that countries like Portugal have to face alone, but one that faces the whole world. The world today is small in the sense that there are no empty spaces out there anymore; we have reached the limits of the model of growth that drove modernity. That model was imperial and wasteful of resources, and it has increasingly turned against itself. The smallness of Portugal, both in political and economic terms, is no longer alone a Portuguese problem, but one of global dimensions: in environmental, legal, financial, and social terms.

References

Axelson, Eric. 1973. *Portuguese in South-East Africa, 1488–1600*. Johannesburg: Struik.

Clarence-Smith, Gervaise. 1985. *The Third Portuguese Empire, 1825–1975*. Manchester: Manchester University Press.

Freyre, Gilberto. 1946. *The Masters and the Slaves*. Trans. Samuel Putnam. New York: Knopf.

Galvão, Henrique. 1975 (1959). *Carta Aberta a Salazar*. Lisbon: Arcádia.

Hannerz, Ulf. 1992. The Global Ecumene as a Network of Networks. In Adam Kuper, ed., *Conceptualizing Society*. London: Routledge.

Mattoso, José. 1993. A formação da nacionalidade no espaço ibérico. In José Mattoso, ed., *História de Portugal*, vol. 2. Lisbon: Estampa.

Mintz, Sidney W. 1996. Enduring Substances, Trying Theories: The Caribbean Region as Oikoumenê. *Journal of the Royal Anthropological Institute* 2 (2): 289–311.

Neto, Vítor. 1993. O Estado e a Igreja. In José Mattoso, ed., *História de Portugal*, vol. 5. Lisbon: Estampa.

Pina-Cabral, João de. 1989. Sociocultural Differentiation and Regional Identity in Portugal. In Richard Herr and John H. R. Polt, eds., *Iberian Identity: Essays on the Nature of Identity in Portugal and Spain*. Berkeley: Institute of International Studies, University of California Press.

———. 2001. Galvão Among the Cannibals: The Emotional Constitution of Colonial Power. *Identities: Global Studies in Culture and Power* 8 (4): 483–515.

———. 2002a. "Agora podes saber o que é ser pobre": Identificações e diferenciações no mundo da lusotopia. *Lusotopie* 10 (2): 215–24.

———. 2002b. *Between China and Europe: Person, Culture, and Emotion in Macao*. London: Continuum.

———. 2005. Listing Rivers and Train Stations: Primary Solidarities and the Colonial Past in Mozambique. *Vibrant: Virtual Brazilian Anthropology* 2 (1–2): 24–51.

———. 2012. Charles Boxer and the Race Equivoque. In Francisco Bethencourt and Adrian Pearce, eds., *Racism and Ethnic Relations in the Portuguese-Speaking World*. London: Published for the British Academy by Oxford University Press.

Pina-Cabral, João de, and Clara Carvalho, eds. 2004. *A persistência da história: Passado e contemporaneidade em África*. Lisbon: Imprensa de Ciências Sociais.

Pina-Cabral, João de, and Rui G. Feijó. 2002. Do Ultimato à morte de Amália: Notas sobre a sociedade e a identidade portuguesas no século XX. In Fernando Pernes, coord., *Panorama da cultura portuguesa no século XX*, vol. 1. Oporto: Edições Afrontamento; Fundação Serralves.

Pulido Valente, Vasco. 2006. *Um herói português: Henrique Paiva Couceiro*. Lisbon: Aletheia.

Russell, Bertrand. 1934. *Freedom and Organization, 1814–1914*. London: Allen & Unwin.

Sanches, Manuela Ribeiro, ed. 2006. *"Portugal não é um país pequeno": Contar o "império" na pós-colonialidade*. Lisbon: Cotovia.

Soromenho-Marques, Viriato. 2002. *A Revolução Federal: Filosofia política e debate constitucional na fundação dos EUA*. Lisbon: Edições Colibri.

Vale de Almeida, Miguel. 2004. *An Earth-Colored Sea: "Race," Culture, and the Politics of Identity in the Postcolonial Portuguese-Speaking World*. New York: Berghahn.

Vidal, Laurent. 2005. *Mazagão: A cidade que atravessou o Atlântico*. Lisbon: Teorema.

CHAPTER 8

Two Countries in the Alps:
Austrian and Swiss Presentations of Self for
Internal and Global Consumption

Regina F. Bendix

Austria and Switzerland have considerable similarities: both are democracies located in the Alps. Mountains and lakes provide excellent conditions for tourism, a major component of the respective national economies. Wealth, neutrality, and providing a home to many international organizations make them attractive to nationals from elsewhere, as did the banking secrecy that has recently brought unwelcome international attention. Nonnatives constitute a considerable component of the workforce from high- to low-skilled professionals, which causes social tension and fosters a climate for antiforeigner political parties. Such similarities in topography, economic institutions, heterogeneous social composition, and political boundary drawing on behalf of "natives" allow for comparison; history, in its master narratives as well as in its latent residue in habits and mentality, contributes to divergence: put concisely, Switzerland has always been and felt small, Austria grew to imperial dimensions that mentally reverberate in its shrunken terrain.

Self-representations are points of departure for understanding the Swiss and the Austrians' experience as members of small countries.[1] National pasts contribute to self-assessments and alternate, habitual strategies to maintain their respective political and economic standing within and outside Europe. This chapter draws on dominant renderings of history as a resource for how small countries conceive of themselves on the global stage. History is a component of what Michael Herzfeld (1997: 3) terms cultural intimacy, that is, "those aspects of a cultural identity that are considered a source of external embarrassment but that nevertheless provide insiders with their assurance of common sociality." Herzfeld is critical of the thin ethnographic foundation of historical and sociological accounts of nationalism, and his explication of surface display and deep knowledge offers a counterweight to Benedict Anderson's (2006) "imagined community." If Ernest Gellner (1978: 144) conceived of nationalism as "a movement which conceives the natural object of human loyalty to be a fairly large anonymous unit defined by shared language or culture," Herzfeld places weight on the scraping within and between the subdivisions of a state. Cultural intimacy contains the necessary knowledge to keep a country's external sheen in shape.

The prevailing histories of Switzerland and Austria have brought forth an active, can-do sense of self in Switzerland that does not shy away from showing some internal scraping. Dominant Austrian narratives, by contrast, employ a passive, occasionally lamenting voice that looks at the country through a filter of "formerly known as the Austro-Hungarian Empire." Feeling and acting as Switzerland or Austria in the contemporary world can be further extrapolated from representations and enactments, iconography, literature, music, and media. Such sources permit a view on what kind of agency is possible within a country, beyond moments of crisis or glory that generate national momentum and reassurance.

Between Tourism and Brand: Passive and Active Fashioning of the Image

Tourism relies on the circulation of images; these dovetail with the consolidation of national images in nation branding. In Austria, the capital Vienna with its reminders of empire and sites associated with art and music heritage dominates in tourist representations; occasionally this is supplemented with Salzburg as home of a world-famous music festival, yet linkages to the imperial center are often part of advertising for locations far from the capital. Throughout the 1990s, touristic referents in Carinthia or Upper Austria included Viennese highlights, from Castle Schönbrunn to Wiener schnitzel. In 2005, Austria even considered nominating *Wiener Schmäh*—"Viennese

Charm"—for intangible heritage (Ritterband 2009: 120). The capital—though politically since 1918 mostly in the hands of the social democrats—is suffused with haptic reminders of imperial history. While the "crown lands," now states, politically signal their distance from the capital, references to Vienna and Emperor Franz Josef I and his wife Elisabeth, "Sisi," remain omnipresent.[2] In 2012, a British veteran of national branding was hired. He found it hard to correct the natives' fondness "for waltzing bliss and Lippizaner romance" (Puchleitner 2012), but a new brand was devised: "Austria, Land of Bridge Builders." This reactivated a 1970s image: socialist chancellor Bruno Kreisky sought to replace the Nazi image of Austria as bulwark against the East. Austria was to be a bridge for encounters between East and West, economically and politically (Gingrich 1998: 124).

The core Swiss visual and mental resources are the mountains. Neither the (rather small) capital Bern nor any other city is as important. Recent Swiss tourism campaigns have drawn on images and sounds of Alpine pastorals, yet equipped them with unexpected technology and reminders of urbanism.[3] Switzerland, too, participates in nation branding and in one report held first place among such brands in 2013.[4] Rather than a slogan, Switzerland uses its flag and the name of the country as icons and appears to be successful with this external presentation.[5] During recent years, however, subversions of the flag have surfaced among the stock tourism images. They unabashedly intermingle with the "proper" postcards and reveal culturally intimate sources of critique (Figures 3 and 4).

These miniature "variations on the flag" create an ironic distance to the country whose appeal to foreign guests is what many residents live off. Themes such as "Confédération Hermétique," "The Clean Country," or "Everybody loves Switzerland" speak of small-minded politics seeking to conserve the country for the Swiss alone, of money laundering and other problematic practices: these topics are vigorously debated in the internal public sphere. Mixed in with regular postcards for tourists, the images subvert the purported smallness of the country and its entanglement with the world—a world that loves Swiss resources and opportunities so much that everyone wants to penetrate the borders. The Swiss are thus openly reflexive, at once critical of their small country and enamored of its archaic customs.

Not only affluent nations engage in nation branding; poor countries like Barbados do it too. To be an economically attractive country on Earth 2.0 requires calibrated use of cultural elements to stylize a national image, rooted in tradition, politically stable while dynamically evolving. Though sharing

Figure 3. Confederation Hermetique.
From the postcard series "Swiss Touch"
by Bertrand Lehmann and Jaques
Vallotton. Permission for publication
granted by Lehmann and Vallotton.

Figure 4. Everybody loves Switzerland. From the
postcard series "Swiss Touch" by Bertrand
Lehmann and Jaques Vallotton. Permission for
publication granted by Lehmann and Vallotton.

not just Alpine terrain but also an economic reliance on the tourist industry, Austria's and Switzerland's imagery is an indicator for how these small countries act in the world.[6] Different voices emerge about who one is as a country and what collective cultural resources there are. Austrian tourism planners, up to the time of their "brand new" nation brand as bridge builders, were caught in the passive voice, still living under the shadows of a shattered empire and polishing the memory; the Swiss, by contrast, act within and react to their national container comfortably. Peter von Matt (2001: 175), reviewing literary representations of statehood, contrasts "monarchies that were made by God himself personally" and "react to mockery as if it were blasphemy" with democracies "that are conjoined to laughter": "Laughter about everything that constitutes [democracies] and in all the acidity and gradations of causticity is not just connected with the freedom of opinion and the freedom of speech and publishing. [This laughter] is grounded more deeply: in the knowledge that the established order is preliminary and that those who have made it or want to have it in just this way at present can be changed again at any time." Austrians hold on to aspects of the subject position—unfortunate things happened to them, most infamous in that presentation of Hitler's annexation of Austria in 1938, which hides the fact that the Germanophile population welcomed the Third Reich. This helps to explain why Austria was less thorough in the postwar scrutiny of fascist offenders than Germany. The story of forced annexation locates war criminals outside one's recovered country. While debating their country with self-deprecating humor, the Swiss, too, have taken a long time to scratch behind the surface of wartime neutrality. Both countries serve as host to the United Nations and other international organizations, but incidents of secret doings behind the citizenry's back are higher in Austria: in Transparency International's "Corruptions Perception Index 2012," Switzerland has risen to sixth place, Austria dropped to twenty-fifth.[7]

Joining a larger territory again, Austria entered the European Union in 1995. When Jörg Haider's Freedom Party (Freiheitliche Partei Österreichs) came into government in 2000, the EU for the first time imposed sanctions on a member country, chastising Austria for electing a party in breach of member states' shared values. No other EU member state has experienced such sanctions, confirming Austrian feelings of being a victim. The Swiss voted against joining the EU in 2001, but opted to accept the Schengen treaty in 2008 and partake of various other EU benefits. Switzerland remains part of the European Free Trade Association (EFTA), which it cofounded in 1960.[8] The intense debates over EU membership and the resulting vote for abstinence from full participation demonstrate citizens' desire to remain independent. Being Swiss means holding on to sole control but does not preclude opportunism in profiting from economic benefits for nonmembers.

Territory and the Place of the Alps in the Imaginary

Sharing the Alps and even the colors of their respective flags, the territorial history and corresponding imaginaries of Switzerland and Austria are nonetheless different. In Austria, the Alps constitute 65 percent of the territory and close to half of the population lives in the Alps; in Switzerland, the relation is 60 percent to one-fourth.[9] In Switzerland, however, the Alps have always been the major geographic and political referent within a territory remaining nearly constant since early modernity. The Austro-Hungarian Empire once was eight times the size of present-day Austria, including vast fertile and industrially productive lands. The territorial shrinkage of 1919 has not been fully absorbed in the Austrian consciousness. A brief look at how political history and vestiges of the Alpine do or do not come together in the two countries will illustrate the differences.

Areas in what is now central Switzerland liberated themselves from the Holy Roman Empire and the growing Habsburg realm starting in the fourteenth century. By 1536, the confederation reached from Lac Léman to Lake Constance and across the Alps to include the present-day Italian-speaking canton Ticino as a subject territory. In the early nineteenth century, Grisons (Graubünden) and the Valais joined. The territory stayed the same to this day, with the additional canton Jura created as late as 1979 from terrain previously part of canton Bern. There was internal strife and bloody warfare within the country along confessional and class lines. The last such war in 1847 ended with the new constitution of 1848. Coming to terms with opposing points of view—once through warfare, now through a federalist political culture offering cantonal freedom and federal initiatives and referenda—contributes to the coherence of what remains a heterogeneous citizenry.

The Alps have been a core Swiss imaginary since Albrecht von Haller published his "teaching poem" "Die Alpen" in 1729. Whether romantic, enriching, democracy-enhancing, leisure-fostering, challenging, healthy, or simply beautiful, the Alps are a literary sine qua non (von Matt 2011: 30–32; Zopfi 2009). They were the designated *reduit* (reduced terrain) the Swiss would withdraw to should Hitler's forces enter; bunkers throughout the Alps remind of the plan.

The Swiss do not describe themselves as multiethnic but rather as multilingual. What has been considered Switzerland's exceptional feat is this combination of four national languages within one small terrain, given that the country is surrounded by one-language states. The confederation was multilingual nearly from the start; the four language areas show dialectal diversity and other than Romansh[10] all use the standard written languages of their large neighbors Germany, France, and Italy—with numerous if small educationally sanctioned standard differences. Andreas Wimmer (2011) regards networks generated within a history of political alliances across linguistic divides as reason for the successful Swiss integration. Multiethnicity is positively valued, however, only for the four official language groups—obvious in antiforeigner initiatives since 1968 and the rise of the Swiss People's Party to the percentage-wise strongest right-wing party in Europe.

The Alps, however, are politically more neutral, evident also sartorially: the classic Alpine cowherd's shirt is worn across ages and political ideologies. Made from light blue and white cotton, with tiny edelweiss—the Alpine flower par excellence—strewn along the stripes, this shirt now denotes coolness; even women occasionally wear it (Schumacher 2012). Austria's territorial history along the Danube begins with the Babenbergs in the late tenth century, superseded by the Habsburgs who expanded the dukedoms of Austria and Styria to include Bohemia, Croatia, and Hungary by the early fifteenth century. By 1780 the Habsburg-Lotharingian dynasty also held Galicia. On the eve of World War I, Bosnia and Dalmatia, previously Ottoman, were part of the Habsburg realm. The Ottoman sieges of Vienna in 1529 and 1683 remain deeply engrained in memory. Both times the forces of the Holy Roman Empire succeeded in driving away the Turkish forces, which is remembered through place names, plaques, statuary, and permanent exhibits in the Vienna Museum of Military History. Pushing the old Muslim foe further out of the Balkan Peninsula was particularly gratifying, bringing forth what Andre Gingrich (1998), coining the term "frontier orientalism," has described as a doubling of the image of the Muslim Other—the bitter enemy on the one hand and the subjected, territorially integrated, hence economically useful Turk on the other.

On the eve of World War I, the Habsburg empire had thus reached an enormous territorial expanse. Yet behind the tolerant label *Vielvölkerstaat*, or "state of many peoples," brewed unrest.[11] The harmonious togetherness of many nations within one state was home to vigorous nationalisms contributing to the war's outbreak and to the dramatic shrinking of the empire into present-day Austria.

The Alps became a dominant part of the Austrian landscape only with the twentieth-century republic and have thus not been the same kind of ideological mainstay as in Switzerland. It was German mountaineering clubs who in a form of leisure colonialism conquered the Austrian Alps, building hiking paths and huts (Tschofen 1999). There is no comparably fierce, Alpine freedom loving among Austrians.

Germans remain the biggest group of foreign tourists. Austrians like to profit from them; the Swiss are no less opportunistic in welcoming members of what is jokingly called "the big canton." But there is no Swiss equivalent to Felix Mitterer's satire *The Piefke Saga* written for television. Narrating the unhappy symbiosis of vacationing Germans and Austrian tourism providers, it aired first in 1990 and enjoyed reruns for fifteen years on Austrian TV, generally at the height of tourist season. The center of the Austrian imaginary remains Vienna. In terms of referents to an Alpine and native sartorial habitus, the green loden jacket spells "conservative," no matter how apolitical the person who wears it. The woman's dirndl bears the stigma of service clothing, otherwise worn only by children or tourists.

Austria now consists of nine states and one official language, German. Croatian, Slovene, and Hungarian are regionally accepted, with certain schooling and administrative dealings in those languages. The recognized minority languages as well as, since 1904, the inclusion of Islam next to Judaism, Catholicism, and Protestantism as a religious option in the school curriculum, maintain aspects of a historical pluralism.

Put side by side on a map of Europe, both countries look small. One has been steadily small, but is proud of the size held over many centuries. The other mourns the loss of terrain and the power that went with it. There is, however, an Alpine fascination that the two countries share: competitive winter sports. Schools encourage learning to ski, and watching ski races is occasionally indulged in, even during school hours. Budgets to support national winter sport teams are sizable in both countries. It is an arena where Austrian and Swiss athletes win medals and thus attract international attention. The Swiss federal sports ministry has consistently fostered fitness across the population, rather than favoring scarce talent. Having to balance a complicated whole, the Swiss have "given preference to compromise; in this avoidance of the exceptional one can see the general tendency for the mean which builds social cohesion by adjusting the differences" (Gamper 2005: 70). In both countries some high schools have a sports, particularly skiing, emphasis. But in Austria, the successful athlete may revel in stardom, and royal nomenclature reemerges: ski aces Karl Schranz and Franz Klammer turned into König Karl and Kaiser Franz respectively, while Hermann Maier adopted the nickname "Herminator"—in allusion to Hollywood star (with Austrian roots) Arnold Schwarzenegger. With winning Swiss athletes like the ski racers Bernhard Russi or Didier Couche or the tennis player Roger Federer, it is their modesty and deference to the whole that supports them and makes them candidates for the sportsman of the year award; as

Michael Gamper (2005: 88) puts it, it is the Swiss collective that decides who gets to be a famous Swiss.

Negotiating History, Collective Biography, and the Place of the Foreign

The official narrative of Swiss statehood maps nicely onto the terrain just described. The core story is rendered most powerfully in Friedrich Schiller's play *William Tell* from 1804, which, despite varied humorous and critical deconstructions, remains read and performed all over the country (Bendix 1989). "We want to be a unified people of brothers" begins the oath spoken by the cowherds and peasants seeking to liberate themselves from the Habsburg yoke. Bertolt Brecht, in his *Refugee Dialogues*, written in the 1940s, saw the plight of this small country differently when he opined that "the Swiss's historical thirst for freedom comes from the fact that the country is inauspiciously situated. They are surrounded by countries that all like to conquer things. So they have to be constantly on the qui vive. If it were different, they would not have to thirst for freedom. One has never heard of the Eskimo's thirst for freedom. They are localized more auspiciously" (von Matt 2001: 21; my translation). Brecht concluded that thirst for freedom is superfluous in countries that are located more fortuitously. Opting for neutrality in the early nineteenth century, the Swiss avoided entanglement in the great wars of the twentieth century. Neutrality, in turn, has made the country a reliable host for international endeavors—including the second largest UN office in the world. It has been a site for peacekeeping negotiations and has itself engaged in peacekeeping missions. The International Red Cross was founded in 1867 on the initiative of the Swiss Henri Dunant in 1867, who in 1901 was the first cowinner of the Nobel Peace Prize.

There is plenty to counter this hegemonic Swiss biography, but it represents a source of satisfaction: The Swiss have not just given the world chocolate, cheese, and watches—they inhabit a beautiful country, have a long record of democratic rule, and do not take sides in military conflict. Looking at the underbelly of the glossy narrative, one will see ferocious civil wars connected to the Reformation; patrician rule within the cities and urban efforts to tax the countryside leading to bloody wars with the peasantry; and Swiss mercenaries opportunistically fighting for money on various sides all across Europe. Foreign intervention—Napoleon's invasion—was necessary to liberate some areas from internal colonial rule and give Switzerland its foundational constitution. Neutrality was an idea Switzerland had to accept as part of the Congress of Vienna in 1814–1815; it has been interpreted rather loosely in profitable arms deals, sheltering moneys of warring rulers, and being available for economic deals among other war profiteers.

Jumping into the recent past and present, the Swiss have been hotly debating the presence of ever more immigrants. Alfred Häsler's 1967 novel *The Boat Is Full* critically depicts Swiss refugee policy toward Jews during World War II; Markus Imhoof's film based on the book was nominated for an Academy Award in 1982. Internationally less known are the various initiatives seeking to tackle what nationalist politicians depict as a small country infested with too many foreigners. Since 1968, there have been no fewer than nine initiatives attempting to reduce the number of foreigners present or to halt immigration. All of them lost narrowly. Christoph Blocher transformed the Schweizerische Volkspartei (SVP) into a right-wing party with a social base no longer just in the agricultural sector but also attracting young urban voters. Blocher's election to the federal council gave the SVP for the first time two seats on the seven-member Swiss executive. His party collected enough signatures for an initiative to send criminal foreigners back to their home country; this was the first successful antiforeigner initiative, in a national vote of 2010.[12]

For this initiative, the SVP developed an ad depicting lovely white sheep whose grazing land needs to be protected against the black, criminal, foreign sheep (Figure 5). The iconographic power, in all its cuteness, was considerable. There were many critical reactions to it. Most satisfying for those who objected to the initiative's inherent iconographic racism was the shift in the federal council shortly thereafter—circulated widely online again with the sheep imagery (Figure 6): Blocher lost his federal council seat due to a show of solidarity across the other parties in parliament. His nonrenewal led to a split of the SVP into two segments.

Better known internationally than the sheep is the SVP's minaret initiative in 2009. Both houses of parliament had recommended against it, but the popular vote was overwhelmingly in favor of banning the building of further minarets. Only the cities of Basel and the cantons of Geneva, Vaud, and Valais voted against it. The outcome unleashed a discussion about national and civic identity (Zeit Online 2009). Vigorous public debates about who the Swiss are may be one of the distinguishing features from their Austrian neighbor: ever since the early eighteenth century a steady stream of Swiss

Figure 5. "Create Safety." Original SVP campaign ad, with the black sheep standing for purportedly criminal foreigners. Culled from Geden (2010).

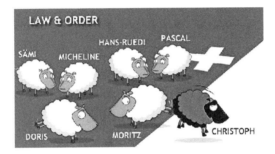

Figure 6. Use of the sheep design by the SVP's opposition, turning the SVP federal counselor Christoph Blocher into a black sheep that is kicked out of the seven-member federal council. Image culled from Dominik's Blog, posted December 2007, http://blog.zindel.org/category/politik.

authors have engaged in this conversation. Max Frisch stands as one representative (von Matt 2001). His sober retelling of the Tell story, *William Tell for Schools*, stripped the freedom-loving ancient Swiss of their heroism and turned the foreign oppressor into a wimpy, puzzled administrator. Neither imagined communities nor cultural intimacy is at issue in this recasting, but, argues literary historian Peter von Matt (2001: 133), patriotism as a public and erotic manifestation. In contrast to the general scheme of love where there are plenty of objects of affection to select from, patriots have only one fatherland to love, and hence "the jealousy in the realm of patriotism invariably turns into a struggle over the right to capture this homeland's true essence" (133). It is a hot fight, says von Matt, with sharp conflicts over what kind of identity this country now truly has. But it is an open and secure conflict: it is not one's place in the world that is at issue, but what this place is, and how one is to identify with it.

The Napoleonic Wars sealed the Swiss territory in 1814, while the Austrian Empire continued to grow until 1918, when it shrank to become the Republic of Austria. With the national contours established over a very long time, scholarly works tackling Swissness abound—exploring self-representational activities in the here and now as well as in the past. In 1985, the Swiss National Science Foundation funded a multiyear initiative entitled "Cultural Plurality and National Identity," charged with examining the state of being and feeling Swiss, both in view of integration challenges within and EU challenges from the outside, and with the goal to foster reflection on potential frailties (Kreis 1994). For Austria, it is much harder to find works willing to tackle "Austrianness," though particularly during the years of Allied occupation after World War II, there were both political and scholarly efforts to build a national Austrian identity distinct from Germany. For the present, there are collections of Austrian cartoons and of Austrian humor, but the view of the whole often stops at the empire as a filter through which to look at the present.

Dorothy Noyes's (2010) concept of the "subjunctive space" is helpful to understand how a narrative about mutual belonging can take shape and fill with substance.[13] The Austrian subjunctive is there and is not. The political past is full of breaks. In the late nineteenth century, after 1945 and again after 1995, when Austria had joined the European Union, reference points to the first written mention of "Ostarrichi" in 996 were celebrated and constructed a *longue durée*.[14] Ostarrichi figured, of course, in the combination *Österreichisch-Ungarische Monarchie* (Austro-Hungarian Monarchy), much as the Nazi regime later built on the quasi-natural link to what Ostarrichi had been in 996: an administrative unit of the dukedom of Bavaria, which, under the name Ostmark, Germany annexed in 1938.

The Austrian subjunctive is thus frail and ambiguous. Key elements that shaped Austrian history are not necessarily such that a citizen wants to identify with them. It seems better, perhaps, to stand next to them—eyes downcast, as subject to, not actor within that history. There were illustrious monarchs such as Leopold I, Maria Theresia, and Franz Josef I responsible for shaping that history, and there was the Ottoman threat with Vienna as the fortress that the Turks could not conquer—but it is particular commanders such as Prince Eugene whose skill is memorialized, not the country as a whole. There is the image of an empire that benevolently ruled and modernized many lands—yet it was also a colonial rule, shaken off violently during World War I. There is the conversion to the Republic of Austria, initiating a politically turbulent era, with votes in several of the states as to whether they wanted to stay with Austria or join one of the surrounding countries. The political instability culminated in Austro-fascism as of 1933, and ended with the annexation by Nazi Germany in 1938. There was the powerful 1815 Congress of Vienna, reorganizing Europe after Napoleon's defeat. The neutral Austria of 1955, however, gingerly emerged from ten years under Allied occupation. The 1952 science-fiction film *1. April 2000*, intended as a gloss on building an Austrian self-consciousness separate from Germany, offers an image of an innocent nation repeatedly accused of breaking world peace (Kieninger et al. 2000). In it, individuals are victims or innocent bystanders whose destiny is guided by others. A cultural intimacy acknowledging the complicity of many is deeply buried.

Since the crumbling of the empire, and with the rise of overt ethnic strife and anti-Semitism, Austrian authors such as Karl Kraus, Joseph Roth, and Robert Musil laid open such buried sentiment and agency. Paradigmatic is Robert Musil's unfinished novel *Der Mann ohne Eigenschaften* (The Man Without Qualities), published in 1932. Musil captured the ambiguous attitude toward one's personal life and the life of a still ever-present dual monarchy (Wolf 2011). He coined two terms that neatly sum up being and feeling Austrian—*Parallelaktion* and *Kakania*. Beginning in 1913, Musil's characters are engaged in the "parallel action"—referring to plans for Franz Josef's seventieth jubilee as emperor, to be parallel to but better than Prussian Wilhelm I's jubilee. To Musil and to the reader, the actors are engaged, absurdly, in planning a jubilee unlikely to happen in a parallel universe, ignoring that World War I is about to shatter their actual world. This world, in turn, Musil names Kakania, derived from the omnipresent descriptor *kaiserlich-königlich* (imperial-monarchical), abbreviated into *k. & k.*: "All in all, how many remarkable things might be said about that vanished Kakania! For instance it was *kaiserlich-königlich* (Imperial-Royal) and it was *kaiserlich und königlich* (Imperial and Royal); one of two abbreviations, *k.k.* or *k. & k.*, applied to every thing and person, but esoteric lore was nevertheless required in order to be sure of distinguishing which institutions were to be referred to as *k.k.* and which as *k. & k.*" (Musil 1953: 33). In the twenty-first century, one still finds stores reminding buyers of their former status as "k & k Hoflieferant"—manufacturers and procurers with the privilege to deliver to the court; "k & k" is one of many abbreviations that remind of a society accustomed to big and small aristocracies, to titles acquired by birth, marriage, service, or purchase. Titles were constitutionally abolished, but the communicative habits prevail—in everyday greetings, in letters. The sense of a parallel world is even transported grammatically on occasion, when people address someone else within a face-to-face exchange in the third person, as when a waiter inquires "has the gentle lady finished with her coffee?"—a habit that linguistically recalls the distance between aristocracy and others. It is a reminder of everyone's performance of self—no one is truly at one with his identity. The gusto with which such deference is remembered, and reenacted, even if done playfully, creates a link to the past; the pretense constructs a present still enamored of pseudo-meritocratic forms of address.

Kakania remains present in tourist marketing. As recently as 1996, the great-grandson of Franz Josef I allowed the community of Bad Ischl to advertise his presence to tourists, clearly assuming that this would provide luster to what was once the imperial summer resort (Kamolz 1996). It is also evident in the big balls punctuating the winter season, with young women making their societal debut and international celebrities arriving as guests of present-day monarchs of the business world—staging grandeur that masks a shrunken importance in the world. Other countries have revived ballroom dancing (not least due to TV shows such as *Let's Dance*, the German version of *Dancing with the Stars*); Austria, however, has an unbroken tradition for this seasonal entertainment in upper-class wardrobe. Many different groups, including craftsmen, hold an annual ball, and the Austrian UNESCO commission placed the "Viennese Ball Tradition" on its budding national register of intangible heritage.[15] One can also see Kakania's power in scholarly efforts, as so much scholarship deals with the classic fin de siècle; even deconstructionist initiatives refer to Kakania, and satirists like to employ the name and all it invokes.[16]

Transcending the concreteness of balls or the Viennese operetta with its "utopia in reverse" (Csáky 1998), one can point to art, particularly music, and recognize a timeless, embraceable field of identification. The sensory power of music and—in the case of the waltz identified with Vienna the world over—dance facilitates an embodied belonging quite different from the patriotism von Matt evoked for the Swiss. Austria's musical protagonists and their histories within and beyond Vienna are known, and while the living history performances in baroque costume are geared to tourists, there is so much music in such a plethora of venues that it can be shared without fear of loss.

Figure 7. "Two Kinds of Nonsense" by Michael Pammesberger: "How Austrians see themselves"; "How others see Austrians." Culled from Ritterbrand (2009: 265).

Turning to Austria's cultural intimacy, it is non-Austrians who remember embarrassing facets, while Austrians focus on the grand moments in history and art, as shown in a cartoon by Michael Pammesberger (Figure 7). Pammesberger entitles the cartoon "Two Kinds of Nonsense"—what Austrians see about themselves and what outsiders see about them. The hidden double of the collective image is suppressed at home, but visible to the rest of the world. Remembering and enacting nobility in titles, ball traditions, and codes of deference and subservience seem to deny the republic and its demand for democratic participation and responsibility. The outside viewer has not forgotten the annexation of 1938 and recognizes that after 1945 former Nazis continued in respectable positions—in the cartoon, it is Kurt Waldheim who poses as a singer. Having served as secretary-general of the United Nations from 1972 to 1981, his election to the Austrian presidency in 1986 coincided with revelations about his service in the German army and his detailed knowledge of crimes of war as an intelligence officer. Due to the fact that Waldheim had previously held the highest UN office, the entire world was shamed by Austria's cultural intimacy—the failure to uncover war criminals and supporters.[17] Austria was internationally sidelined during the six years of Waldheim's presidency, with many countries not permitting him to visit. Undoubtedly it was this public, international shaming, alongside the

1986 Waldheim scandal, that brought the rise of Jörg Haider's Freiheitliche Partei Österreichs (FPÖ).

These events began to move Kakania—if never completely—aside. While research on Austrian wrongdoing in World War II was now taken up more seriously, the FPÖ's nationalist platform and—like Blocher's SVP in Switzerland—its open stance against migrants contributed to a new, problematic Austrianness. Party leader Haider in the 1990s strategically shifted from pan-Germanism toward a rhetoric of the Austrian body politic (*Volkskörper*), using a term intrinsically linked with National Socialism. In 1993 he launched the campaign "Austria First." Haider died in a car accident in 2008; current FPÖ leaders continue to hold a substantial share of votes in Austria. According to Thomas Fillitz (2006), Haider constructed mutually supportive subjunctives of Austrian culture vis-à-vis the Other: one sought to remove immigrants rendering the Austrian body politic impure back to their home countries, the other conceived of Austria as composed of a series of minorities, among whom the German-speaking minority was the majority. The composition of the country in this view no longer harks back to the state of many peoples. Instead there is a focus on the present territory, its borders, and the dangers looming within and without.

With its name, the Austrian Freedom Party recalls the Brecht assertion cited earlier: countries that have to invoke freedom might be less than ideal places to seek refuge. The pathologies of right-wing politics in these two Alpine republics differ, in part due to European Union membership or lack thereof. Austria may have joined not least to belong, once again, to a larger territory whose leadership controls the destiny of large numbers of people. But there was unease from the beginning, and a new "EU-exit" party formed in 2011.[18] One of its adherents wrote the following online comment regarding the party platform: "*Thank God that we have the EU and euro . . . otherwise we would be experiencing life like the Swiss: Growth, prosperity, independence, high-paying jobs, and [our] own currency, which increases in value*" (emphasis in original).[19] The very formulation of this statement, however, again points to the passivity within the Austrian sense of smallcountryness: the author would like to experience the good life, but he does not seem to consider the responsibilities involved in maintaining the desired independence.

The Swiss held elections to both houses of parliament in 2011. A brochure was sent to voters explaining how to vote and which parties were running for office. Each party was associated with a vegetable, and the overall concept was a rather astonishing tongue-in-cheek booklet concluding with a traditional vegetable soup recipe: voting materials for the two houses of parliament encapsulated in a pot of soup. The implicit message was that of a tasty, perhaps somewhat messy soup, with plenty of spice and leading to a strong foundation for being, feeling, and acting in the contemporary world. (Some) Austrians, by contrast, feel, yet again trapped in a vessel. It does not even have the luster of empire but demands submission to European compromises and paying for irresponsible others.

The subjunctive would seem to be a suitable gloss for the resources available to a small country: with the subjunctive voice, a given present may be presented and positioned for outside consumption, with cultural intimacy constituting an internal platform, available for negotiating the (hi)story of just how this space came to be, for keeping check of what kinds of things are bubbling that might chip the varnish, and what needs to be kept in check to maintain the place one has acquired as a small country within the global interaction of political and—even more so—economic spheres. The two small Alpine countries Austria and Switzerland are quite different in their handling of outside gloss and cultural intimacies. Yet in their acting within the world, the Swiss and the Austrians display similar agility and efficiency.

* * *

Many thanks go to the editors of this volume for their patience and vigorous assistance. Colette Rogivue has sent numerous documents helpful for this paper. Christoph Bock and Nora Kühnert have given support in bibliographic and iconographic research. Translations from the German are my own. The comparison provided ends roughly with the year 2012, not taking into account the subsequent populist developments in both countries.

Notes

1. The affective dimensions of nationness are pursued more vigorously in a set of papers assembled by Mookherjee (2011: S17); cf. also Bendix (1992).

2. The 1992 musical *Elisabeth* contributed to this, the 1955 film *Sissi* continues to air annually, and "Sisi" tourist packages are sold. The American musical *The Sound of Music*, based on the von Trapp family's fictionalized story, is a powerful referent to Austria; Austrians take less note of it (cf. Kammerhofer-Aggermann and Keul 2000).

3. See the "Schweiz Tourismus Kampagne" by photographer Robert Bösch, accessed 4 May 2013, http://www.robertboesch.ch/de/werbung/schweiz-tourismus.

4. Cf. "Future Brand," accessed 4 June 2013, http://www.futurebrand.com/foresight/cbi.

5. Until 2012, a site named "Image Switzerland" monitored the image of the country abroad. "Image Switzerland," accessed 30 May 2012, http://www.image-switzerland.ch/index.php?id=10&L=1. As of 2013, the tasks assembled under "communication abroad" have been integrated into the home page of the federal government; accessed 5 May 2013, http://www.fdfa.admin.ch/eda/en/home/topics/prskom.html; cf. also "Swissworld," accessed 7 May 2013, http://www.swissworld.org/en/switzerland/.

6. As of 2014, eleven percent of Austrians are employed in tourism; the annual revenue is nearly 20 billion euros (accessed 4 July 2016, https://www.wko.at/Content.Node/branchen/oe/Tourismus-in-Oesterreich-eine-gesamtwirtschaftliche-Betracht.pdf). In Switzerland, as of 2014, 4 percent of the workforce is employed in tourism, with earnings of 17.4 billion francs—16 billion euros ("Schweizer Tourismusverband," accessed 4 July 2016, http://www.swisstourfed.ch/index.cfm?parents_id=962).

7. Corruption Perceptions Index 2012, http://cpi.transparency.org/cpi2012/results/.

8. The 1985 Schengen Treaty reduced EU-internal border controls and eventually introduced freedom of movement for citizens within the terrain of signatory states. EFTA's other members are Norway, Iceland, and Liechtenstein.

9. Cf. information compiled under "Aplenländer," accessed 4 July, 2016, https://de.wikipedia.org/wiki/Alpenl%C3%A4nder#cite_note-2.

10. Romansh, a group of dialects derived from Vulgar Latin, is spoken by an estimated sixty thousand Swiss within the canton of Grisons; see Cathomas (2008).

11. On the imagination or delusion of a harmonious ensemble in the late nineteenth century, see Bendix (2003).

12. The Swiss government has thus far delayed legal implementation of this initiative; the SVP handed in a further initiative in 2012 that succeeded in 2014, creating massive conflicts and economic setbacks with the EU.

13. Noyes developed the concept to talk about relations between adjoining countries and military knowledge projects generated by army officers trying to understand tribes and nations in conflict. For Noyes (2010: 7), "world making" is a tool used to "predicate a narrative upon the conflict, give us a way of getting a handle on it."

14. Available online under "Ostarrichi Urkunde," accessed 20 May 2013, http://www.univie.ac.at/elib/index.php?title=Ostarrichi_-_Urkunde_-_Otto_III_-_996; cf. Tschofen 1996.

15. Protests against a ball with a Fascist past and present led to the removal of the entire Viennese ball tradition from the listing in 2012; see UNESCO streicht "Wiener Ball" als Kulturerbe. *Der Standard* [online], 19 January 2012.

16. Literature scholar Wolfgang Müller-Funk coordinated a longer research effort on Kakania, *Kakanien Revisited* (Müller-Funk, Plener, and Ruthner 2002), accompa-

nied by an Internet site of the same title, accessed 19 May 2013, http://www.kakanien
.ac.at/. Erich Ledersberger assembles his news columns and books on "Kakania," accessed 19 May 2013, http://kakanien.com/.

17. In 1987, the parliament established a committee of historians to examine the
accusations against Waldheim, who was found not guilty of any war crimes but clearly
in possession of knowledge about atrocities.

18. EU-Austrittspartei, accessed 19 May 2013, http://www.euaustrittspartei.at. The
home page opens with a banner reminding viewers of the new beginning of Austria's
republic in 1955, "Österreichischer Staatsvertrag vom 15.5.1955—'Österreich ist frei'";
thus again it is freedom that is sought, without much thought given to "freedom from
what" and "freedom to do what."

19. Heinz M., 9 May 2012, on "EU Austrittspartei Programm," http://www
.euaustrittspartei.at/parteiprogramm/.

References

Anderson, Benedict. 2006. *Imagined Communities*. Rev. ed. London: Verso.

Bendix, Regina 1989. *Backstage Domains: Playing William Tell in Two Swiss Communities*. Bern: Peter Lang.

———. 1992. National Sentiment in the Enactment and Discourse of Swiss Political
Ritual. *American Ethnologist* 19 (4): 768–90.

———. 2003. Ethnology, Cultural Reification, and the Dynamics of Difference in
the Kronprinzenwerk. In Nancy Wingfield, ed., *Creating the Other*. London:
Berghahn.

Cathomas, Regula. 2008. *Sprachgebrauch im Alltag—Die Verwendung des Rätoro-
manischen in verschiedenen Domänen: Wechselwirkungen und Einflussfaktoren*.
Chur: Institut für Kulturforschung Graubünden.

Csáky, Moritz. 1998. *Ideologie der Operette und Wiener Moderne*. Vienna: Böhlau.

Fillitz, Thomas. 2006. "Being the Native's Friend Does Not Make You the Foreigner's
Enemy!" Neo-Nationalism, the Freedom Party and Jörg Haider in Austria. In
Andre Gingrich and Marcus Banks, eds., *Neo-Nationalism and Beyond*. New York:
Berghahn.

Gamper, Michael. 2005. *Die Schweiz in Form: Sport und Nation in einem kleinen Land*.
Wien: Nagel und Kimche.

Geden, Oliver. 2010. Rechtspopulismus in der Schweiz: Das dunkle Herz Europas. *Süd-
deutsche Zeitung* [online], 17 May.

Gellner, Ernest. 1978. Scale and Nation. In Fredrik Barth, ed., *Scale and Social Organization*. Oslo: Universitetsforlaget.

Gingrich, Andre. 1998. Frontier Myths of Orientalism: The Muslim World in Public
and Popular Cultures of Central Europe. In Bojan Baskar and Borut Brumen, eds.,

MESS: Mediterranean Ethnological Summer School, vol. 2, Piran/Pirano, Slovenia, 1996. Ljubljana: Inštitut za multikulturne raziskave.

Herzfeld, Michael. 1997. *Cultural Intimacy.* London: Routledge.

Kammerhofer-Aggermann, Ulrike, and Alexander G. Keul, eds. 2000. *"The Sound of Music": Zwischen Mythos und Marketing.* Salzburg: Salzburger Landesinstitut für Volkskunde.

Kamolz, Klaus. 1996. Monarch im Hinterzimmer. *Profil* 32 (August): 66–68.

Kieninger, Ernst, Nikola Langreiter, Armin Loacker, and Klara Löffler, eds. 2000. *1. April 2000.* Vienna: Verlag Filmarchiv Austria.

Kreis, Georg. 1994. *Die Schweiz unterwegs: Schlussbericht des NFP 21 "Kulturelle Vielfalt und nationale Identität."* Basel: Schwabe.

Mookherjee, Nayanika. 2011. The Aesthetics of Nations: Anthropological and Historical Approaches. In Nayanika Mookherjee and Christopher Pinney, eds., special issue, *Journal of the Royal Anthropological Institute* 17 (Supplement s1): S1–20.

Müller-Funk, Wolfgang, Peter Plener, and Clemens Ruthner, eds. 2002. *Kakanien Revisited.* Tübingen: Francke.

Musil, Robert. 1953. *The Man Without Qualities.* Trans. Eithne Wilkins and Ernst Kaiser. London: Secker & Warburg. German original, 1930/1932.

Noyes, Dorothy. 2010. From Objects of Intervention to Subjunctive Worlds: On the Proliferation of Military Knowledge Projects. Paper presented at Making Sense in Afghanistan: Interaction and Uncertainty in International Interventions, Mershon Center for International Security Studies, Ohio State University, Columbus, 9 April.

Puchleitner, Klaus. 2012. Nation Branding: Brückenbauer Made in A. *Format Trend— das Portal für Wirtschaft und Geld*, 14 November. http://www.format.at/articles /1246/525/346465/nation-branding-brueckenbauer-a.

Ritterband, Charles E. 2009. *Dem Österreichischen auf der Spur: Expeditionen eines NZZ-Korrespondenten.* Vienna: Böhlau.

Schumacher, Claudia. 2012. Beim Sännechutteli endet der Ethno-Trend. *Neue Zürcher Zeitung Am Sonntag*, 13 May, 75.

Tschofen, Bernhard. 1996. Heimatsymbole der Gegenwart. In Reinhard Johler, Herbert Nikitsch, and Bernhard Tschofen, *Post vom schönen Österreich.* Documenta ethnographica 1. Vienna: Verein für Volkskunde.

———. 1999. *Berg, Kultur, Moderne: Volkskundliches aus den Alpen.* Vienna: Sonderzahl.

Von Matt, Peter. 2001. *Die tintenblauen Eidgenossen.* Munich: Hanser.

Wimmer, Andreas. 2011. A Swiss Anomaly? A Relational Account of National Boundary-Making. *Nations and Nationalism* 17 (4): 718–37.

Wolf, Norbert. 2011. *Kakanien als Gesellschaftskonstruktion.* Vienna: Böhlau.

Zeit Online. 2009. Minarett-Streit: Die Schweizer debattieren über sich selbst. 9 December.

Zopfi, Emil. 2009. *Dichter am Berg.* Zürich: AS Verlag.

CHAPTER 9

Serbia and the Surplus of History: Being Small, Large, and Small Again

Aleksandar Bošković

On Monday, 28 May 2012, the manager of the Serbian national football team, Siniša Mihajlović, decided to expel one of the players from the team because the player, Adem Ljajić, did not sing the national anthem as it was played before the friendly match against Spain a couple of days earlier in Switzerland. According to the officials from the Serbian Football Association, the player was in breach of the special contract that he, like all players, signed with the new manager: one of the provisions was that all the players must sing the national anthem. Actually few people in Serbia know the lyrics of the national anthem, "Bože pravde" [God bring us justice]. It is a relic from the time before 1941, and, with its multiple references to God, Orthodox Christianity, and ethnic Serbs, to the exclusion of other peoples,[1] is not very popular with nonreligious people and non-Serbs.[2] For many, it serves as a stark reminder of the 1990s wars, especially with references to "Serbian lands." Thus many people living in Serbia have problems identifying with it, and the football team incident was widely interpreted as one in which the manager (an ethnic Serb) expelled a young player (an ethnic Muslim) for not being "Serbian" enough.

This is one example of the confusion that arises in Serbia when national symbols are concerned. As far as I know, Serbia might be the only country in the world that is not a monarchy but has a royal symbol (the crown) as part of its national flag, another transplant from the time before World War II.

This is a country where the "surplus of history" seems to be almost a permanent condition.

What makes a country big or small? Are there objective parameters, or does it boil down to self-perception? Obviously, smallness can be related to both. In the case of Serbia, all play a part, with an important caveat: the Serbian elite never considered their country as small. Since the country's formal independence in 1878, they frequently believed that it should be bigger, and it almost doubled in size following the Balkan Wars of 1912 and 1913. This self-perception is primarily the result of its relative size compared to neighboring countries, as well as of specific historical and cultural circumstances. In this chapter, I will outline these circumstances and point to the factors that characterize Serbia as a small country. As its perceptions of smallness and how to transcend it primarily have had to do with issues related to modernity, my focus will be on Serbia's struggles to transcend its smallness (sometimes self-perceived as backwardness), by modernizing itself and adopting values and norms characteristic of more developed, mostly Western European countries.

Throughout most of the twentieth century, Serbia has shifted in size, with the appropriate changes in self-perception about its own importance. As it coped with gaining territories and being part of different political systems (as it was part of the larger South Slav state, between 1918 and 1941, and then again between 1945 and 1991),[3] it also struggled with its own identity and state formation. Thus, Serbia presents a good case of a small country that struggles with its own image, as well as with self-representation. As it was, for most of its recent past (1918–1941, then 1945–1991, and in some forms 1992–2005), part of a larger whole, it did not really consider itself as a small country. On the other hand, according to the census of October 2011, it has 7.3 million inhabitants, which, by UN standards, does put it in the category of "small countries." Of course, the smallness is also a matter of perspective; thus, Serbia is larger than all its former Yugoslav neighbors (Croatia, Bosnia and Herzegovina, Montenegro, Kosovo, and Macedonia), which still makes it *relatively large*, at least in the regional perspective. Overall, the standard of living in Serbia is still higher than one of its two neighbors that are members of the European Union,[4] which also puts things in an interesting perspective.

While Serbia would most obviously fit into the category of "downsized countries," it could also be seen as an "underdog country" (especially in terms of its own self-perception, following the wars of the 1990s), and, especially in recent years, its political elite has promoted the idea of Serbia as a "buffer zone" country. During the Cold War period, former Yugoslavia was perceived as a "buffer zone" country, formally socialist, but with an impressive degree of openness, and certainly open borders since the early 1960s. The politics of the Non-Aligned Movement (NAM), one of whose founders was Yugoslav president Josip Broz Tito, also contributed to this. Yugoslavia was the only prominent European member of this movement, and its first conference took place in Belgrade, in September 1961. I will address some of these issues in this chapter, but especially the reasons for certain ways in which the perceptions of the country's elite are promoted in public and shared by large segments of the general population—through the media, educational system, public discourses, and so on.

What Constitutes a Nation?

As the Autonomous Province of Kosovo declared its independence from Serbia in February 2008 and was subsequently recognized as an independent country by most developed countries of the world, this created a sense of national tragedy, coupled with a feeling of impotence. Serbia lost control of the province following the 1999 intervention by the NATO forces (which included bombing targets in both Serbia and Montenegro, which at the time was still joined with Serbia). Ethnic Albanians (forming up to 90 percent of the inhabitants of Kosovo) for the most part refused to participate in any form in the Serb-run institutions since the early 1990s. However, in the popular Serbian imaginary, Kosovo was and always will be part of Serbia. It was connected through historical and mythical ties. Hence, the "loss" of Kosovo provoked feelings of injustice and anger. Many Serbs felt that they were being bullied by the big powers (led by the United States), and this was the consequence of their being small. On the other hand, this feeling of smallness went hand in hand with the perception that they were right, and that eventually justice would prevail and Kosovo would again be part of Serbia. In this sense, the self-perception of smallness and weakness was coupled with the belief that the cause of their anger against the stronger opponents was just and that they were fighting for the right cause. In more imaginative interpretations, this belief in the "just cause" is perceived as a reenactment of a medieval myth, according to which Serb fourteenth-century nobles chose the "Kingdom of Heaven" (that is to say, to fight the Ottoman Turks, which led to their deaths) over the "Kingdom on Earth."

Being Small and Then Larger Than Life

One of the problems was that Serbia—along with some other Balkan countries—had to deal with the problem of its self-perception. The issue of national identity has been constantly debated in Serbia from at least the mid-nineteenth century. What most authors consider as "the Serb national program" can be traced to the 1844 document called "The Draft" (*Načertanije*), compiled for the Prince Aleksandar Karadjordjević. This paper was actually written for internal use only—it was meant for the foreign policy considerations of the ruling elite. It was produced under considerable influence by the Romanticist movement in Poland. The paper displayed concern for the Serbian "brothers" who lived in other "lands," especially for the Orthodox Christian Serbs, and especially those living within the borders of the Austro-Hungarian Empire. Yet it also promoted the idea of Serbia as the natural "center of gravity" to which (South Slavic) people from the region would naturally gravitate (Garašanin 1939). This idea was frequently recreated in recent years in the statements of leading Serbian politicians, who like to state that Serbia is "the hub" of the Balkans and that the country is crucial for peace and stability in this part of Europe. Here one can see the oscillation between the ideas of the "big" and the "small"—although, for the most part, leading Serbian politicians would regard referring to Serbia as a "small country" as an insult. Thus, smallness was perceived as a temporary condition that would be left behind and from which a stronger and "bigger" country will emerge.

Throughout the nineteenth century Serbia gradually grew in size, acquiring new territories following its recognition as an independent country at the Berlin Congress in 1878, and especially with the territorial gains (most of present-day Kosovo and Macedonia), following the Balkan Wars. In the aftermath of the First World War, political and intellectual elites from Croatia and Slovenia joined the Serbs in supporting a new South Slav state.[5] Serbian political and intellectual elite embraced this state as a way of promoting their own national goals. This state, sometimes referred to as "the first Yugoslavia," disintegrated following the attack by the Axis powers in April 1941, but was formed again in 1945 after the end of World War II. In fact, the Yugoslav partisan army was by 1945 a formidable force, in number of soldiers only behind the United States, the Soviet Union, Great Britain, and France. Serbs identified with Yugoslavia to a great extent. For most of the Serbian cultural elite, the goal of "all Serbs living in a single state" was finally achieved in Yugoslavia. Focusing on the Balkans, contemporary Serb historian Dubravka Stojanović comments that "the greatest Serbian misfortune was that [Serbia] was successful in wars. That fact was frequently used in the beginning of the wars of the 1990s, when, historically not quite accurately, it was repeated that Serbia never lost a war."[6] Yugoslavia as created after 1945 was not a small country, in terms of either size (it was slightly larger than Great Britain), or population (it had around twenty-four million inhabitants before being dissolved in 1991). Sports were a very important marker of national identity, and Yugoslavs were especially proud of their athletes and their successes. This was especially important in team sports, like basketball. In basketball, they saw themselves as "small" in sense of David, defeating the Goliaths of the United States and the Soviet Union, and winning the World Championship in Ljubljana in 1970.[7] The success of several former Yugoslav players, like the Croat Krešimir Ćosić, or Serb Dražen Dalipagić, actually made possible later influx of European players into the world's most important arena, the NBA.

However, while many of its citizens regarded it as a medium-size, but important country, they also regarded it as small in comparison with, for example, Scandinavian countries. While these had rather small populations, their economic might provoked admiration. On the other hand, Greece was always regarded as small, even after it joined the EEC and after its growing economy far surpassed the Yugoslav one. Moreover, Serbs continued to view Greece as small even during the 1990s, when it was perceived to be one of the few allies that Serbia had in the world—even though by then Greece was both larger and more populous than Serbia.

Social Meanings and Political Symbols

Countries are defined by specific symbols (anthem, flag, coat of arms), by their territory (borders)—a bit unclear in the Serbian case—but also by their institutions. Through their political institutions, countries establish themselves, formulate some basic principles of their existence, and are then able to adequately relate to others (other countries, international organizations, and so on).

Serbia provides an interesting case study in considering the rise and development of political institutions. This is a state that came into being after the first "national revolution," as Leopold Ranke has called it, in the Balkan part of the Ottoman Empire, and which, ever since its first autonomous proclamations (e.g., the 1835 constitution) adopted liberal models imported from Western Europe. Throughout the nineteenth century, Serbia gradually incorporated liberal legislature and institutions, and this trend accelerated after its independence. The laws on freedom of press and freedom of association during the 1880s provided conditions for formulating a liberal 1888 constitution based on the Belgian one. That constitution remained in effect for six years, and was reinstituted following the change of ruling dynasty in 1903, beginning what in Serbian historiography is sometimes referred to as the "golden age of Serbian democracy." It provided for the clear separation of powers and democratic procedures based on the most developed European standards of the time. The introduction of quasi-universal male suffrage and the adoption of liberal laws on the freedom of press, assembly, and speech provided the foundations for democratic government.

However, during the same period of institutional changes there was an almost petrified, premodern, and strongly patriarchal society with its own institutions. Poor agrarian people formed 87 percent of the total population. Most peasants owned plots smaller than five acres in size, insufficient for providing for large families. The urbanization process did not really take off until World War I, so the civic class remained small and weak, consisting mostly of petty craftsmen, merchants, and state administrators. There was practically no industry, except for a few breweries and cement factories. These factories were too small to stimulate industrialization and development. The literacy rate, one of the important factors for creating for a democratic society, was extremely low. In rural areas, 76 percent of the people were illiterate, while in the urban areas the percentage was around 45. Overall, this provided unpromising terrain for the transplantation of the most modern European institutions (Stojanović 2013).

When analyzing the way in which that system functioned, one could see that the imported institutions did not operate as intended. According to Stojanović, they were gradually pervaded by a "premodern" idea of politics, which blocked the new institutions and rendered meaningless a well-intended legal framework. A democratic form was filled with an authoritarian content.

The opposition frequently complained about it in its press. One could read in *Odjek* [Echo], paper of the younger democratically oriented generation of intellectuals, mostly educated in Paris, such frustrated statements as: "Serbia accepts from the West all the products of human spirit but in form and not in essence. She uses the laws only as ornaments and not as something really needed." On the opposite side of the political spectrum, progressives and older generation conservatives made almost identical objections. They saw in institutions almost a conspiracy: that is, to keep the same authoritarian political content but to hide it with the change of form:

> This democratism paraded here is democratism by name only. Its purpose is to serve as the veneer behind which it will still be speculated [*sic*], just like behind other veneers. Actually, they want speculators of new order to suppress the ones of the older order. (Stojanović 2011: 207)

In this model of political culture, politics is primarily perceived as a conflict, as a perpetual war in which one is justified in using all means against political opponents—not as a way of articulating and resolving social conflicts. Early twentieth-century nonparty press reported that among the politicians there were high passions that brought Serbia into a permanent sick condition, where "spites and vengeances, hatreds and defamations, persecutions and spying, are characteristics of the era, where political party passions cannot find their own limits." The climate of intolerance that governed political life was described as the one in which political freedom was reduced to the "freedom of brawl." Issues of general interest became subservient to the "fragmentation of political parties, personal strife and conflicts, individual aspirations, insiders' bills, aspirations to any particularity" (Stojanović 2011: 208).

Serbia as a small country in the early twentieth century struggled to catch up with the broader world (Europe). This led to serious debates among the members of the political parties (Perović 2000, 2003; Stojanović 2013), sometimes bordering on what has been described as "political fanaticism" (Stojanović 2011: 208). The harshest accusations were exchanged between the feuding camps, creating an impression that there were no limits to what one could say.

Modernity and Its Discontents

This brings us to the issue of modernity. For most of the twentieth century, Serbia has struggled to catch up with more developed European countries, and some of these struggles continue well into the twenty-first century. As it coped with gaining territories (and peoples that came with them, ethnic groups who were never consulted as to whether they wanted to join a new country or not) and shifting political systems (as it was part of the larger South Slav state), it also struggled with its own identity and state formation. Thus, following the break up of Yugoslavia, other former Yugoslav republics gained independence by voting for it; in Serbia, the situation was quite different: it again became independent (in 2005) only after it was *left alone*.[8] Nobody else wanted to live with Serbia any more.

The developments following the wars of the 1990s (in which, according to the official propaganda, Serbia never took part) dramatically influenced issues of representation related to national identity, but also those of building new institutions. Serbia's political elite seems to be caught between historical goals that actually go back to the nineteenth century and the reality in which global alliances and key concepts have changed. Serb elites seem to be in a particularly awkward spot when it comes to understanding the consequences of the fall of Communism in Eastern Europe. In recent years, there have been some attempts to study some of the institutions involved and to put them in the context of wider social and political shifts (Perović 2003; Stojanović 2010, 2013).

Contemporary struggles with modernity are also reflected in the constant rearticulation of historical goals and political realities, as well also in relation to the country's size—both in terms of territory and in the symbolic sense, in terms of the country's international importance and prestige. The former Yugoslavia was an important player in international politics, especially through the Non-Aligned Movement. The quest by Serbia's elite to understand contemporary global processes and to be understood by other actors in the shifting political landscape of Eastern Europe, has created new ways of dealing with the past. These are visible in changes in education, but also in a whole new set of cultural paradigms supposed to shape national identity. Of course, some of the problems with the shaping of this identity have to deal with the fact that it is not quite clear where the borders of Serbia lie.

However, Serbia presents an interesting case (and possibly a good ethnographic case study) of the phenomenon labeled by historians like Latinka Perović and Dubravka Stojanović as "the alliance of the elites." The actual term was coined by the historian Fritz Fischer (1967), explaining German politics between the 1871 unification and 1945.[9] Numerous examples prove that the elites, consciously or not, kept Serbian society at a certain level of underdevelopment. This was discussed by one of the most important Serbian ethnologists, Tihomir Đorđević (1868–1944), in a two-volume ethnohistorical study reflecting on the 1820s, where he tried to prove how Serbian peasants were the true keepers of the "authentic" culture—unlike the spoiled and "Westernized" people who lived in the cities. His general idea was to show how this "traditional" way of life was superior and should be preserved. The village and the city were "completely different social communities" (Đorđević 1983: 305). The villages are the reservoir of the authentic national energy and culture. In his other works (especially the multivolume compendium on the folklife, 1930–1934), Đorđević emphasized the importance of keeping traditional values against the advent of modernization. While accepting the modernizing values in some aspects, he resented the fact that people were no longer wearing folk clothes. He advocated a level of traditionalism as a defense against the modern culture "pushing in on us" (1930–1934: 4:8).

One of the ways of keeping things as they are was a conscious decision by the elites to preserve a certain level of underdevelopment (Perović 2003). Being small was seen as a good thing, creating the environment where these elites could prosper and flourish—even if it was detrimental for the society as a whole. Serbian elites did little to remove economic or political constraints for the country's development. They had no wish to allow free initiative, as this would have led to the reduction of their almost limitless power. This meant that Serbia would remain outside of the global economic trends as much as possible, so "staying small" was an essential component of the perceived national greatness. Various elite segments, ranging from the church to intellectuals, representatives of the financial sector, and army officers, had an interest in blocking any modernization and Europeanization. Only in an underdeveloped society could they maintain their social standing. Stojanović (2003, 2013) provides numerous examples of this frame of mind, especially through transcripts of the discussions in the National Assembly. It meant delaying decisions that could speed up the country's development (for example, the building of Belgrade's water and sewage system was delayed for administrative reasons for almost four decades), as well as staffing the administration at all levels with people unreservedly loyal to party leaders. Many young Serbs who studied in Western Europe in the late nineteenth and early twentieth centuries returned with strong nationalist feelings. Just as in the case of Germany described by Fischer (1969), the Serbian elite tried to divert the attention the other way, so from its independence until 2000 Serbia was at war every seven years (Perović 2000; Sundhaussen 2007).[10]

What kind of connection do these historical reminiscences have with contemporary Serbia and its ambivalence toward Europe? Just like the rest of Eastern Europe, after the fall of Communism, the former Yugoslavia had an opportunity to transform its own society and, by coming closer to Europe, conduct the transition to a modern society. Yet instead of initiating development processes, Serbia started a process of the dissolution of the Yugoslav state and an attempt at ethnic demarcation, leading to the wars of the 1990s and further distancing from wider integration processes. Serbia's elites saw this dissolution as an opportunity to finally realize aspirations of a unified Serbian state—both in terms of territory and in terms of having all Serbs from the former Yugoslavia still in a single country. When large segments of the society resisted—only around 20 percent of the conscripts answered to the mobilization, independent media criticized the war, and citizens' associations and political parties opposed to the nationalist program were formed. On several occasions, there were protests lasting for several months aimed at deposing President Slobodan Milošević and ending the war politics of his government. However, political and intellectual elites recognized their own interest in the project of creating a great Serbian state, which led them once again at the end of the twentieth century to sacrifice economic and social development, just as they had a century before (Sundhaussen 2007).

After the Milošević regime was deposed in 2000, the main obstacles to Serbia's European integration were its relations to war crimes and the lack of cooperation with the Hague Tribunal. Here one again encounters the same thing: the new elites kept the old national program. They did not openly confront the society with the causes that brought it to the deepest crisis during the 1990s, including the accusations of genocide. That is why many critics in Serbia claimed that there was no essential change in 2000, and that the change of people in power was implemented only in order to keep the unchanged national program, which the compromised Milošević was no longer able to implement. Transformation of the society is still slow and unwilling, even though it again sends a clear signal that it wants change and has entry into Europe as its goal. This was demonstrated in the dramatic way in the 2008 elections, where President Boris Tadić's Democratic Party, proposing the European Serbia, defeated its ultra-nationalist opponents. All the public opinion surveys show that more than 60 percent of the citizens support the European integration. However, even though the society gave a clear pro-European response in all the elections after 2000, with the exception of the most recent ones, the elite, with its hindrance, made the transformation of the Serbian society the slowest of all the Eastern European countries.

Old Dreams and New Realities

Part of the problem (to return to the issue of "big versus small") is that since its independence Serbia has proclaimed certain "national goals" (unification of all Serb lands), and all leading Serbian politicians have felt the need to continue with this policy. When occasional opponents to these policies headed the government (Jovan Ristić in 1878, Zoran Đinđić in 2001/2003), they were assassinated. Attempts to reform society in the early 1880s were violently stopped through armed protests throughout the country. As a matter of fact, so strong was the wish to lag behind that the majority of Serbian politicians at the time were also strongly opposed to railroads—the international rail corridor was introduced only after France and Great Britain threatened Serbia with economic sanctions. Even in the "bigger" South Slav state, Yugoslavia, Serb national goals and aspirations were incorporated in the larger state in the same way as was the case in other multiethnic countries, like the former Czechoslovakia (cf. Holý 1996). This meant that Serbs perceived Yugoslavia as fulfilling their own national goals, even though it was formally a multinational state. Just like the Czechs, Serbs thus "internalized" the larger state as their own, so it was not really necessary to display Serbian nationalism during Yugoslavia's existence.

Serbian intellectuals already felt the need to justify national claims in the nineteenth century. Ethnologists like Stojan Novaković were active in political life. Ethnology, parallel to German *Volkskunde*, prospered. Jovan Cvijić, the internationally recognized "anthropogeographer" at the time, tried to establish character traits that separated Serbs from the other South Slavic peoples (in the sense that made them better and superior). By 1906, Serbia already had a professorial chair in ethnology, a national ethnological society, and a national ethnological journal. Cvijić was also active in politics and was a member of the state delegation at the Versailles Peace Conference following World War I. However, this dramatic influence of ethnologists gradually waned, as its most important representatives died by the end of World War II. But with few exceptions, other intellectuals were more than happy to provide support for the state and state ideology.

Serbia (along with the rest of Yugoslavia) enjoyed dramatic economic development between 1945 and 1980. But when real market economy reforms were implemented in the late 1950s, there was a strong backlash, and the reforms were effectively dead by 1975. Political leaders spearheading reforms were deposed and successful company directors fired.

The dream of territorial expansion, of dominion over lands that were supposed to be Serbian, continued. This dream was expressed in epic poetry and folk literature, but also in the discussions of intellectuals—in the Serbian Academy of Sciences and Arts, in the Writers' Association, and at the University of Belgrade.

Conclusion: The Surplus of History, the Future of Uncertainty

I have outlined some aspects of Serbia's struggles with modernity. At the same time, these were also struggles of a country seeking to establish its place in a changing world. Perhaps the contemporary Serbian historians cited are too obsessed with the idea of modernization. Perhaps the country needs to be left alone, to revel in the feeling that "the international community" unjustifiably denied it its "sacred place" and historical-mythical "place of origin," Kosovo. But the question remains: what would Serbia do with 1.5 million ethnic Albanians who would never recognize its rule?

Serbia's sense of smallness could be seen as a product of a "weak group–weak grid" pattern (Douglas 1970: 56–64), in combination with specific historical developments. As Serbian society went through dramatic changes, part of the adaptation of its population was a fairly relaxed attitude toward cultural symbols. As a matter of fact, as pointed out by Perović and Stojanović, many of them significantly changed over time, due to shifting historical circumstances. The fragmented nature of a peasant-based society precluded formation of any stronger bonds on the national level. On the other hand, modernizing processes were seen as a threat, and history was invoked whenever possible to keep these processes at a safe distance. Smallness was viewed as something essentially positive, characteristic of a rural society where everyone was supposed to know everyone else. In this sense, Serbia was supposed to be better than other countries. At the same time, however, Serbia's elites were well aware that the standard of living was much higher in other (primarily West European) countries, so there was a tendency to strive for accelerated economic and political development. Unfortunately, this development was incompatible with some of the goals of the Serbian elite. To complicate matters further, the "downsizing" of Serbia through the perceived loss of Kosovo reiterated the problem of a small country unable to realize its own goals.

"Being small" in the Balkans is not that different from being small in other parts of the world. While Serbia is a small country, it is still relatively big, compared to its neighbors. It is still struggling to find its place in the processes of globalization, especially with vivid memories of its importance while being part of a much larger country and a respected global player, especially until 1980. What makes it specific is the obsession with the myths of the past, the surplus of history, its shifting between geographical smallness and perceptions of historical greatness, and the intention of its elites to continue bravely leading the country to uncertainty.

Notes

1. It was part of the anthem of the Kingdom of Yugoslavia before World War II (the other part being the current Croatian anthem). The reference to the king was also there, but it was deleted from the new version of the text.

2. I do not wish to dwell here on the issues related to religiosity in the former Yugoslavia. However, there are sufficient data that point to the fact that members of several nations (including Serbs) identified themselves as religious (in the case of Serbs, belonging to Orthodox Christianity) and, at the same time, declared that they did not believe in God.

3. Between 1918 and 1929, Kingdom of Serbs, Croats, and Slovenes; 1929–1941, Kingdom of Yugoslavia; socialist Yugoslavia (the exact name changed three times) between 1945 and 1992; Federal Republic of Yugoslavia between 1992 and 2002.

4. Citizens of Bulgaria and Romania still frequently come to Serbia, looking for work. In most cases, they take low-skill and low-paid seasonal jobs, without any social security.

5. The idea of the unity of South Slav tribes had a long history in Croatia, and it seems that the word "Yugoslavia" (South Slav state) was coined for the first time by a Croatian Catholic missionary in the mid-seventeenth century.

6. Stojanović, personal communication, 2012.

7. Yugoslavia also won World Championships in 1978 and 1990, Olympics in 1980, and European Championships in 1973, 1975, 1977, 1989, and 1991, making it the most dominant national team during the last two decades of the country's existence.

8. Montenegro declared independence in 2005, thus putting an end to the State Union of Serbia and Montenegro, which existed since 2002. Serbia lost control over Kosovo following the NATO intervention in 1999 and the UN Security Council Resolution 1244. Kosovo declared independence in 2008. Serbia and Montenegro also formed the "rump" Yugoslavia since 27 May 1992.

9. I am not claiming Fischer's views were uncontroversial—but the fact is that his thesis is very popular among the new generation of Serb historians (as well as their mentor, Latinka Perović).

10. The mass protests of 1992 and 1996/1997 were skillfully exploited by members of the ruling elite, who basically "co-opted" opposition activists with promises of power sharing at the local levels. Even when Milošević was finally deposed in late 2000, the main criticism directed against him was not that he led Serbia to a series of unnecessary and self-destructive wars during the 1990s, but that he lost them.

References

Đorđević, Tihomir R. 1930–1934. *Naš narodni život* [Our Folk Life]. 10 vols. Belgrade: Geca Kon.

———. 1969. *Krieg der Illusionen: Die deutsche Politik von 1911 bis 1914*. Düsseldorf: Droste.

———. 1983 (1922/1924). *Iz Srbije Kneza Miloša: Kulturne prilike od 1815. do 1839.* [From Prince Milos's Serbia: Cultural Affairs from 1815 to 1839]. Belgrade: Prosveta.

Douglas, Mary. 1970. *Natural Symbols*. London: Barrie & Rockliff.

Fischer, Fritz. 1967. *Germany's Aims in the First World War*. Trans. C. A. Macartney. New York: Norton.

Garašanin, Ilija. 1939 (1844). Načertanije: Program spoljašnje i nacionalne politike Srbije na koncu 1844. godine [The Draft: Program of the Foreign and National Serbian Policies at the End of 1844]. In Dragoslav Stranjaković, Kako je postalo Garašaninovo "Načertanije," [How Garašanin's "The Draft" Came into Being]. *Spomenik SKA* 91:76–102.

Holý, Ladislav. 1996. *The Little Czech and the Great Czech Nation*. Cambridge: Cambridge University Press.

Perović, Latinka. 2000. *Ljudi, događaji i knjige* [People, Events, and Books]. Belgrade: Helsinki Committee for Human Rights in Serbia.

———, ed. 2003. *Srbija u modernizacijskim procesima 19. i 20. veka: Uloga elita* [Serbia in the Nineteenth- and Twentieth-Century Modernizing Processes: The Role of the Elites]. Belgrade: Helsinki Committee for Human Rights.

Stojanović, Dubravka. 2003. *Srbija i demokratija, 1903–1914: Istorijska studija o "zlatnom dobu srpske demokratije"* [Serbia and Democracy, 1903–1914: A Historical Study of the "Golden Age of Serbian Democracy"]. Belgrade: Association for Social History.

———. 2010. *Ulje na vodi: Ogledi iz istorije sadašnjosti Srbije* [Oil on Water: Essays on Serbia's History of the Present]. Belgrade: Peščanik.

———. 2011. In the Quicksand: Political Institutions in Serbia at the End of the Long 19th c. In Tassos Anastassiadis and Nathalie Clayer, eds., *Society, Politics and State Formation in Southeastern Europe During the 19th Century*. Athens: Alpha Bank & Historical Archives.

———. 2013. *Iza zavese: Ogledi iz društvene istorije Srbije 1890–1914* [Behind the Curtain: Essays from Serbia's Social History, 1890–1914]. Belgrade: Association for the Social History.

Sundhaussen, Holm. 2007. *Geschichte Serbiens, 19.–21. Jahrhundert*. Vienna: Böhlau.

PART IV

Struggling with Scales

CHAPTER 10

Blood and Other Precious Resources: Vulnerability and Social Cohesion on the Maldives

Eva-Maria Knoll

"Though the Maldives is a small country it comparatively requires a lot of blood for medical purposes," stated health minister Ahmed Jamsheed Mohamed on the occasion of the inauguration ceremony of a website and a text message system for blood donor recruitment in August 2012.[1] The Republic of Maldives without doubt ranks among the "absolutely small" countries. The land mass of the 1,200 coral islands amounts to just 298 square kilometers; less than half the size of Singapore. The sovereign Maldivian territory of 90,000 square kilometers of Indian Ocean waters, however, is comparable in size with the land mass of Portugal or Jordan. It is a smallness of a unique spatial matter with a land-sea ratio of 1:300, providing a rather difficult terrain for the high intensity of blood transfers between the approximately 340,000[2] citizens addressed in the health minister's speech.

Blood becomes a particularly precious resource when it moves as lifesaving gift between healthy and sick bodies. The reason blood is in such high demand in a place primarily known from tourism brochures as "paradise" lies in the genes of its people. About 19 percent of the Maldivian population carry a defective gene that may result in children being born with a life-threatening blood disorder (Firdous, Gibbons, and Modell 2011: 176–77). These children require regular blood-transfusion therapy throughout their lives. The procurement of donor blood is organized in the Maldives—as in other developing countries—in the framework of a replacement-in-blood policy (cf. Titmuss 1997: 132). If you need blood, you have to bring a donor. Establishing and maintaining a network of appropriate donors—or donating blood on a regular basis—are aspects of acting with limited human resources in a small and developing country's health-care landscape. This chapter considers smallness in relation to both a unique environment and the availability of various resources, ranging from humans and their body fluids to coconuts and shells.

Intersections of Smallness: Islandness and Vulnerability

Working in this coral island world, I developed the habit of evaluating globes and world maps according to whether I can spot the Maldives or if they are missing. Are these islands absent because they are not significant enough, or are they technically too small to be plotted? Granted, in sharp contrast to historical nautical charts featuring the Maldives quite prominently as a dangerous obstacle or vital stopover in the Indian Ocean, on contemporary maps one has to search closely for "what appears to be a splatter of the cartographer's pen," as Amin Didi (1949: 3), who would become the country's first president, put it.

In addition to this elementary problem of visibility, small territories have long been correlated with various disadvantages (Benedict 1967a). If they are not just small but in addition surrounded by water, they are considered particularly vulnerable (Connell 2013; Lewis 2009; Lazrus 2009).[3] In the Maldives some vulnerability results from the high prevalence of a genetic disease embedded in environmental specificities and the struggle for development. Though economically not as vulnerable as small islands in typhoon or hurricane regions, with land surface elevations of just two meters above sea level the Maldives are also exposed to natural extremes: to the long-term effects of climate change, to seasonal impacts of monsoon-related storm flooding, and to the occurrence of noncyclical environmental disasters such as the 2004 tsunami.

The consequences of environmental disasters on small societies in exposed locations are addressed by international and regional bodies as well as by the interdisciplinary research field of island studies.[4] The Maldives have been involved in raising attention for the concerns and in articulating the challenges of small territories at international levels. Health is one of fifteen main topics of the UN organization SIDS (Small Island Developing States), since "countries with small populations and/or limited skilled workforces are particularly vulnerable to the burden of disease due to the impact on the level of productivity and the toll on the social sector."[5] Island studies scholars have analyzed the interconnectedness of insularity and health issues predominantly in the contexts of epidemics, famines, and quarantine (Lewis 2009: 7, 9). Due to their laboratory character, the islands' absolute smallness and population limits make them "good to think with"—Darwin's Galapagos visit is perhaps the most prominent example. Oliver Sacks's (1997) essay on people born color-blind on the Pacific Pingelap atoll is another example, and the hereditary skin disease Mal de Meleda was even named after the island Meleda (now Mljet in Croatia; Saftić, Rudan, and Zgaga 2006: 544). There have been only initial studies so far of the social burdens and challenges of hereditary diseases for small island communities; of emerging genetic identities and marriage strategies (see, e.g., Bornik and Dowlatabadi 2008; Prainsack and Siegal 2006). Some of the Maldivian "sociological aspects of smallness" (Benedict 1967b) that are deeply entangled with this people's genetic destiny and the environmental features of the country are a limited marriage market and costly and time-consuming medical travel activities.[6] The burden of blood donor recruitment will be discussed in detail below.

Despite the fact that the Maldives appear on maps—if at all—as just a double chain of tiny dots in the center of the Indian Ocean, surprisingly, Maldivians basically do *not* consider their country small. Now and then they would refer to it as being small—yet one would hardly hear this reference to absolute smallness without a preceding "though" or a "but." This "though/but" conception of the country often capsizes the prevalent landmass-oriented geopolitical gaze by opposing an "oceanizing" local understanding about size that recognizes the unique environment of the 1:300 land-sea ratio.[7] Island studies would capture this vision islanders have of the space they inhabit with the term "islandness," as "the sum of representations and experiences of islanders, which thus structure their island territory, whereas insularity could be viewed as the particular physical characteristics that define insular space" (Taglioni 2011: 47). Maldivians, it seems, imagine people on densely populated small islands in relation to an enormous connecting water space, rather than imagining the country as relatively small compared, for example, to neighboring Sri Lanka.

Too little and too much population has long been recognized as a particular problem of small island territories (Smith 1967; Rapaport 1990). Immediate

proximity on the small, densely populated Maldivian coral islands is coupled with the enormous dispersal of these islands across central parts of
the Indian Ocean. In Western understanding *the island* is truly an icon of
smallness. The limited space of an island is associated with loneliness, en-
closure, isolation, remoteness, and seclusion. Its archetype is the paradise
island in a romantic version and the prison island in a threatening one (see,
e.g., Picard 2010; Baldacchino 2007). The Maldivian population is both privileged to inhabit some of the most beautiful islands on the planet and doomed
to live on these extremely limited and isolated territories—insularity becoming all too evident when one's child needs a blood transfusion every second
or third week to survive.

Another often encountered Maldivian "small though/but" construction
of islandness resonates with what is experienced as a more or less independent history of the country. In sharp contrast to its neighbors India and Sri
Lanka—and in contrast to the destiny of many other islands and island
countries—the Maldive archipelago has managed to retain some kind of self-
governance throughout most of its history. The colonial power over Ceylon
in general included the Maldives, though usually it was exercised without
much actual interference, respecting the archipelago islanders' handling of
local matters according to their Islamic customs.[8] Yet in the sixteenth century
a fifteen-year period of Portuguese colonial rule (part of the historical expan-
sionism discussed in Pina-Cabral's chapter, this volume) tried to violently
and religiously interfere. Accordingly, this time is still painfully as well as vic-
toriously remembered by reference to the national hero Muhammad Thaku-
rufaanu's triumph over Portuguese aspirations in the archipelago. Dutch
dominance in the Indian Ocean began in the mid-seventeenth century, and in
the early nineteenth century Ceylon became a British colony. The Maldives
requested protectorate status in 1887, and the British era lasted until independence in 1965.

Being Small, Playing Big: Precious Resources
in Past and Present Global Contexts

It would be mistaken to assume that insular smallness automatically results
in scarcity of resources and in being particularly vulnerable or insignificant—
just think of offshore financial centers. Historical and contemporary examples from the Maldives will show that it is exactly scarce and therefore valued

resources through which this country has time and again gained global recognition. It provided goods that acquired luxurious and wealth-generating meaning through long-distance trade in the premodern world. Ibn Battuta's presence as a judge in the fourteenth century and his marriage affiliation to the sultan's family underscore the archipelago's significance in early Arab Indian Ocean trading and religious networks. Ma Huan's report on Chinese-Maldivian merchandising provides an early fifteenth century example: "One or two treasure ships of the Middle Kingdom went there too. They purchased ambergris, coconuts and other such things. It is but a small country."[9] In the twentieth century the remote insularity itself turned into a valued resource and entangled the archipelago once again in diverse global networks; first as a strategic place in the big power game, second as a place of tourist desire.

"It's raining ambergris," exclaimed my language tutor in excitement in 2012, on one of the southernmost islands. Every other day the news reported crews of tuna-fishing boats coming to harbor with ambergris, a waxy substance of musk-like fragrance produced in the digestive system of sperm whales. Before perfume began to be produced synthetically, ambergris was a very precious material—more expensive than gold and gems. Ridiculous sums are allegedly still paid for larger pieces by "unknown French buyers" from the perfume industry, and guidelines on how to identify the valuable substance were printed.[10] I was amazed that this peculiar oceanic resource still has the power to turn tuna fishermen into millionaires overnight and to inspire the imagination of the whole nation. The continuing value-generating power of ambergris contrasts with coco-de-mer and cowries as two other precious resources from the past traceable in the regional culture's folklore (Romero-Frias 2003: 59, 114, 199; 2012: 6, 287).

Coco-de-mer is a rare and unusually shaped double coconut reminiscent of certain female body parts. Accordingly associated with exceptional powers, with sexual desire and fertility, the nut was in high demand both for the sixteenth-century curiosity cabinets of European nobility and, cut in half, as a begging bowl, one of the Persian dervish's insignia (Kläy 1986: 59–65). Before the Seychelles islands were discovered, the mystery of the nut's origin even increased its value. Prevalent currents in the Indian Ocean washed this largest seed in the plant kingdom ashore on the Maldives. Accordingly, the Seychelles nut came to be known as the Maldive coconut, and the scientific name of this seed's palm tree, *Lodoicea maldivica*, still reflects to this assumption.

Cowries—small, oval, shiny porcelain-like shells of a mollusk—played a role in Maldivian exchange, wedding ceremonies, and wealth accumulation (Maloney 1980: 316, 323, 417, 419; Ottovar and Munch-Petersen 1980: 10–12). Beyond this local significance, cowries were also of historic significance. Cowries were used as a "small money" currency in Asia and Africa; they formed the monetary system of the Indian Ocean trade that combined South Asia, West Asia, Europe, Africa, and the New World. Most of the treasured *Cypraea moneta* shells entering world trade were fished in the lagoons of the Maldive Islands and traveled enormous distances in their heyday between the sixteenth and eighteenth centuries (Yang 2011; Hogedorn and Johnson 1986: 7). The Maldivians traded the *moneta* in Ceylon, Bengal, and Indian ports, and the prominent colonial trading companies carried the cowries to the European trading centers. From there cowries went on to West Africa, where they became the shell money of the global slave trade.[11] Taking into account its large spatial and temporal span, the cowry "was probably the first universal money and one that lasted longer than any other kind of money in human history" (Yang 2011: 18, 22).

As the source of cowries, coco-de-mer and ambergris, the Maldives had a "unique position as a supplier" (Yang 2011: 9). The archipelago nevertheless retained a peripheral status throughout the period of changing colonial powers in the Indian Ocean. In World War II, however, the remote islands' location at the very center of the ocean became of strategic interest. In 1942 the British built an airfield on Gan Island, the most southern atoll, as an alternative to their naval base in Ceylon. It was leased by the British from the Maldivian government until 1967 as a strategic stopover between the Middle East and Far East. By the mid-1960s this strategic interest shifted to Diego Garcia on Chagos, the Maldives' neighboring archipelago to the south, from which the entire settled Creole population was forcibly expelled, replaced by a U.S. military base (Vine 2009). As world history has sufficiently proved, insular smallness can represent a certain vulnerability to being bullied, conquered, expelled, even subjected to nuclear contamination. The airstrip on Gan remained, and it turned out to be a scarce resource in the Maldives' world of tiny coral islands. In the 1970s the airstrip was taken over by the up-and-coming transportation and tourism business, and parts of the old Royal Air Force station's sergeants' mess areas were turned into a hotel.

This brings me to two contemporary spheres where the Maldives play a significant role on the global stage and where another understanding of islandness in terms of "though/but" smallness might be rooted. First, with the rise in tourism in the early 1970s, the country's 1,200 remote islands and the 1:300 land-sea ratio became wealth-generating resources and positioned the Maldives in the premier league on the international stage of luxury tourism (Kundur 2012; Faber 1992). Exceeding the threshold of one million annual arrivals in 2013, tourism forms the country's largest economic sector (Ministry of Tourism 2014). Due to long-distance travel, the tropical island became a true "heterotopia" in Foucault's (1984 [1967]) sense, a place imagined and real; a metaphor for a utopian paradise space as well as an accessible holiday destination. In contemplation of climate change, however, the "tropical island" became also an icon of human concerns. In this regard, second, once again Maldivian smallness has achieved global recognition by indicating the climate-change vulnerability of this archipelagic "waterworld" (Hastrup 2009) with a headline-grabbing underwater cabinet meeting in 2009, and with catchy slogans like "if we cannot save the Maldives we cannot save the world."[12]

With the island as a strategic and iconic resource that is endangered and intrinsically entangled with the modern tourism industry, we find some continuity with the bygone resources of cowries, coco-de-mer, and ambergris that also had interlinked the coral islands with translocal profit and luxurious lifestyle desires. Behind the tourist-brochure image of the Maldives, and despite the vision of the islands falling victim to climate change, however, there is a daily struggle for blood, of which hardly any tourists have ever heard. In this regard, the Maldive people are once again astonishing in their achievements.

Numbers Matter: A Small Society's Struggle with a Hereditary Blood Disorder

The Maldives are the smallest but most prosperous "above the regional average" country in South Asia, upgraded from least-developed country status in January 2011, and placed in the "medium human-development group" in 2012 (UNDP 2013). Health care, however, remains a challenging task in the archipelago—especially in treatment-intensive cases of chronic diseases. Every fifth to sixth person in the Maldivian population is a carrier of a defective gene that may result in children being born with thalassemia, a life-threatening disorder of hemoglobin production.[13] Two carriers of the genetic trait (heterozygous) would represent a high-risk couple with a 25 percent chance of conceiving a thalassemic child (homozygous), whose body cannot produce enough functioning red blood cells, and thus would need blood transfusion therapy every two to three weeks throughout her or his life.[14] The Maldives are located in the center of the so-called thalassemia belt. This is an area where malaria is or was widespread, and where an estimated 4.6 million thalassemia patients are living in smaller and larger countries of the Mediterranean, the Indian Ocean, and the Pacific (Weatherall and Clegg 2001: 706).

Thalassemia, the most common genetic disease in the world, has an almost eighty-year time line of discovery and treatment development. For the purpose of this text, I would like to stress two time horizons of discovery. The blood disease was discovered between 1910 and 1925 in patients with a Mediterranean background. The subsequent belief that it was restricted to this area led to its somewhat misleading etymology and to the misnomer "thalassemia."[15] However, case reports from Asia and the Middle East proliferated, and by 1960 the enormous extent of a thalassemia belt in the tropical world and the disorders' high prevalence in certain Asian populations became apparent (Weatherall 2010b: 1114). The frequent occurrence of the thalassemia trait in the Maldives results from malaria, the dreaded "Maldivian fevers" that for centuries had kept Europeans at a distance,[16] from island endogamy (Firdous 2005: 132; Maloney 1980: 336–37), and consanguineous marriages. However, since the Maldivian kinship system with its marriage patterns was built up from the confluence of three systems—Arab, Dravidian, and north Indian (Maloney 1980: 309–51)—first-cousin marriages are less often seen than in other, thalassemia-affected Muslim countries. The environmental factors of malaria and the challenging wind and current conditions for interisland sailing or rowing resulting in a limited marriage market might explain the uneven distribution of thalassemia carriers and cases throughout the country's twenty-one atolls (Firdous, Gibbons, and Modell 2011: 176).

Surprisingly, however, despite having one the world's highest prevalences of the beta-thalassemia trait (Firdous, Gibbons, and Modell 2011: 187), the Maldives long remained almost overlooked in the scientific world. Until very recently (e.g., Weatherall 2011) the "splatter" in the center of the Indian Ocean was largely missing in epidemiological survey maps. Could a small country's population size, resulting in small absolute case numbers despite an extraordinary ratio of prevalence, be particularly vulnerable to being disregarded in the world of science?

I asked Bernadette Modell, a distinguished expert on hemoglobin disorders, why this small country's particularly pronounced struggle with thalassemia has not been more prominently recognized in the scientific world:

> The answer is pretty simple. The Maldives have a small population and no university [until 2011]—people go to Sri Lanka [among other places] for higher education. Therefore there is no one resident with experience in academic publishing. On the other hand, there are some very highly talented people who recognize the importance of thalassemia and do everything they can to ensure treatment and prevention. Dr. Naila Firdous is a Maldivian obstetrician who has spent her life on this work, always an uphill struggle. In the developing-country setting these people are too busy doing their remarkable work to write it up for publication—or, even tougher, to get it through the complex publishing process. If you don't publish, you don't get noticed.[17]

The first documentations of the blood disorder on the Maldives were recorded in the early 1970s (Firdous 2005: 132), and in the late 1980s thalassemia was recognized as a serious health issue. A report of a World Health Organization (WHO) visit in 1988 immediately ranked the Maldives as one of the "world's thalassemia 'hot spots,'" and already in this report the difficulty is mentioned that "the family has to bring a donor for their child" (Modell, Razzak, and Hindley 1990: 1170). Thanks to the promotion of a local health NGO, to a National Thalassemia Program (Firdous 2005: 132), and to the emerging "biosociality" (Rabinow 1996; Gibbon and Novas 2008) in the form of a thalassemics and parents' self-help group, thalassemia treatment, awareness, and prevention programs have almost reached international standards within the last two decades. The blood donor procurement regime, however, is still challenging. Especially "finding an adequate number of donors at the island level is problematic because of the small size of their constituent populations" (Firdous 2005: 133).

According to the Thalassaemia International Federation, at least fifteen million blood units are needed every year to keep the five hundred thousand worldwide thalassemia-major patients alive.[18] On the Maldives 60 percent of the country's entire blood requirement was assigned for thalassemia treatment (Firdous 2005: 133), and by spring 2013 the monthly need for the 574 registered patients amounted to five thousand blood bags.[19] As in many developing countries, in the Maldives blood donation is predominantly organized as a donor-replacement system.

Crucial Recruiting Networks and Compassionate Biosociality

Blood donors are in high demand in the Maldives, yet their numbers are limited by several factors. The blood of close family members may be too similar in its characteristics, so rejection reactions in the recipient are to be feared. Moreover, a thalassemic's family often includes carriers. Although hardly affected by the defective gene in their daily life, carriers' hemoglobin levels are often below average, and according to this mild form of anemia their capacity to replace donated blood is limited (Hazelwood 2001: 98). As a result, private donor networks tend to run along lines of friendship or acquaintance. Due to monthly menstrual bleeding, women's hemoglobin levels also are rather low from the outset. Moreover, although lifestyle diseases (such as being overweight or high blood pressure) are on the rise, most young Maldivian women are still remarkably small and slim, with weights often below forty-five kilograms, and thus have to be rejected as donors. Male donors therefore dominate the thalassemia donation scene.[20] The majority of donors I talked to give *ley hadhiyaa* (lit. "gift of blood") for particular thalassemia patients on a regular basis. Their recruitment works mostly through personal networks, as the following ethnographic vignettes show.

Like the average beta-thalassemia major patient, the teenager Zeenath[21] needs a blood transfusion every two weeks. Her two older sisters help her to recruit donors. The three sisters have a fixed list of donor friends on their cell phones. In this way they always know "who is next on the list; is next in the queue," so they can easily take turns calling them in. Since it is a well-established network, running now for about fifteen years, not much talking is necessary. A short "My sister needs blood. Are you free to donate?" is enough. Like many others, Zeenath and her family do not trust the medical expertise of the small hospital on their home island. Instead, they prefer to take the ninety-minute ferry ride to the capital, where the oldest sister lives, for various health matters, including Zeenath's transfusions. Thus their donor list bypasses their home island and draws from the much larger donor pool in the capital.

Shop owner Mohamed has the rare A-positive blood group, for which it is difficult to find donors in the Maldives. He has brought his employee to the transfusion clinic—by pure coincidence one of the rare matching donors. At the clinic, 450 milliliters of blood will be taken from the donor, and it will take about ninety days for the donor's body to replace the removed vital substance. Thus every three months Mohamed can count on his employee as an easily available donor. In between, Mohamed would call the handful of appropriate donors he knows. He easily gets impatient, however, with the far too small donor pool for his blood group. He would then dial the emergency police number. The police have always found an appropriate donor from their own ranks.

Abdulla, a twenty-three-year-old software engineer from Male, remembers the time when he was too young to organize the donors by himself and yet too old not to recognize how hard this recruiting business was for his divorced, single mother. Sometimes she could not remember whom she had already asked and who had actually given the last time, so she would ask people again, with the result of repeatedly feeling disappointed and embarrassed in equal measure. Occasionally, when she was not able to come up with a donor on time, she left anemic Abdulla in the small children's playground in the courtyard of the transfusion clinic, and she went outside to ask people on the street "please give blood for my son." He could see her crying and stopping strangers on the street to beg for blood.

Donor Ahmed is in his forties. He lives in Male but originates from a southern atoll with a particularly high prevalence of thalassemia. We talk in the waiting room of the clinic's laboratory, where in a few minutes a nurse is due to take his blood. But there is some confusion because another donor has already shown up for the child Ahmed is supposed to be giving blood for. With his twelve years' experience of regular blood donation Ahmed is well aware that such failed coordination happens. Sometimes a donor who promised to come would not show, or two donors have been called in to give their precious gift at the same time. Nevertheless, Ahmed will donate today. In this case his blood will go into the small stock the clinic provides for desperate patients who could not manage to find a donor. There Ahmed's blood will be stored for a maximum of thirty-five days. Blood as fresh as possible, however, is preferable for thalassemia patients, since hemoglobin has a lifespan of 120 days.

These examples show that the Maldivian thalassemic blood recipient is not the rather passive "receiving" actor in the blood transaction (Street 2009: 195). Maldivian thalassemic blood recipients and their parents with their investments in donor recruitment have to be added to what Jacob Copeman

(2005) has argued is a multidimensional economy of blood management. Thalassemics and parents work hard and creatively on their donor networks in order to secure the next transfusion and thus survival. Thereby the proximity of this small societies' *Gemeinschaft* is beneficial in providing family, friendship, and island networks that can be activated in the recruiting process.

In addition to these direct donor network channels the precious body substance may take alternative routes. In "blood camps" donors give their blood *not* for a particular recipient and *without* being encouraged by a familiar person. Blood camps are regularly organized in the Maldives on 14 June (World Blood Donor Day), on 8 May (International Thalassemia Day), and shortly before Ramadan (to take some pressure off regular donors during the physically challenging Islamic month of fasting). In addition to these annual target dates, the outstanding blood demand for thalassemia treatment in the Maldives also resonates in specific PR and charity strategies: some Maldivian companies and tourist resorts organize blood camps and collect blood from their staff when celebrating an anniversary. The Indian Club, an association of Indian expats in the Maldives, for example, organizes a blood camp once a year.

"It Is Very Hard": A Small Country's Compassionate Biosociality

The blood procured in blood camps is collected according to the "voluntary unpaid blood-donor scheme" favored by the World Health Organization (WHO 2011), the Red Cross/Crescent, and by Richard Titmuss (1997) in his classic study *The Gift Relationship* (first published in 1970). The majority of blood bags for thalassemia treatment, however, derive from personally recruited donors. Such "donor replacement schemes" dominate in non-Western, developing countries and contrast with the systems where blood is either treated as a commodity collected from paid donors or where the flows of blood follow the WHO ideal.[22] In the latter systems, the mobilization for voluntary nonremunerated blood donations is often imaginatively stimulated, and ideologically and politically loaded, and in this way is based on what Bob Simpson (2011) has aptly called "blood rhetorics."[23]

The Maldives dismiss these kinds of rhetoric, which connect blood donation with the formation of national identities, because this small country's divides do not run along ethnic or religious lines. The Maldivian population is ethnically and linguistically largely homogeneous and "100 percent Sunni Muslim," as is often stressed—with pride by some, and (internationally) criticized by others—since other religious orientations are not recognized in the country. The archipelago's current ditches and inequalities are rather found between representatives of a more moderate and a rather conservative Islamic orientation, between those profiting to a greater or lesser extent from the luxury tourism business and those who have fewer opportunities to participate (e.g., women; Shakeela, Ruhanen, and Breakey 2010), between people living in the centers (the two urban agglomerations Male and Addu City) and those living in infrastructural disadvantaged "outer islands,"[24] between the 340,000 Maldivians and the estimated 100,000 (predominately male) foreign workforce, and between those affected by acute and chronic diseases who can and those who cannot afford health-care-related travel within the country or across borders.

In the Maldivian thalassemia blood collection system, the donor's blood is *not* replacing the used blood of a blood bank's virtual pool. Here, "direct donors" (Choudhury 2011: 119) give their precious gift for a particular child or an adult thalassemic and are recruited by the thalassemic or her or his parents. As a second contrast to dominant replacement systems, mostly these donors are not family members (as, for example, in Papua New Guinea; Street 2009) but friends and associates. Janet Carsten (2011) reminds us that transfers of bodily substances are imagined in relational terms, Alice Street (2009: 194) has argued that replacement systems give rise to different modes of relatedness and, in his classic ethnography on the Maldives, Clarence Maloney (1980: 331) emphasized friendship connections next to kinship ties as the very "fabric of human relations." All the donors I have talked to knew that thalassemia is a life-threatening and debilitating disorder. Their motivations for regular donations pointed to a particular mode of relatedness, comprising feelings of altruism, guilt, and obligation that centered on the exclamation that "it is very hard for the child and the parents." This remark takes in the aspects of the physical pain of the child or adult thalassemic due to regular pricking for blood tests, transfusions, and iron overload therapy, as well as the emotional suffering, the treatment-related time, and financial exertion of whole families—and the challenge in providing blood donors. Since the population density on the tiny Maldivian coral islands correlates to a certain social density, any small island community is well aware about the suffering, pain, and burdens of particular individuals and families.

Maldivian blood donors see their precious gift as a contribution to shoul-
dering these burdens. Maldivian thalassemics and their blood donors form
more of a *Gemeinschaft* and are less of a *Gesellschaft* (cf. Introduction), addressed and encouraged by blood rhetorics. In smaller societies we see a
higher intensity of relations, since people "are brought into contact over and
over again in various activities" (Smith 1967: 47). Accordingly, individuals
have to take on a greater number of different roles. Comparatively many Maldivian friends and neighbors are also blood donors.

The Maldivian network-dependent direct-donor system is experienced
and emphasized as an enormous burden by adult thalassemics, parents, and
representatives of prevention and treatment programs. Some parents and thalassemics, however, stress that despite this undeniably heavy burden, the
system does not only have disadvantages. It seems to be linked to the kind of
trust experienced by a small country's *Gemeinschaft*. Parents explained that
it "feels good to know the donor," to know what kind of person that is—
especially that a donor does not consume drugs or alcohol. It is reassuring
that the donor eats healthily and leads a generally healthy lifestyle; in a nut-
shell, that she or he "is a good person." The mother of an eight-year-old thalassemic added a sociomedical dimension to this kind of trust based on
knowing a donor's lifestyle when she argued that, based on the long-term
donation relationships, she knows to which donors' blood her daughter
would not show allergic reactions. With these donors she feels more relaxed
during the approximately four-hour transfusion. This kind of a bottom-up
approach toward blood safety based on a face-to-face relationship with blood
donors mirrors and thwarts what has been discussed at length in Western
blood-transfusion discourses, namely, the risks and uncertainties of paid and
anonymous donor systems and the equation of identifiable blood with blood
safety (Titmuss 1997).

By contrast to the average tourist, the Maldivian population nowadays is
well aware of the thalassemia challenge. A screening program was initiated
in 1992, the subject entered the school curriculum in 1996, and premarital
genetic screening has (at least theoretically) been obligatory since 1999. Thus
sooner or later everybody comes to know her or his individual carrier status
(Firdous 2005: 133–34). And since one in five Maldivians is a carrier of the
thalassemia trait, even those who are not directly affected are nevertheless
aware and alert. The step from an imagined community (that shares the burden of a genetic destiny and of anemic suffering) to a real community (that
displays a specific kind of blood-based relation) is perhaps indeed a shorter

one in a small archipelagic community. The shared genetic curse together with the harsh treatment realities and the recurring need for blood seems to create a certain social cohesion and forms a kind of thalassemia-based solidarity that is articulated in a remarkable willingness to donate blood. This might throw new light on a "diffuse solidarity" based on blood relationship, as David Schneider has argued for American kinship (1980 [1968]: 23–25, 50–51). The social thalassemia fabric in the Maldives can be characterized as a shoulder-to-shoulder relationship of mutual awareness and shared burden of a genetic destiny. Following the considerations on the emergence of new group identities around genetic conditions (Rabinow 1996) and related novel modes of activism (Gibbon and Novas 2008), I would characterize this variant of "expanded networks of biosocial involvement" (Gibbon and Novas 2008: 7) as *compassionate biosociality*. Maldivian direct blood donors are not affected at first hand by the thalassemia trait—they are neither heterozygous carriers nor homozygous thalassemics, and mostly they are not involved in lobbying or other group activities. Yet, they are compassionate with these groups and contribute a crucial resource. Thalassemics and their donors form the imagined community of a genetically challenged small society. Compassionate biosociality might perhaps find a more fertile ground in a small country with a particularly high prevalence of a genetic disorder.

Via regular replacement donors for specific thalassemics recruited through personal networks, supported by blood camps' collections among anonymous donors for unspecified recipients, blood flows can be kept within the country. Due to the general scarcity of a small island country's resources, the Maldives otherwise import almost everything, from construction materials to staple diets and products for daily needs. The more than one million annual tourists are not asked for lifesaving gift blood. On the Maldives blood moves between the healthy and the sick, but almost exclusively between Maldivian bodies.[25] In my view, this is an enormous achievement for a small country with a limited population pool and thus with absolute limits regarding body substances.

Conclusion: Smallness Imposes Limits and Calls for Particular Strategies

The thalassemia-centered Maldivian blood economy rests on multiple factors. The burden of procuring blood donations can rely on accessibility and connectivity as specific qualities of a small country's social fabric. In addition to the community's genetic-disorder-centered cohesion there are factors such as the rather close-knit connections accorded to small island communities, the limited health resources resulting from both insularity and underdevelopment, and a religion that provides a specific inventory of social measures for the underprivileged. The flipside of cohesion in the "simultaneity of contrasting possibilities" (cf. this volume's introduction) of a small country's social fabric also becomes obvious, however, since failing in donor procurement seems to point to one's failure in social-networking competence (Street 2009: 208).

The jeopardy of network failure may indicate why compassionate biosociality and insularity may seek technological complicity in equal measure in the Maldives. The new website and text message system for blood donor recruitment referred to at the beginning of this chapter has the capacity to do both—to strengthen and to downplay the contrasting possibility poles of the small country's social fabric. It builds upon and strengthens shoulder-to-shoulder shared thalassemia attention as well as possibly bridging, absorbing, and concealing network failure in donor procurement. The environmental features of the 1:300 land-sea ratio evoke technology of distance management. Cell phones, the Internet, and social networks such as Facebook are extremely popular in the Maldives due to their ability to connect a small community dispersed across a vast oceanic territory and thus to overcome a "feeling of isolation" that plays a crucial role in islandness (Taglioni 2011: 47). The 171.6 "fixed and mobile telephone subscribers per 100 people" in the Maldives is accordingly remarkable (UNDP 2013). The innovative potential of the web- and text-message-based blood-donation procurement system for thalassemics lies in the entanglement of two interacting elements, namely, the usefulness of technological distance management in an archipelagic environment and the small world's social fabric phenomenon of "thinking in networks." Assembling and thus sharing of the existing private donor networks to a country-wide, technologically mediated donor service somehow was a logic next step.

In the Maldives, networks of blood donors are assembled according to matching blood types and proximity to the recipient in need. The system enables thalassemics or their parents to encourage blood donors by simply sending a text message via cell phone or the Internet, indicating the blood group needed and the home area of the recipients. As a spatiotemporal coordination of originating veins with veins in need (Copeman 2005: 466) the system distributes the message to blood-group-matching donors in the vicinity. In Maldivian blood management, blood as a timeless idiom of relationship and solidarity (Copeman 2009b) is linked with cell phones and the Internet as timely idioms of connection and distance management. The future will show if technological mediation in donor procurement can be as effective as the intimacy of direct relationships in personal networks. The future will also show whether the June 2012 fusion of the former National Thalassaemia Centre with the Blood Transfusion Centre to form a new institution called Maldivian Blood Services (MBS) will help to ease the burden of donor procurement for thalassemia treatment, and what kind of blood rhetoric this institution will use to encourage donors. For the ambitious vision of an intensified regional Asian cooperation in blood services (Choudhury 2011), the Maldives' location may perhaps again be too remote.

By spring 2013 the IT-based donor recruitment system had proven some efficacy, according to one of its initiators, a thalassemic himself, though it had not yet reached its full theoretical capacity, which would occur when the data of the more than fourteen thousand blood donors registered with MBS is fed into the system. In 2014, however, the aforementioned initiator and driving force of the system passed away unexpectedly and far before his time. In the aftermath to this tragic event the system dwindled away. Thalassemics and parents have turned to other (not thalassemia-focused) blood donor recruiting social media networks, and the country's reference clinic MBS in Male has substantially increased efforts to enhance its blood bank stock through running blood camps in tourism resorts, companies, and governmental offices almost every week. Though these efforts ease the recruiting pressure, they are still far from being sufficient to meet the extraordinary thalassemica-related blood requirements of this small country. Moreover, these efforts so far are concentrated in the capital island Male. As a result, the majority of Maldivian adult thalassemics and parents of thalassemic children still remain dependent on the compassionate biosociality of their blood-donor networks—that is, on the archipelago population's strength, which emerged from a small country's experience in facing challenges.

*   *   *

I am grateful to the following people for their valuable consultations, discussions, and advice: to my hosts and the thalassemics, their parents and their blood donors for sharing their insights and experiences; to Ibrahim Faisal, Bernadette Modell, Nils Finn Munch-Petersen, Xavier Romero-Frias, Mariya

Saeed, Boris Wille, and the International Small Island Studies Association
(ISISA). My thanks also go to David Westacott for polishing my English.

Notes

1. Mohamed Afrah, Blood Donation Website and SMS System Introduced,
Haveeru Online, 16 August 2012.

2. *Statistical Yearbook of Maldives 2014*, preliminary data, accessed 28 October
2015 at http://planning.gov.mv/yearbook2014/yearbook/Population/3.1.pdf.

3. See also the website Island Vulnerability, http://www.islandvulnerability.org.

4. About 10 percent of the world's population live on islands and "one-fourth of
the world's sovereign states consists of island or archipelagic territories" (Baldacchino
2007: 1).

5. SIDS (Small Island Developing States), accessed 31 May 2013, http://www.sidsnet
.org/about-sids.

6. Medical travel is carried out *within* the archipelago for preventive measures such
as genetic screening and genetic counseling, since this is largely available in the capital,
and *across borders* for prenatal genetic diagnosis and possibly pregnancy termination,
as neither is available on the Maldives (Firdous, Gibbons, and Modell 2011: 185). Travel
can also be necessary for blood transfusions and other forms of treatment.

7. The prevalent geographical gaze that draws the line between what does and does
not belong to a country makes archipelagic countries smaller than they are, even "mi-
nuscules" them. Stefan Helmreich's (2011: 137) concept of "oceanization," that is, "a
reorientation toward the seas as a translocally connecting substance," is helpful in
reassessing current geopolitics.

8. The facts that the tiny Maldivian coral islands did not earn agricultural interest, that the archipelago was malaria-ridden, and that the shallow waters of the coral
reefs were difficult to navigate probably contributed to the lower level of political interference. However, the archipelago was always dependent on trading relationships
and networks with mainland and island neighbors, particularly India and Sri Lanka.
A significant proportion of today's cross-border mobility still involves the same historic trade destinations, for educational, shopping, business, leisure, and medical
reasons.

9. Ma Huan, Chinese Muslim interpreter, traveler, and author of *The Overall Survey of the Ocean's Shores*, as cited in Romero-Frias (2003: 10). Ma Huan accompanied
the Chinese Muslim admiral Cheng Ho on his expeditions. The fourth voyage (1413–
1415) brought him to the Maldive Islands (*The Encyclopaedia of Islam* [Leiden: Brill,
1983], 5:849; cf. Ptak 1987).

10. *Haveeru Online*, 3 June 2012.

11. In the eighteenth century the Dutch Vereenigde Oost-Indische Companie (VOC) and the English East India Company (EIC) shipped 11,436 metric tons—around ten billion individual shells—to West Africa (Hogedorn and Johnson 1986: 58).

12. Cf. Jon Shenk's 2011 movie *The Island President*. The global-warming-related vulnerability of the Maldives has become highly politicized. The understanding of this topic ranges from seeing the Maldives as one of the first victims of sea-level rising (in this case, a symbolic microscopic image of an industrialized world's fears) to the viewpoint that the whole affair is a foreign policy PR strategy of one Maldivian political party.

13. Beta-thalassemia is the most common variant of hemoglobin disorders in the Maldives and beta-thalassemia major is the most severe and most common transfusion-dependent disorder. In addition to beta carriers the contemporary prevention programs screen for alpha and alpha zero, hemoglobin E and D, and sickle cell traits. In the Maldives, everyday encounters with these inherited blood disorder variants are captured by the generic term "thalassemia" (Brit., thalassaemia), which I also use in this chapter.

14. Several factors increase the chances for high-risk couple formations: The density of 19 percent heterozygous carriers in the population results in every fifth person in the already limited small marriage market being a carrier. This situation is fueled by the country's exceedingly high divorce and remarriage rate. Maloney (1980: 309) reported eighty-four divorces per one hundred marriages for the mid-1970s. Court statistics assembled by the Department of National Planning report forty divorces per one hundred marriages for 2008 and 2009.

15. Greek *thalassa* "sea" and *an* plus *haima* (or *haema* in the Latinized version) "no blood," meaning the lack of blood (anemia) occurring around the sea, that is, the Mediterranean in the Greek worldview (Eleftheriou 2003: 7).

16. Although the protective effect is still not entirely understood, research suggests that an evolutionary adaptation means that carriers of the thalassemia trait "are somewhat protected in areas where *Falciparum malaria* is or has been endemic" (Weatherall 2010a: 178–84; Higgs, Engel, and Stamatoyannopoulos 2012: 376). This kind of resistance of thalassemia heterozygotes to the most severe form of malaria increased the number of carriers within a small and highly malarial territory where more non-carriers fall victim to the disease.

17. Bernadette Modell, personal communication, 15 July 2013.

18. Thalassaemia International Federation, accessed 23 May 2012, http://www.thalassaemia.org.cy/did_you_know.html.

19. Ibrahim Faisal, (at that time) deputy director of Maldivian Blood Services (MBS), personal communication, 30 June 2013. The great efforts in treating 574 Maldivian thalassemia patients out of a population of 340,000 become clear when this number is compared to the "more than 2,000" patients among the twenty million inhabitants of neighboring Sri Lanka (Hemoglobal, accessed 6 June 2013, http://hemoglobal.org).

20. Drugs were brought up by my informants as an additional donor-limiting factor, since the illegal consumption might be revealed in the blood screening process. According to the *Guardian* (London), "one in 20 of Male's inhabitants is a regular user of heroin or cannabis" (Burke 2012). The listed factors limiting and aggravating donor recruitment are not only evident on small archipelagic countries like the Maldives. Indonesia with its seventeen thousand islands faces similar challenges due to a dispersed population, a low number of female donors due to their low hemoglobin levels and low body weights, as well as insufficient blood supply during the fasting month (Soedarmono 2010: 45). Though Indonesia, as a large country of 220 million, shares the features of a difficult infrastructural archipelago situation and a challenging donor scarcity with the Maldives, its greater financial and human resources would certainly help ease bottlenecks and emergencies.

21. The core of the data on donor recruitment presented here was gathered in a fieldwork period from November 2011 to January 2012. All names have been anonymized.

22. For an overview of blood transfusion services in Asia, see Choudhury (2011); on gift and economy aspects of blood donation, see Copeman (2009b); on relational aspects, see Carsten (2011).

23. In neighboring Sri Lanka's civil war times, for example, donor campaigns promoted "blood as an anonymous gift" and addressed and encouraged voluntary donors by drawing upon rhetorics of devotional acts of giving in Buddhism, of extended kinship obligations, or of militaristic nationalism in the face of Tamil secessionist encounters, among others (Simpson 2011). In India, the Maldives' second closest neighboring country, national integration of linguistic, caste, and ethnic diversity is addressed by the "difference-traversing gift" (Copeman 2009a: 79).

24. See, e.g., "Service Inequalities Plague Thalassaemia Sufferers," *Minivan News* [online], 8 May 2012.

25. An interesting direction that cannot not be followed here may be to consider current donor willingness in light of the historic significance of blood in the country's folklore as well as of blood sacrifice in relation to epidemics that Romero-Frias identifies as essential to understanding Maldivian mythology (2012; 2003: 88, 113–29).

References

Baldacchino, Godfrey, ed. 2007. *A World of Islands*. Malta: Agenda Academic.

Benedict, Burton, ed. 1967a. *Problems of Smaller Territories*. London: Athlone.

———. 1967b. Sociological Aspects of Smallness. In Burton Benedict, ed., *Problems of Smaller Territories*. London: Athlone.

Bornik, Zosia B., and Hadi Dowlatabadi. 2008. Genomics in Cyprus: Challenging the Social Norm. *Technology in Society* 30 (1): 84–93.

Burke, Jason. 2012. Maldives' Political Instability Allows Gang Violence to Flourish. *Guardian* [online], 22 October.

Carsten, Janet. 2011. Substance and Relationality: Blood in Contexts. *Annual Review of Anthropology* 40:19–35.

Choudhury, Nabajyoti. 2011. Blood Transfusion in Borderless South Asia. *Asian Journal of Transfusion Science* 5 (2): 117–20.

Connell, John. 2013. *Islands at Risk? Environments, Economies and Contemporary Change.* Cheltenham, UK: Edward Elgar.

Copeman, Jacob. 2005. Veinglory: Exploring Processes of Blood Transfer Between Persons. *Journal of the Royal Anthropological Institute* 11 (3): 465–85.

———. 2009a. Gathering Points: Blood Donation and the Scenography of "National Integration" in India. *Body & Society* 15 (2): 71–99.

———. 2009b. Introduction: Blood Donation, Bioeconomy, Culture. *Body & Society* 15 (2): 1–28.

Didi, Amin A. M. 1949. *Ladies and Gentlemen: The Maldive Islands.* Colombo: Novelty Printers and Publishers.

Eleftheriou, Androulla. 2003. *About Thalassaemia.* Nicosia: Thalassaemia International Federation Publications (4).

Faber, Mike. 1992. Micro-States, Increasing Integration and Awkward Imperatives of Adjustment: The Case of the Republic of the Maldives. In Helen M. Hintjens and Malyn D. D. Newitt, eds., *The Political Economy of Small Tropical Islands: The Importance of Being Small.* Exeter: University of Exeter Press.

Firdous, Naila. 2005. Prevention of Thalassaemia and Haemoglobinopathies in Remote and Isolated Communities: The Maldives Experience. *Annals of Human Biology* 32 (2): 131–37.

Firdous, Naila, Stephen Gibbons, and Bernadette Modell. 2011. Falling Prevalence of Beta-Thalassaemia and Eradication of Malaria in the Maldives. *Journal of Community Genetics* 2 (3): 173–89.

Foucault, Michel. 1984 (1967). Of Other Spaces: Heterotopias. *Architecture, Mouvement, Continuité* 5 (October): 46–49.

Gibbon, Sahra, and Carlos Novas, eds. 2008. *Biosocialities: Genetics and the Social Sciences.* London: Routledge.

Hastrup, Kirsten. 2009. Waterworlds: Framing the Question of Social Resilience. In Kirsten Hastrup, ed., *The Question of Resilience: Social Responses to Climate Change.* Copenhagen: Kongelige danske Videnskabernes Selskab.

Hazelwood, Loren. 2001. *Can't Live Without It: The Story of Hemoglobin in Sickness and in Health.* Huntington, N.Y.: Nova Science Publishers.

Helmreich, Stefan. 2011. Nature/Culture/Seawater. *American Anthropologist* 113 (1): 132–44.

Higgs, Douglas R., James Douglas Engel, and George Stamatoyannopoulos. 2012. Thalassaemia. *Lancet* 379 (9813): 373–83.

Hogendorn, Jan, and Marion Johnson. 1986. *The Shell Money of the Slave Trade*. Cambridge: Cambridge University Press.

Kläy, Ernst Johannes. 1986. Die Republik Malediven. In Ernst Johannes Kläy and Daniel Kessler, *Trauminseln–Inselträume*. Bern: Bernisches Historisches Museum.

Kundur, Suresh Kumar. 2012. Development of Tourism in Maldives. *International Journal of Scientific and Research Publications* 2 (4): 1–5.

Lazrus, Heather. 2009. The Governance of Vulnerability: Climate Change and Agency in Tuvalu, South Pacific. In Susan A. Crate and Mark Nuttall, eds., *Anthropology and Climate Change from Encounters to Actions*. Walnut Creek, Calif.: Left Coast Press.

Lewis, James. 2009. An Island Characteristic: Derivative Vulnerabilities to Indigenous and Exogenous Hazards. *Shima: The International Journal of Research into Island Cultures* 3 (1): 3–15.

Maloney, Clarence. 1980. *People of the Maldive Islands*. New Delhi: Orient Longman.

Ministry of Tourism, Republic of Maldives. 2014. *Tourism Yearbook 2014*. Male: Ministry of Tourism.

Modell, Bernadette, Abdul Razzak, and Nicholas Hindley. 1990. Thalassaemia in the Maldives. *Lancet* 335 (8698): 1169–70.

Ottovar, Annagrethe, and Nils Finn Munch-Petersen. 1980. *Maldiverne—et øsamfund i det Indiske Ocean*. Copenhagen: Kunstindustrimuseet.

Picard, David. 2010. Tropical Island Gardens and Formations of Modernity. In Julie Scott and Tom Selwyn, eds., *Thinking Through Tourism*. Oxford: Berg.

Prainsack, Barbara, and Gil Siegal. 2006. The Rise of Genetic Couplehood? A Comparative View of Premarital Genetic Testing. *BioSocieties* 1 (1): 17–36.

Ptak, Roderich. 1987. The Maldive and Laccadive Islands (Liu-Shan 溜 山) in Ming Records. *Journal of the American Oriental Society* 107 (4): 675–94.

Rabinow, Paul. 1996. Artificiality and Enlightenment: From Sociobiology to Biosociality. In Paul Rabinow, *Essays on the Anthropology of Reason*. Princeton, N.J.: Princeton University Press.

Rapaport, Moshe. 1990. Population Pressure on Coral Atolls: Trends and Approaching Limits. *Atoll Research Bulletin* 340:1–33.

Romero-Frias, Xavier. 2003 (1999). *The Maldive Islanders: A Study of the Popular Culture of an Ancient Ocean Kingdom*. Barcelona: Nova Ethnographia Indica.

———. 2012. *Folk Tales of the Maldives*. Copenhagen: NIAS–Nordic Institute of Asian Studies Press.

Sacks, Oliver. 1997. *The Island of the Colorblind and Cycad Island*. New York: Knopf.

Saftić, Vanja, Diana Rudan, and Lina Zgaga. 2006. Mendelian Diseases and Conditions in Croatian Island Populations: Historic Records and New Insights. *Croat Medical Journal* 47 (4): 543–52.

Schneider, David M. 1980 (1968). *American Kinship*. Chicago: University of Chicago Press.

Shakeela, Aishath, Lisa Ruhanen, and Noreen Breakey. 2010. Women's Participation in Tourism: A Case from the Maldives. In Noel Scott and Jafar Jafari, eds., *Tourism in the Muslim World*. Bridging Tourism Theory and Practice 2. Bingley: Emerald.

Simpson, Bob. 2011. Blood Rhetorics: Donor Campaigns and Their Publics in Contemporary Sri Lanka. *Ethnos* 76 (2): 254–75.

Smith, T. E. 1967. Demographic Aspects of Smallness. In Burton Benedict, ed., *Problems of Smaller Territories*. London: Athlone.

Soedarmono, Yuyun S. M. 2010. Donor Issues in Indonesia: A Developing Country in South East Asia. *Biologicals* 38 (1): 43–46.

Street, Alice. 2009. Failed Recipients: Extracting Blood in a Papua New Guinean Hospital. *Body & Society* 15 (2): 193–215.

Taglioni, François. 2011. Insularity, Political Status and Small Insular Spaces. *Shima: The International Journal of Research into Island Cultures* 5 (2): 45–67.

Titmuss, Richard. 1997. *The Gift Relationship*. Expanded and updated ed., ed. Ann Oakley and John Ashton. New York: New Press. Original edition published in 1970.

UNDP (United Nations Development Program). 2013. "The Rise of the South: Human Progress in a Diverse World." In *Human Development Report 2013*. New York: UNDP.

Vine, David. 2009. *Island of Shame*. Princeton, N.J.: Princeton University Press.

Weatherall, David. 2010a. *Thalassaemia: The Biography*. Oxford: Oxford University Press.

———. 2010b. Thalassemia: The Long Road from the Bedside Through the Laboratory to the Community. *Nature Medicine* 16 (10): 1112–15.

———. 2011. The Challenge of Haemoglobinopathies in Resource-Poor Countries. *British Journal of Haematology* 154 (6): 736–44.

Weatherall, David J., and J. B. Clegg. 2001. Inherited Haemoglobin Disorders: An Increasing Global Health Problem. *Bulletin of the World Health Organization* 79 (8): 704–12.

WHO (World Health Organizarion). 2011. Blood Safety. Fact Sheet no. 279. June. http://www.who.int/worldblooddonorday/media/ blood_safety_factsheet_2011. pdf.

Yang, Bin. 2011. The Rise and Fall of Cowrie Shells: The Asian Story. *Journal of World History* 22 (1): 1–25.

CHAPTER 11

Belize:
A Country but Not a Nation

Richard Wilk

People on the mainland can go through their lives oblivious to what
happens on remote islands, but the opposite is hardly true.

—Kuwayama (2003: 11)

When I first proposed doing dissertation fieldwork in Belize, my adviser told
me to be careful about choosing such a small place. If I worked in a large
country like Brazil or Mexico, I would have an established research literature to work with and a community of people who would read my work. I
could make connections with local universities and scholars, and I would
have many other anthropological studies to draw upon. In contrast, research
in tiny countries could be easily ignored—who had even heard of Belize or
of anthropologists who had become well known for their research there?

But from the time I first set foot in what in 1973 was still called "British
Honduras," I was charmed by a country whose new capital city had fewer
than three thousand inhabitants, most of whom fled to Belize City, the old
capital, on the weekends. I loved the fact that I could start the day in a Mayan village full of thatch houses where women still went topless, have lunch
in an Afro-Caribbean town full of strapping Garifuna women farmers, and
then pass the evening drinking beer with Latin American cane cutters. Anyone could walk down the street and knock on the prime minister's door to
ask a question or offer an opinion, and some members of the House of Rep-

resentatives were elected with fewer than six hundred votes. The prime minister was said to know the names and family histories of half the people in the country. The population of 150,000 people was smaller than most rural *counties* in the United States, but it was confusingly divided by ethnicity, class, education, and geography. Rather than feeling particularly small, Belize seemed highly compressed, as if all the elements of a much larger country had been shrunk and squeezed into a smaller space. Things that were normally far apart—the richest and the poorest, for example—could be found right next to each other in Belize. Actually the rich and poor, urban and rural, often shared surnames and close kinship connections.

Nevertheless, in many ways my adviser had been correct about the scholarly drawbacks of working in Belize. The many things I published in local journals were never cited and may have been read by perhaps fifty people. There was no local university until the 1990s, and until recently there was only one Belizean cultural anthropologist (I am currently training the second). But over time the country has become better known by academics, partly because of the large number of archaeologists excavating there, and the many biologists and conservationists attracted by the opportunities to study nature in protected areas. An extraordinary number of cultural anthropologists have worked in Belize over the last forty years, perhaps the highest ratio of anthropologists per capita of any country in the world. While I was just beginning my dissertation research, one of Fredrik Barth's students showed up, expecting to work in the same place, and a month later one of Napoleon Chagnon's students arrived in an adjacent community.

Belize is not only physically small (about 280 kilometers north to south and about 100 kilometers east to west, close to 23,000 square kilometers); for many years it was virtually invisible, in the sense that few people outside the immediate area had actually heard of it. The national motto on the flag, "sub umbra floreo" (in the shade we flourish), expressed a kind of pride in being so out of the way. Belize followed none of the possible paths for small places to come to global attention; no violent revolutions, comically evil tyrants, or natural catastrophes, and no conspicuous economic, historical, or cultural riches. Even its most valuable products—fine hardwoods and lobsters—were never labeled or branded, and Belizean orange juice was blended with cheaper, less flavorful Brazilian concentrate. Mail addressed to "Belize, C.A." (Central America) often ended up in California (CA) or Brazil instead.

The country was uncomfortably ambiguous even at the level of international diplomacy. The U.S. government for many years could not decide whether to treat Belize as part of the Caribbean, because it is English-speaking and populated with the descendants of African slaves, or as part of Central America, because of its geographical position and large Spanish-speaking population. For a brief time, the United States included Belize in both its "Caribbean Basin Initiative" and its "Central America Democracy, Peace, and Development Initiative," allowing Belize to "double dip" and receive the highest per capita allocation of U.S. development assistance of any country in the world, about $900 per household in the 1980s.[1] The Peace Corps, which had more than two hundred volunteers in the country in 1984 (one for every 925 Belizeans!), was sometimes caught in a tug-of-war between Caribbean and Latin American administrators.

The narrative of Belize rests on a widely shared notion of scale in global discourse. It is the tiny untouched place that has been overlooked or by-passed by modernity, a little corner that preserves old ways of doing, seeing, and saying. This is a shared story between locals and tourists, something that makes Belize instantly recognizable. It is the master narrative that makes every tourist an explorer, every cave trip an adventure, every zip-line excursion uniquely dangerous and exciting. Belize is "unexpected," "untouched," and "undiscovered," which requires a fairly elaborate amount of work, when you are moving a couple of hundred thousand tourists through the country every year—far more than the number of inhabitants. It requires the willing collusion of agents, operators, and tourists themselves, so the mystery can be recovered every night, so the next batch can experience it in the morning, much the way some people believe virginity can be restored by magic pills.

Emerging from the Shade

Many events and processes have coincided to bring Belize out of its obscurity, enlarging its presence and increasing the visibility of its land and resources, if not its people and cultures. Political independence came very late in Belize, partially because of outstanding land claims from neighboring Guatemala, a conflict that remains unsettled, though the danger of actual invasion had passed when independence was granted in 1981. Many of the functions of government had been taken over by elected representatives in the 1960s, but independence required the full set of symbols making up the "identi-kit" of a modern country, everything from a national anthem and flag to patriotic poems, a national bird, renamed streets, and a seat at the

United Nations (Löfgren 1993). A national beauty pageant sent Miss Belize to the Miss World competition for the first time (Wilk 1995).

Prior to independence the government had refused to promote tourism, on the grounds that the country should not become a land of "waiters and busboys" (Smith 2011). In 1984 a more conservative, business-oriented governing party began to promote tourism, which overtook agriculture as a source of income in the early 1990s and has since grown to the largest industry, now attracting almost one million tourists a year, most of them on cruise ships. Nature, rather than culture, is at the core of Belize's tourism marketing. Visitors come for the snorkeling, diving, and rainforest, stopping along the way at ancient Maya cities safely stripped of the living.

The concentration of tourists in the offshore cays and the coastal barrier reef has led to a curious geographical inversion. Areas that were once the economic heartland—the sugarcane plantations of the north, the citrus groves of the central valleys, and the commercial hub of Belize City—are now peripheral places. The offshore reefs and islands, once a periphery where a few fishermen made their living, are now the center of the tourist economy. This inverted geography is reflected in a changed vocabulary. In tourism culture, "Belize" is now mapped starting from the cays and Caribbean coast, while the rest of the country has become "the interior," which carries a hint of danger, implying a sort of steamy organic complexity. It does not help that Belize City itself has been beset by an epidemic of violent crime and robbery, driven by the drug trade and gang culture, so that tourists are sternly warned to avoid the place (Matthei and Smith 1998). Instead they are led into a "tourist village" surrounded by walls, where only licensed locals are allowed, and most of the profits are skimmed off by the cruise ship companies.

Tourism is not just a one-way flow. Many Belizeans travel to neighboring countries and the United States, and an increasingly large emigrant population has settled both legally and illegally in Los Angeles, Chicago, Texas, Florida, and many smaller places in the United States. Though they are hard to count, there are probably about 150,000 Belizeans in the United States, compared to about 320,000 in the home country. Reputedly, there are more Belizeans in Los Angeles than in Belize City, making Los Angeles the largest Belizean settlement.

Television and now cell phones and the Internet have done a great deal both to publicize Belize's existence and to inform Belizeans about their tiny place in the global scheme of things. Despite their awareness of coming from a small and insignificant place, a kind of resistant, defiant nationalistic pride is expressed everywhere in the country. In recent years many Belizeans have started to call their country "The Jewel," a name first used on the national radio station in the 1980s (as in "The Jewel of the Caribbean"), and later picked up in tourism promotion.

One striking example of the way television has affected Belizean nationalism dates to the early 1980s, when the only regular station available on Belizean television was WGN, the "superstation" based in Chicago, which broadcast the baseball games of the Chicago Cubs. Many Belizeans became avid fans, and because they knew the games were televised at home, Belizeans in Chicago started going to the games and holding up big signs that addressed their relatives in Belize. Eventually the TV announcers noticed them and started to talk about Belize on the air. When the Cubs made it to the National League Championship games in October 1984, all of Belize took an unofficial holiday. The streets were empty, traffic came to a standstill. After the Cubs lost, they sent several players to Belize on a tour to promote local youth leagues, and the welcome parade drew crowds that rivaled those for the pope and Queen Elizabeth (Wilk 1993).

The Intimacy of Small Places

As the introduction to this volume explains, small countries tend to have higher density of interconnections, shorter pathways between individuals, and informal networks that give the impression that the nation is just a big village. Though Belize is ethnically diverse and class stratified, and half the population is scattered at very low density in more than two hundred small villages and towns, the sense of intimacy is expressed in many ways and places. As in a small family, quarrels and differences can be intense, so injustice always has a human, personal face. Institutional anonymity is impossible. Rather than being a distant impersonal force, government's power usually takes the form of someone you may know from childhood or through a distant kinship connection.

Uncrossable social boundaries are often personalized too. Racism based on skin color is still very much a force, but among a group of siblings or relatives, some will have "good hair" or "clear skin," while others face discrimination in school or the workplace. Recent immigrants cling to the outer edges of society, and it may take more than a generation before unschooled monolingual Mayan people from Guatemala or poor plantation workers become socially connected beyond their immediate neighbors. Chinese, American, and European migrants have tended to gravitate toward enclaves. This heightens the visibility of poverty and disparity, which may help explain the extremely high crime rate. Farmers lose their crops to predial larceny; homes, churches, and schools left empty are quickly broken into; moored boats disappear. In 2012 thieves made off with a barge carrying 125 tons of sugar, which was never recovered.

The intimacy of a small country with a high crime rate means that everyone knows a friend or has a relative who has been the victim of a serious crime. Multiple murders can go unpunished because witnesses are afraid to testify. Even the police have been known to suddenly "forget" about the details of a crime scene or "lose" important pieces of evidence. No witness can be truly anonymous, and there is no way they can be effectively protected after their testimony.

Coupled with an extremely high rate of traffic fatalities, life in Belize often appears precarious, and the lurid treatment of every major accident and crime on television news makes it seem even more so. Corruption in both public institutions and private industry is similarly pervasive; so many people "know someone" who works for customs, the police, the fisheries office, or lands and surveys. Collusion and price-fixing are common in many professions because everyone knows everyone else. There are only about a hundred lawyers in the country, three veterinarians in private practice, perhaps ten dentists, and, for many years, three resident archaeologists and one cultural anthropologist.

Other, more intimate boundaries separate even close kin groups. For such a small country, the number of different churches and congregations is amazing. In one Creole village of about 550 people where I worked for a time, there were seven different congregations. Four of them had direct connections with U.S.-based churches that sent regular missionary groups, money, and material aid.

Party politics is deeply embedded in Belize, where the present two-party structure emerged in the 1960s (Shoman 1987). It is common to hear someone identified as "red" or "blue" after the party flags, and in every town or village families are seen as the partisans for one party or the other. It has become more possible for a person from a red family to marry someone from a blue one, but it can still be difficult for everyone involved. Because the parties are relatively evenly balanced (government has changed hands five times since independence), and there are considerable benefits to being a loyal supporter of the party in power, partisanship is pervasive in public life.

Scale and Proportionality

A key issue in the pervasive effects of crime and corruption, as well as many other aspects of life in Belize is the question of scale. Although the country is small, many aspects of running the nation-state cannot be shrunk in proportion. Belize is a scaled-down country in the sense that it reproduces all the qualities of a much larger country at a smaller scale; it has a legislature, but each representative is elected by about three thousand people. Its military has one general and about two hundred soldiers. The need to reproduce all the bureaucratic functions of a large country leads to many absurdities and an unreasonably high cost of government on a per capita basis.

The small population of professionals is unevenly and spottily distributed in the country. There are not enough soldiers to protect and patrol the borders, so thousands drift in from Guatemala, Honduras, and Mexico to hunt, fish, cut trees, loot archaeological sites, dig for gold, and pillage valuable tropical plants. The tiny environmental department cannot keep up with all the construction projects, development plans, and requests for permits to clear land and cut down mangroves along the coast, nor can the geology office possibly supervise all oil exploration. With only a small fleet of ambulances, large areas are served by only one emergency vehicle. Most services are heavily concentrated in the old capital, Belize City, a stressful and expensive bus ride from distant towns and villages.

Running a small country requires a bureaucracy far larger in proportion to the population than does a large country. Some functions require a large professional staff, the very people who can easily leave the country for a place with better salaries. I once worked on a project with the Central Statistics Office, which then consisted of one trained statistician and two clerical workers, who had to provide social, census, and economic data for hundreds of local and foreign agencies. They were far too busy to install new computers and software, and when the statistician got sick or took a holiday, all functions stopped. There is a constant high turnover in almost every government department and ministry, so many people are just beginning to learn jobs when they either get promoted or leave for the private sector. Projects disappear, sit in stacks of neglected paperwork, or get superseded before they are even implemented.

Diplomacy is very difficult on the kind of budget a small country can afford. The Belize Ministry of Foreign Affairs only has the staff and money to support five embassies at most, which does not even cover neighboring Central America. In most countries there is only an honorary consul. Belize cannot send representatives to most international conferences of the many organizations it belongs to, because government staff would be out of the country all of the time. The UN delegation is three people.

Of course intimacy is often pleasant and comforting. The fact that it is so hard to keep a secret in such a small place has put some limits on corruption and kleptocracy. When a contractor was recently photographed destroying the ruins of an ancient Mayan city as a cheap source of road fill, reporters quickly found connections to a government minister, though it looks like only the equipment operators paid any penalties. It is hard to conceal mistakes, or the sudden wealth from illicit activities, yet at the same time, because there are rarely official investigations, most stories remain at the level of gossip and rumor.

Rosaleen Duffy (2000) calls Belize a "shadow state" for this reason. There is a constant air of mystery about construction projects and developments, which often turn out to be scams or schemes. The drug trade flourishes, money laundering is big business, and the government is rumored to have paid off the gangs that control urban streets to reduce the number of murders during recent elections. Beginning in the 1980s the British government encouraged its Caribbean ex-colonies to take up offshore banking, ship registry, and other financial services to build their economies, and Belize is now home to thousands of paper companies and partnerships that can help anyone conceal assets, avoid taxes, and launder money. It also hosts online gambling and pornography in its national web domain.

Given the small scale of Belize and its relative poverty, someone who is nobody anywhere else can be a big fish. It does not take much in the way of political donations or lucrative contracts to gain influence. For many years the dominant figure in the local economy had an empire based on the Coca-Cola franchise, bottled water, and a brewery, though later in life he toyed with a shrimp farm, a small rainforest resort, and a coffee plantation. Lord Ashcroft, a medium-sized somebody in the United Kingdom as treasurer of the Conservative Party, has become arguably the most powerful person in

Belize, with controlling investments in municipal water systems, electricity, phones, Internet, and a bank.

In a few respects, the problems of scale work to the benefit of Belize. There are so few people in Belize that they are hardly worth the time of large retailers and manufacturers. This is why there are no fast-food chain restaurants in Belize. KFC tried in the 1990s, and Subway had a store, mainly patronized by cruise ship passengers, in the early 2000s, but otherwise you have to go across the border to Mexico to find McDonald's. For the same reason the local TV stations are unbothered by foreign conglomerates, and many resorts and hotels in the country are also independent businesses rather than branches of Club Med or other global companies. Are the economic advantages of small scale overbalanced by the many disadvantages?

The Economics of Scale: Why There Is No National Economy

Much of modern economic development is founded on the principle of economies of scale. The only thing that a small economy can offer is flexibility and agility, but those require good communications and some kind of strategic planning—both things that Belize's neoliberal economy lacks. Most of the central government institutions that used to manage prices, agricultural production, import substitution, and food security were disbanded under pressure from the U.S. government and the IMF back in the 1980s, when they also tried to eliminate the government's cooperative department and development bank.

A national economy depends to at least some extent on controlling the flow of money and goods across borders, hopefully maintaining exports and controlling imports in a way that builds wealth. But in Belize, as in many small nations, the small size of the market puts very rigid limits on what can be produced locally. Because the local market is so small, producers can never make enough money to jump the next level to international trade, with all the required paperwork, certifications, and standardization. The local maker of peanut butter can never sell it for less than the cheap import from the United States or Mexico. The only thing manufactured in Belize that has managed to enter the U.S. market is a line of hot pepper sauces. Because everything that is needed to run a farm or factory is imported and expensive, from fuel to spare parts and Internet access, local products can never be competitive. Equipment of all kinds is designed for much larger countries—you cannot buy a dairy plant sized for Belize's needs, or an efficient soybean oil expeller that uses less than one hundred tons a day, more than a year's production in Belize. Even worse, because markets are small, there is no room for competition, so if one person starts bottling honey for the local market he or she may survive, but if someone else gets into the business, both will probably fail.

The only thing that keeps Belizean export agriculture afloat is the hiring of Hondurans, Guatemalans, and El Salvadorans who are willing to work for lower wages than most Belizeans because their own countries are even poorer. Belize was also given constantly changing "sugar quotas" from the British and U.S. governments that allowed producers to sell thousands of tons at a much higher price than they would get on the open market. Europe continues to buy Belizean bananas and citrus products at a subsidized price, and small-farm cacao gets a premium as organic and "fair trade."

The higher wages in Belize are matched by much higher prices for a panoply of imported goods. Local farmers and food processors can never keep up with the demands of consumers, abetted by a steady diet of TV advertising from the United States, for a full range of convenience foods. Consumer demand is always ahead of supply; no matter what goods Belize can produce for itself, they will never be able to displace imported goods, even in the rare cases when they are cheaper. Local producers can never compete when it comes to advertising and packaging, and Belizean consumers tend to prefer foreign to local.[2] Expensive canned pineapple from Thailand sells in the supermarket and appears on the table, despite the luscious fresh ones available in open-air markets.

So how does the Belizean economy stay afloat? While tourism has become a major source of income, providing for those tourists requires all kinds of imported goods, from sheets and beds to outboard motors, even imported salmon they eat instead of local fish. There is also a huge hidden and unmeasured "black" economy based on the production and transshipment of cannabis and cocaine (Wiegand 1994). But what really keeps the whole enterprise going is the more than $75 million in remittances sent home every year by Belizeans abroad.[3] The country is dotted with households and communities dominated by the elderly and the young, since so many of the working-age people are far away.

Belize also has a long history of overseas ownership, which dates back to the early colonial era when huge tracts of the country were divided up among the mahogany barons who discouraged commercial agriculture because it would compete for labor. In the 1970s, the first and only ownership survey found that over 95 percent of the freehold land in the country was owned by foreigners or foreign corporations (Bolland and Shoman 1977). Given the recent marketing of islands, coastal land, retirement home sites and condos, the expansion of citrus, banana, and shrimp farms, and the sequestering of large tracts of land in reserves and parks, it is hard to imagine that figure has fallen substantially.

In what sense, then, does Belize have a national economy, a system with even a degree of self-reliance, with significant boundaries? The borders are porous to people and money, and almost everything seems to be for sale to the highest bidder, who is rarely a Belizean. Guatemalans walk across the western border at will, and the country is a refuge for gang members and miscellaneous criminals from surrounding countries and the United States.[4] Belize is having a difficult time paying even the interest on its huge foreign debt and has ceded control of many key economic policies to the IMF and other organizations. Bound firmly by international treaties and a vast tangle of international law, it is hard to see what kind of autonomy the government has in social policy (Duffy 2002). The "development space" of small countries, the range of policy options that are still open, has dramatically shrunk in the last few decades (DiCaprio and Gallagher 2006). There are certainly grounds to wonder if Belize is really a functional state at all, or if the state apparatus is more than a sham, a stage show behind which drug lords, gangs, and corporate stooges conduct the real business.

A Small Country, Not a Nation

There is no question that Belizean culture is distinctive. There is an imagined community, a country called Belize to which many people are deeply attached. But even the most patriotic Belizeans seem to hedge their bets. During the 2012 national elections, one candidate had her American passport mysteriously stolen and handed to a TV station just a few days before the election, leaving her without enough time to give up her U.S. citizenship. This has been a perennial problem in beauty pageants; one year Miss Belize admitted she was not a Belizean citizen at all and had only been to the country once. Belize is also imagined by foreign conservationists, indigenous rights activists, oil exploration teams, civil servants, and many thousands of tourists, some of whom might never meet a Belizean who is not a waiter. Some people imagine a beach in Belize as the perfect place for a wedding. Along with other countries in the region, Belize is now trying to enter the imaginations of potential retirees from rich countries and foreigners looking for cheaper dentures or cosmetic surgery. The countryside is abuzz with ambitious building projects built on dreams, fantasies, and imagined tropical paradise, at the same time that it is also littered with the ruins of others' fancies. Sometimes Belize seems like a Rorschach test, a place where people can see either Shangri-la or a squalid impoverished hell.

The political and economic reality is that small nations have little power to control their own internal affairs, their boundaries, or their place in the international community. The structural problems they face cannot be solved through their own efforts, even when they band together in weak organizations like CARICOM (the Caribbean Common Market), they have little bargaining power when faced with the policies of global giants like the United States or the European Union, or any multinational corporation. From this vantage point, Belize is in the same position as the U.S. Commonwealth of Puerto Rico, neither independent from nor a part of the United States, except that Puerto Ricans get much better public services and medical care. Many skeptical observers of independence in the Caribbean and Africa have argued that nationhood is not all it seems; that it ushers in new forms of dependency and neocolonialism (e.g., Sheller 2003; Barongo 1980; Henke and Reno 2003). The balance of colonial power has not changed, it has just become less visible.

In 2006 when Belize celebrated its twenty-fifth anniversary of independence, I was invited to write for a set of essays published in Belize to mark the occasion. My paper asked exactly what was being celebrated. In what sense had Belize become independent? I argued that Belize did not have the smallest measure of economic and political freedom on the international stage, while much of the local political class seemed more interested in looting the state than in crafting an independent polity. The trappings of nationhood, which seemed so important in 1981 are looking distinctly ornamental today, branding to attract tourists, and keep Belizeans entangled in a project of nation building that can never succeed.

Even that project seems halfhearted, sometimes ironic and quixotic. The most popular local television program is a local copy of *American Idol*, where the performers lip-synch to popular tunes from the United States, or sing their own versions, often off key or worse. The Kekchi Maya people, the independent rainforest farmers I worked with in 1981, are switching to a diet of tortillas made from imported wheat flour served with a tin of Vienna sausages, the dregs of the U.S. meatpacking industry, washed down with sugary drinks. And as I write this the country is reeling from an ignominious defeat in its first international football match against the United States in the Gold Cup tournament, with a score of 6–1. The minister of state responsible for sports was interviewed shortly afterward, and in just a few moments he expressed all the contradictions of living in a small country.[5]

> *Hon. Herman Longsworth, Minister of State/Sports:* I think we did as well as could have been expected; I believe that we still have a long way to go in football in Belize, but we've made the first step and I was very happy with the outcome of the game and I expect to see a better game on Saturday, I really expect to see a better game on Saturday [against Costa Rica].
>
> *Daniel Ortiz [interviewer]:* As well I am very sure that as a Belizean you felt a little bit down when you saw them loading us up like that!
>
> *Hon. Herman Longsworth:* You bet I was, because you got emotional and you got into the game but when you sat down after the game and you thought about it, you couldn't have expected anything better, really. I believe that the team felt very strongly that they were representing Belize as Belize was behind them. I certainly told them, you know, on certain terms that whatever the outcome was for that game—that we were extremely excited that they had already gotten to that stage and that, that alone for us was a win.

Notes

1. This figure is calculated for the years 1984–1990, when Belize received development assistance through the U.S. Agency for International Development. It does not include military aid, or loans and aid that passed through international NGOs, or agencies like the World Bank or the Pan American Health Organization.

2. The reasons are complex and historically variable; basic foods like corn and rice are supported by import restrictions and high tariffs (see Wilk 2006).

3. This is only counting remittances in cash that passed through legal channels; the actual amount is probably much higher.

4. There was a dramatic incident in 2013 when the unbalanced American inventor John McAfee, a "person of interest" in the murder of a neighbor, hid from Belize authorities while sending taunting e-mails, before escaping to Guatemala and then the United States.

5. Quoted from Hon. Longsworth Hopeful for the Jaguars, 7 News Belize [online], posted 10 July 2013.

References

Barongo, Yolamu R. 1980. *Neocolonialism and African Politics.* New York: Vantage.

Bolland, O. Nigel, and Assad Shoman. 1977. *Land in Belize, 1765–1871.* Kingston: Institute of Social and Economic Research, University of the West Indies.

DiCaprio, Alisa, and Kevin P. Gallagher. 2006. The WTO and the Shrinking of Development Space: How Big Is the Bite? *Journal of World Investment and Trade* 7 (5): 781–803.

Duffy, Rosaleen. 2000. Shadow Players: Ecotourism Development, Corruption and State Politics in Belize. *Third World Quarterly* 21(3): 549–65.

———. 2002. *A Trip Too Far: Ecotourism, Politics and Exploitation.* London: Earthscan.

Henke, Holger, and Fred Reno. 2003. *Modern Political Culture in the Caribbean.* Mona: University of West Indies Press.

Kuwayama, Takami. 2003. "Natives" as Dialogic Partners: Some Thoughts on Native Anthropology. *Anthropology Today* 19 (1): 8–13.

Löfgren, Orvar. 1993. Materializing the Nation in Sweden and America. *Ethnos* 58 (3–4): 161–96.

Matthei, Linda M., and David A. Smith. 1998. Belizean "Boyz 'n the 'Hood"? Garifuna Labor Migration and Transnational Identity. In Michael Peter Smith and Luis Eduardo Guarnizo, eds., *Transnationalism from Below.* Comparative Urban and Community Research 6. New Brunswick, N.J.: Transaction.

Sheller, Mimi. 2003. *Consuming the Caribbean.* London: Routledge.

Shoman, Assad. 1987. *Party Politics in Belize, 1950–1986.* Benque Viejo, Belize: Cubola.

Smith, Godfrey. 2011. *George Price: A Life Revealed; The Authorized Biography.* Kingston: Ian Randle.

Wiegand, Bruce. 1994. Black Money in Belize: The Ethnicity and Social Structure of Black-Market Crime. *Social Forces* 73 (1): 135–54.

Wilk, Richard. 1993. "It's Destroying a Whole Generation": Television and Moral Discourse in Belize. *Visual Anthropology* 5 (3–4): 229–44.

———. 1995. The Local and the Global in the Political Economy of Beauty: From Miss Belize to Miss World. *Review of International Political Economy* 2 (1): 117–34.

———. 2006. *Home Cooking in the Global Village.* Belize City: Angelus Press; and London: Berg.

CHAPTER 12

A War and After:
Sierra Leone Reconnects, Within Itself
and with the World

Jacqueline Knörr

Sierra Leone is small in terms of population and territory—six million people living on 72,000 square kilometers—but also when it comes to economy and infrastructure. In the Human Development Index of the United Nations, Sierra Leone has been listed among the least developed and least livable countries worldwide for many years. The country suffered a civil war from 1991 to 2002, marked by extreme violence against civilians, primarily by the rebels of the Revolutionary United Front (RUF). This war has also had the effect of decreasing the already low self-esteem of Sierra Leoneans, which had resulted from many years of poor political leadership, economic decline, and from what many Sierra Leoneans regard as their poor performance as a nation. The fact that it was Sierra Leoneans who kept killing, mutilating, and displacing their fellow countrymen has left Sierra Leoneans with little trust in their ability to take care of themselves in a responsible and dignified manner. Hence, in contemporary postwar society, Sierra Leone's smallness in populational and territorial terms correlates with a sense of national inferiority.

Thinking about Sierra Leone's smallness and about whether and how it matters, I wondered if concentrating on that topic would add fuel to the fire. Without wanting to overestimate my own impact, would I not contribute to making Sierra Leone look even smaller, less important, and less livable by dealing explicitly with its smallness? It is not my intention to belittle Sierra

Leone. I therefore depict smallness both in terms of its drawbacks and its virtues.

As one of the major potentials of smallness is its ability to connect, I will focus on some of the ways Sierra Leoneans transcend their smallness by connecting themselves and their country both within their own society and to the world beyond Sierra Leone. I will address both the divisive and the cohesive dynamics of some of the major sociocultural structures and institutions that characterize Sierra Leonean society and explore how they are affected by Sierra Leone's smallness. Light shall be shed on the question how historical experiences, sociocultural configurations, and institutions, as well as the narratives related to them, are engaged to enlarge the social and physical space within which Sierra Leoneans make sense of their lives. The phenomena under study will be situated in an ethnographic and historical frame, which may allow for the analysis of the dynamics of smallness in light of their potentials for connectivity and coherence, on the one hand, and division and partition, on the other. I will employ a bottom-up perspective, which depicts a view of smallness from below.

The Civil War (1991–2002)

The Sierra Leonean civil war had many roots, among them the continued deterioration of the economy, bad governance, regional instability, and a pronounced cleavage between Freetown and the rest of the country.[1] Conditions of life had become increasingly intolerable for the majority of Sierra Leoneans by the end of the 1980s. In 1991, Foday Sankoh and his Revolutionary United Front (RUF) entered Sierra Leone from Liberia and, with the support of Liberian warlord Charles Taylor, managed to gain control over diamond-rich areas in northern and eastern Sierra Leone. The ensuing civil war lasted more than a decade and was characterized by widespread violence and gross abuse of human rights, including mass murder. The war came to involve troops from other West African countries as well as South African mercenaries. A government was elected, only to be deposed in a military coup. But the elected president was returned to power and signed a cease-fire with the RUF. The rebel leader Foday Sankoh was given the post of minister of mines. Then later British troops intervened, nominally to evacuate compatriots; Sankoh was captured, and, in a final step, UN troops and British-trained Sierra Leonean forces together began taking over rebel territories. The end of the war was declared in 2002. The war had claimed more than a hundred thousand lives. An untold number of people had been injured and around a million exiled as refugees.

Postwar Society: The Role of NGOs/CSOs in Connecting Sierra Leoneans

Since the end of the civil war, Sierra Leone has witnessed the formation of an abundance of nongovernmental organizations (NGOs) and civil society organizations (CSOs),[2] which provide a wide range of services aimed at the reconstruction of Sierra Leone's social and economic infrastructure as well as at the revitalization of traditional, and the development of new, participatory structures and institutions. NGOs/CSOs assume different forms in Sierra Leone, ranging from big international NGOs, community-based organizations, religious bodies, secret societies (Poro, Sande, Odelays, and so on),[3] trade unions, and student organizations. NGOs/CSOs have not merely supplemented the government's efforts to rebuild the country, but in many ways provide services that the state fails to provide. Thus they have gained a rather high level of acceptance and legitimacy in Sierra Leone's sociopolitical arena.

There are CSOs whose operations follow "Western" or "global" principles and models of policy making. Others are ideationally rooted in more indigenous convictions and customs (such as traditional secret societies). However, most NGOs/CSOs—like the people engaged in them—draw on ideational sources of different origins and combine them so as to suit given situations, contexts, and interests.

Concerning the issues at stake here, it is interesting to see whether and how the abundance of NGOs/CSOs connects Sierra Leone to the national and international arena.[4] It is the more internationally set-up "new" NGOs that give people a feeling of being connected to the wider world, with its more global models of social relationships and policy making. However, as we shall see, more locally set-up NGOs/CSOs with more traditional and indigenous roots may well function as a nexus between social and spatial margins and local and global centers as well.

The small size of Sierra Leone has the effect of giving the impression that NGOs/CSOs are more or less omnipresent: "NGOs are everywhere in Sierra Leone. In every village there is some NGO," a trader who travels upcountry a lot said to me in Freetown. This may not be quite true, but as the country is small, it leaves little distance between the many NGOs/CSOs, which have established themselves in Sierra Leone after the war.

However, it is not so much the spatial proximity of different NGOs/CSOs that affects Sierra Leone and Sierra Leoneans, but the combination of traditional institutions and convictions having been shattered during the war, on the one hand, and the existence of (international) organizations offering alternative models of social relations and policy making, on the other. As one result of the war, the traditional system of mutual dependencies and obligations has been seriously undermined. "Patrons"—whether politicians in Freetown, senior members of secret societies, or landlords—were incapable of protecting their dependents from terror, violence, and loss, and thus they had failed in the eyes of many.[5] The increased presence of international NGOs and Western models of democracy, freedom of speech, gender equality, and meritocracy serve as additional challenges. Traditional generational and gender hierarchies—with older men (and some women) at the top—which had already begun to wane, particularly among the youth, continued to fall into disfavor during and after the war. Thus nonnative social and political models have gained acceptance, whereas native ones have lost their exclusivity in terms of legitimacy and credibility. The fact that Sierra Leone is a small country facilitates the spread of new ideas concerning policy making and the configuration of social relationships.

Connections and Divisions—Past and Present

Sierra Leone hosts around twenty different ethnic groups, with the Mende and the Temne each making up about one third of the entire population. Ethnic specificities in social and cultural practice do exist, but there is much exchange and mutual incorporation of social and cultural traits as well as people. Sierra Leone is renowned for experiencing less ethnic conflict than many other countries in Africa. There have always been some tensions between the two major groups, also reflected by the two major political parties, but violence has been rare. Ethnic conflicts did not play a major role in the civil war either. The war was rather about underprivileged youth engaging in profitable crime (Smillie, Gberie, and Hazleton 2000).

People say that everyone knows everyone else in Sierra Leone due to the country's small size and the transethnic nature of secret societies. The existence of Krio as a nationwide lingua franca also facilitates exchange and interaction between ethnic groups. That the Krio language managed to spread nationwide is related to the role the Krios have played in the educational sector of society as well as in the spreading of Christianity (cf. Oyètádé and Luke 2008).

It seems that the same factors facilitating interaction and exchange across ethnic and religious boundaries—namely, proximity, the transethnic organization of secret societies, and Krio as a lingua franca—have also facilitated reintegration in the aftermath of the civil war. An often-heard statement goes like this: "We are a small country, we have to stick together, and we have to forgive even those who harmed us badly, because after all they are our brothers."

Most Sierra Leoneans, on the other hand, see the nepotism of those in state power, as well as the dividing line between Freetown and the so-called provinces, as major forces undermining national unity. Particularly people in the provinces—Sierra Leone beyond Freetown—tend to feel alienated from the nation's capital. Sierra Leone's "hinterland" has been neglected not only by the Freetown elite and the colonial masters but by postcolonial leaders as well. This division between Freetown and the provinces, and between the Krios and the "natives," is an enduring result of the divide that came about with the ideological and administrative divisions established by the British colonizers and missionaries. With regard to the dynamics of connectivity and divisiveness that may be impacted by Sierra Leone's smallness, the settlement of different groups of liberated slaves in Sierra Leone and the experience of British colonialism are of particular relevance.

Between the end of the eighteenth and the early nineteenth century, different groups of former slaves, freed from slavery in America, were settled in what had been established by British philanthropists as the Province of Freedom, declared a British crown colony in 1808. Following the British abolition of the Atlantic slave trade in 1807, thousands of freed slaves—soon to be called Liberated Africans or "recaptives"—were released from slave ships bound for the Americas and brought to the Freetown Peninsula, where settlements were established for them. These disparate groups of people from diverse ethnic and regional backgrounds passed through a process of creolization, developing an increasingly exclusive identity as "Krio" and perceiving Freetown and the Freetown Peninsula as their homeland (Fyfe 1962; Fyle 2004, 2011; Knörr 1995). This Krio homeland constituted almost the entire colony over which the British started ruling in 1808. In 1896, a protectorate was declared over the hitherto independent communities in the hinterland adjoining the colony.

The colony and protectorate were administered separately. While the Krio inhabitants of the colony were designated "British subjects," the inhabitants of the far bigger protectorate were designated "British protected persons." This administrative division fostered notions of superiority and distinctiveness among the Krios, many of whom provided foster parentage for children from the protectorate. These notions of superiority were encouraged by the paternalism of the British, who put the Krios in charge as missionaries, teachers, and civil servants to "civilize" the local population. As a result, the Krios came to represent a significant part of the first Western-educated elites in British West Africa (Wyse 1991; Spencer-Walters 2006).

However, from the 1920s onward, native elites started competing with the Krios for high political offices, a development that generated hostile exchanges between the inhabitants of the colony and the protectorate, as well as discontent against the colonialists among the Krios (Knörr 1995; Porter 1963; Spitzer 1974).

Being a small minority living almost exclusively in Freetown and its environment, the Krios were seldom considered for political office beyond the local level in the later phases of colonialism and after independence had been achieved in 1961.[6] However, the Krios continued to figure prominently among the educated elite, serving as a model of modernity and civilization within Freetown and beyond. They were major players in the judiciary and the educational sector, and as such exerted considerable influence over the institutional dimensions of the postcolonial order.

The question here is whether the Krios' impact also has to do with the smallness of Sierra Leone. Comparing their influence with the influence of other Creole groups settled in different colonial settings, this seems to be the case. In Sierra Leone, the Krios did not merely maintain a distinct identity but often set themselves apart from the native population by claiming non-indigenization, nonmixture with natives. In fact, the Creoles *did* intermarry with the local population, but they incorporated those they married into the Krio group, forcing them to give up their original ethnic identities. In other, larger countries, processes of creolization were marked by a higher degree of indigenization—by Creoles becoming natives in the process of creolization rather than natives becoming Creoles. My main comparative case is Jakarta, a very large city and the capital of a very large country. Here, processes of creolization also led to the emergence of distinct Creole groups during colonial times, but their members did (and do) not celebrate distinctness based on being different from—or rather, better than—the native population (Knörr 2007, 2010a, 2014). Little comparative research has been done on Creole identities and groups, and the question concerning the impact of the relative size of the country on the different types of Creole integration and differentiation in colonial and postcolonial societies still needs investigation. Scale may well be one contributing factor. A larger hinterland would likely not have let itself be ignored for so long. The development of national identity has thus not been hampered by a primordial character of ethnic identifications or by a lack of transethnic ties, but by the social and economic cleavage between Freetown and the rest of the country.

Nationhood Versus Statehood

The way Sierra Leoneans perceive the relationship between the Sierra Leonean state and themselves is impacted by the small number of Sierra Leoneans and the small size of the Sierra Leonean territory. Most Sierra Leoneans feel that being a nation and having a state is important to be considered part of the "civilized" world. Being a small and poor country, they think, makes it even more important to be united as a nation and represented by a state. Smallness matters here: because "we are a small country and we are all connected, everyone knows everyone through someone" (female informant in Freetown).

However, nationhood and statehood are in many ways viewed as being in opposition to one another. Sierra Leoneans often complain about the weak identification of political stakeholders with their nation, their people, with their Sierra Leonean "brothers and sisters." They complain about the state's selfishness as its stakeholders try to gain as much as they can in terms of power and material wealth without redistributing to the people. An older man in Freetown, a low-ranking civil servant himself, told me: "Once they are in power, they want to fill their own bellies as quickly as possible and the bellies of their families and the bellies of those who are back home in their village. They also care about their own tribe more than about Sierra Leone as a whole, as one nation. The closer you are to one of these big men, the better for your own belly and for the belly of your children."[7]

National identification is regarded as lacking in substance most prominently among those who are expected to represent the entire nation. Sierra

Leoneans also claim that the state should be able to govern Sierra Leone more effectively than it does, and that the smallness of the country should be a facilitating factor in this regard: "I mean, America is such a big country and they manage—why shouldn't our politicians manage to run a small country like Sierra Leone?" a young man said to me.

In its small territory Sierra Leone also hosts an abundance of resources in terms of minerals and natural beauty. It is a widespread view that politicians should make sure that the country's wealth is distributed more equally among its people. On the one hand, the proximity of resources and people—resulting from the small size of the territory in which both are located—is experienced as a threat. This is not surprising given the fact that it was the illegal diamond exploitation and trade that fueled the violent civil war. On the other hand, this proximity is also seen as a potential for the just distribution of wealth resulting from fair trade not least with diamonds: "So much in terms of resources and so few people to share it among," claimed a young professional woman.

But Sierra Leone is also seen as too small to effectively oppose being exploited and misruled both by internal, selfish politicians, who do not sufficiently identify with the Sierra Leonean nation, and by external actors, like powerful international companies that manage to take over the country's resources by paying corrupt state actors. People perceive the smallness of Sierra Leone both as a potential for more equal access to resources and as a reason why this is not realized in practice.

Odelays: Empowering the Margins by Connecting Them to the Center

Sierra Leone's smallness influences the ways in which the relationship between state power holders and politically organized margins of society are shaped. Political power is concentrated in Freetown—but here the social as well as spatial margins are broad and in some specific ways rather powerful. The margins are organized mainly in Odelays, urban secret societies,[8] which are influential not merely because of their secret core, which is associated with spiritual power and support in times of crisis, but also because they provide social services—basic infrastructure, wells, schools, land to farm.

Odelays derived from two older secret sodalities, namely, Agugu[9] and Hunters, both having their roots in Yorubaland, from where many of the

Liberated Africans originated (Fyfe 1962; Peterson 1969). Both the Agugu and Hunters societies—as well as the Masonic lodges, whose members largely descended from transatlantic freed slaves—increasingly tended toward exclusivity. For large parts of the Freetown population, Krios and "natives" alike, it became more and more difficult to attain membership. Since the early 1950s, when the first Odelays were founded, they have become the secret societies for the urban poor and for migrants from the interior. Odelays have developed mechanisms that allow for mutual solidarity and identification among the disadvantaged and serve as vehicles for social integration in Freetown (Nunley 1987; cf. King 2012). They function as bridges across ethnic groups, link the powerful with the powerless, and connect Sierra Leoneans living at home with fellow countrymen living in the diaspora.

In contemporary Sierra Leonean society, the state and the Odelays are connected in a complex network of mutual dependencies. At the social margins of Freetown urban secret societies are experienced as a kind of semiofficial state representing the nation "from below." The state needs the support of these marginal, yet powerful Odelays to maintain its power at the center. It needs them to ensure at least some basic social infrastructure at the margins, so that these will not turn to rebellion. It also relies on their support in elections. Apart from the mere manpower of the Odelays, it is also their spiritual power that is both admired and feared across different groups and classes. Vice versa, the Odelays demonstrate their connections to the state and its representatives by making the latter turn up at important Odelay events, such as masquerades and the inauguration of schools.

Odelays nowadays are also transnational institutions, with branches in several countries where Sierra Leoneans reside. I know of branches in the United States, Great Britain, and the Netherlands. Many diasporic Sierra Leoneans send remittances back home to support their respective Odelays in Sierra Leone. Nathaniel King's (2012) informants claim that the financial and material contributions of Sierra Leonean diasporas accounted for 40 to 60 percent of the resources that went into annual Odelay performances. Diasporic Sierra Leoneans stage parades in their countries of residence, not least to collect money for the "real" parade back home, where many of them travel for the event. According to King again, diaspora members spent entire days at their Odelay headquarters on home visits. Meanwhile, in appreciation of the contributions of the diaspora, members at home would display the flags of the countries where the diaspora members resided in their annual parades. Some wore stars-and-stripes bandannas; a few wore Barack Obama T-shirts. Relationships between members help empower the social margins in Sierra Leone, as well as to cope more successfully with life in the diaspora. So through their Odelays, modest townspeople in "small Salone"[10] connect to the big wide world.

Krio Narratives of Transnational Connections

Sierra Leoneans generally tend to refer to the past when explaining what makes them specifically Sierra Leonean and what makes them take pride in being Sierra Leonean. Following a self-destructive war, they still find little to be proud of in the recent past. Rather, references are made to the "Athens of Africa," which Sierra Leone used to be called, to some of the first secondary schools in Africa, to the role of Freetown as a haven for liberated slaves, and to the fact that Sierra Leone was among the most developed African countries in early postcolonial times (Knörr 2010b).

The historical dimension of diaspora in Krio identity is particularly obvious and evident, with many ancestors of the Krios having returned from the Americas or from other places outside of Sierra Leone. Contemporary differentiations with regard to this historical heritage also reflect internal differentiations in Krio identity and their relationship to different groups of compatriots in the diaspora.

Among the Krio elite, both the Krio Descendants Yunion (KDY)—refounded as the successor of the Settlers Union[11] in 1990—and the Freemasons enjoy support among the mostly elder and conservative in both Freetown and the diaspora. They allow for a connection with the Krios' past and serve as a link between the Krios in Sierra Leone and those in the diaspora. I will focus on the KDY here. Despite the fact that many younger Krios have misgivings about the KDY because of its retrospective outlook, they usually acknowledge its role in maintaining links with the past and with the diaspora. A young Krio teacher explained to me: "You know, these are mostly old people dwelling on past glories of Krio society. They can be quite nostalgic about the Krios' past, and they like the idea of connecting themselves to the Americas and to England. I think they should be more future-oriented and more integrative. However, they are also important because they make sure we won't forget about our roots and about our history. So, I honor them for that although I am not a member and wouldn't want to be."

Krios tracing their roots to Nova Scotia and Jamaica[12] often consider themselves as the Krio elite. A Krio who claims that his ancestors have come to Sierra Leone from Nova Scotia said to me in 2005: "We who can actually claim having come to Sierra Leone from Jamaica and Nova Scotia are the real Krios. So we like to connect to our heritage, which is connected to Jamaica and Nova Scotia. Sometimes, the natives in Sierra Leone still deny us the status as real Sierra Leoneans, which makes it even more important for us to connect to the places we once came from." This statement shows that reaching out often goes with a feeling of not being accepted as native Sierra Leoneans. It is not surprising that particularly elder Krios connect to roots beyond Sierra Leone, as they have experienced more severe rejection than their children and grandchildren have in their lives.

The KDY considers the Krios to be both Sierra Leoneans and people in the diaspora. Some of the elder and more traditionally minded Krios still look across the Atlantic to find a place to relate to as home. "The Krio[s] can be seen as a Diaspora. The roots of their society came from the returnees from Europe and the Americas and from the coastal tide of slaves from all over the sub-region who were being taken across the seas to the 'New World.' . . . In this diasporic constituents efforts are now being made to re-new links between the Krios in Sierra Leone and the blacks in Nova Scotia and Jamaica" (KDY 2016. That this desire to connect "their" Freetown to somewhere beyond Sierra Leone has grown as a result of the war comes as no surprise. During the war many Krios experienced a fear of being trapped. Diasporic society also "represents human suffering, survival, and triumph" (Steady 2001: xv), a representation that suits the postwar Krios' state of mind.

The appreciation of the diasporic dimension of Krio as well as Sierra Leonean identity has also increased since the end of the war because diasporic Krios and other Sierra Leoneans have shared in the effort to reconstruct Sierra Leonean society. Krios in the diaspora also engage more specifically in the restoration of old Krio houses in Freetown and Krio villages on the peninsula by sending money back home.

Although the Krios connect their heritage to the Americas, many among them also emphasize the African input in the formation of Krio identity, thereby aiming to enhance their acceptance as Sierra Leonean citizens. While the firstcomers in the formation of Krio identity—who came to Freetown from the Americas (black poor, Nova Scotians, Maroons)—are held in high esteem by many, the by far largest group of Krio descendants, namely, the Liberated Africans who were settled in Sierra Leone after having been freed from slave vessels, are situated within a discourse that emphasizes the African dimension of Krio ethnogenesis. When stressing the Liberated Africans' input, the Yoruba influence in particular is foregrounded. Thereby the African dimension of Krio identity is highlighted: "The Yorubas were the largest single ethnic group among the liberated Africans hence the culture of the Krios was profoundly influenced by the Yoruba culture" (KDY 2016).[13]

Many Krios feel that emphasizing their Yoruba heritage is more credible and authentic than claiming a Western identity. By Africanizing themselves "Yoruba-style," they may enhance their indigeneity and retain a certain sense of superiority at the same time. Connecting themselves to the Yoruba also serves as a means to connect themselves to the largest and most influential country in West Africa, namely, Nigeria.

The African, and particularly the Yoruba, dimension of Krio identity is also emphasized in recent academic writing (see Sengova 2006; Spencer-Walters 2006). However, most writers—in the tradition of Akintola Wyse (e.g., 1991)—also draw attention to the native Sierra Leonean impact on Krio culture and identity. It is the mixture of people and the amalgamation of different cultural traits that are emphasized, by means of which not merely the Krios but Sierra Leone as a whole are globally connected.

Notes

1. For a more detailed analysis of the Sierra Leonean war, see, for example, Alie (2006); Conteh-Morgan and Dixon-Fyle (1999); Richards (1996, 2005); Reno (2003).

2. The terms "NGO" and "CSO" are mostly used synonymously. I use "NGO/CSO" as the encompassing term here. Both are legally constituted corporations that (ideally) operate independently from any form of government. They are typically nonprofit organizations and pursue wider social and political aims.

3. Sierra Leoneans are traditionally organized in (gendered) secret societies (Poro for men, Sande/Bundu for women). Concerning more "modern" urban secret societies (Odelays), see below. See Højbjerg (2004).

4. On discourses and controversies concerning the role of NGOs in Africa (and beyond), see Hudock (1999), who includes a chapter on Sierra Leone and The Gambia.

5. On the system of patrimonialism along the Upper Guinea Coast, see Knörr and Trajano Filho (2010); Mouser (2010); Murphy (2010).

6. As of this writing, the position of mayor of Freetown has always been occupied by a Krio despite recent contestations.

7. Concerning the "belly" dimension of African politics, see Bayart (1993).

8. These societies are secret in that their members share secret knowledge, which may only be communicated among its initiated members.

9. Also known as Egungun, Egugu, and Ogugu.

10. "Salone" is the Krio and affectionate name for Sierra Leone.

11. The Settlers Union was founded by the Krios in the 1950s in reaction to the native Sierra Leoneans challenging their supremacy.

12. The Nova Scotians among the Krios are descendants of black Loyalists, American slaves who had fought with the British during the American Revolutionary War (1775–1783) to earn freedom. More than three thousand freed slaves were settled in Nova Scotia after the war, from which they emigrated to Sierra Leone (1792). Much of the Western influence in Krio society is owed to the Nova Scotians who continued to be a distinct group until the 1870s. The Jamaican Maroons were runaway ex-slaves who, before emigrating to Sierra Leone, had settled in Trelawny Town, one of the Maroon towns in Jamaica (see Fyfe 1962; Knörr 1995; Porter 1963; Wyse 1991).

13. In this context it is interesting to note that Yoruba identity may itself to some extent be a result of the interactions across the South Atlantic, namely, between Brazil and what became Nigeria, from the slave trade onward (see Matory 1999). On the Yoruba dimension of Krio society, see Fyle (2004); cf. Knörr (2010b).

References

Alie, Joe A. D. 2006. *Sierra Leone Since Independence*. Accra: Africa Future.

Bayart, Jean-François. 1993. *The State in Africa*. London: Longman.

Conteh-Morgan, Earl, and Mac Dixon-Fyle. 1999. *Sierra Leone at the End of the Twentieth Century*. New York: Peter Lang.

Dixon-Fyle, Mac, and Gibril R. Cole. 2006. Introduction. In Mac Dixon-Fyle and Gibril R. Cole, eds., *New Perspectives on the Sierra Leone Krio*. New York: Peter Lang.

Fyfe, Christopher. 1962. *A History of Sierra Leone*. London: Oxford University Press.

Fyle, C. Magbaily. 2004. The Yoruba Diaspora in Sierra Leone's Krio Society. In Toyin Falola and Matt D. Childs, eds., *The Yoruba Diaspora in the Atlantic World*. Bloomington: Indiana University Press.

———. 2006. Foreword. In Mac Dixon-Fyle and, Gibril R. Cole, eds., *New Perspectives on the Sierra Leone Krio*. New York: Peter Lang.

———. 2011. *A Nationalist History of Sierra Leone*. Freetown: Self-published, Securicom.

Højberg, Christian K. 2004. Universalistic Orientations of an Imagistic Mode of Religiosity: The Case of the West African Poro Cult. In Harvey Whitehouse and James Laidlaw, eds., *Ritual and Memory*. Walnut Creek, Calif.: AltaMira.

Hudock, Ann C. 1999. *NGOs and Civil Society: Democracy by Proxy?* Cambridge: Blackwell.

KDY (Krio Descendants Yunion). 2016. Website, accessed 25 June, http://slbtbhm .homestead.com/kdy.html.

King, Nathaniel. 2012. "Contested Spaces in Post-War Society: The Devil Business in Freetown, Sierra Leone." Ph.D. thesis, Martin Luther University, Halle-Wittenberg.

Knörr, Jacqueline. 1995. *Kreolisierung versus Pidginisierung als Kategorien kultureller Differenzierung: Varianten neoafrikanischer Identität und Interethnik in Freetown, Sierra Leone*. Münster: LIT-Verlag.

———. 2007. *Kreolität und postkoloniale Gesellschaft: Integration und Differenzierung in Jakarta*. Frankfurt am Main: Campus Verlag.

———. 2010a. Contemporary Creoleness; or, The World in Pidginization? *Current Anthropology* 51 (6): 731–59.

———. 2010b. Out of Hiding? Strategies of Empowering the Past in the Reconstruction of Krio Identity. In Jacqueline Knörr and Wilson Trajano Filho, eds., *The Powerful Presence of the Past: Integration and Conflict along the Upper Guinea Coast*. Leiden: Brill.

———. 2014. *Creole Identity in Postcolonial Indonesia*. London: Berghahn.

Knörr, Jacqueline, and Wilson Trajano Filho. 2010. Introduction. In Jacqueline Knörr and Wilson Trajano Filho, eds., *The Powerful Presence of the Past: Integration and Conflict along the Upper Guinea Coast*. Leiden: Brill.

Matory, J. Lorand. 1999. The English Professors of Brazil: On the Diasporic Roots of the Yoruba Nation. *Comparative Studies in Society and History* 41 (1): 72–103.

Mouser, Bruce. 2010. Insurrection as Socioeconomic Change: Three Rebellions in Guinea/Sierra Leone in the Eighteenth Century. In Jacqueline Knörr and Wilson Trajano Filho, eds., *The Powerful Presence of the Past: Integration and Conflict along the Upper Guinea Coast*. Leiden: Brill.

Murphy, William P. 2010. Patrimonial Logic of Centrifugal Forces in the Political History of the Upper Guinea Coast. In Jacqueline Knörr and Wilson Trajano Filho, eds., *The Powerful Presence of the Past: Integration and Conflict along the Upper Guinea Coast*. Leiden: Brill.

Nunley, John W. 1987. *Moving with the Face of the Devil*. Urbana: University of Illinois Press.

Oyètádé, B. Akíntúndé, and Victor Fashole Luke. 2008. Sierra Leone: Krio and the Quest for National Integration. In Andrew Simpson, ed., *Language and National Identity in Africa*. Oxford: Oxford University Press.

Peterson, John. 1969. *Province of Freedom: A History of Sierra Leone, 1787–1870*. Evanston, Ill.: Northwestern University Press.

Porter, Arthur T. 1963. *Creoledom*. Oxford: Oxford University Press.

Reno, William. 2003. Sierra Leone: Warfare in a Post-State Society. In Robert I. Rotberg, René Lemarchand, and William Reno, eds., *State Failure and State Weakness in a Time of Terror*. Washington, D.C.: Brookings Institution Press.

Richards, Paul. 1996. *Fighting for the Rain Forest: War, Youth and Resources in Sierra Leone.* Oxford: International African Institute.

———, ed. 2005. *No Peace, No War.* Athens: Ohio University Press.

Sengova, Joko. 2006. Aborigines and Returnees: In Search of Linguistic and Historical Meaning in Delineations of Sierra Leone's Ethnicity and Heritage. In Mac Dixon-Fyle and Gibril R. Cole, eds., *New Perspectives on the Sierra Leone Krio.* New York: Peter Lang.

Smillie, Ian, Lansana Gberie, and Ralph Hazleton. 2000. *The Heart of the Matter: Sierra Leone, Diamonds, and Human Security.* Ottawa: Partnership Africa Canada.

Spencer-Walters, Tom. 2006. Creolization and Kriodom: (Re)Visioning the "Sierra Leone Experiment." In Mac Dixon-Fyle and Gibril R. Cole, eds., *New Perspectives on the Sierra Leone Krio.* New York: Peter Lang.

Spitzer, Leo. 1974. *The Creoles of Sierra Leone: Responses to Colonialism, 1870–1945.* Madison: University of Wisconsin Press.

Steady, Filomina C. 2001. *Women and the Amistad Connection.* Rochester, Vt.: Schenkman.

Wyse, Akintola. 1991. *The Krio of Sierra Leone.* Washington, D.C.: Howard University Press.

PART V

Grandeur, Irony, and Small Worlds

CHAPTER 13

An Emirate Goes Global:
The Cultural Making of Abu Dhabi

Sulayman Khalaf

Abu Dhabi emirate is considered small in relative terms, even though it is the largest emirate within the federation of the United Arab Emirates (UAE). With a land mass of only 83,600 square kilometers (116th in the world), this is a small country in relation to many of its neighbors, such as Saudi Arabia, Iraq, Iran, and Pakistan. Yet Abu Dhabi emirate and the UAE act large. What are those factors empowering Abu Dhabi as a visible global actor?

Several empowering factors can be identified. The most significant is oil wealth, enabling Abu Dhabi to transform itself over the last fifty years into a magnet, attracting global flows and raising its global image. Increasing oil revenues, coupled with a small population and a stable modernizing political elite, has transformed Abu Dhabi and the UAE from a land of scarcity to a land of unlimited good. Oil-generated income has been invested to create infrastructure, a high quality of life, and a flourishing modern metropolis. The World Bank ranks the UAE as the world's sixth richest country in terms of gross domestic product (GDP) per capita. Abu Dhabi city is viewed as the richest and newest city in the world.

Economic factors are now evident in all aspects of the Emirati way of life. Until the mid-1960s, Abu Dhabi's inhabitants lived their traditional way of life, characterized by scarcity, illiteracy, and harsh poverty. Nowadays the city's continuously expanding skyline bombards its multinational inhabitants with all things modern and global. Here we will focus on the story of

Abu Dhabi's cultural making, and refer to its economic transformations only as a background to the main theme. The discussion will be guided by a few major questions. How has this new oil wealth empowered Abu Dhabi to go beyond its relative smallness and invent itself as a pioneering and leading capital in the domain of culture? Why and how has Abu Dhabi established itself as a promising and vibrant arena, attracting large numbers of Arab and international actors and agencies to participate in the making of a new Arab/ global space? How is the media capitalizing on this culture-building process to project the image of Abu Dhabi as one of empowerment and strength? This chapter looks at how the ongoing construction of various cultural heritage projects is leading Abu Dhabi to reach beyond its small local capacity and geographical boundaries and invite global art institutions, expertise, and agencies to build a world-class cultural capital.

The media inform UAE citizens that their sense of smallness is being counteracted by the creation of a global position of importance, not only in economic domains but also in developing culture and heritage to realize multiple goals: fostering tourism, supporting future economic diversification, raising the image of Abu Dhabi as a regional cultural capital, and supporting national identity, which is currently contested in the midst of large expatriate multiethnic communities.

The production of culture on the scope and scale currently being undertaken in Abu Dhabi can inform us how an emirate, small as it is in terms of geography and national population size, manages resources and plans cultural strategies to invent itself as a local/global actor. It will illustrate how financial capital surplus is being transformed into cultural capital that will complement its economic power and enhance its international prestige and standing. It promotes national identity as a cultural construct embracing both traditional heritage and modern global culture. It is also constructing the image of the UAE as modernizing nation-state, building its ideological aspects with aspirations for global reach.

Abu Dhabi Among the Emirates

Despite its very small resident population of about one million national citizens and eight million expatriate migrants of various nationalities, the United Arab Emirates has been ranked for several years as the second largest Arab economy after Saudi Arabia. Abu Dhabi is the largest among the seven emirates, constituting over 85 percent of the nation's total land area. It also possesses 10 percent of the world's oil and 5 percent of its gas reserves, and produces 90 percent of the oil in the UAE. With plans for increasing oil output in the future, Abu Dhabi aims at controlling tremendous financial resources to realize its vision as a global player, particularly in overseas investment.

In economic terms Abu Dhabi's current state of wealth is simply staggering. Since independence in 1971, under the stable leadership of the late Sheikh Zayed, this superrich oil-exporting emirate has carried forward the union of the country. It has not only provided for much of the expenditure of the federal ministries but also given generously to support modern development in the smaller, less wealthy emirates of Ajman, Ras Al Khaimah, Umm Al Quwain, and Fujairah. More recently it has come to the aid of Dubai in managing its debt crisis after the 2008 collapse of the real-estate market. Dubai's leadership hastened to rename its most valuable and prestigious iconic building, the highest in the world, after Sheikh Khalifa, at the time ruler of Abu Dhabi and UAE president.

Being empowered by such immense wealth, Abu Dhabi has begun turning its attention over the last decade to assert itself globally. The process of inventing itself as a global hub is reflected in the construction of several large and ambitious economic, educational, and cultural projects. The Formula One racetrack was completed to host championship races held since 2009. A cluster of five international chain hotels were hurriedly constructed near the racetrack to host thousands of racing enthusiasts from around the world. Nearby, Masdar City, built in 2007, is a world-leading experiment in building a carbon-neutral green city in the desert. Masdar, which means "source" in Arabic, employs scores of international scientists working in the field of alternative energy sources. It also manages the Masdar Institute of Science and Technology, which was developed with the support of the Massachusetts Institute of Technology. It is a graduate-level research-oriented university focusing on alternative energy and sustainability.

The establishment of the Masdar Institute has generated other projects that will further reinforce Abu Dhabi's global interconnectivity. It has attracted the headquarters of the International Renewable Energy Agency, seen the establishment of the World Future Energy Summits, and inspired the Zayed Future Energy Prize for the Environment. This represents a comprehensive and unified undertaking. The already-functioning campuses of La Sorbonne Abu Dhabi and New York University Abu Dhabi are fully financed and supported primarily for the purpose of enhancing the global image of a rising superrich city. The speedy development of formerly barren outlying islands is a visible statement that the city is expanding to invent itself in ways compatible with its economic might and future-oriented outlook.

The Cultural Making of Abu Dhabi

How has the new oil wealth, along with other factors, empowered Abu Dhabi to go far beyond its relative smallness and invent itself as a leading cultural capital in the Gulf region, the Arab world, and beyond? To answer this broad question we need to frame presentation and explanation within the broader contexts of the evolving society of Abu Dhabi, UAE nation building, and the new political and cultural economies.

Abu Dhabi's ambitious ongoing cultural projects can be viewed as an embodiment of its vision of developing a contemporary national identity, which is being forged by being anchored in elements of a heritage from the past while at the same time embracing the modern world (TCA Abu Dhabi 2012). Currently Abu Dhabi has more than twenty cultural projects, heritage annual festivals, and institutions engaged in the celebration of culture and heritage, and these carry the promise of transforming it into a leading cultural capital in the Gulf region and beyond.

The four examples presented here reflect this vision, a political cultural ideology that is an integral component of the larger nation-building process that Miriam Cooke (2013) refers to as the "tribal modern." While a few examples will refer to the UAE at large, the focus for illustrative data will mainly be drawn from the Abu Dhabi emirate, as my primary observation field. My knowledge of the emirate is a result of twenty-two years of living and working in the country, what Anh Nga Longva (1997) termed "living observation," although certain research topics have also required the traditional methods of participant observation and interviews.

The selected projects that will be described briefly in this paper include: (1) the building of global brand-name museums, (2) the Poetry Academy and poetry competitions, (3) invented camel annual heritage traditions and festivals, and (4) falconry and work with UNESCO for the promotion of the

2003 Convention for the Safeguarding of the World Intangible Cultural Heritage (ICH).

Al-Saadiyat Island Cultural District

Saadiyat Island is only five hundred meters from Abu Dhabi's main island and is now undergoing a remarkable transformation, unprecedented in scale. Once barren and uninhabited, the whole island is to be developed and by 2020 be home to 145,000 people. In the domain of developing itself as a cultural capital in the region, an entire district on Saadiyat is to be devoted to culture and the arts. Abu Dhabi is building two satellite branches of the Louvre and Guggenheim museums, which together with the Performing Arts Center, Zayed National Museum and Marine Life Museum will create a world-class cultural district. This is intended to transform Abu Dhabi into an international arts capital and tourist destination. By using well-known architects as well as branded museums, the project establishes its international credentials and when completed will be one of the largest concentrations of cultural institutions in the world. As Sarina Wakefield (2013) comments, it is through the development of this "world class" notion of heritage that Abu Dhabi intends to place itself on the map of globally significant cities and promote itself as a cosmopolitan center within the Gulf region. Each museum will be housed in iconic buildings representing the finest architecture at the beginning of the twenty-first century. It will be a center for global culture, attracting local, regional, and international visitors to view its unique exhibitions, permanent collections, and performances. An exhibition showing large-scale plans for the island and models of its museums has been on display for several years. The organizers of the project devoted a section in the display to explaining the benefits of what has been termed "the Bilbao effect" (Rybczynski 2002)—the transformation of a city by a new cultural facility into a vibrant and attractive place. Saadiyat Island was named as the Middle East's leading tourism project by the 2009 World Travel Awards.

Louvre Abu Dhabi will be the first museum in the Arab world to exhibit global art. With a 2016 opening date, it is designed to house the aesthetic expressions of different civilizations and cultures, ancient and contemporary. Born from an agreement between the governments of Abu Dhabi and France, it is designed by the world-famous architect Jean Nouvel. The Abu Dhabi government paid U.S.$525 million to be associated with the Louvre name, with an additional U.S.$747 million in exchange for art loans, special exhibitions, and management advice (Riding 2007).

Designed by the world-renowned architect Frank Gehry, Guggenheim Abu Dhabi will be a platform for global contemporary art and culture. It will display the most important artistic achievements of our time, as well as acknowledging the specific identity derived from the cultural traditions of Abu Dhabi.

Zayed National Museum will be the national museum of the UAE. It tells the story of Sheikh Zayed, the UAE's founding father, and of the unification of the country. It will exhibit the history of the region and its cultural connections across the world. Designed by Foster+Partners, it will be built in the shape of a falcon's wing feathers. The British Museum has a consultative role in developing the museum collection.

In Phase Two of the Saadiyat Cultural District, the Performing Arts Center will be home to various genres and traditions of music, dance, and theater. It is set within the futuristic contours of Zaha Hadid's organic design. The Maritime Museum is being built to exhibit Abu Dhabi's maritime heritage, and to explore the Gulf population's long relationship with the sea.

The project has experienced some delays since the economic crisis of 2008, and although construction is under way for the first three museums, Phase Two has yet to be tendered. Abu Dhabi has a challenge in developing its own trained staff to sustain this museum project; otherwise it will remain heavily dependent on expatriate expertise.

Poetry Academy and Million's Poet Competition

The example of the Poetry Academy illustrates Abu Dhabi's empowerment to reach out to poetic voices throughout the Arab world. The Poetry Academy was established in 2007 under the Abu Dhabi Authority for Cultural and Heritage (ADACH)—more recently integrated into the Abu Dhabi Tourism and Culture Authority—for the purpose of safeguarding and promoting Arabic poetry. Its stated aims are promoting and developing poetic talent, collecting traditional Emirati poetry from elderly living poets, encouraging young poets, publishing books, and supporting researchers, as well as formulating criteria for the evaluation of poetry and the enhancement of poetic appreciation among the public. Another unstated aim is that the poets lavish praise on Abu Dhabi and its enlightened visionary rulers.

The Academy offers training courses for young poets to develop their skills, as well as an annual course for twenty-eight participants to develop further their talent for Nabati poetry. Budding poets come from around the Gulf and Arab countries and receive certificates of attendance. The Academy has published sixty-one books on poetry, including Nabati (twenty-eight books), classical poetry (seventeen) and research (sixteen). For the last six years it has produced a monthly elegant glossy magazine. This is sold in the UAE for U.S.$2.80, but in reality it is distributed freely as gifts to government ministry staff and individuals.

The Academy also arranges an annual Nabati poetry competition, the "Million's Poet," with very large cash prizes (the first prize is five million UAE dirhams, or U.S.$1,363,000). This takes place in the Academy's large purpose-built theater and is covered by its own television channel. It is an extremely popular poetry competition, with audiences of thirteen million regular viewers from around the Arab world, and seventy million for the final. About five thousand competitors apply each year to take part. Large numbers of Nabati poetry enthusiasts travel from the Gulf and surrounding regions to attend the competition, and Abu Dhabi sheikhs usually attend the final rounds.

The Prince of Poets is another annual competition for formal classical Arabic poetry. It also attracts poets from all over the Arab world, who go through a rigorous competitive selection process. The winner receives a million UAE dirhams (U.S.$273,000), and the Poet Prince's cloak and ring, with runners-up also receiving prizes. There is a panel of three or four judges, and the competition is produced with theatrical extravaganza and light shows.

Camel Racing: An Example of Invented Annual Heritage Festivals

The unprecedented changes experienced in Abu Dhabi as a result of its oil wealth have generated serious concerns related to the preservation of national identity and a strategy of safeguarding and activating traditional heritage. A large-scale heritage revival (*ihya al turath*) process has been embraced by Emiratis and, in particular, by the people of the Abu Dhabi emirate.

Over the last thirty years, the Abu Dhabi government has encouraged greater numbers of people to be involved in safeguarding their traditional heritage. This is regarded as the major pillar in supporting national identity—increasingly becoming a matter of debate due to the emirate's own ambitions to achieve rapid modernization. On one hand, this has weakened traditional life in visible ways. On the other, it has empowered authorities, groups, and communities to return to this heritage and reproduce it, even reinvent it, in new festival forms now celebrated by the nationals as an ongoing series of heritage events. Camel culture provides a link to the historical nomadic way of life. Camel racetracks provide the Emirati community with a ritually constructed theater to celebrate its own political ideology, cultural traditions, and values (Knoll and Burger 2012).

In Abu Dhabi and the UAE, camel racing is now a multidimensional cultural heritage celebration. It has grown over the past twenty-five years to reach levels of a national heritage industry, involving the mobilization of labor, capital, and integrated organization of many people, agencies, institutions, and sheikhly patrons. Around 120,000 workers (mostly migrant labor) are currently involved in the annual production of these heritage-sport races throughout the UAE, which occur during the six mild winter months (Khalaf 1999).

Camel races in pre-oil times were performed by the local communities on festive social occasions: religious feasts, celebration of rainfall, weddings, circumcision, perhaps the occasional visit of a prominent tribal sheikh. Now the scope and depth of change has touched all aspects of the races, so much so that they would appear beyond recognition for many elderly citizens. New organizational innovations have evolved around camel racetracks built with stadiums on the outskirts of most cities, developing the races into an "invented tradition" (Hobsbawm 1983). The Camel Racing Association organizes different races for each breed of camel and different distances for various age groups. The training of the camels is usually carried out by Bedouin camel experts, at the camel farms of the sheikhs or on their own small farms. The trainer (*mudhammer*) is assisted by a large cast of camel laborers, from countries such as Bangladesh, Pakistan, India, Sudan, Oman, and Baluchistan (Iran).

The races embody both economic and political aspects. For the Bedouin, camel racing is a field through which they can reach the bounty of the oil-state, personified by the ruling sheikhs as patrons of camel heritage. Salaries and wages are paid according to the hierarchy of work and the laborer's status and citizenship. Camel markets enable the Bedouin camel breeders to exhibit their fine racing camels (*al-hejin*, as they are known locally) with hopes of selling them for a good profit; camels with winning records sell for more than half a million U.S. dollars. The commercialization of camel traditions is evident during the final races, when large corporations make their presence felt. The modern market, represented by these trading companies, contributes to the success and development of the races by sponsoring prizes of luxury cars. The sight of hundreds of European and Japanese cars shining under the sun is attractive, enticing the Bedouin camel trainers and breeders. Other prizes and awards include cash and gilded swords and daggers, presented by the ruling sheikhs and the Camel Racing Association.

Television has played a significant role in the evolution and popularization of this camel heritage. It has been "the medium" and "the message" at the same time (McLuhan 1964: 23). Television is essential in following the races, as the tracks are huge and the races can only really be viewed by cameras mounted on jeeps following the racing camels. The races are widely broadcast on free public channels. TV and print media highlight the political and cultural aspects of the races, by emphasizing the positive role of the state and the importance of camel heritage for national identity. Bedouin Nabati poetry is recited during the races to express nationalist messages, such as praise for the sheikhs and modern national development, praise for the camels in action and their trainers, and an emphasis on cultural authenticity (Khalaf 2000). Framing these cultural celebrations with Bedouin poetics and cultural aesthetics provides a voice to the changing lives among Emirati Bedouins.

Al-Dhafra Camel Festival

The Camel Festival was initiated by the Abu Dhabi government in 2008 to celebrate desert camel culture. The declared objectives are to preserve the purity of Asayel and Majahim camel breeds, to celebrate Bedouin culture, and to activate cultural tourism. In addition, the festival promotes development in the Western Region of the emirate and creates a market for camels. The festival is supported by leading figures, including its patron, the crown prince of Abu Dhabi, Sheikh Mohamed bin Zayed (Abu Dhabi Events 2012).

This festival of twelve days takes place during each year's local winter season, in December. Since its first occurrence, it has been transformed into a large international event that has caught the attention of media. In 2012 there were around twenty thousand camels participating in the various camel beauty competitions, with more than eight hundred camel owners coming from different parts of the Arabian Peninsula. Each year sees an increase in the number of camel owners participating.

The camels are judged on various criteria, and the examining committee deliberates for hours. The Emirati winner of the one million dirham prize in 2011 for the black Majahim is a passionate camel lover, empowered by personal wealth. He told me that he spent more than eighty million UAE dirhams (U.S.$22 million) to buy the best camels he could find. What he celebrated most, when surrounded by media, is *al-namous*, the symbolic prize of social honor and pride. This camel beauty festival reflects that much wealth has trickled down to the Emirati citizens in large ways. This has enabled some groups and individuals to indulge in camel competitions that carry potlatch aspects, as the camel owners perform some type of what Thorstein Veblen (1973) terms "honorific waste"—a large amount of capital is used up in order to obtain increased measures of *namous* (social honor).

In addition to the camel beauty contests, Bedouin poetry recitals, heritage camel races, and camel auctions and sales, the festival presents a wide range of heritage activities for visitors, spread across several square miles of undulating red sand dunes. There are also various competitions for traditional handicrafts, as well as falconry competitions, date competitions, and a children's village. All the daily activities are crowned with free Arabic hospitality of coffee, dates, cold drinks, and lunches. Water, wood, fuel for fires, coffee, sugar, rice, tea, and lambs are freely provided throughout the festival's duration.

Nomination of Falconry on the UNESCO ICH Representative List

In the sphere of domesticating animals, falconry represents one of the oldest relationships between humans and birds. It is the traditional art and practice of keeping, training, and flying falcons to take quarry in their natural state. Falconry has been practiced in Arabia for centuries. In pre-oil times it was popular among the Bedouins as competition among their elites, but also as a way of supplementing their simple diet. Although changing life conditions have meant that the need to hunt for food has disappeared, falconry as an elite competition has remained. Indeed, material wealth has given a new impetus to the practice of falconry as an outdoor recreational heritage activity, with estimates of five to seven thousand falconers. The heritage legacy of the late president Sheikh Zayed bin Sultan as a renowned and passionate falconer has been a source of inspiration for thousands of Emirati citizens to take up this heritage sport. Throughout his presidency, Sheikh Zayed promoted sustainable falconry by regulating its practice and establishing institutions to preserve falcons, the quarry, and the natural habitat. The Emirates Falconers Club was set up in 2001 with the aim of supporting falconers and promoting falconry as a national heritage, and it has a membership of around three thousand. Falconry is associated with Bedouin rituals and poetry. Today the falcon has become the primary unifying symbol of the entire nation, being the state emblem on postage stamps, bank notes, coats of arms for police and army, identity cards and passports, as well as all state letterheads and logos of state companies.

What is of relevance here is to explore how the UAE, led by Abu Dhabi, has for several decades been at the forefront of numerous local and international initiatives to promote falconry and build transnational heritage culture. These started as early as December 1976, with the first international conference on falconry, bringing together Arab, European, and Asian experts to share their knowledge. Decades later, the UAE led ten other countries in preparing a multinational nomination file for falconry to be inscribed on the UNESCO Representative List of Intangible Cultural Heritage of Humanity. The participating countries were Belgium, Czech Republic, France, Republic of Korea, Mongolia, Morocco, Qatar, Saudi Arabia, Spain, Syria and the UAE. Falconry was inscribed on 16 November 2010, and is the largest multinational file to date. Two other European countries, Austria and Hungary, joined in 2012, reflecting the popularity of falconry as a global heritage. The submission also reflects the financial and logistical support the UAE provided to enable other countries to be part of this project. The nomination file took three years to prepare, with five workshops held in Abu Dhabi to enable the participants to come together and submit a six-hundred-page file. All expenses in organizing and hosting these meetings were carried by Abu Dhabi, including air travel and hotel hospitality.

The interest in safeguarding falconry at both a local and an international level has provided the UAE with appropriate wings to reach out to the world. What is regarded by Emiratis as a core heritage symbol of their country has been used to exercise its soft power and promote cultural exchange and dialogue. Falconry is practiced in more than sixty-five countries, and falconers share values, traditions, and practices. The methods of training and caring for birds, the equipment used, and the bonding between a falconer and his bird are similar throughout the world.

In addition to the UNESCO file, Abu Dhabi has been involved in other falconry-related activities. These include the sponsorship of the International Festival of Falconry, the largest international gathering of falconers in the world. The third festival was held in Al Ain, UAE, in December 2011. Abu Dhabi also hosts the Annual Hunting and Equestrian Exhibitions, the Avian Research Center, the Sheikh Khalifa Houbara Breeding Center, and extensive breeding programs in Morocco and other countries that are supported financially by the UAE. The UAE also hosted the fourth session of UNESCO's Intergovernmental Committee for the Safeguarding of Intangible Cultural Heritage in 2009, with more than five hundred delegates from 130 countries as guests in Abu Dhabi for six days.

Conclusion: Small, Yet Empowered

My concluding notes will focus on the implications of Abu Dhabi's small scale, its empowerment to go beyond "being small" toward "acting large," and how this has been translated into its ambitions to be a global player in the cultural domain. Discussion of Abu Dhabi's perception of its relative smallness and how it is being counteracted by perceptions of empowerment and strength requires that we provide multiple contextualizations of the evolution of Abu Dhabi society.

What are some of the sociological implications related to Abu Dhabi's smallness and empowerment? Its small population size, coupled with huge oil wealth and restrictions on naturalization, has enabled it to give its citizens a life of plenty. It has established for its national citizens an unmatched welfare state with a wide range of benefits from womb to tomb, without having to resort to taxation. Families have acquired an aristocratic lifestyle, with an average of two to three domestic servants in each household. This "image of unlimited good," which has evolved as an aspect of citizens' lives, is basically a function of the "small size/large wealth" equation particular to the UAE and other similar oil-rich Gulf states (Khalaf 1992).

The small-scaled size of the population has promoted greater social networking among nationals. People are known to each other, and this is experienced frequently among the citizens in their daily lives. The "imagined community" (Anderson 1991) and the "real community" overlap and fuse to a great extent. Smallness has also enabled closer social and political intimacies between the people and the ruling sheikhs, which in turn has strengthened national identity.

Wealth and a generous caring welfare state have transformed the small population of Abu Dhabi into a managerial class, with over 90 percent being employed in the state bureaucracy. This fact generates a psychology of power vis-à-vis the larger number of expatriates they manage and control. Nationals perceive themselves as a privileged social class, especially because they are a small minority (10–15 percent) in their own country.

However, the presence of large numbers of expatriates has intensified the sense of small "Emirati-ness," with nationals expressing a psychocultural state of being under siege by the huge presence of such diverse immigrants and their cultures (Khalaf 2006: 260). This has induced the citizens to present to the world a cohesive and distinct community image by upholding age-old customs and traditions as identificational factors (Ansari 1987). The wearing of traditional dress as a national uniform indicates this sense of identification of self from others, and the national dress is now used as a boundary-maintaining marker.

Being small, yet empowered, has enabled Abu Dhabi to project its image as large. This in turn is externalized to provide the citizens with the framework within which they view the rest of the world. UAE nationals view larger neighboring countries (such as Iraq, Iran, Pakistan, and Egypt) as negative reference groups. They are perceived as countries plagued with poverty, political instability, turmoil, and arrested development.

While small in its population and technical capacities, Abu Dhabi has relied on oil wealth to make up for such shortages and opened its door wide for global expatriate labor and skills to achieve an extremely rapid transformation in society, polity, and culture over the last five decades. Unlike the development of many countries, in the UAE "social organization and ideology build the economy" (Fox, Mourtada-Sabbah, and al-Mutawa 2006: 4).

This development policy is in itself an act of performing large. The UAE total population in the early 1960s was only around sixty-five thousand. After fifty years of development it has reached nearly nine million. About 90 percent of this population growth is the result of a continuing influx of migrant labor. UAE statistics often refer to the country's size in terms of a relatively large total population. This is an act of appropriating the global other as an added dimension to country size.

Being small twice (that is, by geographical size as well as by national population) explains the emphasis on constructing national identity through celebrating heritage as a generalized strategy to project the nation as large, both to itself and to the world outside. However, it is important to note that traditional ideology has become synthesized with a modern lifestyle, and it is because of this duality that modernization is not seen as interfering with tradition (Heard-Bey 2004: 419). Rather, tradition has become rearticulated within the modern process through cultural conversion (Garcia Canclini 1995). The popularity of the Million's Poet competition, where traditional poetic forms are used to address contemporary issues, serves as an example of this.

In Abu Dhabi, the selective use of elements from modernity through which to articulate a specific local experience takes place within the structure of traditional ideology and kinship. The focus on national identity reinforces the "tribal modern" component of this identity, which in turn reinforces and maintains the hereditary political system. As Sayyid Hurreiz (2002: 60) notes, "Since the present leadership is a legitimate outcome of traditional heritage, and since such heritage enhances their presence and continuity, it is only logical that they promote folklore."

The large-scale ongoing cultural development that Abu Dhabi is undertaking represents multiple things at the same time. While having huge capital surpluses, the emirate aims to diversify its future economic base (Abu Dhabi Urban Planning Council 2007). Cultural tourism is one area that has been identified, and part of the strategy is the proposed creation of Abu Dhabi as the cultural capital of the region. There is a move toward transnationalism, as identity is shaped toward securing a new economic role for the emirate.

Cultural development also supports nation building, as past and future projects reflect both the traditional and modern, the local and global. These project the image of a pioneering nation taking the lead, for example, of many world countries to submit falconry as the Intangible Cultural Heritage of Humanity.

Being small has been (and continues to be) counteracted through large world cultural initiatives over the last several decades. Building the Louvre and Guggenheim museums and having the New York University Abu Dhabi and Sorbonne Abu Dhabi universities, as well as other cultural and educational institutions, are statements of the power to act large, localizing the global. Abu Dhabi's newly established institutions have become vibrant arenas attracting large numbers of Arab and international actors and agencies.

Depending primarily on oil wealth and expatriate labor and expertise, Abu Dhabi has managed to transform itself into acting large in the cultural arena, although several issues and challenges remain. While much has been achieved within a short time frame, the dependency syndrome on expatriate labor carries with it numerous political, economic, and cultural challenges and risks. There is a recurrent debate within the UAE on the threat to "national identity" due to the large number of expatriate residents. Moreover, the cultural projects focusing on attracting interest within the Gulf region and the Arab countries, notably the Million's Poet competition and the camel races and heritage festivals, have undoubtedly been successful and continue to grow in popularity. Yet ambitions to promote Abu Dhabi as a cultural destination to a wider international audience remain largely untested, and the question still remains as to whether cultural tourism is a viable strategy. The coming years will provide the answer as to whether the Al-Saadiyat Island museum project will succeed in supporting Abu Dhabi's goal to be a global cultural destination.

References

Abu Dhabi Events. 2012. Al Dhafra Camel Festival (2012) brochure. Accessed 5 June 2013, http://abudhabievents.ae/uploads/Al-dhafral_brochure%20EN.pdf.

Abu Dhabi Urban Planning Council. 2007. *Plan Abu Dhabi 2030: Urban Structure Framework Plan*. http://www.upc.gov.ae/abu-dhabi-2030.aspx?lang=en-US.

Anderson, Benedict. 1991. *Imagined Communities*. Rev. ed.. London: Verso.

Ansari, Ghaus. 1987. Urbanization and Cultural Equilibrium in the Arabian Gulf States. *Bulletin of the International Committee on Urgent Anthropological and Ethnological Research* 28:19–23.

Cooke, Miriam. 2013. *Tribal Modern: Branding New Nations in the Arab Gulf*. Berkeley: University of California Press.

Fox, John W., Nada Mourtada-Sabbah, and Mohammed al-Mutawa. 2006. The Arab Gulf Region: Traditionalism Globalized or Globalization Traditionalized? In John W. Fox, Nada Mourtada-Sabbah, and Mohammed al-Mutawa, eds., *Globalization and the Gulf*. London: Routledge.

Garcia Canclini, Néstor. 1995. *Hybrid Cultures*. Minneapolis: University of Minnesota Press.

Heard-Bey, Frauke. 2004. *From Trucial States to United Arab Emirates.* Dubai: Motivate.

Hobsbawm, Eric. 1983. Introduction: Inventing Traditions. In Eric Hobsbawm and Terence Ranger, eds., *The Invention of Tradition.* Cambridge: Cambridge University Press.

Hurreiz, Sayyid H. 2002. *Folklore and Folklife in the United Arab Emirates.* London: RoutledgeCurzon.

Longva, Anh Nga. 1997. *Walls Built on Sand.* Boulder, Colo.: Westview Press.

Khalaf, Sulayman. 1992. Gulf Societies and the Image of Unlimited Good. *Dialectical Anthropology* 17 (1): 53–84.

———. 1999. Camel Racing in the Gulf: Notes on the Evolution of a Traditional Cultural Sport. *Anthropos* 94 (1/3): 85–106.

———. 2000. Poetics and Politics of Newly Invented Traditions in the Gulf: Camel Racing in the United Arab Emirates. *Ethnology* 39 (3): 243–61.

———. 2006. The Evolution of the Gulf City Type, Oil and Globalization. In John W. Fox, Nada Mourtada-Sabbah, and Mohammed al-Mutawa, eds., *Globalization and the Gulf.* London: Routledge.

Knoll, Eva-Maria, and Pamela Burger, eds. 2012. *Camels in Asia and North Africa.* Vienna: Austrian Academy of Sciences Press.

McLuhan, Marshall. 1964. *Understanding Media.* New York: McGraw-Hill.

Riding, Alan. 2007. The Louvre's Art: Priceless. The Louvre's Name: Expensive. *New York Times* [online], 7 March.

Rybczynski, Witold. 2002. The Bilbao Effect. *Atlantic Monthly* [online], September.

TCA Abu Dhabi (Abu Dhabi Tourism and Cultural Authority). 2012. http://tcaabudhabi.ae/en/culture/Pages/default.aspx.

Veblen, Thorstein. 1973. *The Theory of the Leisure Class.* Boston: Houghton Mifflin.

Wakefield, Sarina. 2013. Hybrid Heritage and Cosmopolitanism in the Emirate of Abu Dhabi. In Pamela Erskine-Loftus, ed., *Reimagining Museums: Practice in the Arabian Peninsula.* Boston: MuseumsEtc.

CHAPTER 14

Smiles and Smallness:
Jokes in Yemen and Palestine

Andre Gingrich, with Zulfokar Al-Dubai and Noura Kamal

In the Arab-speaking world, explicit forms of public awareness about living in a small country emerged only fairly recently, during the late twentieth century. For the cases of Yemen and Palestine, this chapter discusses how the topic is addressed through certain jokes and witty riddles.

Context: Smallness in the Arab Middle East

During the colonial period, political notions of either Pan-Islamic or Pan-Arabic belonging were often much more influential than their smaller-scaled counterparts. The tension between appeals to religious awakening and pan-national unification in its more secular versions in fact had inspired many in the Arab anticolonial movements since the early nineteenth century. Both of these broad wings of anticolonial cultural and political mobilization usually had thought in terms of self-understood "greatness" as part of the general visions that mobilized many (Gingrich 1999): "great" visions of the entire Muslim community, or of the complete Arab homeland. That homeland usually was seen in its three major parts: the "East" (al-Mashriq,[1] east of the Red Sea), the "West" (al-Maghrib, between Libya and Morocco), and Egypt in the "middle" of it all. In those anticolonial discourses, "smallness" was not a topic frequently activated, except in negative ways—that is, as a colonial scheme to divide and rule the rising masses.

First generations of royal leaders in independent Arab countries of the nineteenth century (Saudi Arabia) and early twentieth century (North Yemen, Egypt, and Iraq) in practice pursued more pragmatic attitudes. In their ideological orientations and rhetorical prose, however, notions of grandeur remained prominent. This was reinforced by the leadership of newly independent regimes that came to power between 1945 and the 1970s, wherever Pan-Arab military regimes seized control in the region. By their respective leaders, and through corresponding ideological emphasis, most of them— Nasser's Egypt, Gaddafi's Libya, Hafez Assad's Syria, Saddam Husain's Iraq, Yasser Arafat's Palestine Liberation Organization (PLO)—presented themselves as vanguards of the glorious Arab nation, marching toward happy unification under their victorious leadership. Corresponding counterarguments from the various facets of the religious wing in the political spectrum about a "new Caliphate" or a new Islamic "empire" or republic became increasingly popular together with the reemergence of political Islam since the late 1970s and early 1980s (whether in Palestine or Egypt, in Syria, Iraq, Yemen, or Sudan), and with the gradual crumbling of Pan-Arabic illusions.

It was during those years I first became aware that in some corners of the Arab world, "our country's smallness" was becoming addressed at all by some of my hosts: at first in the 1970s, in the course of my encounters with Palestinian refugees in Lebanon, and then in 1980 while traveling in Central and Upper Yemen. It was explained to me as an outsider that the topic of smallness entailed some embarrassment—and the gestures and grins accompanying several of those conversations indicated that as well. In terms of reputation and honor, the argument went, it would be better if one were strong. It is difficult to be strong, however, the argument continued, if your country is small, weak, and helpless. It should be added that these circles of hosts were all male. For them, the notion of smallness conveyed an additional threat of possible allusions to a "lack of size" of male genitals.

Yet "smallness" as a descriptive and symbolic category of relevance for society's current position was being addressed *despite* the embarrassment. What followed in several of these conversations were jokes—more or less harmless little tales with a punch line that made everybody in the room smile or laugh. The laughter dissolved some of the embarrassment, at the same time creating an implicit consensus about the insight highlighted by the punch line, such as: "the influential Arab countries are using us Palestinians merely as bargaining chips for their own interests"; or "the Emirates and the Saudis can push us Yemenis around in whatever ways they choose"; and so on.

It appears to me that it is indeed only since the 1970s and 1980s that one's country's smallness thus has become a topic to be positively addressed at all in relevant corners and arenas of the Arab world. The Cold War was coming to an end, and many in the Arab world felt increasingly frustrated with Pan-Arab nationalism and its discrepancy between rhetorical thunder and meager results. Some were simultaneously concerned about the reemergence of political Islam. It was this incipient skepticism about the potentials of those "big" ideological and cultural visions among both wings of the political spectrum that created new discursive spaces and arenas for soberly addressing—perhaps even for the first time in history—one's country's smallness.

In Tunisia, Lebanon, Palestine, Yemen, and several of the smaller Gulf countries, many began to realize that it had to be *here* that one would have to engage with the making of a future. No longer could one wait for initiatives and possible solutions from the outside. The Arab-speaking Middle East has dramatically changed since the end of the Cold War (Korany and Dessouki 2008). Yet the topic of smallness among Arab countries, and its intersections with jokes and humor, continued to accompany me. It will be at the core of this text from today's perspective.

Outline: Jokes, Concepts, Research Approaches

Humor has not really been a central topic of study for disciplines such as sociology, history, or sociocultural anthropology whose records are fairly thin in this regard. Fields with closer leanings to the life sciences—physical anthropology, clinical psychology—often displayed a stronger interest in the topic. This might relate to the possible eruptive or healing effects of humor, but also to its obvious universal dimensions.

The actual enactment of interpersonal humor always being deeply contextualized, most sociocultural anthropologists would agree about the difficulty in translating humor for other audiences and readers. This critical awareness about the limits of cultural translations has kept verbal and situational humor at the margins of research by sociocultural anthropologists—while the study of literature, media studies, musicology, and art history have developed some remarkable expertise. Usually these analyses by studies in arts address humor by known professionals and entertainers, whose nonanonymous works feature wider ranges of dissemination and a smaller impact of situational contexts and local constellations.

A cursory glance over sociocultural anthropology's record (including folklore studies) with regard to the study of humor indicates three main lines of research (Driessen 2015). The first and more traditional one was concerned with *documentation*, in line with how ethnographers collected local myths, fairy tales, or legends in various continents since the nineteenth century. An example is the Aarne-Thompson classification system for Euro-American humor (Dundes 1997). The second and more recent legacy is *analytical* and dates back to insights in the British tradition,[2] by A. R. Radcliffe-Brown (1940), Mary Douglas (1968), and others, on the functional and symbolic aspects of humor and related institutional aspects; Mahadev Apte's 1985 study represents a more recent landmark publication in this regard. Finally, a third strand is primarily *self-reflexive*, discussing and ridiculing the anthropologists' misconceptions, confusions, and adventures in fieldwork. That legacy ranges from Horace Miner's (1956) "Nacirema" satire to Nigel Barley's humorous self-reflections (e.g., 1983). An important link between the first and the third strand was established by the work of Alan Dundes (e.g., 1987). Notwithstanding a few allusions to the first legacy, the present text is largely situated within the second tradition.

As standard humorous forms of expressing narrative culture, jokes in the eastern parts of the Arab-speaking world (al-Mashriq) represent a genre of verbal presentation and entertainment that is fairly similar to jokes in Europe and the Americas. Narration is expected to rarely last longer than one or two minutes, ending with a self-explanatory punch line. Jokes usually have no known author, and many of them may follow some standard plot that would involve a sequence of several steps leading to, or culminating in, the punch line. In some parts of al-Mashriq, the jokes' plots may often be arranged around a popular humorous figure, such as Ibn Za'id in Central Yemen (Lambert 1985). Fictional humorous figures in south Arabia would correspond to certain equivalents in northern Arabia such as Juha or in Turkish (Nasreddin Hoca) and other languages.

In Islamic times, Arab societies provided public appreciation for the arts in ways that often prioritized spoken or written language over other forms of artistic expression and performance. To this day, popular and elite respect for calligraphy or poetry finds fertile cultural environments anywhere in Arabia. The popular role of good storytellers among adults, or of good narrators of fairy tales for children and adults, also is legendary in Arab history. Written collections of humorous tales and jokes in Arabic have a legacy that in al-Mashriq dates back to the tenth to thirteenth centuries C.E. (Marzolph

1992). Today, knowing good jokes, and being able to present them in an entertaining and acceptable manner, also counts as a personal asset and an enhancement of reputation—although this entails less prestige than storytelling and is rarely considered as a form of popular art. Still, telling jokes is more widely accepted among male and female laypersons in al-Mashriq than, say, in continental Europe, and it has less of a competitive male bias to it. In most parts of al-Mashriq, telling jokes is a welcome ingredient to distraction, entertainment, and socializing—whether this takes place in mixed gender groups of relatives or among gender-specific gatherings.

I have chosen the Palestinian West Bank and Central Yemen for the present analysis for the obvious reason that I am fairly familiar with both contexts after many years of academic interest.[3] Moreover, it seemed appropriate for the present purpose to also discuss and compare these two among the less influential cases of "smallness" in al-Mashriq, while the two much more powerful examples of Israel and the Emirates are discussed by other contributors (see Dominguez, Chapter 6, and Khalaf, Chapter 13, in this volume). An additional advantage in choosing jokes on smallness from Central Yemen and the Palestinian West Bank lies in the fact that to a certain extent, public culture in both areas is fairly permissive with regard to humor—more so than in some other parts of al-Mashriq: certain denominations and theological orientations in Islam such as the "Tawhid" school of thought (outside Saudi Arabia known by the somewhat pejorative term of the "Wahhabi" direction) and several Salafi versions of Sunni Islam tend to frown upon the public display of humor and entertainment. In the Palestinian West Bank and in Central Yemen, such religious orientations do exist, but they have not risen to any hegemonic position. Therefore from most religious perspectives in both cases of small countries, the public display of humor is acceptable and legitimate—at least within those limits that do not question the foundations of Islam per se.

A few words on methods will conclude this section. It has already been indicated how this small project gradually grew in a cumulative manner through occasional encounters, readings, and ethnographic observations in rather pedestrian and casual ways across the years. This gained additional momentum when Ulf Hannerz and I began to prepare for the conference preceding this book. Between January and May 2010 I compiled my relevant field materials—as previously gathered in Ramallah, in Sana'a, and in their vicinity—which resulted in a first set of commented jokes from both areas. On that basis I formulated a loose hypothesis claiming that jokes were a convenient outlet to informally address and discuss concerns about the country's smallness in Palestine and in Yemen, as compared to neighboring countries. In addition, it was posited that smallness would be addressed primarily in metaphorical forms rather than descriptively, and that these metaphors would widely differ—including references to Palestine's and Yemen's very different sociopolitical and military contexts.

In 2011/12, I then closely collaborated in this project with Dr. Zulfokar Al-Dubai (Dhu 'l-Fuqar al-Duba'i) and (then) doctoral candidate Noura Kamal. Dr. Al-Dubai, with whom I am very well acquainted since the 1980s, is a Yemeni-Austrian psychiatrist with family roots in Central Yemen. With a doctor of medicine degree from the University of Vienna, he has more than twenty years of professional experience in Austrian clinics. Dr. Kamal is a native from Nablus (northern Palestine) with a master's degree in sociology from BirZeit University, and now with a Ph.D. in social anthropology (2015) from Vienna University. I have cooperated with Dr. Kamal since about 2006, at first in the context of an EU-sponsored cooperation project with BirZeit University, and later as principal adviser to her Ph.D. project. For the second phase of the present project, Zulfokar launched an inquiry in 2012 through his family members in his home area in Central Yemen, and Noura investigated through her relatives in Nablus—both about current jokes that would relate to the hypothesis above. In this manner, they collected about a dozen jokes each. This second double set of jokes, like the first set, happened to relate in a substantial manner to the initial hypothesis.

A final phase of the inquiry was then marked by researching relevant and active Yemeni and Palestinian Arabic websites. This phase delivered a third set of about the same number of jokes, among which several were more or less identical to those collected previously. I have treated the website format for the present purposes as an interface between the spoken and the written, in view of authors' anonymity in both forms of communication, and also in view of the significant intersection that became apparent in our respective harvests of jokes. Because of this project's emphasis on "verbal and quasi-verbal, anonymous" jokes, I refrained from extending the analysis into certain genres of printed collections.

Out of our overall collections of some twenty jokes per region, most of them in several versions, I have chosen basically four per region for the present text. This choice followed several criteria. First, the selection should be fairly diverse, representing the wider range within the sample, accumulated through phases one to three as described above, from which the selection was taken. Second, these jokes should be easily comprehensible for a readership of nonspecialists—thereby minimizing the notorious labors of cultural translation. Last but not least, the choice should convey at least a spicy taste of what Noura, Zulfokar, and I have come to appreciate as indigenous approaches to humor in Palestine and Yemen.

In short, what follows are the results of a qualitative analysis. If there is any bias in these materials and their representation here, then it may be urban and liberal middle-class in the socioregional sense, and moderately nonaggressive in the directions these jokes take. The analysis thus cannot possibly strive to achieve any exhaustive representation, certainly not along any quantitative criteria. Yet along the qualitative dimensions outlined here, a few significant albeit incomplete glimpses into al-Mashriq interrelations between a country's smallness and publicly accepted humor should be provided.

Ethnography: Jokes on Smallness from Nablus and Sana'a

We shall first discuss the Yemeni jokes, which feature one recurrent theme related to the country's relative smallness as a sense of "being backward." That topic is often addressed by modernists. They often are groups of intellectuals and upper-class citizens in families with stronger international connections. Many among them relate the country's strong tribal element and a correspondingly weak central state as main causes to the theme of "hopelessly lagging behind." One joking riddle from Sana'a, for instance, asks: "Why is it that in 2080 the Yemen will rule the rest of the world?" The joke solution to the riddle is: "Because in 2080, everybody else will be living on Mars. So the world will be left behind to the Yemen alone." The same set of themes is addressed in another joke:

> Allah and Archangel Gabriel are revisiting the world in 2050. They want to find out what has become of each country Allah had once created. They come to Morocco, but that country has changed so much they don't recognize anything. The same is true for Egypt, and for Saudi Arabia. Then they come to the Yemen—and here, Allah turns to Gabriel and says "Now finally, there's at least one country in the world that hasn't changed a single bit ever since I created it."

A second set of Yemeni themes that are informing jokes with some intersections regarding the country's relative smallness has to do with labor migration to the Gulf countries. For a long time, labor migration to Saudi Arabia and to the smaller Gulf countries has been among the most important income sources for many male Yemenis. Although that pattern changed repeatedly, Yemeni out-migration into the oil-exporting countries of al-Mashriq is still highly relevant—to the extent that many inside Yemen criticize the apparent eagerness for out-migration as a sign of the country's weakness, dependence, and inferiority.

The implicit message in the following joke is that Yemenis are so eager to earn their money through well-paid employment elsewhere that they do not care enough about what is really important, that is, in their own country and even in the face of God. This is a joke that I have also heard among rural and tribal people in Upper Yemen.

> A country guy has received a letter from his cousin in the Saudi Gulf region, informing him that there is a job waiting for him there. He is asked to come. So this country guy rushes to a travel agency in Sana'a to buy the flight ticket. That being done, he is told that he still needs a Yemeni exit visa. So he rushes to the Ministry of Interior to obtain that exit visa, after which the officer tells him he would still need a Saudi entry visa. Time is getting short before the plane's departure. Our country guy breathlessly rushes across Sana'a's main street where the Saudi Consulate is. Yet before he reaches the other side, a car knocks him over and kills him.
>
> Like every good Muslim, he has to wait until the Day of Judgment comes when his final fate is decided. Finally it is his turn, and he steps forward. Archangel Gabriel, sitting to the right of Allah, looks into his face and says to him: "We're not quite sure about your record—there were good things but also bad things in your life. So we let you have a say in this: Where do you want to go from here, to heaven or to hell?" And our failed emigrant answers: "I want to go to Saudi Arabia."

In a third set of jokes that have emerged during the past few years, the country's deplorable status is also taken for granted. But now there is one factor that is identified as being primarily responsible for the country's weakness, poverty, and backwardness. That primary responsibility is attributed to Ali

Abdallah Salih, president of Yemen for thirty-five years until January 2012. In this last Yemeni joke, the Arab Spring's mass protests have already started, and the outgoing dictators experience their last few months in office.

Mubarak, Gaddafi, and Ali Abdallah Salih sit together under a palm tree. The transistor radio reports about mass demonstrations everywhere, which makes Mubarak jump up in fear. He is so afraid that he climbs on the top of the palm tree. Ali Abdallah Salih looks up and shouts: "This is totally useless, come down immediately!" But Mubarak is too afraid and refuses to come down again. Ali Abdallah Salih shouts back that he will pay him ten million dollars if he comes down, but still Mubarak refuses.

Gaddafi then gets angry, and shouts up to Mubarak: "You old fool, if you don't come down by yourself right now I'm gonna shoot you down, and will castrate you afterwards!" Mubarak climbs down immediately. Ali Abdallah Salih is offended and says: "My suggestion was much more reasonable, why didn't you follow my offer?"

To which Mubarak replies: "Well, Ali, we all know that Mu'ammar Gaddafi is crazy and so unpredictable that you never know whether or not he means what he says. But with you, Ali, the whole world already knows that you're nothing but a liar. So with you, I knew straight away that you wouldn't give me any dollars."

One could of course insist that none of these jokes refer in any explicit way to the country's relative smallness. That is true as long as we look at each of these jokes separately, that is, in an isolated manner. Taken together, however, crosscutting layers of recurrent themes can be identified. These layers of recurrent themes all concentrate in a self-criticizing manner on what is communicated as the country's negative situation: stagnating, backward, deplorable, dependent, badly governed. This becomes conspicuous especially when Yemen is compared to others. In the case of God and Gabriel visiting many Arab countries before looking at Yemen, they single out this country as the one that has never changed. In the case of the country guy trying to emigrate, the man is so obsessed with his wish to find work in Saudi Arabia that nothing else matters.

One could therefore speak of layers of collective autocritique and of mocking Yemen's inferiority. These thematic layers contextualize an implicit topic of relative smallness. In these jokes, relative smallness is imbued with the sense of being inferior and worse off than the others, of lagging behind more than the others, of being ruled in the worst possible way without the world really caring about it. We shall leave it at that for the moment, while keeping in mind the notions of layers of collective autocritique and mocking Yemen's relative inferiority. As an intermediate result, these layers implicitly address Yemen's relative smallness.

The Palestinian jokes chosen as having something to do with smallness, at least in a relative way, take a different general orientation. They very rarely are engaging with one or the other form of autocritical mocking. By contrast, they usually are soaked with black or sad humor. In addition, they display a certain form of sarcasm and also a dosage of cynicism that alludes to the Palestinian condition in a variety of ways.

The few jokes from Palestine that actually do address Israel in a more explicit manner are sad rather than black jokes, and, while they clearly allude to the Israeli presence, they do so in a rather decent, not personal way. A case in point is a riddle, originally known to have come from Christian Palestinian residents of Bethlehem: "How would Christmas happen if Joseph and Mary were following their star not in Roman times, but in the present?" The answer is: "They would get stuck along the road like all Palestinians. For this reason, long before his parents were ever able to make it to Bethlehem, Jesus would have to be born alongside the tarmac road at an Israeli military checkpoint."

One alternative trope addresses the widely held Palestinian conviction that the whole world makes life easy for Israelis but untenably hard for the Palestinians. This becomes dryly visible in the joke about an Egypt Air flight from Amman to Cairo.

In the air, the plane's engines begin to show serious problems. Upon consultation with his deputy, the captain has to announce through the loudspeaker: "Unfortunately, the engines' problems are so grave that we would not be able to fly on with the plane's load as it is. One passenger will have to be thrown out of the plane so that the rest can safely fly on. The second captain will ask questions to each passenger, and the one who can't answer the question will be thrown out."

One after the other, a number of Egyptian and Jordanian passengers are presented with one question each, and they all manage to respond accordingly. Then the second captain approaches the Israeli passenger on board and asks him: "How many inhabitants live in

Egypt?" The Israeli passenger thinks for a moment and then says: "More than eighty million people, I believe."

"Correct," says the second captain. Now, turning to the Palestinian passenger sitting in the next row, the second captain asks: "And what are the names and addresses of those eighty million people?"

Parts of this theme are also addressed in the Palestinian version of a much more widely employed joke pattern:

A Kuwaiti, a Japanese, and a Palestinian are traveling in a small sailing boat. A storm comes up and the three are unable to reach the coast. Despite their desperate efforts, the boat keeps filling with water to the point that it may sink.

The Japanese suggests that each of them throws out something to make the boat lighter. He grabs his huge film camera, throws it into the water and says, "We have enough electronic devices in Japan, it doesn't really matter if I throw away this one."

Hearing and seeing this, the Kuwaiti grabs the Palestinian, throws him into the ocean and says to the Japanese: "We have so many Palestinians in Kuwait—it doesn't really matter if we throw out this one."

Again, the Palestinian person in this second version of the same trope *suffers*—he is thrown out into a fatal destiny—without being responsible for the situation that has led to this emergency and without being given a chance of doing anything else. Actually, this Palestinian version represents the Palestinian in the joke as a mere object.

In both jokes the Palestinian has done nothing wrong. It is remarkable though, that he suffers in the end as a victim of bad treatment by other Arabs. Interestingly, some of these jokes do not address Israel directly at all. Several of those that do, such as the first joke about Bethlehem or the next one, present "the Israeli(s)" as not doing much except being or representing the occupying power.

The same remains basically true for a third trope in jokes related in some way to Palestinian smallness. These are jokes addressing the unbearable situation in the Palestinian West Bank and its division into "Zones A, B, and C" forms of administration. Allusions to that situation then may or may not be combined with indications that the world either is not even aware of this situation or is aware but obviously finds it normal. The world therefore is not portrayed as treating the Palestinians primarily in an unjust manner, but it does not notice how bad the Palestinian situation is because this is not important to the world. This line of reasoning comes out in the following joke.

> An American, a Frenchman, and a Palestinian each has recently died, and because they have not exactly led decent lives they are now being sent to hell. But before they enter, the devil (al-Shaytan) is granting each of them one last phone call to their relatives.
>
> The American calls his only daughter in Tucson, Arizona, and they talk to each other for one hour. Afterward, that man has to pay one hundred dollars for his phone bill. The Frenchman calls his wife in Marseille, and he talks to her and to his son and his daughter for two hours. So he has to pay two hundred dollars.
>
> Then, the Palestinian is given his last phone call, and he dials Nablus. He talks to his three cousins and his four brothers and his five sisters, and to his wife and their three sons and their four daughters, all of which takes five hours. Afterwards, however, he only has to pay one dollar to Satan. The American and the Frenchman are furious. They ask the devil why they had such huge phone bills whereas the Palestinian, who talked much longer on the phone than they did, had to pay almost nothing. To which al-Shaytan answers:
>
> "Well, the Palestinian phone call was so cheap because THAT was a local phone call—from hell to hell."

It should have become obvious at this point why our overall sample of Palestinian jokes did not include a single example of self-mockery and autocriticism, so common among the Yemeni jokes presented in the first group. In general, these jokes address Palestinians' situation as something that is caused by many other factors, all of them being basically outside the reach of Palestinians' themselves. The Palestinian laughter, as it echoes in these jokes, is about others' ignorance of, or more or less intentional and careless shaping of, that desperate Palestinian condition.

Palestinians get stuck in roadblocks, are being thrown into the water or out of planes, and live in hell. The "relative smallness" in Palestinian jokes is related to this sense of being absolutely powerless. Israel, the Western powers, other Arab countries all have access to power and access to agency, whereas the Palestinians in the jokes' narratives can do very little if anything at all to actually change their condition.

If we take these particular jokes as a specific set of vignettes of Palestinian self-portrayals, then it does appear as if they outlined Palestinians as "passive victims." This certainly is merely due to this particular sample, and thus to an investigative bias, in which we searched for possible connections to smallness and its metaphors. There are in fact many jokes that address Palestinians as active resistance fighters, but for obvious reasons, they then do not focus on Palestinian inferiority by demographic or territorial size or its correlates. On the other hand, the apparent absence of collective Palestinian self-ridiculing is perhaps more than balanced by a plethora of "regional jokes" in everyday Palestinian lives, as, for example, jokes about people from al-Khalil (Hebron), or jokes about people from Ramallah, and so forth.

If we now seek to apply similar formal criteria as employed for the Yemeni jokes, the argument can be spelled out as follows: Palestinian jokes addressing the country's and the refugee diaspora's smallness in an indirect and metaphorical manner do so through crosscutting layers of black, sad, and sarcastic humor in which the laugh is about others, about external forces. The ways in which the "world," big powers, and the occupying Israeli presence treat Palestinians obviously is the thematic environment within which Palestinian smallness is contextualized as being helplessly exposed.

Analysis and Interpretation: Searching for Alternatives?

It is now common academic knowledge that the formulation of a research question has its influence on the outcome. Had we asked about jokes on more general subjects—such as, say, about the discrepancy between Islam's values and the ways many people live up to them—then the inquiry might have yielded several jokes that are shared by Palestinians as well as by Yemenis. A very specific topic such as smallness, however, generates with a certain necessity results that are relatively specific for each of the two countries in question.

It might also be helpful to remember that Yemen and Palestine are installed in very different if not contrasting positions along a wider spectrum of al-Mashriq constellations. These constellations—rearranged after the end of the Cold War, the watershed events of 11 September 2001, and the "Arab Spring" of 2012 and its aftermath—make up the condition of the Middle East today. One could even argue that since the turn of the century Yemen has turned into a "failing state" torn apart by civil war, while Palestine may be presented as an "emerging state" since the establishment of some autonomy in its "zones A."

Like any simple contrast along two shorthand formulas, this one between Yemen as failing and Palestine as emerging state of course simplifies a complex condition to an almost untenable extent. Since Ali Abdallah Salih was forced to give up some of his personal hold on power, the Yemeni state has continued to disintegrate under conditions of increasing international military involvement (up to the time of writing in late 2015). The notion of Yemen as a "failing state" thus is somewhat misleading (at least in 2015), because it ignores that international military involvement. Something similar but different is also valid for the notion of Palestine as an "emerging state." This at least is the opinion expressed by the European Eminent Persons Group (including, for example, former NATO secretary-general Javier Solana and the former prime ministers of Italy, Ireland, the Netherlands, and France) who in an open letter from April 2013 address "the continuing destruction of the Palestinian people's right to self-determination" (EEPG 2013: 20). In short, the notion of Yemen as a failing state may convey a somewhat too narrow assessment, while the idea of Palestine as an emerging state may encourage too much optimism.

Still, these two shorthand formulas help to highlight why current contexts and conditions in both countries are so different that the contrasts between our two selections of jokes in fact entail few surprises. We were able to identify two main sets of thematic layers that contextualize these jokes in different ways. Palestinian smallness is portrayed and discursively represented with sad or black humor about the absence of local power and in the face of injustice by others. In Yemeni jokes, the country's relative smallness is portrayed and discursively represented in self-ridiculing ways as a self-inflicted situation of being backward, dependent, and badly governed. Despite the bizarre and absurd settings inherent in these jokes, one may state that these main discursive themes and symbolic patterns are relatively realistic in some ways, by at least truly reflecting certain basic elements of the respective country in the real world.

In both sets of jokes, "smallness" never is a topic in its own right. As postulated in the initial hypothesis, smallness as a joke's trope occurs only in metaphorical ways and disguises. The most common thematic metaphors are "vulnerability" in both regions, with a factor of "haplessness" in the Palestinian case and a factor of being "backward" in the Yemeni case. Two sets of factors appear to be primarily responsible for this permanent metaphorical disguise of the topic of smallness. One set of factors is the fairly recent emergence of arenas and spaces in which it is possible to reflect on the topic of "being small"—notwithstanding much stronger, long-established legacies of "great" political and cultural visions. To then actually occupy in discursive ways these spaces and arenas, however, a second factor of symbolic obstacles has to be overcome. These symbolic obstacles are sociocultural and relate to honor: they implicitly suggest that people who openly admit "being small" might make themselves vulnerable and exposed to attacks against their honor. In principle, this is valid for all adults—whether male or female, but with a special emphasis on men nevertheless since they are perceived as the main representatives of collective honor, and given the fact that all the Arabs who appear in our jokes are male.

Occupying the discursive space of "smallness" therefore continues to come along with a sense of tension and potential embarrassment—about being as vulnerable as one is by being small and by addressing it and about being ridiculed about it. This, precisely, is the key reason why jokes seem to be not just one but in fact a very privileged form of carrying out discourses about smallness in al-Mashriq. Jokes are a fairly safe form of addressing and mastering the potential embarrassments related to the topic of smallness. Their more or less standardized format and the social settings in which narrating jokes and listening to them include strong elements of ritualized speech behavior (Gingrich 2010) offer the advantage of a relatively safer journey through somewhat troubled waters. At the same time, the permanence of metaphorical disguise continues to protect the symbolic content of these jokes, so they cannot become offensive for people who should not feel offended. And last but not least, the laughter triggered by the punch line in fact does have the potential of dissolving some of the tension that comes along with the topic.

Dissolving the tension of embarrassment, and actually making a consensus visible and audible through laughter when otherwise the actual existence of such a consensus could easily be contested and put to doubt, is a primary result of these jokes' circulation and narration. The elicitation of consensus through laughter also confirms the "realism behind the absurd" that we have referred to above as being symbolically inherent in these jokes. That realism reminds us that jokes have a general quality already noted by Sigmund Freud, who once remarked that jokes (as well as lies, as Freud maintained) have an important feature: the more truth they address behind their stories, the better they are.

Through their references to the real world, their anonymous circulation, which today is enhanced through the new media, and by their potential of making consensus visible and audible jokes and witty riddles have the additional potential of overcoming isolation by sharing with each other the many dimensions of laughter—dimensions that, in these instances of jokes about relative and metaphorical smallness, focus on the sharing of laughter as critique.

Telling these forms of jokes, and listening to them, creates, enhances, or reactivates circles of a certain version of "cultural intimacy" (Herzfeld 1997), which is shared by insiders while outsiders rarely gain access into these circles at all. Perhaps inside these circles today, therefore, jokes and witty riddles are attaining new social significance for reflections about a country's smallness—at least in the Arab world of al-Mashriq with its limited space, until recently at least, for public spheres of debates and for democratic media. In this regard, the role of the new social media was not only relevant as a methodological device for the present research. Much more important, in fact, is social media's role in bridging the gaps of embarrassment and for widening the small arenas of critical laughter inside the societies in question.

One may wonder if, simultaneously, the role of the narrator is perhaps diminishing while the relevance of the new social media grows for telling stories, jokes, and witty riddles. A certain decontextualization certainly is unavoidable as soon as the jokes discussed in this chapter, as well as others, may become more easily accessible through the new media. Yet at the same time, this seems to also encourage off-line narration in the sense that people feel less inhibited than before to tell jokes to each other in dialogical face-to-face encounters. So for the time being, it seems that the impact of the new social media upon cultural and discursive diversity in the Arab world has enriching and stimulating aspects—especially, with regard to laughter and humor.

The current phase of globalization offers unprecedented facilities and arenas to have jokes circulated more easily and more widely through new technologies and formats of communication. Similar to what Claude Lévi-Strauss (1970 [1964]) said about myths, one may argue that new technologies of communications emphasize and accelerate the capacity of jokes to "narrate themselves." In a global context where small Arab countries have left Pan-Arabism behind and often are becoming weary of Pan-Islamism, jokes about one's country's smallness thus help communicate shared forms of alternative meaning. The alternative meanings addressed by many of these jokes and riddles ask in ways that are tailored to the prevailing discursive moods in each of these small Arab countries: Isn't it time to stop accepting the status quo? How long should we continue taking this? Isn't it time to move in a different direction?

*   *   *

For their comments and suggestions on earlier versions of this chapter, I would like to thank Ulf Hannerz as my coeditor, Lori Allen (London), Regina Bendix (Göttingen), Amahl Bishara (Tufts), Eva-Maria Knoll (ÖAW Vienna), Bambi Schieffelin (NYU), Daniel Varisco (Doha), and Cathryn Marshall (Grand Haven, Mich.).

Notes

1. The transliteration of Arabic terms in this chapter follows (except for cases where an Anglicized form is recognized) a simplified version of the *International Journal of Middle East Studies* (IJMES) rules.

2. Marcel Mauss's 1928 article "Parentés à plaisanteries" (now available in a fine English translation [Mauss 2013]) represented an important pioneer work and precursor for this legacy.

3. The Palestinian interactions were funded in part by the EU-sponsored TEMPUS cooperation projects (2003–2004, 2006–2011), "Capacity Building in Social Science Methodologies for Palestine (CASOP)" between BirZeit University, Université Aix-Marseille II, and the Austrian Academy of Sciences.

References

Apte, Mahadev L. 1985. *Humor and Laughter.* Ithaca, N.Y.: Cornell University Press.

Barley, Nigel. 1983. *The Innocent Anthropologist.* London: British Museum Publications.

Douglas, Mary. 1968. The Social Control of Cognition: Some Factors in Joke Perception. *Man,* n.s., 3 (3): 361–76.

Driessen, Henk. 2015. Humor. In James Wright, ed., *International Encyclopedia of Behavioral and Social Sciences,* 2nd ed. Oxford: Elsevier.

Dundes, Alan. 1987. *Cracking Jokes.* Berkeley: Ten Speed Press.

———. 1997. The Motif-Index and the Tale Type Index: A Critique. *Journal of Folklore Research* 34 (3): 195–202.

EEPG (European Eminent Persons Group). 2013. A Letter to EU High Representative Catherine Ashton. In European Eminent Persons Group and John V. Whitbeck, Two Views: What Next for the "Peace Process"? *Washington Report on Middle East Affairs*, June–July, 19–21.

Gingrich, Andre. 1999. *Erkundungen: Themen der ethnologischen Forschung*. Vienna: Böhlau.

———. 2010. Blame It on the Turks: Language Regimes and the Culture of "Frontier Orientalism" in Eastern Austria. In Rudolf de Cillia, Helmut Gruber, Michal Krzyzanowski, and Florian Menz, eds., *Diskurs, Politik. Identität / Discourse, Politics, Identity*. Tübingen: Stauffenburg.

Herzfeld, Michael. 1997. *Cultural Intimacy*. New York: Routledge.

Korany, Bahgat, and Ali E. Hillal Dessouki, eds. 2008. *The Foreign Policies of Arab States*. New rev. ed. Cairo: American University in Cairo Press.

Lambert, Jean. 1985. La geste d' 'Ibn Zâ'id ou la sagesse de l'honneur. *Cahiers de Littérature orale* 17:163–94.

Lévi-Strauss, Claude. 1970 (1964). *The Raw and the Cooked*. Trans. John Weightman and Doreen Weightman. London: Jonathan Cape.

Marzolph, Ulrich. 1992. *Arabia Ridens*. Frankfurt: Klostermann.

Mauss, Marcel. 2013. Joking Relations. Trans. Jane I. Guyer. *HAU: Journal of Ethnographic Theory* 3 (2): 317–34.

Miner, Horace. 1956. Body Ritual Among the Nacirema. *American Anthropologist* 58 (3): 503–7.

Radcliffe-Brown, A. R. 1940. On Joking Relationships. *Africa* 13 (3): 195–210.

CHAPTER 15

Greater Than Its Size:
Ireland in Literature and Life

Helena Wulff

Approaching it by air, the sight of Ireland emerging from the sea is spectacular. All of a sudden it is there: the beaches meandering along the coast interrupted by cliffs, then the buildings of Dublin and the flat fields extending farther behind. You get a sense that the island is so small you can see all of it from above.

Down on the ground, arriving in Dublin, visitors would note the small-town quality of this city of only five hundred thousand inhabitants: no subway, no blocks of skyscrapers. People often take strangers into friendly account in a way that would be rare in a big city, in a big country. There is a habit of connectedness in Ireland, of inclusion. The fact that it is an island also matters.

Ireland is a small country in both absolute and relative terms.[1] The distance from Dublin on the east coast straight to Galway City on the west coast is 186 kilometers, that from Cork City in the south to the Northern Irish border is 281 kilometers. There are two Big Others: Great Britain, the former colonizer, represents a lingering Hegemony while the United States represents Hope. But in one way Ireland is Big. It is indicative of its rich literary tradition that Ireland, with a population of only four and a half million, has produced four Nobel Prize winners in literature: W. B. Yeats, George Bernard Shaw, Samuel Beckett, and Seamus Heaney. This literary tradition also contributed to Ireland's trajectory into political independence.

And writing continues to play an important part in defining what kind of a country this is. Contemporary fiction writers such as John Banville,

Roddy Doyle, Anne Enright, Joseph O'Connor, and Colm Tóibín are the protagonists of my study of the work and the social world of Irish writers.[2] Frank McCourt, best known for *Angela's Ashes* (1996), died in New York in 2009. His memoir trilogy is included here as a forceful illustration of issues on migration and diaspora. A young writer, Belinda McKeon keeps up the tradition of contextualizing Irish fiction in the countryside with *Solace* (2011). The novel makes a poignant point about the link to the Irish land (Wulff 2007a).

This is a study I conduct in large part through "yo-yo" fieldwork (Wulff 2002), back and forth from Stockholm. The project requires recurrent visits (over more than the classic one-year-in-the-field) in order to enable my presence at focal events taking place regularly but occasionally in Ireland: literary festivals, book launches, prize ceremonies, readings, creative writing workshops. I have visited writers' retreats, one way to spend time with writers informally. Additional data come from in-depth interviews with writers, as well as with publishers, editors, and agents. Texts are central for this study, both literary texts and journalistic articles by the writers. I also make use of newspaper features about the writers, book reviews and reports from literary festivals and similar events. Writers' blogs and tweets are there, too.

Ireland forms an eloquent ethnographic case. It speaks to issues of postcoloniality, migration and diaspora, borders, religion in national politics and violent conflict, and the cultural consequences of sudden prosperity brought by the European Union, but followed by an even quicker downturn. With their background in journalism, contemporary writers become public intellectuals as they regularly also write cultural journalism: primarily for the *Irish Times* and magazines such as *London Review of Books* and *New York Review of Books*.

In this chapter, I engage with the smallness of Ireland at three levels. It is there in the literary texts. The intimacy of local life was already evident in the classics of Irish ethnography, such as the monographs by Conrad Arensberg (1937) and Arensberg and Solon Kimball (1940). Current literary writing also often portrays small groups of people, family, and friends, who move in dense, interconnected circles two or three generations deep. But these circles now sometimes reach to Britain or the United States. Smallness is also there in the social world of the writers, closely knit, with a core of people who have known each other since they went to university in the 1970s. And this in turn relates directly to a methodological need for social sensitivity in a small-scale field.

It is easy to study people who know each other: I just follow their network links. Their recommendations take me past gatekeepers. But the fact that these networks are multiplex and intertwined also calls for caution. I have reached a point when those I meet may want to know what their colleagues have confided in me, especially about career drawbacks: rejections from publishers or writing blocks. Fame is no guarantee against declines, but might in fact make people even more vulnerable. So I do not pass on pieces of information that might be hurtful or threatening, as I move around in the sometimes competitive small literary world. I have also been careful when asking a writer to connect me to another one, as they may in some way be rivals. I have even conducted interviews with writers I am not really interested in, but feel I have to include, as they have been suggested by important main informants (cf. Wulff 2012b).

Ireland's Smallness

The meaning of smallness varies between countries. The main aspect of Ireland's smallness is that the country is greater than its size, as it has a committed diaspora of an estimated eighty million people claiming Irish descent, distributed across the world in the United Kingdom, the United States, Canada, Australia, Argentina, New Zealand, Mexico, South Africa, Brazil, and the states of the Caribbean and continental Europe. Their commitment to Ireland has partly to do with its vulnerability. What is now the Republic of Ireland was under brutal British colonization for at least four hundred years, until as recently as 1921. It is likely that the hurt of history runs deep in a small country, and among its diaspora.

Ireland's smallness is also reflected in tourist industry branding. In a study of travel images, I found that "images of Irish journeys stand out for their particular combination of portraying hospitality, traditional culture in music and dance, wit and loquacity" and that "Ireland generates dreams of peaceful country life, childhood summers, and a happy, old-fashioned past." There is also an "abundance of pastoral landscapes" in the images (Wulff 2007b: 532). Closeness to the countryside is a frequent feature of Irish life. One reason is that it is more common than not to have a rural family background only a generation or two back. A hurtful history of English landlords is another reason why the link to the land is significant. Although countryside was a central topic of writers such as John McGahern, the land continues to play a major role in contemporary Irish novels too. Belinda McKeon's *Solace* (2011) focuses on a generational conflict over a farm where a father, Tom, wants his son, Mark, to continue the rural life, while the son is looking toward the city and doctoral studies at the university. Then they are hit by mutual grief, as both the wife of the father (also the mother of the son) and the fiancée of the son die in a car accident. Eventually, the link to the land makes the two men reconcile: "It had been years since Tom's son had spent so long at home. He stayed almost the whole summer, working the farm every day, and sleeping in his old room, with the child's crib at the foot of the bed" (McKeon 2011:1). While Mark is out in the field saving the hay, Tom takes his grandchild there in order to "show to her the way it was done: the lines of grass, the huge yellow bales lurching out of the red machine, and the shape of her father in the tractor cab, a hand on the steering-wheel, and his head turned to watch the progress of the baler hitched behind" (McKeon 2011: 1). Like many great works of fiction, *Solace* contains unexpected connections and events. Mark meets a young woman in Dublin who becomes his fiancée, but before long they realize that they grew up close to each other. The dramatic twist is that her father had once wronged Mark's father, so badly that he was still devastated decades later. This raises a crucial question about smallness: can a small country, where many people are closely connected, be a scene for unexpected connections? Or does smallness imply predictability? Surprise is clearly a literary strategy, but from my field observations I know that what are regarded as unexpected connections also happen in real life. It can be the young woman dancer who marveled over how her husband had known her brothers at school—long before he knew her. The point here is that smallness certainly is predictable in many ways, but particular connections may still be unexpected.

Interestingly, this can also be extended abroad. Once when Belinda McKeon was arriving at Kennedy Airport in New York, and the immigration officer asked her with his professional sternness, "What do you do for a living? What are you coming over here for?" her polite reply was: "I'm a writer of fiction." He relaxed and went on: "Do you know Colm Tóibín?" In her capacity of Colm Tóibín's protégée, McKeon certainly knows him. They appear in public together for readings, and when she interviews him at literary events. McKeon had just not expected the New York immigration officer to make a connection between the two of them (Tóibín and McKeon 2012).

An understanding of Ireland's particular smallness, moreover, includes two unifying events that occurred at different junctures in the political history of the nation. The first one was the "dream speech" delivered by Eamon de Valera, prime minister and the founding father of the Republic, on the radio on St. Patrick's Day in 1943. In the speech, de Valera famously described his vision of an ideal Ireland of rural harmony with "comely maidens dancing at the crossroads." Since then the notion "dancing at the crossroads" has been a key metaphor in Irish political and social life. De Valera's "dream speech" was a part of his nation building (cf. Wulff 2007a).[3] The second unifying speech took place more recently, in 2010. This speech became a response to the financial crisis that had replaced the unprecedented economic boom, the "Celtic Tiger" in the late twentieth century. After years of euphoria, the atmosphere in the country was broken by the bad news of a deepening recession. People in Ireland were very worried, and felt even worse when they realized that the rest of the world was being fed humiliating news stories about their situation. This was the atmosphere when Colm Tóibín (2010) gave a keynote speech at the Irish Literature Exchange in Dublin, celebrating 1,500 books in translation. Summoning his ill-at-ease compatriots to a more positive image of Ireland, he pointed at the power of its cultural impact abroad. The speech was printed on the front page of the *Irish Times* under the headline "Spreading the Real News from Ireland." The first lines read:

> This country's economic crisis may be making headlines, but a much more serious and deeply influential image of this country emanates from the culture we send out to the world. And now, more than ever, that mission is vital.
>
> I think it is possible to argue that both trade and diplomacy are culture for slow learners, that what happens with music and books, with painting and poetry, how they move and spread, how they do not recognise borders, how they find translators, is a blueprint for what happens later with goods and services and with treaties between governments. . . .
>
> Our duty is to make good sentences, and that is our responsibility too.
>
> Beyond that, nothing much. But maybe good sentences stand for other things that are good, or might be improved; maybe the rhythms of words used well might matter in ways which are unexpected in a dark time.

This speech is an act of Colm Tóibín as a public intellectual. He certainly has the attention of Dublin intellectuals, academics, and artists. They read what he writes, watch him on television talk shows and festival panels, and discuss his ideas in conversations with each other. I have often noticed that Tóibín's assessments capture what has not yet been formulated by others, or even predict the course of events. In his article "The Public Role of Writers and Intellectuals," Edward Said (2002: 25) notes that "during the last years of the twentieth century the writer has taken on more and more of the intellectual's adversarial attributes in such activities as speaking the truth to power, being a witness to persecution and suffering, supplying a dissenting voice on conflicts with authority." Said mentions Ireland as one country where issues on "freedom of speech and censorship, truth and reconciliation" have been addressed by "the writer as an intellectual testifying to a country's or region's experience, thereby giving that experience a public identity forever inscribed in the global discursive agenda." As to Irish intellectuals, Said interestingly identifies "an impressive battery," such as the novelist and poet Seamus Deane, and the literary scholars Declan Kiberd and Luke Gibbons. It was Gibbons who famously identified Ireland as "a First World country, but with a Third World memory."

"Everyone Knows Everyone"

The social world of Irish writers is indeed close-knit. Not only does everyone know everyone, but in many cases writers, critics, editors, literary scholars, and journalists are related. They are in-laws, cousins, even siblings, uncles and nephews and nieces spanning two generations, even back to a grandparental generation. Going back to the inner circle of writer friends in the current Dublin literary world, they were born in the mid-1950s and have known each other since they went to university, mostly to University College Dublin, such as Roddy Doyle, Colm Tóibín, and Dermot Bolger. Founded in the mid-1800s as the Catholic University of Ireland, University College Dublin has been closely connected to the Irish nationalist movement. Among its eminent alumni are Irish politicians, actors, and writers, notably James Joyce. Anne Enright is a part of the same friendship group, although she went to Trinity College Dublin, the Protestant university (and the oldest university in Ireland, founded in 1592). John Banville, a little older, never went to university as he wanted to make a living on his own as soon as possible, which he did as subeditor and literary editor at Irish newspapers. Again, cultural journalism in Ireland, as well as in Britain and the United States, keeps being a part of the literary writers' work. The prominent journalist Fintan O'Toole is also included in the network, as are some publishers and editors. The writers, mostly male, connect each other to publishers, review each other, appear together in public and in the media.

Yet the small scale breeds not only friendship and collegiality but also competition, which in a small place can be difficult to run away from. This is captured in the novel *Fox, Swallow, Scarecrow* (2007) by Éilís Ní Dhuibhne, a satire of Dublin's literary world during the greedy Celtic Tiger economy. A case of apparent rivalry in Dublin's literary world also emerged when Anne Enright was awarded the Man Booker Prize for her novel *The Gathering* (2007b). At first this news was received in Dublin with great enthusiasm and pride. This is the most distinctive literary prize in the Commonwealth and the Republic of Ireland. The winner receives £50,000, and the novel will be prominently marketed across the globe. The Man Booker Prize is made public at a black-tie ceremony at the Guildhall in London, broadcast live. Short-listed writers are present, but do not know who the winner is before it is announced. This is a moment of major uneasiness for Irish writers, who often are short-listed and sometimes win the prize.

But it did not take long after the initial euphoria over Enright's prize before a media campaign attacking her began, not least in blogs. This campaign focused on Enright's article "Disliking the McCanns" (2007a) in the *London Review of Books*, where she accused the McCann couple (whose daughter Madeleine had disappeared on a holiday in Portugal) of being neglectful parents. Why Enright wrote the provocative article remains unclear. It is also difficult to trace the origin of the campaign against her; it might well have been launched by an envious writer. Enright apologized to the McCanns, and eventually the campaign ceased. But when it was at its height, literary Dublin was fiercely for or against Anne Enright. Her friends and fans wrote supportive cards and called her, while her competitors were full of spite (Wulff 2012a).

The importance of the Man Booker Prize is noteworthy in its own way, too, as an example of the place of Irish writing in the world. Despite the fact that Irish literature has some clear characteristics of its own, in a global literary landscape, both classical and contemporary Irish writers are often taken to be English. In bookshops outside Ireland, the works by Oscar Wilde or John Banville, to name just a couple of Irish writers representing different epochs, are usually displayed under signs saying "English literature." In Dublin's literary world this is taken as an instance of postcoloniality—of how "the former colonizer appropriates Irish writers taking the credit for their success, rather than allowing the Irish their independence, and to shine in their own right" (Wulff 2012a: 238).

Éilís Ní Dhuibhne, one of the writers in my study, also writes under the pen name Elizabeth O'Hara. She has a Ph.D. in Irish folklore, and, as her late husband was Swedish, she knows Sweden. She has written some academic articles but is mainly a fiction writer. In addition to her English language publications, she publishes in Irish. I sent her the outline for the conference that this volume is based on. Her e-mail reply to me is worth citing at some length:

I think Ireland is a "fragile" country, as described. Perhaps also an "underdog"?

But "fragile" is an interesting adjective for us. The literary situation in Ireland is interesting in the context of this conference. First, the Irish publishing industry was shattered in the early 1800s, after the Act of Union abolished the Irish parliament (and moved Irish MPs to Westminster). Before that there was a fairly vibrant publishing industry in Dublin. The Irish publishing industry has never recovered from the move, one could say. The important locus of publishing is still London. (E.g., there is nothing like Norstedts or Bonniers in Dublin: I'm always astonished when I see the huge building Norstedts has—any Irish publisher has a staff of only a handful of people.)[4] This has important implications for Irish writing. For instance, it explains why some writers would translate basic phrases in Irish, which any Irish person who is half way intelligent would understand, to English. It also means that we have an essentially postcolonial attitude to our writing. Success happens in England, it is perceived (although in fact the main sales for Irish writers are in Ireland, which is why a few English publishers, such as Penguin, Transworld, and Hodder, have recently opened small branches in Dublin). This fits in with the idea expressed in the conference description: the middle classes measure themselves against another country. That's spot on, as far as literature is concerned.

Of course it has to do with the language situation. If we spoke Irish, we would have to have a vibrant publishing industry here. But since we don't, London can take over. It's a weird aspect of literary economics that the tax breaks etc enjoyed by Irish writers mean that when an Irish author is very successful, absolutely none of the profit, apart from that earned by bookshops, accrue to Ireland. The author doesn't pay tax; the publishers are in England. (It's stupid, from an economic point of view.)

The language issue also means that Irish authors are constantly in competition with English and American (and of course others.) There are advantages and disadvantages to the situation.

You should perhaps remember to say something about literature in the Irish language? Minority of writers writing for a very small readership, state funded publishing industry, tiny circle so that the writer can practically anticipate who the readers will be, personally.

Of course, everything you know about the small networks, everyone knowing everyone, etc, is true. I get the impression that in literary circles in England everyone knows everyone too. But I'd guess it's more hierarchical; there's circles within circles. Here there's a bit of that, but it's more like one circle. Just as, I suppose, everyone has met the president, lots of people have visited the president's house (Aras an Uachtarain). It's different from say America, where you don't expect to have dinner with the Obamas occasionally. . . .

This makes reviewing very difficult. No doubt Sweden is not much different.

It comes as no surprise that Éilís Ní Dhuibhne prefers the notion of Ireland as a "fragile" country rather than an "underdog"—who wouldn't?—although I keep noting instances of the latter as well, in life and literature. The Irish are famous for creative wit, which has to be understood in relation to its many dark political and economic dramas, not least postcolonial ones. This is an interactive type of wit, often executed by throwing a question back to the questioner. It can also take the form of saying something in a deadpan serious tone of voice—while meaning the opposite.

In an interview I did with John Banville, he identified an Irish writing style in fiction in terms of "grim comedy." And in a *New York Times* article from 2011, entitled "The Grim Good Cheer of the Irish," accentuated by the current emigration, he describes the pain of parting from loved ones and "homesickness in the vast world of exile": "Our most effective succor, however, may rest in what has not changed at all: our persistently grim cheerfulness. One could say, as some do, that we Irish are congenitally masochistic, that we secretly welcome misfortune. But it does not feel like that. Rather, we have always had a propensity to laugh at ourselves, which stands us in good stead in these melancholy times, when laughter, even the self-mocking kind, is at a premium."

A part of the social life of Irish writers is enacted at writers' associations events—particularly at the annual Irish PEN dinner when prizes are awarded by the president of Ireland. Events organized by Aosdána, the Irish arts academy, also offer opportunities to meet, as do literary festivals and conferences. But this is only the public social life of Irish writers, distributed all over Ireland, while the private social life tends to take place in Dublin, at restaurants, bars, and homes, and includes smaller groups than those getting together at organized events. The smaller informal groups of friends usually consist of writers of about the same level of fame.

But then there is again the complex relationship to the world outside Ireland. There is a distinction between writers with an international reputation who publish in Britain and the United States—the inner circle—and writers with a national reputation, mostly publishing with Irish publishers. More often than not they move in separate circles, while young aspiring writers (with a recent degree in creative writing) who have published one book, or are trying to get published, form a third group (Wulff 2012a). Individual young writers can be seen with established writers who function as their mentors; established writers may also write glowing endorsements of new books by unknown writers. Some of these established writers have taught creative writing. Among those who have known each other since they went to university in the early 1970s, friendship groups are not completely intact after a number of decades. One friendship, between two women of national fame, turned into a purely professional relationship after one of them had an international breakthrough.

Contrary to their classic predecessors, such as Brendan Behan, who are reputed to have lingered in certain bars in Dublin, I have heard several contemporary male writers state emphatically that they do not spend a lot of time in bars—"we write!" One reason may be that many have younger children, and nowadays men take more active care of their children than in the past. The idea of Irish writers meeting in bars has been taken up by the Irish tourist board, with Dublin Literary Pub Crawls every summer season. At the "crawl," actors perform classic writers, reading from their works in one legendary pub after another. I have been taken to a couple of bars in central Dublin where contemporary writers are regular customers, at least now and then. One of them is more of a private hangout, not perceived as a literary place—unlike the bars included in the Dublin Literary Pub Crawl.

In an interview with Colm Tóibín, he told me that he did not think of the literary world in Dublin as a community of colleagues that is a whole; but, rather, he thinks of it in terms of a number of small groups of friends. To him, traveling and living abroad is crucial, so "some writers are in France, the United States, all you want is three writers who share the same jokes. . . . How people know each other is through travelling!" (Wulff 2010: 110)

Again, there is the more cosmopolitan context. I have encountered Anne Enright in Leuven at a literary conference where she gave a keynote reading, in Dublin at a poetry festival and for an interview, in Hong Kong for a reading she did in a book store, in Galway at a literary festival for a reading, and in Stockholm when I was her moderator at a panel in a bookstore. Meeting abroad for readings on panels at literary festivals is in a sense when writers have time to meet. Irish writers often make friends abroad, or get to know each other better, and then continue these friendships back in Dublin. Frequent travel is part of life for other Irish intellectuals, as well. We may remember the names Edward Said noted as public intellectuals: Seamus Deane, Declan Kiberd, Luke Gibbons. It so happens that all of them have a base at the University of Notre Dame, Indiana, in the United States, rather than in Dublin only—and this could well be one reason why Said was aware of them. Other writers in my study, such as Colm Tóibín, are also a part of this group of intellectual friends and colleagues. And the University of Notre Dame, a diaspora academic center for Catholics, is an enduring institutional base. (Another well-known attraction at the university is its football team, "The Fighting Irish.")

In the end, however, writers must sometimes be alone. Some who are in especially high demand for public events and readings simply take a break from public appearances for a few months each year, or even for a whole year when they do not accept invitations. They also seem to reduce getting together with friends. The need for isolation when being in "the whirlwind of writing" has led Joseph O'Connor not to allow anyone, not even his wife (he claims), into his study located at the back of the garden and, he stated in an interview, "I don't pick up the phone for six months!"[5]

The Irish Border: Short but Significant

The Republic of Ireland is surrounded by sea borders on three sides: east, south, west. The land border separates it from Northern Ireland, a province of the United Kingdom since the 1920s. Writing about the Irish border, Hastings Donnan and Thomas Wilson (1999: 73) note that "the visibility of state markers such as guard towers, road signs and national flags, however, are shadowed by other signs whose significance may be less obvious to the uninformed." These signs pertain to the Troubles and post-Troubles. With its 360 kilometers, the Irish border is short compared to many state borders. It is crossed routinely by trains, buses, and cars. But because the Republic of Ireland is a small country, when violent activities happen on the Irish border, they reverberate around the whole country. This border is "the gateway to a province which may be viewed, in its entirety, as a borderland, a frontier zone of disputing nations and ethnic groups" (Donnan and Wilson 1999: 74). It is also a bridge, however, when it comes to institutions of religion and schooling (not including the universities that north of the border are in the British system) that are partly shared.

Colm Tóibín's book *Bad Blood: A Walk Along the Irish Border* (2001) is a literary reportage drawing on his walk from Derry (Londonderry is the official, Protestant name of the city) in Northern Ireland to Newry. It can be seen as a way for someone who was brought up as a Catholic in the Republic of Ireland to make sense of the Troubles. The walk took place more than a decade before the breakthrough in the peace process that would come with the Good Friday Agreement in 1998. There had been political talks attempting to put an end to the Troubles, but as Tóibín notes, tension and fear were still prevalent. As he walked, he met people from both sides of the community and observed rituals from marches to funerals. As the Twelfth of July approached, to be celebrated by Protestants with marches that had been connected with violence, Tóibín found himself in a small village, Ballinamallard, in Fermanagh in Northern Ireland. Before he went to bed in a hotel, he noticed how the local people were getting ready for the annual Orange parade (Wulff 2010). But "it wasn't long after midnight when I was awakened by sounds beneath the window." A loud voice said: "Fuck the Pope!" (Tóibín 2001: 53–54). Tóibín was amused, thinking to himself that "the man below the window had been drinking." Tired from his walking, Tóibín was having a rest. He had been "drinking in Blake's, swimming in the public baths, and exerting myself as little as possible. I hadn't walked an inch, let alone a mile. Soon I would start walking again, but not yet, O Lord, not yet. Now I was in bed wondering if the man below the window had any idea that up above him was a papist from Wexford."

A Legacy of Leave-Taking

Emigration has been integral to Ireland for centuries. The most momentous emigration took place in connection with the Great Famine in the mid-nineteenth century when Ireland was still occupied by Britain. As two million people were forced to leave the island, and one million people starved to death, the entire population was reduced by 20–25 percent. It is a frightening fact that the population has still not reached the same level as before the Famine raged (Whelan 2005). In the twentieth century, unemployment again triggered a number of emigration waves (Brown 1985). Emigration was at its height in the 1950s and the 1980s. Then in the 1970s, immigration had started slowly and has increased steadily since then. Return migration has kept accelerating, as has the new immigration including refugees from different parts of the world (Tovey and Share 2000). With the economic downturn in 2008, however, young people have again started to leave Ireland in search of work.

As emigration and diaspora have defined so much of Irish life for such a long time, they are obvious literary topics, ranging from loss and longing to displacement. Ireland's small scale is brought out in emigration stories about unexpected encounters, emotional comfort, and practical support by fellow Irish people in foreign places, but also about how a close-knit society produces tensions through social control.

Joseph O'Connor's historical novel *Star of the Sea* (2002) is a racy thriller set in 1847 on an overloaded ship, carrying emigrants away from the Famine in Ireland to New York. On board are people who knew each other back home and realize that their past is catching up with them. In *Brooklyn: A Novel* (2009), Colm Tóibín paints the portrait of a young woman in 1950s Ireland who emigrates to Brooklyn in order to get a job. This is arranged by an Irish priest, and she starts working in a department store. She is chaperoned by her Irish landlady and goes to the Catholic church, where she eventually meets an Italian man. When her sister suddenly dies, she goes back to her mother in Ireland. But in the end, the young woman decides to return to Brooklyn and lead her life there.

With the exceptionally successful memoir *Angela's Ashes* (1996), Frank McCourt established himself as a major diaspora writer. It was made into a film and translated into German, French, and Spanish. McCourt was awarded the Pulitzer Prize for this late debut, at the age of sixty-six. Having practiced storytelling since an early age, McCourt tells a riveting tale about growing up during miserable conditions, first during the Depression in New York and then in the slums of Limerick. As soon as he can, he moves back to New York, having saved and stolen enough money for the ticket. The following quote, written in a certain tongue-in-cheek manner, summarizes what the reader has learned about this young man's beliefs and dreams about America—America as the Big Other of Hope. As the ship sails into New York at dawn, McCourt (1996: 359) is on deck thinking he is in a film that will end, and he will find himself back in the cinema in Limerick: "I can pick out the Statue of Liberty, Ellis Island, the Empire State Building, the Chrysler Building, the Brooklyn Bridge. There are thousands of cars speeding along the roads and the sun turns everything to gold. Rich Americans in top hats, white ties and tails must be going home to bed with the gorgeous women with white teeth. The rest are going to work in warm comfortable offices and no one has a care in the world." The sequel to *Angela's Ashes*, entitled *'Tis* (1999), continues the story about McCourt as a young man in New York. He gets a job at a hotel, where he is confronted by the class system he had thought did not exist in America. This is the time of the Korean War, so he is drafted and sent to Germany, where his task is to train dogs and type reports. Back in America, he works on the docks, but having left school at fourteen he has a strong drive for more education. At New York University he meets a long-legged blonde, and things start falling into place. But finally it is his job as a teacher that really makes the difference. As he goes on to describe in *Teacher Man* (2005), the third memoir in his trilogy, he has an outstanding pedagogical talent. For thirty years he taught writing to unruly teenagers in an underprivileged area of New York. While not hiding one or two setbacks, he details how he managed to relate to his students and capture their interest in storytelling. In the process, he became a writer himself.

But again, Ireland is now also an immigration country. How is this mirrored in fiction? Roddy Doyle has taken on the topic in his collection *The Deportees and Other Stories* (2007). In light of Ireland's conflicted and fractured ethnic and religious history, the new immigration can be said to accentuate the issue of who exactly is Irish. In Doyle's satirical, yet serious short story "57% Irish," the protagonist considers how to measure Irishness. He invents a test based on people's reactions to video clips of the Irish dance show *Riverdance*, the traditional song "Danny Boy," and a goal scored by the Irish player Robbie Keane against Germany in the 2002 World Cup in football. In Doyle's touching story "Guess Who's Coming for the Dinner," an

Irish girl introduces her Nigerian boyfriend to her slightly taken aback but well-meaning working-class family. "The Pram" is Doyle's chilling story about a Polish child-minder in Dublin. Unsurprisingly, these stories show how immigrants stick together. They are, however, in many cases taken through the close-knit networks of native Irish people.

Yet as immigration has so far been a rather marginal aspect of Irish society, this is a literary theme still in its infancy. There are short stories and plays by Nigerian writers living in Dublin, but they hardly mention the immigrant experience. As Colm Tóibín reflected in a conversation with me, it will be the second generation that will reveal what it is like to be newcomers, and children of newcomers, in Ireland.

Notes

1. Although my usage of the term "Ireland" mostly refers to the Republic of Ireland (with its twenty-six counties), I also discuss Northern Ireland (with its six counties).

2. The study "Writing in Ireland: An Ethnographic Study of Schooling and the World of Writers" was funded by the Swedish Research Council.

3. In *Dancing at the Crossroads: Memory and Mobility in Ireland* (Wulff 2007a), I apply the idea of "dancing at the crossroads" by arguing that this metaphor captures how Ireland is now situated at the crossroads between Irish tradition and European and cosmopolitan modernity; see also Wulff (2005). Journalist John Waters's essay book entitled *Jiving at the Crossroads* (1991) is an example, as it discusses Ireland between the past and the present, the urban and the rural. As an instance of the close-knit networks of the Irish literary world, Waters used to be married to the flamboyant singer Sinead O'Connor, who is the sister of author Joseph O'Connor.

4. Norstedts and Bonniers are major Swedish publishing houses.

5. Joseph O'Connor, public interview, Stockholm, March 2012.

References

Arensberg, Conrad. 1959 (1937). *The Irish Countryman*. Gloucester, Mass.: Peter Smith.

Arensberg, Conrad M., and Solon T. Kimball. 1968 (1940). *Family and Community in Ireland*. Cambridge, Mass.: Harvard University Press.

Banville, John. 2011. The Grim Good Cheer of the Irish. *New York Times*, 17 December.

Brown, Terence. 1985. *Ireland: A Social and Cultural History, 1922–1985*. London: Fontana Press.

Donnan, Hastings, and Thomas M. Wilson, 1999. *Borders*. Oxford: Berg/Bloomsbury.

Doyle, Roddy. 2007. *The Deportees and Other Stories*. London: Jonathan Cape.

Enright, Anne. 2007a. Disliking the McCanns. *London Review of Books*, 4 October.

———. 2007b. *The Gathering*. London: Jonathan Cape.

McCourt, Frank. 1996. *Angela's Ashes*. New York: Scribner.

———. 1999. *'Tis*. New York: Scribner.

———. 2005. *Teacher Man*. New York: Scribner.

McKeon, Belinda. 2011. *Solace*. London: Picador.

Ní Dhuibhne, Éilís. 2007. *Fox, Swallow, Scarecrow*. Belfast: Blackstaff.

O'Connor, Joseph. 2002. *Star of the Sea*. London: Vintage.

Said, Edward. 2010. The Public Role of Writers and Intellectuals. In Helen Small, ed., *The Public Intellectual*. Oxford: Blackwell.

Tóibín, Colm. 2001. *Bad Blood: A Walk Along the Irish Border*. London: Picador. Originally published as *Walking Along the Border*. London: Macdonald, 1987.

———. 2009. *Brooklyn: A Novel*. New York: Scribner.

———. 2010. Spreading the Real News from Ireland. *Irish Times*, 18 November.

Tóibín, Colm, and Belinda McKeon. 2012. In Conversation: Colm Tóibín and Belinda McKeon. 1 March, www.youtube.com.

Tovey, Hilary, and Perry Share. 2000. *A Sociology of Ireland*. Dublin: Gill & Macmillan.

Waters, John. 1991. *Jiving at the Crossroads*. Belfast: Blackstaff Press.

Whelan, Kevin. 2005. The Cultural Effects of the Famine. In J. Cleary and C. Connolly, eds., *The Cambridge Companion to Modern Irish Culture*. Cambridge: Cambridge University Press.

Wulff, Helena. 2002. Yo-Yo Fieldwork: Mobility and Time in a Multi-Local Study of Dance in Ireland. In Ina-Maria Greverus, Sharon Macdonald, Regina Römhild, Gisela Welz, and Helena Wulff, eds., Shifting Grounds: Experiments in Doing Ethnography, special issue, *Anthropological Journal of European Cultures* 11:117–36.

———. 2005. Memories in Motion: The Irish Dancing Body. In Bryan S. Turner, ed., The Dancing Body, special issue, *Body & Society* 11 (4): 45–62.

———. 2007a. *Dancing at the Crossroads*. Oxford: Berghahn.

———. 2007b. Longing for the Land: Emotions, Memory and Nature in Irish Travel Advertisements. *Identities* 14 (4): 527–44.

———. 2010. Colm Tóibín as Travel Writer. *Nordic Irish Studies* 9:109–16.

———. 2012a. An Anthropological Perspective on Literary Arts in Ireland. In Ullrich Kockel, Máiréad Nic Craith, and Jonas Frykman, eds., *Blackwell Companion to the Anthropology of Europe*. Oxford: Wiley-Blackwell.

———. 2012b. Instances of Inspiration: Interviewing Dancers and Writers. In Jonathan Skinner, ed., *Anthropology and the Interview*. Oxford: Berg/Bloomsbury.

CHAPTER 16

Swedish Encounters:
End Notes of a Native Son

Ulf Hannerz

About the time when the project of putting together this book got under way, I read a newspaper column in one of the Stockholm dailies, by Richard Swartz (2010), a well-known Swedish foreign correspondent. Here was a column on the characteristics of small countries; Swartz could draw on extensive personal experience of three: Sweden, Austria, and Croatia.

In a small country everybody knows everybody else, Swartz suggests—and then quickly admits that this is a slight exaggeration. Anyway, members of the elite have gone to the same schools, meet each other at the same dinners and exhibitions, read the same papers. They are related to each other or marry each other. The familial atmosphere decreases social cleavages, but also differences of opinion and belief. Such a country becomes less colorful, but at the same time solid, to the point of getting boring.

I have long enjoyed Swartz's skills of reporting and commentary and have met him a couple of times. We attended a conference together once, arranged by a Swedish foundation (I do not remember the topic), and participated in the same panel, on "Cosmopolitanism," at the annual Swedish book fair. In recent years he has stationed himself in Vienna. Over the years, he has built his reputation particularly through reporting from Eastern and Central Europe, not least when much of that was on the other side of the Iron Curtain. I have also met his sister, at another conference—she was the director of a major commercial television channel in Sweden before she became the head of a respected book publishing company. (Another Swartz, a relative

of theirs, was briefly Swedish prime minister, in the restless years at the end
of World War I.)

It struck me that Swartz's commentary on small countries partly ran parallel to lines of thinking we were exploring in our group, although we were
academics and he was a veteran news reporter. Some of his claims were provocative, too, satirical—intended perhaps to get his readers to wake up on a
lazy Saturday morning. In a small country, the café is more important than
the parliament? Anybody who can read and write will sooner or later become
a cabinet minister? Not likely in Sweden at least, particularly as the turnover
in high political offices is mostly not so quick. It is true, however, that if their
cabinets are about the same size and with the same standard structure (see
Introduction), Swedes would seem to have about ten times as much chance
as Germans to become ministers.[1]

That, again in the terms of the introduction to this volume, would be a
matter of absolute smallness. So is Swartz's claim—which, as he says, goes a
bit too far—that everybody knows everybody else. But he notes some of the
umbrella devices that would at least strengthen such a tendency: the schools,
the media, the exhibitions. He goes on to refer to the "Jante Law," also referred to in the introduction, according to which nobody is allowed to be
much superior (or, he points out, much inferior) to anybody else. It would
also presumably be a sense of absolute smallness that makes compatriots
convinced, as Swartz argues, that they are all in the same boat—and must
therefore row in the same direction.

The small country, however, also suffers from bad nerves and can only
deal with one thing at a time. But, as it fails to deal with anything conclu-
sively before some new issue claims attention, this goes on and on; the small
country survives, believing that it is busy with its own affairs. Yet actually,
according to Swartz, these are all generated by the outside world or reflections of it.

So here Swartz shifts to a portrayal of the implications of relative smallness. The small country almost always perceives itself as larger, greater, than
it really is. It is at the center, never at the margins. But it worries about what
the surrounding world thinks about it. And when it discovers that the wider
world really does not think much about it at all, it is offended. Some small
countries have persuaded themselves that the only way of drawing the attention of the world is to behave as brashly and insolently as possible toward
it—Swartz will not name names, to avoid diplomatic complications. There is
a pendulum swing between grotesque overconfidence and dejection, espe-

cially obvious in sports. A sports commentator in a small country is a cross between a chauvinist high priest and a masochistic flagellant.

Toward the end of his column, Swartz has some rather debatable suggestions about small-country language. Frequently, he notes, the small country has a language it shares with nobody else. This language lacks the concepts and intellectual tools of the large language, so it thinks less well—no philosophy, just a very impoverished prose. But it is more sensuous, as it is stuck with senses and passing impressions. Swartz refers to a line by the nineteenth-century poet Carl Jonas Love Almqvist, familiar to all Swedes: "Only Sweden has Swedish gooseberries." And a small-country language can blush.

In one way, however, Swartz concludes, the small country is almost always superior to the large country: it is not provincial. As a matter of self-preservation whoever comes from a small country must always explain where he is from, learn foreign languages and customs, and accept without protest that both Shakespeare and Picasso are part of his cultural heritage, despite the fact that neither of them was born in Sveg. Only such a person, in Swartz's view, can be a true internationalist, despite the fact that he lives his life on the edge of the plate. (Sveg? Not quite officially a town, yet the largest settlement in one northerly Swedish province—any native Swede would know that.)[2]

I am a bit skeptical, finally, about those comments on the capacity of small-country languages. Indeed, the mere challenge of trying to do justice in English to Swartz's own subtle formulations in his newspaper column casts some doubt on this in my mind.

So much for Richard Swartz's column itself; in no small part, what follows is in response to it. Of course, by academic standards of comparative studies and generalization, making statements on the basis of knowledge of three cases could seem a bit dubious; moreover, the three countries Swartz identifies are all European. So how would his claims fare when confronted with ethnography from Laos, Fiji, or Paraguay? But then within the space of a newspaper column, there is not room for much evidence. And again, Swartz writes to amuse as much as to analyze.

Togetherness in Sweden and Very Special Gooseberries

Yet one of these three countries is my own, where I have spent much of my life. I have never done what would formally count as field research in

Sweden, but the line between ethnographic observer and native participant should probably not be drawn too sharply. My sense is that living in some particular country is a rather constant reality, which, however, becomes more noticeable in a rather off-and-on manner, in ways that very likely vary between different kinds of inhabitants. It may be a kind of experience and a sensibility most effectively communicated through rather anecdotal evidence. So in what follows, I will offer some more or less auto-ethnographic notes.

What, then, do I recognize in Swartz's picture of Sweden, how does it resonate with my recollections and interpretations of events and situations? The presence of institutions recurrently bringing at least some kinds of people together, and sharing understandings, seems real enough. The fact that I have met both Richard Swartz and his sister, on separate occasions, is a case in point. When he suggests that public opinion can only deal with one thing at a time, I come to think of the dominant role of the op-ed page in the largest Stockholm morning newspaper in setting the agenda and the pace of debate. (That happens to be the paper for which Swartz now does his column.)

On the other hand, I would also believe that this kind of small-country social cohesion and cultural coherence may have passed its climax. By the mid-twentieth century, Sweden had one state church (although with several other denominations, mostly variations of Protestantism, outside it), a largely unitary state school system, one radio channel and one television channel, and compulsory military service for men. This has all changed—toward greater institutional diversity. There was at the time little migration, in or out. Since then, there has been a considerable influx of labor migrants and refugees. These are at least not yet so fully covered by umbrella institutions, and hardly any of them arrive knowing that exotic Swedish language. So network accessibility and transparency have decreased and become more unevenly distributed. Yet such qualities of the fabric of social life may remain relatively strong by the standards of larger countries.

Again, I do not doubt that the awareness of living in a particular country, and specifically in a small country, is stronger for Richard Swartz, as a journalist and a foreign correspondent, and for me (not least as an anthropologist) than for many of our compatriots. With different perspectives, not least professional perspectives, go different horizons. In the southern Swedish village where I have long been spending summers, and where my family has deep roots, many of my neighbors probably see their lives in more local terms, although there are variations among them as well. I find, too, that even as their everyday networks are more local, they sometimes make assumptions about accessibility at a certain remove; my neighbors are inclined to take for granted that people in Stockholm, the capital, are more closely linked together than they really are.

The suggestion that there are limits to the diversity of opinions and beliefs is now perhaps less true than it used to be, since the arrival of newcomers from the outside world. (It is striking that many of Swartz's most visible colleagues in Swedish journalism and commentary are first- or second-generation immigrants.)[3] Even so, the claim is made again and again that the Swedish word *lagom* has no precise counterpart in other languages; it means something like "just right," "not too little, not too much." And Sweden is taken to be *Landet Lagom*, "the *Lagom* country."

Swartz's comment on the place of sports in small-country sentiments is surely appropriate. Sports commentators in the national media can in themselves become stars; occasionally there have been very successful Swedish practitioners in world sports who have become globally famous. True, some of the national heroes have been in sports where the competition is not so great—cross-country skiing is not big outside the subarctic regions of the world.

Then there are these mood swings, not only in sports but, more generally, with regard to global recognition. The American sociologist Neil Smelser (1998) once proposed that "ambivalence" as a mental stance has received less scholarly attention than it actually deserves. It may be conceptually and methodologically inconvenient and is therefore pushed aside. While Smelser does not dwell on questions of nations and national identity, I would suggest that ambivalence is common in the stances of inhabitants toward their small countries. On the one hand, there may be a certain patriotism, even a pride in the quality of life and the accomplishments of the country; on the other hand, the realization that this is not really "the indispensable nation" to anybody else. This ambivalence can take various forms, personal or collective. When Swedes quote that line from Almqvist's poem, "Only Sweden has Swedish gooseberries," it entails some mocking self-celebration; it goes with a sense of ironic distance.

A Royal Encounter

Swartz partly retracts the claim that in the small country "everybody knows everybody else"—this is only true of the elite, he immediately admits. Yet I would suggest that network connectedness does not entirely follow class lines. There was a time when the Scandinavian countries were referred to as "bicycle monarchies." By now you are not likely to find members of the royal families pedaling through city streets, and my sense is that their more private social circles, at least as they enter their more mature years, mostly do not show great diversity. Yet as young adult singles, Swedish royals have been on the Stockholm party scene. The present crown princess fell in love with her personal trainer, a likable young man from a small community in a northern province, and married him. And the crown princess of Norway, before she became that by marrying the crown prince, had been a waitress and an anthropology student at the University of Oslo.

I had my own experience of this sort of network connectedness some years ago, when I went to the royal palace in Stockholm to receive a medal from the hands of His Majesty the King, in a small ceremony.[4] The king inquired about my scholarly interests; we conversed for a while about the fact that global interconnectedness does not necessarily lead to total cultural uniformity but may even stimulate creativity. When he had recently opened an exhibition of Saami crafts, the king pointed out, he could see that some of the new wooden sculpting was still from birch roots but drew on new sources of inspiration. Then we talked about his forthcoming official visit to Shanghai. As my encounter with the king was drawing to a close, I thought I might experiment with a more personal line. So I told him that he and I had at one time had the same physical education teacher. He looked a bit startled, asked who that was, and as I mentioned the name, the most idiomatic translation of his response might be, "I'll be darned!"

I did not tell him why I remembered this network linkage. I had been in my early teens, in an ordinary state school in a middle-class Stockholm suburb, and the physical education teacher had a second job teaching in the small private elementary school in central Stockholm where the then crown prince spent his first school years. At my school, there were times when the gymnasium had to be used for other purposes, while the teacher felt that the weather outside was not too appealing. No outdoor exercise, then; he took my class down in the school basement, where he would show us his home movies of going skiing in the northern Swedish mountains with his royal pupil. I and my classmates referred to this facetiously as "theoretical gymnastics."

It turned out that the king and I had both seen the small advertisement marking our teacher's death a few years earlier in the family pages of the newspaper—it did not get any other public attention, as few would have been aware of his one claim to fame.

Danger in Traffic Relationships, and Sweden at the Center of the World

What my conversation with the king may be taken to show is that "everybody knowing everybody" could be less of a restrictedly elite characteristic than one might expect. In this case, my having had the young crown prince only two network links away in my youth, although we never met at the time, was by way of a quite ordinary physical education teacher. And at the time, by way of that teacher, perhaps several hundred other pupils at my school shared that same royal connectedness. I would suspect that in the Swedish case, such connections crossing the routinely assumed group boundaries are not so rare, whether the people involved happen to be aware of them or not.

Often such awareness is certainly one-sided: in my early teens, I knew of the social proximity of the crown prince, but he surely did not know of me. In the case of "traffic relationships," this tends to be even more likely (Hannerz 1980: 105; 1981: 24). The stranger you hardly even notice in some momentarily shared public space is indeed a stranger; but he or she could just possibly recognize you. It may remain a passing copresence—you only need to avoid bumping into each other. Yet it could be transformed into something else.

One late Friday evening, at the end of February 1986: a middle-aged couple has been to the movies, and they are walking home through the streets of central Stockholm. Normally, it will take them fifteen or twenty minutes. But this is not a normal evening, and the husband in the couple will never reach home. At a street corner a stranger appears, with a gun, and fires two shots at him; he dies very quickly. The dead man is Sweden's prime minister, the leader of the Social Democratic Party, Olof Palme. The assassin disappears into the side streets.

I know that street corner well—it is just a few steps from the office building where our anthropology department was once located. Now a plaque has been inserted into the sidewalk, to remind passersby of what once happened there.

The general point about traffic relationships in relation to scale is that where the physical space is limited, the probability increases that anybody can run into anybody. Sweden is not such a small country with regard to territory—much of its space is largely uninhabited. But in the public space in use, few mechanisms or regulations keep categories of people apart. (Even privately owned but uninhabited forestland is treated as a commons where anyone can take a walk or pick berries or mushrooms.) In principle, people can walk in the same streets, shop in the same stores, go to the same movie theaters. The familial atmosphere to which Richard Swartz referred translates in public space and traffic relationships as a relative egalitarianism and accessibility. I know of no "gated communities" in Sweden.

Olof Palme seems to have had a somewhat complicated relationship to accessibility. As a young politician, he perhaps made a point of living with his family in an ordinary suburban row house. (A film team was asked to turn off their camera when he needed to retrieve the front door key from its hiding place.) Later he moved to the Old Town of Stockholm, to what had previously been the home of another prominent Swede, the economist-politician Gunnar Myrdal. This was certainly more exclusive, but surrounded by lively, mostly pedestrian streets (and this is where he was heading when he was assassinated). On the other hand, his summer home was in a remote location, on an island where he was more out of reach. And it is said that he relished more anonymous vacations on the Mediterranean.

Who killed Palme? There have been many attempts to answer that question. The Swedish police have devoted much effort to the case, pursuing different possibilities. More than three years after the assassination, one man was indeed found guilty of the crime: a street person with alcohol and drug problems, an inclination toward violence, some theatrical training in his youth, and connections to the Stockholm underworld. But the verdict was thrown out by a higher court, as the evidence was found insufficient. So the man was out in the streets again, although now as a sort of celebrity in his circles. (Before his death, he once confessed to the crime, but by then few people had much confidence in his credibility.)

The identification of this prime suspect suggested that the murder could have been a matter of chance, a fateful copresence in the street. But alternative theories were more complex. They had to do with what kind of place Sweden was, and what was understood to be its part in the world.

While Palme identified with what he described as "democratic socialism," he was of upper-middle bourgeois background. He had been radicalized in his youth, supposedly in no small part during his time as an exchange student at Kenyon College, Ohio (with GI Bill war veterans among his American fellow students), and had then had a rapid political career. Inclined toward dramatic formulations in a rather un-Swedish manner, he had a polarizing influence on Swedish politics. He had his warm admirers, and there were people who loathed him. (I remember a bumper sticker on some Stockholm cars from the time before his death: "America has Ronald Reagan, Johnny Cash and Bob Hope. Sweden has Palme, no cash and no hope.")[5] At least one of the assassination theories pointed toward a clique within the Stockholm police force.

Not all theories, however, stayed within the Swedish borders. After many years as either prime minister or leader of the parliamentary opposition, Palme was apparently bored with Swedish domestic politics. And so we get to another facet of how Sweden could see itself as a small country.

In the 1940s, two individuals with well-known last names had laid a foundation for a kind of national imagery with which many Swedes had become quite comfortable. Raoul Wallenberg, who disappeared into a Soviet prison after a dramatic period as a diplomat in Budapest, saving Hungarian Jewry from Nazi death camps, was a member of *the* leading Swedish financial family. Count Folke Bernadotte, assassinated by terrorists in Jerusalem as he was trying to mediate in the Jewish-Arab conflict just after the establishment of the state of Israel, was a nephew of the then king of Sweden (the great-grandfather of the present king). Then for a decade or so the country had a low profile internationally, while the government was more busy expanding the welfare state. By 1960, however, there was another local hero on the global arena, the secretary-general of the United Nations, Dag Hammarskjöld (son of an earlier Swedish prime minister). Hammarskjöld stood up to the Soviet leader, Nikita Khrushchev, and then died under mysterious circumstances in or after a plane crash in central Africa, as he was trying to deal with the armed conflict in newly independent Congo. But before that, he had recruited Swedish troops for the United Nations peacekeeping forces there. So Sweden came to consider itself as a staunch supporter of the world organization, and its soldiers would again and again become "Blue Berets" in remote lands.

In a leap of anthropological imagination I am reminded of a classic figure of political anthropology, the leopard-skin chief among the Nuer, portrayed in E. E. Evans-Pritchard's (1940: 174–175) ethnography. The leopard-skin chief had little power of his own, no steady allies. He was just a mediator in specific situations, given some recognition by the parties to a conflict when they wanted to avoid further hostilities. Something like this may sometimes be the role of small countries in the world: They are harmless, not a threat, or at least not to big-country people. Their own interests are not very weighty. Thus they can sometimes be useful.

The representatives of Sweden in international arenas, or international functionaries who happened to be Swedish, like Dag Hammarskjöld, could sometimes be rather like leopard-skin chiefs. But then at times the imagery might change. The ambition might be to speak the truth to power, on behalf of all small countries, or impartially on behalf of humanity. Olof Palme as prime minister had that inclination. He spoke out eloquently against the American war in Vietnam as well as against Kremlin stooges in East Germany. Through state as well as party machineries, he was involved in many ways with the international scene—sometimes taking sides, sometimes trying to mediate. In this period a notion became popular in some Swedish circles that their small country could be "a moral superpower."

In the 1980s, I was on the board of a small United Nations research institute, a task that took me every year to a meeting in Geneva, where it was embedded in a wider set of international agencies. A few months after Palme's death, I was at one such meeting. It was striking how many in the temporary assemblage of scholars, diplomats, and scholar-diplomats I talked to around the halls, with their diverse global preoccupations, offered me their own opinions about who had killed Palme: Iran or Iraq (Palme had been engaged in attempts to end their ongoing war); BOSS, the South African bureau of state security (this was in the apartheid era, and Palme was against apartheid); the CIA; Mossad, Israeli agency for intelligence and special operations; Chile, under the Pinochet regime (Sweden had supported the resistance). I could only marvel at the varieties of international imagination, and at the same time sense that Olof Palme had been understood, by some at least, as a significant figure in a number of problematic contexts, distributed over several continents.[6]

Meanwhile, and during the times that followed, it also semed to me that there was noteworthily little interest in the wider Swedish public in the different conspiracy theories suggesting either foreign or domestic bases. Some few commentators tried to draw attention to various leads, but mostly interest in them was tepid and did not last very long. Could it have been that in a country so accustomed to relative transparency, there was little fertile ground for conspiracy theorizing?

Moreover, a number of years later, in 2003, another leading Swedish politician was assassinated in Stockholm. Anna Lindh, foreign minister, had taken an afternoon break to go shopping with a friend, and in one of Stockholm's major department stores she was attacked by a young man with a knife. Lindh died in the hospital the next morning. Her assassin, quickly apprehended, was a young immigrant from a Balkan country, with a history of mental problems and a dislike for Lindh's recent pronouncements on Balkan conflicts. (Lindh was otherwise quite popular, a less controversial figure than Olof Palme.) In this case it quickly became clear that it was just a matter of too much accessibility, a chance copresence going wrong in a moment.

Stockholm, 10 December

Now some entirely different case materials, although again starting out with one prominent Swede. The enormously wealthy multinational industrialist Alfred Nobel died in San Remo, Italy, on 10 December 1896. Above all, his name was connected with the invention of dynamite.

But Nobel was born in Stockholm, and the prizes bearing his name have been primarily linked with Sweden. (One of them, the Peace Prize, became based in Norway, as at the time of the creation of these awards Norway was the junior partner in a binational union.) Apparently, the prizes came about to a certain extent due to a mistake: when one of Alfred's brothers died, a French newspaper published an obituary for Alfred, announcing that "the merchant of death is dead." Alfred Nobel, still alive and well, became concerned with the way he would be remembered and wrote in his will that these prizes should be established, in a certain set of fields, to be awarded to the persons who had done the greatest services for the benefit of humanity. He also stipulated that they should be awarded without regard to the recipients' nationality—a remarkably cosmopolitan idea, which at the time disturbed some Swedes greatly.

Since 1901, however, on the anniversary of his death, 10 December, Nobel Prizes are awarded in Stockholm, surrounded by public events that have only grown in scale over time. Certainly many people largely ignore them, but one can hardly fail to notice that they are there; in the national calendar this is a day to hoist the flag. (Taking place in dark and wintry December, they somehow also become a part of the early Christmas season.) In 1968, when the Bank of Sweden celebrated its tercentenary, it added a prize in economics, which became somewhat ambiguously assimilated into the complex as a quasi–Nobel Prize. The Royal Swedish Academy of Sciences is responsible for deciding on recipients for three of the awards, and since I am a member of the Academy section linked to the award in economics, I have attended the ceremonies involved regularly for a number of years. Here, then, is some Nobel ethnography.

The festivities have two parts: attendance is by invitation only. In the late afternoon, the award ceremony is held at the Stockholm Concert Hall. On the podium, the king, the queen, and other members of the royal family are seated on one side, and the prizewinners on the other side, in a semicircle. Behind them are a few rows of seats, mostly for academic notables, including those who will make the short speeches introducing the prizewinners and describing their achievements. These presenters face a challenge: trying to describe intricate scholarly work, in medicine, chemistry, physics, and economics, and its consequences, in terms that are reasonably understandable and even entertaining to a lay audience. The presenter of the winner of the prize in literature tends to have an easier task. (All these presenters speak in Swedish, but the prizewinners can follow what goes on in the English-language translations in the printed program.) The winners then step forward to receive their prizes from the hands of the king. Mostly this goes without a hitch; it has been well rehearsed. Occasionally there is an endearing human factor, as when an eighty-nine-year-old laureate has some trouble grasping the prize, shaking hands with the king, and holding on to his cane at the same time—he would have needed three hands.

In no small part, however, the real stars of the show are the royal family. The entire audience in the hall will stand when the king, the queen, and their children (now adults) enter and sing the "Song to the King" (although some will be silent, either of political principle or because they do not quite remember the words). Then, the entire occasion ends as more or less everybody participates in singing the national anthem. This is a late nineteenth-century creation, backward-looking and a little embarrassing if you actually consider the words: "You rest on the memories of past great days, when your name flew honored across the world." Well, Sweden was not always a small country. But such nostalgia would hardly be so prominently displayed in a text originating in more recent times. With regard to the more distant past, Swedes are now more inclined toward amnesia.

Then everybody gets into the chartered buses, for a ten-minute ride through city streets to the Stockholm City Hall, where the Nobel banquet takes place—a more extended event, beginning with toasts to the king and to the memory of Alfred Nobel. There will be some entertainment during the dinner, and at the end prizewinners will make short speeches. It is a three-course meal, and the idea is that it should include the best of Swedish cuisine, with only local ingredients. It is also an important consideration that it should be possible to serve all the 1,300 guests quickly and without mishaps. The members of the royal family, the prizewinners, and various other notables are at the long central table, other guests are at the many other tables on the sides. At the end of the dinner, they all move slowly up the wide stairs to another hall, where the dance begins.

The Nobel banquet may be viewed as one of those events that really bring a certain range of Swedes together, with some number of foreign guests. The royal family is there, and probably most cabinet members. The diplomatic corps is represented, and a certain number of members of the business and financial elite are in place, often in their capacity as prominent donors. The national academic establishment is also there in strength, from the minister of education to heads of universities and research councils; a fair number of professors are drawn, like me, from those sections of the Royal Swedish Academy of Sciences most involved with the prizes. And here and there at the tables are also media people, there simply to do their reporting work.

Actually, togetherness is not total: the placements at the tables tend to be according to categories, so that those who have been to many of these dinners will see more or less the same people one year after another—people with whom they may also serve on one committee or another. Then on the other hand, the guests whose academic or other positions qualify them for invitations are usually accompanied by their spouses, or some other close family member, and this brings people from other walks of life to the event. I remember once being seated next to a lady who turned out to be a retired secretary from a construction company in a provincial town. This did not seem such a promising point of departure for several hours of dinner conversation, but it turned out that her son the physics professor had spent time at Stanford University, and she had visited him there. Moreover, I could quickly guess that being of that age, and from that town, she would have had a former Swedish prime minister as a local age mate growing up—someone I had also met. My hunch turned out to be correct, so there was quite enough to talk about.

Later, on the dance floor, the chances of quick mingling between categories may in principle be greater. In fact, it seems people dance mostly with their spouses. Yet you do spot some boundary transgressions, perhaps not least among those who make a deliberate point of them: a prominent feminist, also an ex-leader of the post-communist party, swirling around with a somewhat notorious figure from the national world of finance.

What happens in Stockholm, at the Concert Hall and the City Hall, however, is only a part of the Nobel Day. This is also a media event. Looking at the program table for national television, you may find that between them, the two main public service channels devote more than ten hours that day to Nobel-related broadcasting: beginning around lunch with the award of the Peace Prize, across the border in Oslo, Norway, in another city hall, with another royal family present; and ending, a little before midnight, after a live transmission from the dance floor in Stockholm. Showing the award ceremonies, in Stockholm and Oslo, is a fairly easy task. Keeping the television audience interested during the hours when the dinner guests are just there eating and drinking, and when the dancing is hardly of *Dancing with the Stars* entertainment value, must be a greater challenge. Yet this is the Nobel Day program, year after year, so even if not everybody will be watching all the time, it is obviously taken to be of public interest. In fact, you learn that there are people out there, in Sweden's towns and villages, who prepare a very special festive dinner that evening, to be consumed at a table in front of the TV screen.

On Nobel Day, the two Stockholm morning newspapers carry several pages of materials relating to the day's particular events and personnel; in 2012, the front page of one of them has the headline "Everybody on Their Toes in the Kitchen," with a large picture of the chef and his staff, preparing the Big Dinner. And the day after, both have big pictures of the crown princess, heir to the throne, on the front page—a very popular figure who became a mother earlier in the year. Here she is, beaming at the dinner table, with her plate and all three glasses in front of her. And there is much more Nobel reporting inside the papers. The two afternoon tabloids devote eight and six pages, respectively, to the previous day's festivities, but most of this is a picture spread of the gowns worn by the female guests at the banquet (the men, of course, were all in tails). By 2015, the front page headline of one Stockholm morning paper on 11 December was "Successful Feast for Research," while that on the other paper read "Glittering Jewels and Silk over Pregnant Princess Bellies."

So over all, there is something for everybody in the Nobel reporting: some science and science policy; a bit of retrospective overview for the history buffs; a strong dose of royalism; celebrity gossip for those who never tire of that; menus for gourmets; and a lot of fashion news and fashion critique.

Yet what is it that Swedes actually celebrate every year on 10 December? Perhaps what they really celebrate is themselves, the brand of their small country, and their sense that, for once, it draws the attention of the world: the periphery becomes a center for a day.[7] And then one could speculate, counterfactually, that if the multinational industrialist Alfred Nobel had decided that his home was really in one of the other places where he had major business interests, this might not have been Sweden's big day. He and his brothers for some time had one of the major petroleum businesses in the world, for instance, centered in Baku. (I happen to be aware of that, as a distant relative of mine long ago moved to that city as a Nobel employee.) So if the political conditions around the Caspian Sea had been a little different around the next-to-last turn of the century, and if Azerbaijan had been and remained an independent country, perhaps 10 December could instead have become every year a very big day in Baku.[8]

Notes

1. That calculation disregards the fact that Germany is a federal republic. If the number of ministers in the *Bundesländer* governments is included, the chances of reaching cabinet rank become more even.

2. Perhaps Swartz knew that the detective story author Henning Mankell, one internationally well-known Swede, grew up in Sveg. Nordic noir, of course, has been a notable part of the Scandinavian cultural brand in recent times (Hannerz 2013).

3. The notion of a "second-generation immigrant" may seem like a contradiction in terms. But it is commonly used in Sweden (and perhaps in various other European countries) to allude to the fact that children growing up in an immigrant household, even when born in Sweden, are in some ways like immigrants.

4. The medal was awarded by the Swedish Society for Anthropology and Geography, of which the king is the patron.

5. Since only the name of the local politician had to be changed, basically the same bumper sticker might well have been found in a number of countries at about this time.

6. After Olof Palme no other Swedish politician has had an equally high international profile. The internationally most visible Swedish politician in recent times, Carl Bildt, once Conservative prime minister, more durable as foreign minister, has appeared more preoccupied with the European arena. However, a characterization of Bildt by an American diplomat, passed on confidentially to the State Department in Washington but more widely publicized by WikiLeaks, goes with our interests in this book: "A medium size dog with big dog attitude."

7. Quite concretely, of course, and more continuously, the prizes bring prestige to at least some sectors of the Swedish scholarly community, which are involved in the procedure of deciding on the awards, but which probably otherwise would have seemed more peripheral in the research world. (Since 1970, Sweden has had eight Nobel Prize winners in physics, chemistry, medicine, and economics, the same number as the Bronx High School of Science, New York.)

8. After I wrote this, I have found that Azerbaijan actually wants to revive an old Nobel Prize of its own, awarded several times in the early twentieth century and named after Alfred Nobel's nephew Emanuel Nobel, who was active in the Baku petroleum industry (Nygårds 2013).

References

Evans-Pritchard, E. E. 1940. *The Nuer.* Oxford: Oxford University Press.

Hannerz, Ulf. 1980. *Exploring the City.* New York: Columbia University Press.

———. 1981. The Management of Danger. *Ethnos* 46 (1–2): 19–46.

———. 2013. A Detective Story Writer: Exploring Stockholm as It Once Was. *City & Society* 25 (2): 260–70.

Nygårds, Olle. 2013. Azerierna vill ha eget Nobelpris. *Svenska Dagbladet,* 14 September.

Smelser, Neil J. 1998. The Rational and the Ambivalent in the Social Sciences. *American Sociological Review* 63 (1): 1–16.

Swartz, Richard. 2010. Lilleputtarnas land. *Dagens Nyheter,* 12 June.

CONTRIBUTORS

Regina F. Bendix is professor of European ethnology at Georg-August-University in Göttingen, Germany. Her current research focuses on the constitution of value in tourism and heritage settings, the ethnography of speaking and narrative, including the realm of popular seriality. Among her recent publications is *A Companion to Folklore* (2012, coedited with Galit Hasan-Rokem).

Aleksandar Bošković is professor of anthropology at the University of Belgrade (Serbia), where he also directs the Center for Political Studies and Public Opinion Research at the Institute of Social Sciences. His most recent books are *A Brief Introduction to Anthropology* (in Serbo-Croatian; Zagreb, 2010), and *Other People's Anthropologies: Ethnographic Practice on the Margins* (editor, 2008). His main research interests are history and theory of anthropology, psychoanalysis, myth and religion, nationalism, and gender.

Virginia R. Dominguez is the Edward William and Jane Marr Gutgsell Professor of Anthropology at the University of Illinois-Urbana/Champaign, and cofounder of the International Forum for U.S. Studies. A political and legal anthropologist, she has been president of the American Anthropological Association and editor of *American Ethnologist*. Among her books are *White by Definition: Social Classification in Creole Louisiana* (1986) and *People as Subject, People as Object: Selfhood and Peoplehood in Contemporary Israel* (1989).

Thomas Hylland Eriksen is professor of social anthropology at the University of Oslo, Norway. His research and publications have largely concerned social and cultural dynamics in complex societies, including ethnicity, nationalism, and globalization. He has also written many nonacademic books on various topics, including a four-book series on unintended consequences of modernity, as well as two novels. Among his recent books are *A World of Insecurity* (2010, coedited with Ellen Bal and Oscar Salemink) and a biography of Fredrik Barth (2015).

Andre Gingrich obtained his doctoral degree in sociocultural anthropology, which he combined with studies in Arabic, sociology, and Middle Eastern history. His ethnographic field sites primarily are in the Arab Peninsula, including Yemen, Saudi Arabia, and Syria. His book publications include *Anthropology, by Comparison* (2002, coedited with Richard G. Fox), and *Neo-Nationalism in Europe and Beyond* (2006, coedited with Marcus Banks). He directs the Institute for Social Anthropology at the Austrian Academy of Sciences and is a full professor of sociocultural anthropology at the University of Vienna.

Goh Beng Lan is an associate professor and currently head of the Department of Southeast Asian Studies, National University of Singapore. She researches on issues of knowledge production, intellectual history, urbanism, postcolonial identities, and the visual arts in Southeast Asia. She is the editor of *Decentering and Diversifying Southeast Asian Studies: Perspectives from the Region* (2011).

Ulf Hannerz is Professor Emeritus of Social Anthropology, Stockholm University, Sweden. A former president of the European Association of Social Anthropologists, he has also taught at several American, European, Asian, and Australian universities. He has conducted field studies in West Africa, the Caribbean, and the United States and a multisite study of the work of news media foreign correspondents. Among his books are *Foreign News: Exploring the World of Foreign Correspondents* (2004) and *Anthropology's World: Life in a Twenty-First Century Discipline* (2010).

Sulayman N. Khalaf is a Syrian anthropologist working with the Abu Dhabi Tourism and Culture Authority as an expert on heritage. With twenty-five years of teaching experience, his main research interests are on contemporary Arab society, the Euphrates region in Syria, and the Arab Gulf. He is particularly interested in the impact of globalization on Gulf societies and issues revolving around modernity, state, identity, and heritage revival. His recent publications have focused on the reconstruction of local heritage culture in the United Arab Emirates.

Eva-Maria Knoll is a research group coordinator at the Austrian Academy of Sciences' Institute for Social Anthropology. Her research interests focus on anthropology at the intersection with life sciences and health-related mobility. Currently she investigates the treatment and prevention of the inherited blood disease thalassemia in the Republic of Maldives. She has coedited *Lexikon der Globalisierung* (2011) and *Camels in Asia and North Africa* (2012).

Jacqueline Knörr is a research group head at the Max Planck Institute for Social Anthropology and an adjunct professor at Martin Luther University in Halle/Saale, Germany. She has conducted extensive field research in Indonesia, West Africa, and Central Europe. Her research and publications focus on issues of identity, integration, migration, creolization, diaspora, gender, nationalism, and childhood. She coedited *The Powerful Presence of the Past: Integration and Conflict Along the Upper Guinea Coast* (2010), and her most recent monograph is *Creole Identity in Postcolonial Indonesia* (2014).

Orvar Löfgren is Professor Emeritus in European ethnology at Lund University, Sweden. The cultural analysis and ethnography of everyday life has been an ongoing focus in his research. His central research fields have been studies of national identity and transnational mobility, as well as media and consumption. Among his most recent publications are *The Secret World of Doing Nothing* (2010, with Billy Ehn) and the coedited volume *Managing Overflow in Affluent Societies* (2012).

João de Pina-Cabral is professor of social anthropology at the University of Kent at Canterbury, UK. He has published extensively on matters related to kinship, personhood, and ethnicity in postcolonial contexts. He has carried out fieldwork in Portugal, Macau, and Brazil. Among his principal publications are *Sons of Adam, Daughters of Eve: The Peasant Worldview of the Alto Minho* (1986) and *Between China and Europe: Person, Culture and Emotion in Macau* (2002).

Don Robotham is professor of anthropology at the Graduate Center, City University of New York. Previously, he was pro-vice-chancellor at the University of the West Indies, Jamaica. His fieldwork has been in Ghana and in various Caribbean countries. His major interests are anthropological theory, development, and crime. Among his books and articles are *Culture, Economy and Society* (2005) and "Anthropology and the Present Moment," in *Transforming Anthropology* (2011).

Cris Shore is professor of social anthropology at the University of Auckland (New Zealand). His main research interests are political anthropology, particularly European ethnography, university reform, and the anthropology of policy. He is founding editor (with Susan Wright) of the Anthropology of Policy series for Stanford University Press. His most recent book is *Up Close and Personal: Peripheral Perspectives and the Production of Anthropological Knowledge* (coedited with Susanna Trnka, 2013).

Richard Wilk is Provost Professor of Anthropology at Indiana University, where he directs the Food Studies program. His research ranges from the cultural ecology of indigenous Mayan farming and family organization to consumer culture and sustainable consumption, globalization, television, beauty pageants, and food. His most recent book is *Rice and Beans: A Unique Dish in a Hundred Places* (2012), coedited with Livia Barbosa.

Helena Wulff is professor of social anthropology at Stockholm University. Her research is in the anthropology of communication and aesthetics, based on a wide range of studies of the social worlds of literary production, dance, and visual arts in a transnational perspective, presently on contemporary Irish writers as cultural translators and public intellectuals. Among her publications is the monograph *Dancing at the Crossroads: Memory and Mobility in Ireland* (2007).

INDEX

ACKNOWLEDGMENTS

This book is the result of collaborative activities in several stages. Andre Gingrich and Ulf Hannerz began exploring the topic in Vienna, while Hannerz was a visiting scholar at the Internationales Forschungszentrum Kulturwissenschaften (IFK) during the fall and winter of 2007–2008. In May 2010, a small internal workshop was held at the Institute for Social Anthropology of the Austrian Academy of Sciences, Vienna, with Gingrich, Hannerz, Regina Bendix, Virginia Dominguez, Thomas Hylland Eriksen, and Eva-Maria Knoll as participants. The Austrian Academy of Sciences' financial assistance for this meeting and for overall management procedures is much appreciated. In June 2012, the contributors to the present volume came together at Landskrona, Sweden, to exchange views; we are very grateful to the Bank of Sweden Tercentenary Foundation and its director Göran Blomqvist for supporting this encounter financially and organizationally.

We are very pleased that all the participants in these activities have contributed chapters to *Small Countries: Structures and Sensibilities* and responded constructively and patiently to our editorial efforts. For organizational support during the editing process we are grateful to Verena Baldwin of the Institute for Social Anthropology at the Austrian Academy of Sciences. Two anonymous readers for the University of Pennsylvania Press offered constructive comments on the manuscript, and we are also very grateful for the generous and very useful comments volunteered by Professor Gordon Mathews, Chinese University of Hong Kong. Finally, we wish to offer our warm thanks to Peter Agree of the University of Pennsylvania Press for his friendly and very efficient ways in moving the manuscript to publication.

While the project was ongoing, Hannerz had opportunities to present aspects of it in the Department of Anthropology, Princeton University; the Department of Arts and Cultural Studies, University of Copenhagen; and the Department of Social Anthropology, Stockholm University. He wishes to thank participants in discussions on these occasions. Gingrich acknowledges with gratitude the occasions for presenting and discussing aspects of this project in the Department of Sociology, National University of Singapore; the Austrian Cultural Forum in Zagreb; the Max Planck Institute for Social Anthropology in Halle/Saale; and the Department for Social and Cultural Anthropology, Vienna University.

UH & AG